NEW THINKING IN
INTERNATIONAL RELATIONS THEORY

New Thinking
in International
Relations Theory

EDITED BY

Michael W. Doyle
Princeton University

and

G. John Ikenberry
University of Pennsylvania

WestviewPress

A Division of HarperCollinsPublishers

Copyright © 1997 by Westview Press, A Division of HarperCollins Publishers, Inc.

Published in 1997 in the United States of America by Westview Press, 5500 Central Avenue, Boulder, Colorado 80301-2877, and in the United Kingdom by Westview Press, 12 Hid's Copse Road, Cumnor Hill, Oxford OX2 9JJ

Library of Congress Cataloging-in-Publication Data
New thinking in international relations theory / edited by Michael W.
Doyle and G. John Ikenberry.
    p.   cm.
Includes bibliographical references and index.
ISBN 0-8133-9967-X (hc).—ISBN 0-8133-9966-1 (pbk.)
1. International relations.   I. Doyle, Michael W.   II. Ikenberry,
G. John.
JZ1305.N49   1997
327'.09'049—dc21   97-15796
                                                                            CIP

The paper used in this publication meets the requirements of the American National Standard for Permanence of Paper for Printed Library Materials Z39.48-1984.

10   9   8   7   6   5   4   3   2   1

Contents

Preface

Trotsky once remarked of his own era, "it is a curse to live in interesting times." For those who study international politics, we surely live in such times. The Soviet Union has collapsed, the Cold War has ended, some states in what was once called the Second (Soviet bloc) and Third Worlds (developing countries) are "failing," democratization is changing the face of world politics, the United Nations has emerged as a significant actor—and so have a host of nongovernmental organizations—while publics in the industrial democracies appear to be tempted by a turn inward toward isolationism.

Although dramatic global change is perhaps a curse to some old theories and conventional wisdoms, it is also an opportunity. This volume brings together provocative essays by scholars who, taken together, represent a wide range of working theoretical traditions in international relations scholarship. Moreover, our contributors reflect on how their theoretical orientations come to grips with contemporary global change. Their views range over changes in the structure of the international system, the identity and interests of the major actors, the effects of recent developments in military, industrial, and communications technology, strategies of foreign policy, and perceptions of the fundamental visions, goals, and parameters of world politics.

The essays comprise a showcase of the currently diverse theoretical agendas in the field. But the essays are also united in their attention to theoretical analysis that bears on the issue of change in global politics. Together they reflect important strands of "new thinking" in international relations theory. We, the editors, chose contributors who are interested in work currently under way outside of the mainstream of international theory, such as feminist and postmodernist theory, as well as authors who are developing theoretical advances within traditional realms, such as various international or domestic structural theories. We have selected authors and categories according to how they conceptualize the task of international political analysis, from formal modeling to discursive soliloquy, and how they categorize the important sources of change, whether they derive from the systemic interaction of states or the output of domestic politics, from ideas or material forces. We begin with the end of the Cold War, how publics interpret change, and how the classic tradition of international theory—realism, liberalism and socialism—defines change. The classical approach is pluralistic—an approach that the volume taken as a whole illustrates.

We wish to thank Peter B. Lewis, who generously provided the funding that sustained the lecture series from which this volume grew. We also want to express our gratitude to Henry Bienen and John Waterbury, who, as directors of the Center of International Studies at Princeton University, offered wise counsel and material support. Peter Furia and Chandra Sriram ably assisted us and made valuable suggestions for revising some of the chapters. Philomena Fischer patiently helped us manage the process and kept track of the various drafts.

Michael W. Doyle
G. John Ikenberry

1

Introduction:
The End of the Cold War,
the Classical Tradition,
and International Change

MICHAEL W. DOYLE AND
G. JOHN IKENBERRY

In the late 1980s, as the Cold War began to thaw and then melt, politicians, pundits, and scholars disputed among ourselves what the changes meant. For some observers of the international scene the long-frozen war was ending at last. For others it was entering an even more dangerous, because more ambiguous, phase. Change itself was not new, but in 1979 the collapse of the brief détente of the 1970s seemed to confirm a bedrock enmity between the United States and its "free world" allies on the one side and the Soviet Union and its communist allies on the other. Then in the late 1980s that fierce, refrozen enmity thawed into protestations of personal friendship between President Ronald Reagan and President Mikhail Gorbachev, into public and official acts of mutual sympathy for the victims of natural disasters in Armenia and of international terrorism in the skies over Britain, and into negotiated accords to stem the arms race. That there was change was clear, but what was changing and what remained the same, whether the change was to be welcomed or doubted, and what should be done in response to either assumption was not so clear and shaped the policy debate both in the West and in the Soviet Union. In the course of the debate the participants delved further and further into interpretations of what constitutes international amity, enmity, respect, and fear. From there analysts turned to questions of what values, institutions, and interests determine which state is a friend and which an enemy. And thus, usually implicitly rather than explicitly, they practiced international theory.

In order to understand international politics we need international theory. In this chapter, we would like to show that international theory can be useful in accounting for international change. We begin with the public debate over the end of the Cold War, the most significant international change of our decade. We then explore a classical approach to international theory that draws on the political theories of international politics, one that revives the contributions of classical political theorists and understands international relations as world *politics*. This, after all, is where international theory began. We begin here not just because it is a waste for any field to reinvent the wheel and because we should understand the assumptions on which the field was built but also because the classical theorists invented "wheels" whose importance we have unduly neglected. We conclude with a brief guide to how the contributors to this volume explore new paths in international theory.

The End of the Cold War[1]

Let us begin with the rhetoric on the demise and rise of the Cold War. Prime Minister Margaret Thatcher offered the least equivocal judgment, saying quite simply, "The Cold War is over." President Reagan went even further, announcing as he left office, "We won the Cold War." But what they meant (what their statements meant) was far from evident. We cannot forget that lengthy cold wars are also, by definition, "long peaces"[2] in that they remain "cold" and do not turn into "hot" wars. But the Cold War at its height also seemed to differ from ordinary relations among independent powers, great or small, in other periods of peace. So the debate centered on such questions as whether there is change, and if so, what the change is and whether we should promote, applaud, or resist it.

The Cold War was an intense competition distinguished by extreme hostility between the Soviet Union and the United States. It differed from normal interstate relations in its win-or-lose (zero-sum) competition—the extreme competition that characterizes "hot" wars. This competition, moreover, extended outside the narrow arena of bilateral relations to competition across the globe between blocs on both sides of the iron curtain and to almost all issues of social life, from ballet to science to sport to—most important—what President Harry Truman called the "ways of life" that he in his "Truman Doctrine" saw as a choice between freedom and its opposite, tyranny.

In the debate on the possible demise of the Cold War we saw reflected a variety of views. Some perceived what might best be described as a surge of prudence—a long-delayed recognition both of the danger of nuclear weapons and of the two superpowers' growing ability to manage a dangerous relationship.[3] Others, attuned to the past chills and thaws in the Cold War and the purposes that seemed to lie behind them, tried to elucidate what Secretary of State James Baker (citing Benjamin Cardozo) called the basic "streams of tendency" that shape our worldviews.[4]

Three prominent streams seemed to contribute to the public debate on the end of the Cold War. We can identify them conventionally as Liberal, Realist, and Marxist. Following the synopsis of the debate, we explore their foundations in classical political thought.

Some—let us call them progressive liberals in the United States and social democrats in Europe—thought that the Cold War could be brought to an end just because it was an extraordinary departure from normal relations among states and because the reasons that once may have justified it were now absent, or were at least starting to become so.

According to these liberals, the domestic reforms announced by President Gorbachev after he came to power in 1985 offered a significant promise of a moderation in the competition between the two superpowers. Driven by a desperate need for domestic reform, Gorbachev sought a tranquil international environment—one that would benefit the United States as well. The Soviet Union was becoming an "ordinary state"—domestically legitimate and nonexpansionist, and it accepted the basic norms of international order. Foreign enemies and international expansion no longer seemed necessary for domestic political stability. Gorbachev seemed to have rejected the traditional communist view of demonic world capitalism as the essential enemy and irremediable threat to the survival of the Soviet Union. And the Soviet public seemed to accept the Gorbachev regime. All these developments promised a more stable and tranquil world that would promote Western interests as well. A decentralizing, democratizing, reforming Soviet Union would be a moderate Soviet Union. The United States, they argued, should thus accommodate by freeing the Soviet Union from the Cold War restrictions on trade and welcoming it as a participant in international institutions, such as the General Agreement on Tariffs and Trade (GATT) and the International Monetary Fund (IMF), in which it sought legitimate participation.[5]

Conservative liberals shared a commitment to the preservation of individual freedom and a strategy focusing on domestic change in the Soviet Union, agreeing that together these were the key to the ending of the Cold War. But they denied either that change had taken place or that it was taking place in the direction or to the degree that should have led the West to change either its policies or its view of the Soviet Union.[6] The Soviets, they said, have been at war with the free world for more than forty years, and some traced the origin of the conflict to the Russian Revolution in 1917. These liberals accepted the view that the Soviets did not seek to start a hot war; they sought victory in peace. Détentes were strategies with a hostile intent. The Soviet "leopard" may have changed its spots, but it was still a leopard.[7] Gorbachev's efforts at reform had not yet changed the communist, dictatorial character of the Soviet Union. Indeed, Gorbachev's very popularity may have been misleading, these conservative liberals warned. It may have resulted less from the changes he introduced than from the (false) perception on the part of the Russian people that Gorbachev was somehow an opponent of the current system he led and that he may have been trying to preserve. Until true liberal—democratic and capitalist—reforms succeeded, therefore, the domestic regime was as illegitimate as ever, and the Cold War was still a war. The chances of success, moreover, seemed to be quite remote. A protracted crisis, a reversion to Brezhnevian stagnation, or a military coup were the more likely outcomes of the nationalist rebellion both in Eastern Europe and within the Soviet Union that perestroika, glasnost, and democratization were likely to bring.[8]

Thus until the Soviet Union recognized and implemented fundamental political freedoms at home and freed its satellites in Eastern Europe, domestic *economic* reforms merely served, if successful, to strengthen the free world's most dangerous enemy.[9] World politics understands power, former President Richard Nixon added, and Gorbachev, like his predecessors, sought to expand the power of the Soviet Union in pursuit of global predominance, which must come at the expense of the security of the free world.[10] The persistence of hostile communist ideology, the Soviet bureaucratic state, the insecurity of the Russian people, and the continuing evidence of aggressive policy all indicated that the Soviets—despite reforms—continued to be the most perilous security threat that the West faced.[11] Hence the West should continue the Cold War, vigilantly guarding against any increase in Soviet strength. West German Chancellor Helmut Schmidt expressed a similar warning: "Am I mad? Will I give Gorbachev a Marshall Plan so that his successor can resume Russian expansionism with a strong economy behind him?"[12]

Only with the rise of Boris Yeltsin and the affirmation of power of the Russian parliament following the overturned coup of August 1991 against Gorbachev did these liberal hard-liners reconsider the Russian threat. In a widely publicized pronouncement, former President Nixon made a case for aiding the newly democratic and capitalist Russia, citing its pivotal role in the stability of central Asia. But even in 1992 and 1993 caution was the dominant theme. Democratic optimists hailed the victory of democracy in the former USSR and saw it as responsible for the end of the Cold War. With the completion in January 1993 of the historic START II treaty, which cut the nuclear arsenals of Russia and the United States by more than two-thirds, one "senior official" thus opined, though wanly, that "'democracy is the best form of arms control,'" noting (much too simply) that "democratic nations do not start wars."[13] Other liberals worried as they contemplated a "Weimar Russia" and the shallow roots of democracy, capitalism, and liberalism in the former USSR.[14]

But Liberals did not monopolize the Cold War debate, even in the United States. *Realists,* unlike both progressive and conservative liberals, discounted the importance of differences in domestic structures—particularly in the distinctions between "free" and "unfree" societies, liberal and communist ideologies, and democratic, authoritarian, and totalitarian regimes. Statesmen, they said, choose their foes and friends by a different, specifically international, logic. Whatever the differences in domestic politics and economics, the ineluctable tendency toward war that all states share makes them perceive states as equivalent national persons. The Soviet Union is Russia rather than a union of Soviet socialist republics, just as the United States is America rather a federal democratic republic of free citizens and property owners. For them national interests and power count more than institutions or "merely" ideological goals.

Realists shared President Nixon's view that to the extent that Gorbachev's economic reforms strengthened the Soviet Union, they threatened the United States. But Realists differed in that they believed that any increase in the power of any state—democratic, totalitarian, authoritarian, capitalist, socialist—creates insecurity for other states, also irrespective of their political regime. And in response, states increase their arms spending or alter their alliances. This view tends, as a consequence, to downgrade the special significance of the Cold War, seeing it as one among a number of historical rivalries between great powers. Realists, too, applauded President George Bush's desire to test any new departures in relations with the Soviet Union by the question of whose advantage is served. Not until the USSR broke up in December 1991 did Realists advocate active aid toward former Soviet republics. Former Secretary of State Henry A. Kissinger and National Security Adviser Zbigniew Brzezinski recommended balancing against Russian power in the region by aiding the Ukraine against Russia, in a classic balance-of-power logic.[15]

Also in a Realist spirit, however, were very different views perceiving a need to end the Cold War with Russia. The most straightforward of these stressed that the Soviet Union no longer posed a subversive threat to Western Europe, as it may have in the immediate postwar period. The two nuclear superpowers had (and have) rational, overwhelmingly mutual interests in arms control and in curbing their arms race.[16] Security is necessarily mutual in the nuclear age; it requires accommodation, not confrontation. Other, more indirect, Realist views emphasized a supposed increase in Asian power (Japan and China), leading to a relative decline in Soviet and U.S. power. Following the logic of traditional Realist balancing of power, this provided an incentive for a realignment of interests and allegiances, with the United States and the Soviet Union joining to contain the new Asian center of world power.[17]

The most striking dissolution of Cold War worldviews, however, appeared to be taking place on the *communist* side of the Cold War divide. No major political figure in the West had so categorically denied the relevance of Cold War modes of thought and policy as had President Gorbachev. Gorbachev, even more than the progressive Western liberals, saw the Cold War as over. It had become utterly useless in an age threatened by nuclear destruction and deeply in need of the international peace and "comprehensive security" that economic revitalization as well as the "universal human idea" required.[18]

In speeches directed at fellow communists, Gorbachev was revolutionary in his rhetoric. He reaffirmed his identity as Marxist-Leninist as well as that of the Communist Party of the Soviet Union (CPSU), and he reiterated a fundamental fraternal solidarity with all other socialist countries and revolutionary movements.[19] Commentators who portrayed a complete dissolution of communist ideology clearly exaggerated. Democratic centralism—the scientific socialist justification for the monopoly of political power in the hands of the Communist Party—class struggle, and world revolution still had a place within Gorbachev's communist reforms. He himself discounted the degree of change his politicoeconomic restructuring and political openness (perestroika and glasnost) portended—comparing them not to a new revolution but to a new "stage" or task, like victory in the Civil War (1918–1920), the Great Patriotic War (World War II), or the collectivization of Soviet agriculture (1928–1932).

In 1988, however, the revolutionary task was to achieve an international system of security that, on the one hand, promoted domestic glasnost and perestroika and, on the other, curbed and then reduced the danger of nuclear destruction.[20] These were not seen as arbitrary choices but as necessary adjustments to the stagnation of the Soviet economy and "objective" changes in the world, particularly the advent of mutual assured nuclear destruction affecting socialist and capitalists alike. According to Gorbachev, historic contradictions between the world bourgeoisie and the proletariat recede before the dangers provoked not by world capitalism per se or by the international bourgeoisie but by "reactionary circles of the bourgeoisie" and by the "military-industrial complex" in the United States (borrowing the words of President Dwight D. Eisenhower!). Leaving ample room for accommodation by others, *these* narrow cliques threatened alike the legitimate national interests of the American people, the world peace movement so especially prominent in Western Europe, and, of course, "universal human values."[21]

Elsewhere in the communist world, diversity seemed to be on the rise. The debate within the Soviet Union was mirrored by a transnational debate in Eastern Europe. On the one hand, ruling parties in East Germany and Czechoslovakia took conservative positions (sometimes going so far as to censor *Soviet* publications) while the public often seemed to support Gorbachev and his reforms. In Hungary and then in Poland, on the other hand, both the parties and the public found echoes of their own reforms in Gorbachev's initiatives. And Gorbachev's unwillingness to enforce Soviet predominance (the so-called "Sinatra Doctrine") opened up the possibility of national routes to democratic reform, the collapse of East European communism, and the ironic revival in the mid-1990s of socialist-communist parties in a democratic context.

In Western Europe, the nonruling communist parties appeared to be caught between the new attractions that Gorbachev represented to the mass public and the historic rivalry of communist vanguards with mass-based social-democratic parties. As their own declining electoral base continued to shrink, a nostalgic air entered communist discourse. They reaffirmed the attractions of class solidarity and basked in the credit won by the communist role in the anticolonial movement. For a few (such as French worker Jean-Pierre Quilgars, interviewed by the *New York Times*), the personal satisfactions derived from socialist solidarity in the workers' movement and a now nearly archaic-sounding solidarity with global class struggle continued to animate their allegiance. Nationalist hostility—that is, directed toward *U.S.* capitalist imperialism rather than toward domestic West European capitalism—also appeared to motivate them.[22] These traditional socialist suspicions of capitalist America found an echo in the public; socialist suspicion became hard to disentangle from nationalist concerns about an aggressive American behemoth.

Traditional communism seemed most politically alive in the Third World, where it had served as the single most effective organizer of resistance to the most oppressive of colonial and quasi-colonial (South Africa) regimes. There, in a myriad of nationalist tones, communist solidarity in the international class struggle against imperialism seemed to retain much of its hold, and for that very reason criticisms of Gorbachev's turn away from class struggle drew voices of protest. But there, too, it was also ideologically challenged. Criticisms of the Soviet "hegemonism" and of Cuba's lack of domestic freedom increasingly characterized the expressed views of Nicaraguans and others.[23]

Theorizing Change

As these scholars, political leaders, and citizens sought to come to terms with a confusing present and an uncertain future, we can see them considering in various ways—usually implicitly—three sets of questions.

First, what should we want? What is required to promote justice or human welfare, or our national security, welfare, or prestige and power, or class solidarity and socialist revolution?

② Second, what obstacles threaten the achievement of these goals? How might these obstacles change? Why do such obstacles arise? What are the most effective ways to achieve the changes we want or to avoid the changes we do not? Or, more generally put, how does the relevant world work?

These two sets of questions—the normative (What *should* we do?) and the analytic (What *will* happen?)—are bridged by a third question, an implicit question of identity—Who or what are *we*? These questions, of course, are typical of any policy analysis.[24] They probe prospective political choices, political ends and means, causes and consequences. They also tend to be related: Those who seek to guarantee U.S. power see the Soviets as similarly driven; those who seek class solidarity and social revolution see class domination and capitalist imperialism as their leading threats; those who seek individual freedom and the enjoyment of democracy see authoritarian and totalitarian threats. But the connections are not inevitable, nor are they always so clear. Political actors, as eighteenth-century philosopher Jean-Jacques Rousseau once said, make their political schemes "rotate"—they pursue power in order to become wealthy, wealth in order to exercise power, justice in order to be strong, and strength in order to protect just institutions.[25]

These questions also can help us to understand important aspects of the pattern of events of the past, when earlier political actors attempted to interpret and change their worlds and to make political choices and succeeded or failed in them. With the advantage of hindsight, moreover, we as historians and social scientists can begin to do our own secondary analysis of their political ends and means. We can ask not just which policies were good but also which were most influential, when and for whom. We can ask which of the analyses the participants made were accurate and which were not and why. We can of course judge the results of the ends pursued and the views held as a way of refining our own political choices.

We can also assess how *much* change took place. Robert Gilpin has suggested that we distinguish among a "systems change" in the basic actors (from city-states to empires to nation-states), a "systemic change" of leadership (e.g., from one hegemon to another) within the system, or an "interaction change" in the patterns and rules of the system (a shift of alignments or a new regime).[26] If we want our international theories to help us interpret the history of change in the present and the past, what should our theories be able to do?

First, they will need to acknowledge the significance of competing ends—within and among individuals and states.[27] International politics, like all politics, is driven by concurrences, clashes, compromises, and coordinations of wills as well as the capabilities actors can bring to bear to make their will effective. These wills are normative, expressing the "political objectives" that Clausewitz found to be the essence of strategy. They encompass both values and interests. Political leaders, like all individuals, have complex motivations; moral values mix with numerous competing as well as compatible material concerns, both personally and politically. We are driven by "a desire to be able to justify our actions to others on grounds they could not reasonably reject."[28] We cannot separate these drives from those that increase our power, profit, or prestige. We uneasily combine these drives in our own wills; we contest over them with our fellow citizens; and, representing our states, we compete and cooperate with other representatives of other states.

Second, theories should be able to interpret how we assess threats and opportunities. We especially need to know whether (and if so, why) those assessments differ within and between states. Does the mere power of foreigners threaten us? Should capability be read as intention when we, lacking world law and order, necessarily lack any guarantee that capability will not be used against us? Or do we need to look at other indications that mix apparent intentions with capabilities?[29] Do states have strong incentives to behave in differing ways because their bureaucracies, interest groups, classes, structure of public opinion, or federal or constitutional structures prejudice them in one direction or another? Do monarchies differ from democracies? Capitalists from socialists? Theories should give us an account of how the environment operates around us.

Third, in the process of addressing the first and second desiderata, theories will inevitably wind up addressing questions of identity, simply because what we should want and how we see the world serve to define who we are. World politics is defined by the identity of actors who see themselves as representatives of nations, free citizens, members of a class, or some combination of all three—each of whom is acting a world political environment that lacks a global source of law and order. This is what makes world politics different from national politics, urban politics, organizational politics, and family politics.[30] Yet within this shared realization of anarchy, identities differ.

Theories help us to identify who the actors are by telling us what certain kinds of actors should want. When we analyze what they do want and what they actually do, we establish effective guides to explaining and changing world politics. Theories cover the larger issues, but they will not enable us to retrace the exact process of decision that led to the onslaught of the Cold War. What theory surrenders in order to answer the broader questions are the particularities of the moment and the individual. They miss insights into how individuals, groups, and states assess willingness to bear risk. Are we optimists, pragmatists, captives of a single approach, pessimists?[31] Such factors can influence policy judgments, making idealists behave like realists and vice versa. Moreover, theories do not give us specific accounts of the capacities of states in the international system in the particular case at hand.[32] Which state is more powerful, where, on what issues? Theory, therefore, can never serve as a recipe; it is a guide to how to analyze and justify policy, now and in the past, and not a replacement for strategy.[33]

Theory can lend coherence to observations and thereby structure them into the interpretations that make sense of otherwise meaningless or at least confusing events, such as the endings and beginnings of cold wars. But even as it does that, it necessarily begins to do something more, which is to explain why one interpretation is more plausible than another.

The Classical Tradition

To interpret the choices made by political leaders in 1989 we will need to examine the differing interpretations of ends, interests, and institutions that each actor expressed. In order then to interpret the shaping of policy in specific issue areas at specific times we will need a theory that describes how ends, interests, and institutions are related to one another. Interpreting history thus leads us into theory. But theories are composed of interpretations of relations among self-conscious political leaders and the ends that motivate them, the interests that they serve, and the institutions that shape their behavior. Understanding theory leads us into an emphasis on interpretation. That is just what the classics of Realism, Liberalism, and Marxism do. How do they account for international change?

Realism

The Realist's worldview was shaped by the ancient Greek historian Thucydides, writing 2,500 years ago. Niccolò Machiavelli in the sixteenth century, Thomas Hobbes in the seventeenth century, and Rousseau in the eighteenth century laid the modern foundations that are the core of contemporary Realism. The Realists hold in varying degrees that the best description of world politics is a "state of war"—not a single continuous war or constant wars but the constant possibility of war among all states. Politics is gripped by a state of war because the nature of humanity, or the character of states, or the structure of international order (or all three together) allows wars to occur. This possibility of war requires that states follow "realpolitik": be self-interested, prepare for war, and calculate relative balances of power. This view is reflected in simple, hard attitudes, such as those expressed by Prince Bernhard von Bülow (German chancellor from 1900 to 1909), who in 1914 declared: "In the struggle between nationalities, one nation is the hammer, the other the anvil, one is the victor, the other the vanquished." This attitude has led to violent campaigns of national aggrandizement and imperialism. But it also shapes desperate efforts to preserve peace through isolation and minimal conceptions of national security. Realist international political science has led the study of international relations during the postwar period.

Although Realists often portray themselves as being free of idealism, accompanying their view is Realist moral philosophy, which holds that individuals should accept the "national interest" as an ideal, as the one true guide to the formulation of the public policy of states in this dangerous international system.[34] Failing to follow the national interest, or reason of state, is a prescription for national disaster, for an increase in unnecessary global violence, and for irresponsible acts of statesmanship that place private interests or ideals above public needs. Science and morals are not separate endeavors. Realist moral philosophy makes Realist political science coherent; Realist political science provides an essential description that is needed to justify Realist ethics.

Once effective states characterize an international system, little systems change takes place. Continuity is the dominant theme of Realism as the state of war forces states to behave in similar, rational, power-maximizing ways, or fail and be conquered.[35] Change is constant at the systemic level, however, as powerful hegemons rise and fall, as did Athens, the Habsburgs, Napoleon, and Bismarck. This in turn results in interaction changes as alliance patterns shift in response to these seismic upheavals, as do the prospects of order and effective regimes. The end of the Cold War, in this view, may resemble earlier systemic changes, when shifts in power produced significant effects. But proponents of the Realist paradigm have produced conflicting, indeed opposite, estimates of its likely effects, reflecting unresolved differences over whether the Cold War system was a global hierarchy dominated by the United States or a bipolar contest between the two blocs: one dominated by the Soviet Union, the other by the United States. Hence the Soviet decline brought down the Soviet bloc but left the American bloc either relatively stronger and perhaps more stable (the hierarchical view) or divisive and prone to conflict (the bipolar view) now that its anti-Soviet polar glue had dissolved.[36]

Liberalism

The Liberals draw on British philosopher John Locke's seventeenth-century view of liberal individualism—a government of free individuals defending law and property—as well as the eighteenth-century view of liberal commercialism, producing material incentives that promote peace. At the end of the eighteenth century Immanuel Kant's liberal republicanism brought markets, rights, and republican institutions together, reaffirming the centrality of liberal politics and setting out the bases of modern theories of individual responsibility, representation, and liberal internationalism. Rejecting the view of world politics as a "jungle," the Liberal view of world politics is one of a cultivable "garden" that combines a state of war with the possibility of a state of peace. For Liberals the state is not a hypothetical single, rational, national actor in a state of war, as it is in some of the Realist models, but a coalition or a conglomerate of coalitions and interests representing individuals and groups. Not only are a state's interests determined by its place in the international system, but also its place is determined by which of the many interests, ideals, and activities of its members captures (albeit temporarily) governmental authority.

Differentiating between representative republics and autocratic dictatorships, Liberals regard representative states as reflections of individual consent; conversely, they regard autocratic states as instances of the repression of individual rights. (Liberals come in conservative, even Reaganesque and Thatcherite, and not merely social-welfarist varieties.) Domestic values and institutions shape foreign policy, and thus representative and autocratic states are assumed to behave differently. For some, domestic structures themselves determine international outcomes; for others, domestic structures open up the possibility of international systemic changes—pacific unions or peaceful dyads. The state of war for many Liberals only holds outside of the separate peace that liberals have established among themselves.

Liberal moral theory supports the liberal peace with a prescriptive force. Liberals thus argue that foreign policy should reflect the rights and duties of individuals. It should serve to support whatever institutional measures would enhance the ability of morally equal human beings to live their own lives, here and everywhere else. But Liberals differ greatly on the practical import of their principles—whether these principles dictate a strict observance of national sovereignty or permit the possibility of justified intervention and redistribution.

For Liberals the end of the Cold War counts as a significant confirmation of their theory; the collapse of the Soviet empire and the moves toward liberal democracy in Eastern Europe pave the way for a significant increase in international accommodation across the former Cold War divide.[37] They see the driving forces of this transformation in the domestic democratization sweeping the world and in the systemic promise of interliberal peace that may have reassured democratizers when they took their risky reforms. Liberals face confusing problems, however, when elected governments pursue nonliberal policies.

Socialism

Marxist socialist international theory is by far the most clearly defined of the three modern traditions. (Unlike in the two other "churches," its apostles have had to answer to "bishops" and, occasionally, a "pope" or two.) From Marx and Engels's work we can follow a distinct dialogue through the democratic socialists to Lenin, Stalin, Mao, and current-day inter-preters—democratic and nondemocratic—of the canon. For them world politics is intraclass solidarities combined with interclass war waged both across and within state borders. Descriptively, they agree with the Liberals that domestic interests define the political character of a state and that this definition then influences the state's foreign policy. They disagree with Liberals, however, in their argument that the constitutive feature of the state is not a matter of pacific unions of pacifying commerce, but of the war between classes that takes place within and across national boundaries.

Despite an analytic tradition that (as does Realism) explicitly describes normative questions as ideological, Marxists, too, rely upon an idealistic commitment to human welfare that makes the determination of interna-tional progress an essential feature of both their scientific explanation and of their plan for revolutionary liberation.

The end of the Cold War presents an especially difficult case for the so-cialists. A unilinear model of progress seemed to move into reverse. In the early post–Cold War days the spread of democracy and the market seemed to illustrate instead a neo-Hegelian "end of history" for communism as it was rejected by the mass of the people for whom it was designed.[38] A sig-nificant theoretical reevaluation of communism, lending retrospective sup-port to dissenting views of communism as a form of state capitalism, was reinforced by the anomalous end of the communist experiment. Incentives for theoretical revision and constructive reformulation were strengthened as well by the revival of socialism in Eastern Europe in recent years. Democratic socialism in a far-from-clear guise has been adopted by demo-cratic pluralities in a number of democratic Eastern European countries (in-cluding Poland and Hungary).

New Directions

In this volume we seek to go beyond the traditional contests and the tradi-tional theoretical pluralism of the classical tradition to a new pluralism that explores the insights to which the complexity and dynamism of contempo-rary international relations give rise. We asked the contributors to open up the question of changes in identity, interests, and institutions and to explore each of these with methods ranging from the most empirical and behavioral to the most abstract or interpretive.

We begin with two surveys of the state of the field. The first is the present chapter, in which we have outlined the heritage of theoretical pluralism em-bodied in the classic traditions. In the second, Miles Kahler examines the accomplishments of professional postwar international political science. He focuses on its origins and evolution and presents a critical sociology of how it came to be that a structural approach dominated U.S. international political science after World War II.

The chapters that follow develop new or neglected strains of international theorizing. They challenge many of the assumptions and conclusions of both traditional theorizing and postwar political science, either by rejecting their assumptions altogether or by suggesting ways to make the more descriptive methods of traditional analyses more systematic and, in some cases, parsimonious.

A first set of papers represents newly emerging bodies of theory that explicitly reject conventional international relations theory. James Der Derian presents a "poststructural" approach to international politics that attempts to call into question the core features of traditional understandings of interstate relations (Chapter 3). The challenge of the poststructural (called by some "postmodern") approach is to reconceptualize the language and images of contemporary international relations scholarship by exposing what it regards as simplistic understandings of politics. Jean Bethke Elshtain examines the newly emerging feminist critique of international relations theory (Chapter 4). She employs the template of gender to reenvision how one should go about understanding some of the fundamental aspects of interstate relations. Just as a perspective on gender questions some of the conventional assumptions and usual practices of domestic politics, so too it opens for debate the value of traditional ideas of security. Daniel Deudney presents a newly reformulated geopolitical theory of global politics (Chapter 5). Challenging the "idealism" of both traditional and new theory, his geopolitical approach advances a "materialist" conception of politics that emphasizes the central and dynamic significance of physical and technological features of international relations. James DeNardo discusses the limits and possibilities for developing formal mathematical models of international change that specify in much more rigorous ways the traditional assumptions of international theory and illuminate the debate over nuclear deterrence (Chapter 6).

A second set of papers presents "new thinking" that has emerged within more traditional areas of international relations. Joseph M. Grieco presents a recent reworking of structural realist theory that emphasizes the specific logic of competitive state actions within the global political economy (Chapter 7). He distinguishes between the structural incentives that lead to a preference for security and those that lead to power. Matthew Evangelista offers new work in the tradition of international relations theory that focuses on domestic structures and institutions (Chapter 8). Finally, Steve Weber presents recent advances in the area of international institutions and norms (Chapter 9). He focuses our attention on both the origins and the actions of institutions as determinants of changes in "state" behavior, with a special focus on the current evolution of institutional identity in Western Europe.

We have asked the contributors to follow two very general guidelines in their chapters. First, we want each chapter to be a synopsis of a theoretical approach and to highlight what is new within that approach. We left it up to each author to decide how this was best to be done. For those presenting work that lies outside the mainstream, the chapter tends to involve a self-conscious "dialogue" with mainstream theory. For those presenting work within a well-established tradition, the chapter shows where innovation and refinement have been proceeding.

Second, we asked each contributor to reflect on his or her theoretical model, assessing its capacity to explain some aspect of contemporary global change. The authors tackle both the meaning of change in the international system and the cause for it within the perspective of the theory they are presenting. Collectively, the contributors show us the effects of normative and material forces on changes in identity, perceptions of interest, and roles of institutions. They consider:

- Who are the "actors" that drive international change (the structure of the international system, states, classes, genders, individuals)?
- What are the motive forces that move those actors (material and ideal interests)?
- How do those actors interrelate (through institutions or other processes at the domestic or international level)?
- How do observers weigh evidence of change (through scientific or reflectivist methods)?
- And how do observers judge (normatively or instrumentally) the change they observe?

In the final chapter, by John Ikenberry and Michael Doyle, the editors reflect on the various choices and opportunities that "new thinking" in international relations theory provides. The contours of international politics are changing rapidly. The challenge to thoughtful observers of these changes is to reflect also on the theoretical tools that we have available—to build upon traditional theories and methods as well as to encourage new thinking.

We present these essays in the spirit evoked by Arnold Wolfers when he recommended a credo for the international political theorist: "If there is any difference between today's political scientist and his predecessors (the classical political theorists)—who, like himself, were confronted with such problems as alliance policy, the balancing of power, intervention in the affairs of other countries, and the pursuit of ideological goals—one would hope it might lie in a keener realization of the controversial and tentative nature of his reply, in a greater effort to consider alternative answers, and in a more conscious attempt to remain dispassionate and objective."[39]

Notes

Michael Doyle bears primary responsibility for this chapter; he wishes to thank Peter Furia, Chandra Sriram, Paul Sanz, and the reviewers of Westview Press for their comments on this chapter.

1. This section draws on arguments in Michael Doyle's *Ways of War and Peace* (Norton, 1997).

2. John Lewis Gaddis, *The Long Peace* (New York: Oxford University Press, 1987).

3. John Lewis Gaddis, "How the Cold War Might End," *Atlantic Monthly*, November 1987, pp. 88–100.

4. Such worldviews tend to be less than philosophically rigorous. Secretary Baker, in his appointment hearings testimony, assured the Senate that his own tendency was "Texas Republican" and thereby reliably conservative, even though he was known for a certain degree of pragmatism ("Transition in Washington, Excerpts from Baker's Testimony Before Senate Committee," *New York Times*, January 18, 1989, A16).

5. The clearest expression of this widely shared liberal viewpoint that we have found is Richard Ullman's insightful essay, "Ending the Cold War," *Foreign Policy*, vol. 72 (Fall 1988):130–151. The spiritual ancestor of these analyses is George Kennan's "America and the Russian Future," *Foreign Affairs*, vol. 79, no. 3 (April 1951):351–370, in which he sets forth the conditions needed for a "peace" in the Cold War. There he stressed three changes: (1) a lifting of the iron curtain, allowing for an openness and moderation in Soviet foreign policy; (2) the detotalitarianization of Soviet domestic society, particularly its refraining from enslaving its own labor; and (3) the freeing of oppressed nationalities both within and outside the Soviet Union. By the end of the 1980s Kennan's conditions appeared to be more modest (see Kennan, "After the Cold War," *New York Times Magazine*, February 5, 1989, pp. 32–33). An analysis along these lines may also be found in G. John Ikenberry and Daniel Deudney, "The International Sources of Soviet Change," *International Security*, vol. 16, no. 3 (Winter 1991/1992):74–118.

6. Richard Nixon expressed this skepticism most forcefully in *1999: Victory Without War* (New York: Simon and Schuster, 1988). It might appear odd, however, to call him a liberal, but by "liberal" I mean here nothing more than an expressed commitment to the importance of individual liberty, private property, and representative institutions as goals of state policy, as explained later in the chapter.

7. Richard Nixon quotes Dimitri Simes to this effect in *Victory Without War*, p. 45.

8. Zbigniew Brzezinski, "Will the Soviet Empire Self-destruct?" *New York Times Magazine*, February 26, 1989, pp. 38–52.

9. Nixon, *Victory Without War*, p. 46; Richard Pipes, "Paper Perestroika," *Policy Review*, no. 47 (Winter 1989):18–19.

10. Nixon, *Victory Without War*, pp. 21, 33.

11. Ibid., pp. 40–43.

12. "Gorbachev's Everest," *Economist*, December 1988, p. 40. The Group of Seven meeting in France on July 15, 1989, achieved a compromise of progressive

and conservative views when it offered aid to the democratizing Soviet bloc while asserting that complete democratization and liberalization, together with "commercial" relations, were prerequisites of economic aid and peaceful relations (Maureen Dowd, "Leaders at Summit Back Financial Aid for East Europe," *New York Times*, July 16, 1989).

13. Quoted in Steven Erlanger, "A Last Treaty of Its Kind," *New York Times*, January 4, 1993, pp. A1, A9.

14. Good accounts of these events and their possible significance may be found in Timothy J. Colton, "Politics" (pp. 17–48), and Robert Legvold, "Foreign Policy" (pp. 147–176), both in *After the Soviet Union*, edited by Colton and Legvold (New York: Norton, 1992); and in Stephen White, "Russia's Experiment with Democracy," *Current History* (October 1992):310–313.

15. A good account of these debates on U.S. foreign policy may be found in Alexander Dallin's "America's Search for a Policy Toward the Former Soviet Union," *Current History* (October 1992):321–326.

16. See, for example, Kennan, "After the Cold War."

17. George Liska, "From Containment to Concert," *Foreign Policy*, no. 62 (Spring 1986):3–23.

18. Mikhail Gorbachev, Address to the United Nations, December 7, 1988, excerpted in the *New York Times*, December 8, 1988.

19. CPSU Report to the 27th Congress, 1988, in Mikhail Gorbachev, *Documents and Materials: 28th Congress of the Communist Party of the Soviet Union* (Moscow: Novosti, 1990).

20. Gorbachev, interview in *L'Humanité*, 1988.

21. Gorbachev, CPSU Report to the 27th Congress, 1988. Andrey V. Kozyrev, a senior official in the Foreign Ministry, echoed these views ("Why Foreign Policy Went Sour," *New York Times*, Op-Ed page, January 7, 1989) while seeming to go even further in the rejection of the utility and "realism" of class struggle as a guide to international politics. In the Third World, he said, Moscow has repeatedly aligned itself with dubious military dictatorships professing revolutionary ardor against world imperialism. This alignment tends more to the polarization of the Third World than to social or economic progress, which is not incompatible with trade with the capitalist West. He advocated instead a foreign policy rejecting dogma and based on "realism" and the "interests of our fatherland" and yet—expressing the same tension found in Gorbachev's speeches—"a return to Leninism."

22. See the excellent survey of communism in the *New York Times* entitled "Communism Now: What Is It? In the Words of the Faithful": Serge Schmemann, "In Hope and Dismay, Lenin's Heirs Speak," January 22, 1989; James M. Mackhay, "Voices of the Party Faithful: Searching for a Path in a New Era: Across a Divided Europe, an Ideology Under Siege," January 23, 1989; and Michael T. Kaufman, "In Third World, the Legacy of Marx Takes Many Shapes," January 24, 1989. For a more critical account and for background, see Joan Barth Urban, "Afterthoughts in Light of the August 1991 Coup" (pp. 189–200), and Federigo Argentieri, "The Role and Limits of Reform Communism in East-Central Europe: Is Anything *Left* Still Left? (pp. 160–188), both in *Moscow and the Global Left in the Gorbachev Era*, edited by Joan Barth Urban (Ithaca: Cornell University Press, 1992).

23. See Kaufman, "In Third World, the Legacy of Marx."

24. Alexander George discusses fundamental beliefs about human nature and instrumental beliefs about effective strategy as two essential elements of the "operational code" method of analysis. See "The Operational Code: A Neglected Approach to the Study of Political Leaders and Decision-Making," *International Studies Quarterly*, vol. 13 (1969):190–222.

25. "The prince always makes his schemes rotate; he seeks to command in order to enrich himself, and to enrich himself in order to command." Jean-Jacques Rousseau, *A Lasting Peace Through the Federation of Europe*, translated by C. E. Vaughan (London: Constable, 1917), p. 99. The best account that we know of the strategies of statesmen involved in the ending of the Cold War is Don Oberdorfer's *The Turn* (New York: Simon and Schuster, 1991), which illustrates the complex mix of the worldviews—the interpretations and goals, some compatible with Realism, others with Liberalism—that shaped the diplomacy of Reagan, Gorbachev, George P. Shultz, Eduard Shevardnadze, and James A. Baker.

26. Robert Gilpin, *War and Change in World Politics* (Cambridge: Cambridge University Press, 1981), pp. 40–49.

27. Arnold Wolfers stresses the interrelations of goals and means, ultimate and proximate ends. See "The Goals of Foreign Policy," in Wolfers, *Discord and Collaboration* (Baltimore: Johns Hopkins Press, 1962), pp. 67–80. Interrelating ends, explanations, and policies has long been recognized as central to the project of international relations theory. See the report on the state of the field by Kenneth Thompson, "Toward a Theory of International Politics," in *Contemporary Theory in International Relations,* edited by Stanley Hoffmann (Englewood Cliffs, N.J.: Prentice-Hall, 1960), 17–28.

28. Thomas Scanlon, "Contractarianism and Utilitarianism," In *Utilitarianism and Beyond,* edited by Amartya Sen and Bernard Williams (Cambridge: Cambridge University Press, 1982), p. 116; for discussion, see Michael Walzer, *Interpretation and Social Criticism* (Cambridge, Mass.: Harvard University Press, 1987), pp. 46–48.

29. Stephen Walt, *Origins of Alliances* (Ithaca: Cornell University Press, 1988).

30. This is why Raymond Aron and Stanley Hoffmann begin their discussion of international relations theory with the assumption of a "decentralized milieu" (for Hoffman, see "International Relations as a Discipline" in Hoffmann, *Contemporary Theory*, p. 1).

31. For another example, see the discussion of the significance of personality factors in John P. Burke and Fred Greenstein, "Presidential Personality and National Security," *International Political Science Review*, vol. 10, no. 1 (1989):73–92. Their example is drawn from Vietnam War decisionmaking.

32. Richard Ned Lebow's study of international crises, *Between Peace and War* (Baltimore: Johns Hopkins University Press, 1981), draws useful distinctions between context and event that parallel the differences between general theory and reconstructing specific policy choices.

33. For example, an empirical statistical demonstration of the limitations of purely power-oriented analysis may be found in Bruce Bueno de Mesquita and David Lalman, "Empirical Support for Systemic and Dyadic Explanations of International Conflict," *World Politics,* vol. 41, no. 1 (October 1988):1–20; and a

formal demonstration in James D. Morrow, "Social Choice and System Structure in World Politics," *World Politics,* vol. 41, no. 1 (October 1988):75–97.

34. Hans J. Morgenthau, *Politics Among Nations* (New York: Knopf, 1973).

35. Robert Gilpin, "The Richness of the Tradition of Political Realism," and Kenneth Waltz, "Reflections on Theory of International Politics," both in *Neorealism and Its Critics,* edited by Robert Keohane (New York: Columbia University Press, 1986), pp. 301–321, 322–345.

36. See William Wohlforth, "Realism and the End of the Cold War," *International Security,* vol. 19, no. 3 (1995):91–129, for the first view, and John Mearsheimer, "Back to the Future: Instability in Europe After the Cold War," *International Security,* vol. 15, no. 1 (Summer 1990):5–56, for the second.

37. See Ikenberry and Deudney, "The International Sources of Soviet Change"; and Michael Doyle, "Liberalism and the Transition to a Post–Cold War System," in *The International System After the Collapse of the East-West Order,* edited by Armand Clesse, Richard Cooper, and Yoshikazu Sakamoto (Dordrecht: Martinus Nijhoff Publishers, 1994), pp. 85–105.

38. The *locus classicus* is Francis Fukuyama, "The End of History," *National Interest,* vol. 16 (Summer 1989):3–18.

39. Arnold Wolfers, "Political Theory and International Relations," the introduction to *The Anglo-American Tradition in Foreign Affairs,* edited by Arnold Wolfers and Laurence Martin (New Haven: Yale University Press, 1956), and in *Discord and Collaboration* (Baltimore: Johns Hopkins Press, 1962), p. 237.

2

Inventing International Relations: International Relations Theory After 1945

MILES KAHLER

The term "inventing" has become a flag for postmodern questioning of so-cial facts and the historical process that has given them weight. At its most subversive, "inventing" implies the subjection of scholarly endeavors to the microscope of skepticism: Knowledge is neither cumulative nor defined by accepted methods that align it ever more closely with an external and objec-tive truth. Instead it is a human creation subject to many influences that may not coincide with an agreed-upon understanding of scientific progress.[1] My purpose in reexamining the ways in which the new field of international re-lations dealt with the problem of international change after 1945 is less sub-versive in its intent. This revisionist review of the history of international re-lations does, however, fit within a recent wave of disciplinary introspection that has called into question triumphalist and Whiggish views of knowledge creation.[2] The history of such a young field, which only crystallized as part of the social sciences during the 1920s and 1930s, may appear to pose few issues of interpretation. Nevertheless, exploring and explaining the evolu-tion of international relations serves three important ends.

Intellectual archaeology of this kind may produce a less tendentious ac-count of intellectual activity over time, unearthing theoretical alternatives that have been consigned to darkness for other than scientific reasons. The privileging of particular approaches to international relations may result from both an internal logic of scholarship and from the social and political context of intellectual production. Although both external and internal explanations will be presented, a field so recently professionalized and so attuned to policy demands and contemporary history is likely to be influenced by its external context.[3]

Secondly, how we understand the history of international relations will also influence the future contours of the field; an understanding of our collective past is one determinant of our direction. Comprehending the invention of our traditions may be both illuminating and intellectually significant. Nor would international relations be the first or the oldest sphere of action that displayed recently invented traditions.[4]

Finally, an examination of our past may lead us to a better understanding of how to exit from our current discontents; we may come to understand not only why we have done what we have done but also why we are where we are. Like other, less significant events in the past, the end of the Cold War has introduced a large measure of either disarray (if one was previously content) or effervescence (if one was not) into the study of international relations. The past may provide guides to better and worse ways to resolve our current disciplinary dilemmas.

The historical retelling that follows is self-consciously centered on North America and, to a lesser degree, Britain and Western Europe. The issue of whether international relations remains "an American social science" and the implications of one's answer to that question have been discussed elsewhere.[5] An overlooked benefit of the Cold War's end is the lowering of ideological barriers to the construction of a field that is genuinely international. As the scope of its contributors expands across national borders, a disciplinary narrative that is broader than the one offered here will be required.

History and Great Debates:
Thinking About the Past

A stylized version of the history of international relations theory is typically framed by successive "great debates" that haunt countless undergraduate and graduate course descriptions. Although other fields mark their histories with grand theoretical controversies, the choice of "great debate" to describe the engine driving theoretical advance is unusual. The foundational myth of the field is an initial great debate between, on the one hand, idealists, wedded to legal and institutional analysis and blind to the requirements of power politics, and on the other, realists, armed with a theory grounded in human nature and state action and therefore prescient in their reading of interwar international relations. The idealists went down in deserved defeat; realism established itself as the reigning theory in the field.

A second great debate, between science and tradition, occurred in the 1960s. Misguided, principally British, proponents of the traditional study of international relations, which emphasized law and diplomatic history, went down in defeat (at least on this side of the Atlantic), and the grounding of international relations in a behavioral view of the social sciences was accomplished. Finally, the mainstream now confronts the clamor of a diverse group of critics attacking its scientific pretensions and normative biases, perhaps attacking the entire totalizing metanarrative of a field from a postmodern perspective. These outsiders have argued that they are defining a third great debate; the mainstream, satisfied with its progress, thus far fails to recognize it as such.[6]

Pervading this portrait of six decades or more is a strong belief that each debate has ended in scientific advance. Unfortunately, a reexamination of the field's history calls into question this benign interpretation. The protagonists in the debates are often misidentified. The outcome of the debates are misspecified: Winners and losers are rarely as clear as the official version. Some significant controversies are not included and others that should have occurred but did not—the debates that did not bark—drop from view.

Simply stripping away layers of disciplinary mythology and reconstructing intellectual discourse more completely and accurately would be valuable.[7] Explaining the course of invention in international relations must be far more tentative. At least four explanations for the field's evolution can be advanced. Two are internal to the field and its relations with other social sciences. International relations specialists, as members of one of the youngest social sciences, have been absorbed (occasionally obsessed) with their professional standing. Many "advances" were seen as such because they hardened the professional boundaries and barriers to entry in the field. At the same time, international relations began as a self-consciously interdisciplinary field. Its borrowings over time have shifted from one discipline to another, but its eventual capture by political science could not have been predicted at its beginning. The evolution of international relations was not hermetic, however. Its broader political and social context influenced its intellectual development as well. Many historians of the field have emphasized the influence of events—apparent anomalies presented by contemporary world politics—on the field of international relations. Brian Schmidt argues that the effect of international context has been exaggerated; nevertheless, such influence is not simply inferred by observers after the fact.[8] Those engaged in the invention of the field often acknowledge the impulse given by a turn in international events. The longer sweep of international history has seldom been given the weight of immediate and politically significant developments. Finally, international relations has been driven by demand. Its audience typically includes practitioners as well as scholars; at moments of international change or high uncertainty, policy demand may drive research as much as a purely internal logic. Each of these explanations is related to the others—events-driven and demand-driven periods of evolution tend to coincide; professional hardening over time has reinforced the boundaries of the field and weakened its earlier extravagant borrowing from outside.

Idealists, Realists, and the Hardening of International Relations

The first great debate between idealists and realists is a suitable place to begin excavating the field, since this episode and its misinterpretation have profoundly influenced subsequent development of the field.[9] The much disparaged idealists have nearly been erased from our collective intellectual memories, so thorough has the realist rewriting of history been. Few actually read them, since they have been caricatured as airy and naive proponents of the League of Nations, oblivious to the underlying and persistent realities of power and, above all, as amateurs rather than scholars.[10] Although a complete survey of all those later labeled "idealist" is impossible, two prominent examples, Norman Angell and James T. Shotwell, provide evidence that the interwar "idealists" have been misunderstood and their arguments misrepresented.

Norman Angell, author of *The Great Illusion* and many other works, has long served as a target for those undermining the importance of economic interdependence in shaping state behavior. Repeatedly and falsely, he has been portrayed as an exponent of the impossibility of war in an age of interdependence. Angell argued instead that enhanced economic interdependence among the industrialized nations of Europe had altered the economic calculus of warmaking: Any gains from territorial conquest within Europe could not equal the losses from disrupting patterns of trade and investment. This narrower argument was part of a broader case made by liberals before World War I and during the interwar decades that emphasized joint gains (the struggle of central concern is one of man with the universe, not man with man) and attacked the primacy of the state by exploring the development of transnational communities of opinion. But the underlying argument was not idealist, it was materialist: The contemporary state system and its competitive nationalism was a poor fit with underlying economic reality. "International politics are still dominated by terms applicable to conditions which the processes of modern life have altogether abolished."[11]

James T. Shotwell, a Canadian brought up in a setting of nineteenth-century liberalism, was in many ways the model interwar scholar-activist. He became involved with the U.S. government's propaganda machine during

World War I, worked with Colonel House in the preparations for the Paris Peace Conference, and later was instrumental in pressing for U.S. involvement in the League of Nations and in the Kellogg-Briand Pact. An often overlooked part of his career, however, was his role in stimulating large-scale research on international relations and serving as an entrepreneur to obtain funding for such research through institutions such as the Carnegie Endowment for International Peace. Despite his training as a medieval historian, Shotwell developed an early interest in the impact of the industrial and scientific revolutions.[12]

Shotwell's immersion in European history made him sensitive to the central role of war in creating European states and the European state system; he could construct blood-curdling passages about the predatory behavior of states.[13] Nevertheless, he argued, like Angell, that industrialization and science had made war "too dangerous to employ" and virtually impossible to limit.[14] Not only was war more costly in the new era, but also the territorial state system was no longer the only "map" of relevance; science and the growth of economic interdependence has created a new web of relations among peoples. In Shotwell's view, this material underpinning separated the post–World War I peace movement from earlier movements based solely on ethical principles or idealism.[15]

Angell and Shotwell could be described as liberals and institutionalists, but they were hardly idealists. What later critics pilloried as idealism in the interwar decades is better described as liberal materialism, neither so deterministic nor so infatuated with international institutions and law as the current image suggests. Shotwell and Angell were not seduced by a pacifist teleology—an inevitable evolution toward more cooperative states in international politics. Neither believed that material trends had eliminated war or had even touched all parts of the world; the conditions of interdependence existed in spatially limited parts of the international system. Although his prescriptions emphasized international institutions, Shotwell did not make exaggerated claims for the achievements of organizations like the League of Nations. More significant was an emphasis on democratic activism to change international relations. Belief in the power of public opinion is often portrayed as another illustration of hopeless liberal naïveté, but public opinion and its influence on diplomacy was one of the striking aspects of the peace-making process after World War I. Discovering that politicians were forced to respond to popular pressures—a source of great anguish to such realists as Harold Nicolson—was a revelation to the interwar liberals, since it offered an instrument by which the lessons of industrial warfare could be translated into policy.[16]

If the content of interwar liberalism has been distorted, its hegemony was also limited: Realism did not mount its theoretical charge against a field that was monolithic in its allegiances. Many active in defining the new field of international relations during the 1930s—Arnold Wolfers, Frederick Dunn, and Frederick Schuman, a University of Chicago historian who authored an influential text—displayed little of the idealism that was later described as dominant. In the first edition of his work, Schuman devoted scathing comments to overly optimistic accounts of progress in international politics, but he also borrowed materialist premises from some of those he criticized, arguing that the study of politics could not ignore "the 'social' and 'economic' configurations of human relations."[17] In a close examination of textbooks from the interwar decades, William C. Olson and A.J.R. Groom discovered neither internationalist nor idealist predominance. Of about forty titles in the mainstream of the new field from 1916 to 1941, "even if by 'idealist' we mean no more than stressing the efficacy of law and organization, only about half of these can be said to be even primarily idealistic in tone."[18]

Realism, the competitor to Anglo-American liberalism, was in large measure a transplant from continental Europe. The great transatlantic emigration of scholars influenced the development of fields as diverse as nuclear physics, sociology, and political theory.[19] The influx of scholars had an even greater impact on the institutionally weak and ill-defined field of international relations. Key members—Hans Morgenthau, Nicholas Spykman, John Herz—introduced a profoundly pessimistic and continental European emphasis on power politics into a field that was beginning to harden and professionalize. Just as idealism has been misportrayed, however, it is important to emphasize the deep pessimism of many realists regarding the rationalism and positivism that they associated with their scholarly foes. Hans Morgenthau, in particular, noted his early reaction against Marxism and Freud and his discontent with the "rationalistic pretenses" of his philosophy courses at Frankfurt in the 1920s. Like other realists, he reflected the turn toward and fascination with irrationalism that characterized European culture after World War I.[20] This aspect of transplanted realism is particularly ironic given the later wedding of realism to rational choice in the neorealist synthesis.[21] A deep distrust of any claims for a scientific study of international politics was also characteristic of realist practitioners such as George Kennan.[22]

This attack on liberalism and reason by some realists could be seen as simply another fusillade aimed at the idealist project that World War II had already fractured. Their critique was also directed at another target, however, one far more influential in the long run, a group that intersected with the so-called idealists more than would be admitted after 1945. This third contingent can be labeled the "scientists." International relations, one of the youngest of academic fields, lagged behind the other social sciences and history in its institutionalization and professionalization. What was later encapsulated as an interwar ideological battle between realism and idealism was coincident with the professionalization of the field and the adoption by many of its members of the model of natural science for their research. For those shaping this professionalization, the natural science model represented an inevitable and desirable maturation of international relations; for critics, such as Dorothy Ross, international relations simply joined other American social sciences that were marked by "liberal values, practical bent, shallow historical vision, and technocratic confidence."[23]

At the core of this movement was the Chicago school that spearheaded efforts to transform political science during the 1920s and 1930s. Charles Merriam, Harold Lasswell, and Quincy Wright all contributed to the study of world politics as part of a broader analysis of power and political actors ranging from individuals and groups to national governments.[24] As William Fox has described, for these intellectual godfathers of postwar behavioralism, power was the organizing principle of analysis, but no particular place was given to states or to military power. International relations was embedded in a broader political analysis.[25] Their point of agreement with the realists was narrow—that international politics should be studied as it is and not as it might be. This shared antinormative stance disguised divisions that would reemerge in later decades. The scientists embraced their version of a positivism modeled on the natural sciences; the realists were deeply skeptical of scientific pretensions defined in this way. Each group also held distinct views on the degree of disjuncture between domestic and international politics, with the scientists building out from domestic politics and the realists theorizing in from international anarchy and the security dilemma.

To many in the interwar years, the advance of the scientists, not the debate between realists and idealists, was the most significant development in international relations. When Hans Morgenthau arrived at Chicago, he confronted Quincy Wright and a research enterprise with which he could have had little sympathy. In the words of one of his students, "Power politics was a dirty and forbidden word in the Chicago of his time."[26] The scientific movement of the 1920s and 1930s shared more goals (and personnel) with the idealists or liberals than it did with the realists. Shotwell, in his introduction to an early survey of international relations in the United States, lauded the scientific enterprise and the embedding of international relations within the coalescing social sciences. Science led, in his view, to "constructive planning," which was "the supreme task of the social sciences, and the field of international relations offers the best of laboratories for their study."[27] Shotwell was one of the founding research entrepreneurs of the field.[28] The infrastructure of research that was part of social-scientific enterprise in the 1920s—Merriam was instrumental in founding the Social Science Research Council in 1923—had already been extended to international relations. In the 1930s, university research institutes were devoted specifically to the new field.[29] This burst of foundation-supported research was part of a broader desire to affect public policy and social change through research. Both interwar liberals and many scientists of the era shared a program to bring knowledge to power.[30] Their chosen targets differed, however: Many liberal internationalists aimed to influence broader public opinion and the educational system; the scientists more often turned to direct policy advice. The line was not sharp, however, and the success of the scientists waxed and waned in political science and in international relations during the interwar decades. Their project was sharply criticized by more traditional scholars, including William Yandell Elliott, future mentor of the realist Henry Kissinger.[31]

Postwar Consensus and the Hardening of the Discipline

Early postwar conferences and surveys of international relations quickly rescripted interwar debates as a battle between a feckless "utopianism" that had "cast a shadow of academic disrepute over the new field" and a new emphasis on power politics as a "natural reaction to the excesses of sentimentalism."[32] Even William Fox took a less measured and tolerant view of interwar research than he later would; his evaluation was later assimilated by others reviewing the postwar state of the field, reinforcing a view of the inevitable joint triumph of realism and science.[33] Interwar scholarship had been disparaged to such a degree that Dwight Waldo admitted in his 1956 survey that it may have been "discounted unduly."[34]

Vulgarization of the interwar record in the decade after 1945 resembled the "counterprogressive" tendency in postwar history: Both constructed a straw man whose hegemony in the field was exaggerated and whose accomplishments were dismissed.[35] The preferred account of the postwar consensus in international relations was events-driven; interwar scholarship could not deal with the anomalous events of the 1930s, World War II, and the Cold War. A threatening international context was only one explanation, however. Professionalization and new external demand also served to tilt the intellectual balance. A new generation of Young Turks, impelled by their service in government and the military during World War II, were intent on overturning their predecessors, a familiar battle between scholarly generations. The new cohort also accelerated the professionalization of the field. International relations, as noted earlier, was among the last of social science fields to achieve disciplinary status. As in history and the other social sciences before it, those defining the field felt it necessary to separate themselves from what was portrayed as an amateurish past. Amateurism was part of the image of interwar liberalism that was transmitted to the postwar generation, a past of League of Nations societies and peace movements. Both realists and scientists rejected that past, not only for its alleged disregard for the realities of power but also for the obstacles that it presented to achieving professional esteem.

Realists and scientists were also sustained by a new demand for the product of their labors, a demand that offered burgeoning institutional support in exchange. The international relations infrastructure that had begun to appear in the 1930s exploded after World War II as government and foundations increased their demand for knowledge to match the new global interests of the United States. Realism was doubly favored: Not only did it benefit from the same research infrastructure, but also its theoretical stance fit with renewed government emphasis on international commitment and on meeting the Soviet threat; realism was "interpreted as providing a rationale for not appeasing the presumably unappeasable and therefore for the cold war."[36]

Just as later portrayals of the interwar period deserve scrutiny, so too the solidity of post-1945 realist hegemony and the alliance of convenience between realism and science should be carefully qualified. Realism quickly took on the ideological coloration of its new American environment. Even in early realist works, such as Nicholas Spykman's *America's Strategy in World Politics*, liberal institutions make a surprising appearance: Spykman, for example, urged a "regional League of Nations" for East Asia rather than a "one-sided treaty of alliance."[37] Much as American historians blithely reinterpreted Leopold Ranke as a "scientist" of the American kind in the nineteenth century and political science had "Americanized" earlier in the century, so American international relations quickly gave realism what Fox called a "pragmatic meliorist" cast, accepting the reality of the security dilemma in international politics but urging its mitigation through gradualist, liberal prescriptions.[38] This process of amalgamation reached its endpoint when realist John Herz, who coined the phrase "security dilemma," urged "realist liberalism" on his colleagues.[39] The rationalist, improving, progressive strand in American culture transformed the antiscientific pessimism of realism and incorporated it.

Many on the scientific side of the postwar consensus continued to express skepticism about realist pretensions, particularly when voiced in philosophical rather than positivist vocabulary. Quincy Wright, a senior member of the scientific wing, wrote sardonically of Herz's work: "This analysis suggests that 'realism' and 'idealism' have functioned as propaganda terms according to which everyone sought to commend whatever policy he favored by calling it 'realistic'. . . . From this usage we learn that in the past two decades political propagandists have regarded 'realism' as a plus term and 'idealism' as a minus term."[40] Another icon of behavioralism, Harold Lasswell, described "power politics" as a "sentimentalized term," an ironic twist of a favorite realist adjective.[41] A new generation of scholars openly took up the idealist cause, although most seemed to prefer putting the tired and increasingly irrelevant great debate behind them.[42]

Other young scholars, such as Ernst Haas, subjected realist terminology to the scientific microscope and found it wanting.[43] The outcome of World War II could, in any case, be interpreted as much as a triumph of liberal internationalism, particularly in the sphere of economic organization, as one that confirmed realist postulates.[44] As a result, the study of international organizations, despite the setbacks of the 1930s, displayed considerable resilience, although the study of international law began its lengthy divorce from international relations.[45]

International relations was not marked by a clear Kuhnian paradigm shift after 1945; the field remained heterogeneous and continued to include a liberal (or at least nonrealist) corps of practitioners. The often tense alliance between realists and scientists did have significant and often unrecognized consequences, however. For both wings of postwar international relations, power became the core analytic concept. Since the scientists yearned for professionalization, the field became embedded in academic political science. Much of the interdisciplinary richness of the 1930s (which had made professional self-definition difficult) was lost.[46] International political economy, whether of the liberal or the historical-materialist variety, was tainted by its association with Marxism during the Cold War.[47] Study of international organizations continued and investigation of regional integration began in the 1950s, but international institutions more broadly defined (including international law) were hardly regarded as the most exciting frontiers of research in the field. For the scientists, individuals and groups were the core units of analysis; for the realists, it was the state in an anarchic international environment. Institutions had been tarred with the idealist brush and would take some time to be reestablished as central to the field.

The environment of postwar professionalization and demand for research from government consumers virtually eliminated any search for an audience beyond one's colleagues and the modern prince and dampened normative inquiry. Advice directed to popular audiences and efforts to influence public opinion were labeled "propaganda." As Novick describes in the case of history, "the approved postwar sensibility was 'the tragic sense,' and the approved posture, spectatorial."[48] To change the world (not a goal to which one would easily admit), an elitist model was prescribed: At a conference on institutes and their publics in 1953, near unanimity was voiced for the view that "the primary task of the institutes must be to influence the minority that shapes public opinion."[49] Gabriel Almond's classic study of public opinion both reflected and influenced this elitist view of foreign policy.[50] Research directed to particular international goals, such as a more peaceful world, carried the whiff of interwar "utopianism" that alarmed specialists during the Cold War. At best such normative speculation was postponed to a time when the requirements of science had been satisfied.[51] At a time when the parameters of U.S. policy were widely per-

ceived as set by an overwhelming threat from Soviet communism, normative debates were shelved for the duration.[52]

A final consequence of the alliance of realists and scientists was neglect of
explanations for international change. Realists argued for regularities across
time in the domain of power politics; scientists sought their own lawlike
generalizations about human and national behavior. Explanations of change
were not central to either research program. In a Cold War world systemic
change was assumed to occur at a glacial pace in any case. International relations had taken its first step toward a future of comparative statics and
equilibrium analysis, a future that resembled its past of balances of power
and cycles of great-power rise and decline. In this it resembled other social
sciences that had moved away from "historico-evolutionary models . . . to
specialized sciences focused on short-term processes rather than long-term
change over time."[53] It was an oddly comforting, if limited, vision for a field
born in a century marked by violent ruptures and revolutionary upheaval.

Realism and Science: End of Alliance

The second great debate bore little resemblance to the first. It was not stimulated by cataclysmic international events; it occurred at a time of superpower dominance and economic tranquillity, before the Vietnam War had
rattled American social science. It represented a late and somewhat faint
echo of the behavioral revolution in political science played out in the pages
of *World Politics* and *International Studies Quarterly*.[54] The debate was
not theoretical in content. The proponents of tradition (Hedley Bull in the
lead) and science (Morton Kaplan as protagonist) held theoretical and policy positions that cut across the divide that defined the debate. In light of
the history already recounted, however, one can interpret these competing
definitions of international relations as the end of a tenuous alliance between realists and scientists that had defined the postwar consensus. Many
realists shared Bull's unease about the direction of the field: Morgenthau
had situated himself squarely on the antibehavioral side and launched a
vigorous attack on works by Lasswell and Kaplan in a review article.[55] To
members of a field that has, whatever its theoretical and methodological
disagreements, defined itself as a social science, this great debate now seems
a nondebate. Our reaction, however, suggests its larger consequences for
the evolution of international relations.

The second debate concerned methodology, not theory or the sources of
theoretical innovation. In a telling contribution to the debate, Marion Levy
replied to Morton Kaplan:

> I deeply regret that studies in methodology show no promise whatsoever of
> leading to this kind of knowledge [about international phenomena]. Studies of

methodology improve the probability of making something of a good idea. But nothing will replace the importance of creativity in discovering ideas that can be stated with rigor, care, and precision, and creativity in discovering those which can be stated in terms of a small number of variables and among which deductive interdependencies can be shown.[56]

Theory in international relations remained underdeveloped (or implicitly realist) in an era of competing methodologies. Method, so important to Bull and others, proved of little significance in explaining theoretical evolution.

The second great debate also gave an inaccurate impression to many Americans that the study of international relations in Britain and the rest of Western Europe—carried out by the second largest national concentration of scholars and a useful antidote to American ethnocentrism—was incurably hidebound and antiscientific in its orientation. The debate only deepened the parochialism that, paradoxically, has long characterized the study of international relations.

Perhaps most important, the debate symbolized the loss not of "tradition" but of a larger conception of international relations; an argument about method was confused with an argument about scope. Although Bull's views borrowed much from the realists, others have included him in a neo-Grotian strand of international relations theory that is concerned with "deep" institutions in an international society that constitutes and defines individual states.[57] Interest in those institutions would not revive for nearly two decades. Bull's criticisms of the scientific approach, which are not a model of clarity, also resembled later postmodern assaults on the lack of a self-conscious and critical stance in mainstream international relations theory:

> [The scientists'] thinking is certainly characterized by a lack of any sense of inquiry into international politics as a continuing tradition to which they are the latest recruits; by an insensitivity to the conditions of recent history that have produced them, provided them with the preoccupations and perspectives they have, and colored these in ways of which they might not be aware . . . by an uncritical attitude toward their own assumptions, and especially toward the moral and political attitudes that have a central but unacknowledged position in much of what they say.[58]

The apparent defeat of the traditional or classical approach in this second great debate imposed losses even on the empirical program that the victorious scientists would pursue. International relations was severed from political philosophy, diplomatic history, and international law. The latter was gradually expelled from political science departments, and even after international relations reinvented the study of institutions in the 1970s, the empirical value of legal studies would remain unrecognized. Within the narrower field that emerged from the second debate, Hedley Bull's exasperation suggested that security studies—in which he played an important role—was also drifting away from the research programs defined by the scientific wing. As professional self-definition continued to sharpen methodologically, those who defined themselves in other terms were quickly consigned to the "amateur" status previously reserved for interwar idealists.

The field of security studies was also undergoing a transformation and division at this time, one that pitted scientist against scientist. The development of deterrence theory in the 1950s and 1960s was a rare example of genuine interdisciplinary collaboration, a rapidly advancing research frontier, and immediate effects on national policy, particularly in the area of nuclear strategy and arms control. Indeed, demand from the policy community and newly forged links to the national security bureaucracies may explain why the second wave of deterrence theory in the late 1950s had a far greater impact than the first wave of the immediate postwar years.[59] The new methodology of game theory figured prominently in the development of deterrence theory; its rational-choice microfoundations, useful in illuminating strategic interaction, marked an important first step toward the neorealist synthesis of the 1980s.[60]

Nevertheless, links between second wave deterrence theorists and the U.S. government as well as the implicit acceptance by many strategists of Cold War realism stimulated dissident currents among international relations specialists. Peace research was the most important reaction to the melding of realism, nuclear weapons, and the new demand from government. The connection to interwar international relations was direct in the case of peace research: The venerable figure of Quincy Wright wrote the first article in the *Journal of Conflict Resolution* in 1957. In place of the underlying realist basis of much strategic thinking at this time, peace research submitted claims of the inevitability of violent conflict to scientific scrutiny and took a more activist stance toward policy debates, particularly over nuclear weapons. The postwar distaste for "utopianism" was dissipating under the shadow of nuclear weapons. Studying what is no longer implied that fundamental change was impossible. Peace research borrowed its methodology from the scientists and also its belief that the dynamics of violence among individuals, among groups and among states displayed similarities: interstate violence and the realm of international anarchy were no longer privileged.[61]

The Great Debate That Failed: Neoliberalism, Dependency Theory, and Neorealism

Peace research was only one manifestation of a resurgence of neoliberal theorizing that appeared during the 1960s as the Cold War lost its chill. Peace research found much of its support and research infrastructure in

Western Europe. Europe, where long-standing nationalist conflicts had apparently been tamed and a much imitated experiment in regional integration was under way, provided new grounds for challenging realist assumptions, whether in the evolution of security communities, examined by Karl Deutsch and Bruce Russett, or in the exploding field of regional integration, in which Ernst Haas, Leon Lindberg, and others proposed a neofunctionalist mode of explanation. Students of integration undermined realism by first selecting developments in international relations that fitted realist predictions poorly and then explaining those developments by processes and actors outside the state.

Interwar liberals had been absorbed by the issues of war and peace. Neoliberalism in the 1960s and 1970s was drawn to the implications of international economic change. A long postwar economic boom, combined with concerted liberalizing measures among the industrialized countries, produced rapid growth in trade and financial flows. Large-scale American investment in Western Europe and European reactions to "the American challenge" directed public and scholarly attention to the multinational corporation and its potential for reshaping international politics. Growing cross-border trade and investment provoked the interest of both political scientists and economists and produced a rebirth of international political economy. International organization, which had become a backwater of postwar international relations, revived as the collaborative management of international economic relations rose on the scholarly and policy agenda.[62]

Economic interdependence could be narrowly defined, as it was in the influential work of Richard Cooper, but in other hands, it became a full-blown alternative to the dominant realist conception of international order. Edward Morse challenged the state-centric assumptions of realism, asserting that the growth of economic interdependence and transnational actors had fundamentally altered the classical Westphalian state system.[63] Robert O. Keohane and Joseph Nye's formulation of complex interdependence summed up a decade of neoliberal scholarship that had introduced or reintroduced transnational relations, economic interdependence, security communities, international organizations, and the broader concept of international regimes.[64]

The Vietnam War undermined realism by calling into question the assumption of tight international constraints on national policy. The war also produced a burst of interest in foreign policy and its determinants. Widespread opposition to the war created an audience for revisionist diplomatic historians who disputed conventional accounts of Cold War origins and undermined prevailing images of a reactive United States and a ceaselessly expanding Soviet Union.[65] Convinced that the United States did have a wider scope for choice in its foreign policy, researchers on national policy moved beyond the descriptive studies of decisionmaking characteristic of the early postwar years to theoretical approaches that provided clear cautions for policymakers, whether on the costs of misperception (as social-psychological insights were imported into the field) or on the dangers of organizational slippage and bureaucratic competition.[66]

As these neoliberal innovations challenged an apparent realist hegemony in the United States, another theoretical combatant appeared from an unlikely quarter. Dependency theory responded to many of the same international economic changes as neoliberalism and, like neoliberalism, redefined system structure to emphasize economic links between center and periphery (rather than interstate competition) and disaggregated domestic politics in peripheral societies. Unlike neoliberal theories, however, structuralism, promoted by the Economic Commission for Latin America (ECLA), and Marxism—central theoretical influences on dependency theory—assigned these systemic and internal constraints a negative (dependence not interdependence) rather than positive value.

The emergence of dependency theory and its rapid acceptance in North America and Western Europe depended on both external context and apparent theoretical anomalies that dependency theory could claim to resolve. Dependency theory was a collective product of the social science research infrastructure that had been constructed in Latin America after 1945. That constellation of research institutions attracted an interdisciplinary group of scholars who shared a belief that there was some blockage in the development of Latin American capitalism. This perceived anomaly (lack of integrated industrialization after more than a century of political independence) is itself puzzling from the vantage point of the 1990s: Latin American economies enjoyed relatively high growth during the late 1950s and early 1960s, and the international economic environment was more benign than it would be in any other postwar period.[67] As Fernando Henrique Cardoso commented, the creators of dependency theory "were seeking new ideas that could explain why the early optimism about development in the postwar years was turning into bitter frustration."[68]

Receptivity to dependency theory in both Latin America and the United States was heightened in the late 1960s and early 1970s by renewed attention to U.S. intervention in the Third World. Theories of imperialism that had been submerged during the Cold War received greater attention and shifted the theoretical base for dependency analysis away from its structuralist roots toward a Marxist perspective.[69] World-systems analysis, which took shape around this time, borrowed much of its vocabulary from structuralist and dependency analysis without adopting Marxist dynamics as the engine for global change. Compared to dependency theory, however, the world-systems approach awarded an even more dominant role to the system in shaping individual societies. In both cases explanations for development or underdevelopment on the periphery were rooted in the evolution of international capitalism, not the state system.

By the mid-1970s the theoretical claims of dependency theory had been taken up by mainstream political scientists in North America (to the dismay of some dependency theorists).[70] Two challengers, liberal and radical, offered potent alternatives to realist hegemony within international relations. Both emphasized system defined in economic rather than power-political terms; both rejected the state-centric emphasis of realism. In each, domestic development was shaped by the system through transnational linkages that were only partially mediated or not mediated at all by the state. In certain versions of both liberal and dependency theories, the state lost its crucial gatekeeping role vis-à-vis the international system. Despite the apparent strength of these challenges, however, both contenders failed to survive the following decade. Neoliberalism was redefined away from complex interdependence toward a state-centric version more compatible with realism. Dependency theory was virtually driven from the theoretical field. What might have been another great debate faded as realism, redefined and rendered more acceptable to the scientists in international relations, reclaimed a central theoretical position.

The persistence and reassertion of realism during the 1980s has been well documented. K. J. Holsti carefully examined leading textbooks and the works to which they refer, not only in the United States but also in other countries. He found that at the start of the 1980s realism remained the dominant paradigm in each of the countries, with the exception of Japan; in the United States there was a slight shift in favor of neoliberal and dependency theory after 1970, but it was not great.[71] Kenneth Waltz's *Theory of International Politics* was central in stimulating a new generation to become interested in neorealist theory; his efforts to transform the vague and imprecise tenets of classical realism into a form more acceptable to the scientific mainstream of the field attracted some who had labored on alternative approaches.[72] The turn of realism in a more self-consciously scientific direction occurred at the end of a decade in which criticisms of the realist paradigm from scientists testing hypotheses based on realism had grown louder.[73] By the mid-1980s not only had neorealism claimed a central position in the study of international security (where realism had never been seriously challenged), but also it had, in the form of hegemonic stability theory, claimed a central place in international political economy, which had been the primary source of alternative theoretical viewpoints within international relations.

The rise of neorealism in the 1980s and the fading of both neoliberal and radical (dependency) analyses is not a puzzle for neorealists: In the selective process of theoretical elaboration and testing, neorealism had simply offered more parsimonious explanations. More recent developments suggest that such purely internal and theoretical explanations for the consolidation of neorealism are partial at best. Certainly, the alternatives to neorealist analysis demonstrated shortcomings in elaborating a research program and explaining critical international developments. As Keohane and Nye argue in their perceptive retrospective on *Power and Interdependence*, the concept of complex interdependence was not designed as a theory "but as a thought experiment about what politics might look like if the basic assumptions of realism were reversed."[74] Particularly at the systemic level, it did not seem to present an alternative that could compete with structure defined as distribution of power without including the goals and instruments of state policy. Other elements of neoliberal theory, such as interdependence and international regimes, could be accommodated within neorealism; in certain respects, they were captured by the emerging neorealist synthesis.

Dependency theory's decline was also due in part to its internal and theoretical treatment of two apparent anomalies: rapid industrialization in parts of the periphery (particularly the newly industrializing countries) in the late 1960s and 1970s and a turn toward democracy in Latin America in the 1980s. This degree of variation among the trajectories of developing countries was a major anomaly for a theory that emphasized systemic determinants of national development. Dependency theorists dealt with these developments by amending and supplementing the theory with domestic variables, particularly state capabilities in encouraging industrialization and bargaining with foreign investors. A better fit with existing patterns of industrialization on the periphery was won at the cost of both parsimony and the original systemic emphasis of the theory.[75] Paradoxically, in emphasizing the state, revised dependency theory paralleled the state-centrism of neorealism and redefined neoliberalism, theories with very different images of system structure.

A final, internal explanation for the widespread acceptance of neorealism was its compatibility, after translation, with the rational-choice and game-theoretic approaches that were winning widespread acceptance in international relations and other social sciences. The transmutation of neorealism from its original Waltzian structuralism—Waltz had explicitly argued that his theory did not require rationalist microfoundations—to an approach with rationalist and individualist premises was crucial to its success.[76] The rational and state-centric postulates of revised neorealism attracted many who were less interested in its structural features.

These conceptual and internal explanations for the fading of dependency theory, the redefinition of neoliberalism, and a wider acceptance of the neorealist research program in the early 1980s are only partly convincing. The theoretical weaknesses of neorealism—easily as great as those of its competitors—were overlooked in ways that suggest other explanations for its popularity. One argument for neorealism's success is familiar from the history of international relations since the interwar period: A rise in international insecurity, specifically the onset of the "new" Cold War in 1979 and 1980, added to the appeal of realism, as it had in the past.[77] The field had entered yet another of its events-driven cyclical swings in the realist direction.

Apparent disorder in the international political economy of the 1970s and the adoption of defensive national policies in the face of that turmoil had shifted attention from the new features of economic interdependence to the political prerequisites of a liberal economic order. Robert Gilpin and Charles Kindleberger staked out theoretical ground for what would become the theory of hegemonic stability.[78] At the same time, a neoliberal experiment, the European Community, reached a temporary hiatus in the face of external economic shocks. The leading exponent of regional integration theory—perhaps the most fully elaborated body of neoliberal theory—declared that "regional integration in Western Europe has disappointed everybody: there is no federation, the nation-state behaves as if it were both obstinate and obsolete, and what once appeared to be a distinctive 'supranational' style now looks more like a huge regional bureaucratic appendage to an intergovernmental conference in permanent session."[79]

These international events posed questions for competing theoretical stances, but they hardly signaled a return to the military insecurity and state-dominated world economy of the 1930s. Economic integration in the world economy proceeded apace, particularly in the sphere of financial liberalization and globalization of markets. New forms of multinational investment and novel linkages among international firms appeared. Coincident with the fading of dependency theory in the 1980s, debt-ridden economies in Latin America and sub-Saharan Africa were more deeply influenced by the capitalist world economy than they had been at any time since 1945.

Events supply only part of the answer to the faltering of these alternatives to neorealism. The spatial distribution of international relations research offers some additional purchase on the shifting balance in theoretical allegiances. National parochialism in the field of international relations combined with the continued central position of the United States to support the agenda of neorealism, an agenda infused with the concerns of anxious Americans. The implications of hegemonic decline (if U.S. decline could be demonstrated) drove the neorealist agenda in international political economy. National setting may have had a second effect: individualist and rationalist models (exemplified by a transformed neorealism) have enormous appeal in American social science. As Dorothy Ross argues, they best "embody the individualistic and ahistorical premises of liberal exceptionalism."[80] In this sense neorealism marked the final stage in the Americanization of realism.

Demand from policymaking consumers of international relations research spurred some earlier theoretical developments in the field, particularly second-wave deterrence theory. Such demand had little to do with the popularity of neorealism, however: Academic neorealists (including Kenneth Waltz and Robert Gilpin) had little time for the revived Cold War views of American conservatives; neorealists were often explicitly critical of Reagan administration defense and foreign policies. Reaganite anticommunism was marked by a revival of ideological competition with the Soviet Union. Neoconservative champions of the ideological battle had little in common with realists like Henry Kissinger or academic neorealists.

Although realism may have served to legitimate U.S. competition with the Soviet Union in the 1940s and 1950s, academic neorealism argued for managing and tempering that competition in the 1980s. University research had become disconnected from the policy because of the Vietnam War and a key institutional innovation of the 1970s: the Washington think tank. Policymakers in search of foreign policy advice or a new agenda did not need to turn to the university, as they often had in the 1950s. New suppliers of ideas—tailor-made for policy appetites—now existed within easy reach; many of these suppliers were former policymakers themselves.[81] The new, politically connected think tanks competed successfully for policymaking consumers, but few scholarly members of the field of international relations seemed to care.

Although the policy community exercised less and less influence on the course of international relations research in the 1980s, foundations, through the pattern of their funding, could still shift incentives, particularly for younger scholars. Large-scale funding of security studies in the 1980s undoubtedly strengthened neorealism, since many in the new generation of security specialists, whatever their policy preferences, identified themselves as neorealists. As for the research infrastructure in Latin America that had produced dependency theory, it had been eroded by repressive authoritarian governments in the 1970s. During the following decade academic attention in the region turned toward concrete and pragmatic measures to escape economic crisis rather than systemic explanations for underdevelopment.

Whatever weight is attached to internal and contextual explanations for the evolution of international relations theory in the 1980s, the promised great debate among neoliberals, neorealists, and dependency theorists did not occur. By the end of the 1980s, the theoretical contest that might have been was reduced to relatively narrow disagreements within one state-centric, rationalist model of international interaction. The crucial distinction between neoliberal institutionalism and neorealism came to lie in their assessments of the importance of absolute gains or relative gains calculations among states.[82]

Another Theoretical Turn: Postmoderns and Sociologists

For those content with the Tweedledum of neorealism and the Tweedledee of neoliberalism, the subsidence of great debates was simply a sign that the pre-paradigmatic phase in international relations research was over.

However, the history of the field—its evolution shaped by international events, its professionalization, and demands from competing audiences—casts considerable doubt on this comfortable assumption. The proclamation of a Kuhnian paradigm shift is often a signal that such a shift has probably not occurred; paradigm is as often a weapon used in scientific battles as a description of theoretical achievement.[83] By the 1990s a combination of internal dissatisfaction with the progressive narrowing of the research agenda and dramatic, unexpected international events combined to give a new turn to theoretical debates, much as they had in the past.

Those dramatic events included the end of the Cold War, which represented a fundamental change in great-power competition for the first time since 1945, one that presented a deep challenge to neorealism. Although a complete explanation for the changes that ended the Soviet empire in Eastern Europe and then the Soviet Union itself will not be offered for some time, structural realism is unlikely to contribute much to that explanation. The world was bipolar in 1989 and, some would argue, remains bipolar in military terms today, yet all agree that international politics has been profoundly transformed. Of equal significance, that transformation, which included the rapid demise of an imperial power, occurred with no great-power conflict and remarkably little loss of life.[84]

As might be expected, these events and others, such as accelerated institution-building in the European Community and widespread opening to the international economy by developing countries, revived interest in a broadened liberal theory. The new turn in research addressed the role of international institutions in facilitating cooperation and the transformations produced by economic integration (or the desire for such integration). Above all it represented the triumph of reductionism. Structural realism and its research agenda had gone the way of its system-level rivals—complex interdependence and dependency theory. The explanatory power of structural variables—defined as the distribution of power—was demonstrated to be exceedingly weak. Hegemonic stability theory had been theoretically undermined and empirically challenged: A "strong" version of the theory that relied solely on hegemonic power distribution without accounting independently for the preferences of the hegemonic power seemed to explain very little in the history of international cooperation, the rise and fall of regimes, or the stability of the international economic order. Even the presence or absence of a liberal hegemonic power did not seem necessary to explain the persistence of institutions or habits of cooperation.[85] The same questioning of the importance of polarity as an explanation for international conflict was carried out by scholars using a wide range of methodologies over a considerable historical span.[86] Those who continued to elaborate neorealist theories were forced to improve the empirical fit by adding a domestic (and often subjective) dimension to the explanation.[87] Parsimony was sacrificed to obtain adequate explanatory punch.

Renewed interest in the sources of national policy ranged well beyond the old decisionmaking frameworks or social-psychological critiques of rationalist assumptions. The pattern of research also displayed refreshing differences from the past. Islands of research interest—such as the aversion of democracies to war with one another—attracted scholars using diverse methodologies who conversed with one another. A healthy eclecticism was complemented by clear preferences for particular styles of explanation, from sectoral interests to government institutions to ideational clusters. Few seemed intent on establishing a new dominant paradigm that would render illegitimate alternative research programs. A broad if rough-and-ready agreement on what constitutes "science" in international relations was apparent.

Into this healthy confusion stepped two new challengers that did not fit the old and often poorly defined contenders of realism, liberalism, or Marxism (or their more refined descendants). The appearance of these newest contenders represented the unearthing of some of the buried elements in the history of international relations and also the injection of European social theory into an increasingly Americanized and remarkably parochial field. Although Robert O. Keohane grouped these critics of the neorealist consensus as reflectivist, their numbers included at least two tendencies: a more radical group of critics that centers its attacks on questions of method and epistemology (the postmoderns) and a second group (the sociologists) that does not question the scientific enterprise of the field (whatever its qualms about positivist methodology) but does reject the individualist and state-centric premises of both neorealism and neoliberalism.

The postmoderns and their onslaught on the scientific pretensions of international relations represent the revenge of classical realism on its neorealist heirs. Postmoderns such as Richard Ashley transform an irrationalism and critical stance derived from the European origins of realism into a profound skepticism about scientific claims. Although the affirmative postmoderns (as labeled by Pauline Rosenau) may widen the scope of the field, unearthing the buried strands that were omitted in the writing and rewriting of our short history, one can predict that the postmoderns will fail in their effort to launch a third great debate for two reasons.[88] Postmodernism rejects the totalizing claims of mainstream theory. Therefore, any great debate would be one in which one side refuses to win and also refuses to accept defeat. An intellectual guerrilla war is the most that can be expected. More important, despite frequent theoretical importations into international relations, professionalization over five decades has erected formidable barriers to imports from the humanistic disciplines. The postmoderns must win converts from among individuals who are self-selected and self-defined as social scientists, whatever their methodological choices. Few are likely to forgo that identity for the unsatisfying toil of postmodern analysis, an analysis that proudly rejects the claims of scientific certainty in favor of an interpretive stance.

If the postmoderns represent a challenge to the scientific pretensions of international relations, another group, the sociologists, take on its current individualist and state-centric premises. Their criticism centers in part on the narrow neoliberal definition of international institutions as an expression of exogenously defined state interests. At least in the case of "fundamental" institutions, the sociologists argue that institutions constitute states and their practices; such institutions are "preconditions for sovereign states and meaningful state action rather than consciously chosen artifacts."[89] Although this view of institutions and their constitutive character parallels that in contemporary sociology, particularly the structuration theory of Anthony Giddens and the new institutionalism of John Meyer, it also recalls the neo-Grotian and traditionalist views that departed American international relations after the second great debate.[90]

Like the postmoderns, the sociologists work against strong investments within international relations. Even those skeptical of the more austere variants of neorealism tend to transfer more and more explanatory power to the level of domestic politics and thus move further away from the system-constituting image presented by the sociologists. The sociologists attempt a revival of system-level theorizing at a moment when most in the field have lost interest in previous systemic projects.

Explaining Theoretical Evolution in International Relations

A Kuhnian model of scientific revolution bears no resemblance to the evolution of theory in international relations. Neorealists proudly trace their origins to classical Greece—revolution is hardly the dominant metaphor for theoretical change in the field. Paradigms do not topple and destroy older foes, although the ability of realism to bury the record of interwar idealism would come close to the Kuhnian model if international relations had existed as a well-defined field at that time. Instead, the history of the field demonstrates the rise and fall of theoretical alternatives over time, according to a rhythm that is often driven by international events: Realism increases its appeal and extends its research program during moments of international insecurity; its critics extend their arguments during moments of relative international stability (in this history, during the 1920s, the 1960s, and perhaps the 1990s).

Even a crude internal account of theoretical development that begins with theoretical variation and proposes a model of testing, selection, and revision in the face of anomalies hardly matches the post-1945 history that has been described. Initial theoretical variation and innovation has by some measures been excessive: As Holsti noted, there are incentives for apparent innovation in international relations and other American social sciences; grand and middle-range theories proliferate. From another perspective, there has been relatively little genuine innovation, since so much theorizing has centered on realism and liberal and Marxist critics of realism.[91]

Rather than occurring within professional confines, theoretical selection has been influenced at times by external events and the context of the field. Some theories have been buried and others privileged, not by careful tests internal to the discipline but by apparent anomalies thrown up by recent history. The importance of "current events" anomalies gives the development of the field a peculiar volatile quality: Rather than confronting anomalies in the broad stretches of international history that remain unexamined, theoretical "testing" occurs in a random and often surprising fashion.

Finally, the field has also been driven by anxiety about its professional self-definition and concern over its boundaries and membership. These concerns were particularly acute before the field was firmly implanted in political science, but they remain today in the uneasy relationship between the scholarly community and foreign-policy practitioners. Demand from the world of practitioners undoubtedly strengthened the theoretical hold of realism in the immediate postwar years, although policymakers often chose one set of realist recommendations and ignored others (as both George Kennan and Hans Morgenthau discovered). During and after the Vietnam War, however, scholarly and policy worlds drifted apart. Academics became averse to reputations as pundits; policymakers found scholarly theorizing beside the point. This separation was a question of infrastructure (for example, the rise of the Washington think tanks); it was also grounded in the insecurity of university specialists. An easy flow across the boundaries between university and government might endanger the reserved skills and arcana that support professional standing in a field with blurred boundaries and uncertain membership.

Recent scholarship in international relations confirms these historical patterns and also carries suggestions of change. The end of the Cold War set off a predictable new round of rethinking within the field. Whatever the value of this theoretical ferment, one shrewd observer warned before the Cold War ended of "the tendency of academics in our field to develop theoretical innovations on the basis of recent diplomatic developments—even before these developments have assumed the character of long-term trends or patterns of behavior."[92] Increasingly, particularly among those investigating national policies, old realist and liberal labels are difficult to apply. Despite the challenge of the postmoderns, a broad consensus on what constitutes evidence and scientific technique has developed across methodological divides. The second great debate no longer rocks the field. Connections to the study of comparative politics and political economy have been strengthened by the burst of research activity at the level of national policy, remedying a long-standing weakness in liberal, realist, and radical analysis. The relationship with other disciplines, which has often been characterized by indiscriminate borrowing, appears to rest on a more symmetric basis.

The other contributions to this volume are a strong demonstration of renewed theoretical innovation in the field, innovation that avoids old patterns and old labels. At the risk of reviving old conflicts, it may be said that the research agenda and dilemmas that confront international relations in the 1990s bear some resemblance to those of the 1920s, which was the last decade in this century when great-power conflict did not threaten. From many perspectives, the core concepts of international relations, particularly anarchy and sovereignty, are reexamined and questioned. Rather than erecting a sharp divide between international and domestic politics, anarchy is no longer seen as a unique province of interstate relations (particularly in an era of failed states and vicious ethnic strife). Sovereignty, the irreducible attribute of states, is given a more contingent and historically fluid character.[93] The sovereign territorial state becomes problematic and its dominance of international relations bears historical explanation. Pushed along by these theoretical developments and by strong interest in domestic political institutions, a unified politics may be in view, one that uses similar theoretical approaches and methodological tools to examine institutions and politics, whether international or domestic.[94] The ambitions of the Chicago school of Merriam and Lasswell are reborn. Finally, the material basis of global politics, particularly the advance of economic integration, receives renewed attention from researchers after years of neglect.

One dilemma of the interwar decades also remains for international relations scholars, and that is the field's relationship to politics and policy. Is there a role for political intervention beyond advising the prince? The cautions and skepticism of most postwar scholars may be ending. Nongovernmental organizations advancing the cause of human rights, the global environment, and equitable development are increasingly visible players in a redefined world politics. Scholars, on the model of the 1920s, are increasingly participant-observers, advancing changes that often run counter to state interests. Public intellectuals, virtually an extinct species by the 1980s, have reappeared; international relations may eventually reclaim the wider audience that it gave up in the post-1945 retreat to the academy.

This portrait of change and effervescence in international relations might be labeled progress without qualification were it not for two shortcomings in recent theorizing. One is the decline of system-level theory. Dependency theory and neoliberalism conceded this dimension of theory first, but structural realism has also failed to develop a convincing research program at this level of analysis.[95] The second is a persistent unwillingness, at least since the rise of realism and science after 1945, to offer explanations of international change. As described earlier, realism was interested in explaining not change but rather enduring regularities, a feature adopted in the comparative statics of its more scientific descendent, neorealism. Its static quality was reinforced by the equilibrium analysis that characterizes many rational-choice and game-theoretic accounts. Liberalism, which often endorsed a progressive view of history, has been more confident of change, but, in the worst case, change was equated to vague hopes of progress or, in more analytically sound variants, was reduced to economic and political change within societies. Dependency theorists and other radical theorists accepted a broad, Marxist-inspired, and rather deterministic account of the sources of international change that required constant revision in the face of a slippery, chameleon-like capitalism.

The dynamic for international change may finally be sought at the level of developments within societies; the current turn toward second-image theorizing could be a healthy response to the overblown claims of past systemic theory. Before transforming international relations into a branch of comparative politics, however, it is worth considering whether international change can be adequately explained at the level of national politics and policy. Some link between system (however defined) and unit that couples relative analytical precision and dynamism, an engine that drives international change, is required. Two approaches at the center of research programs in other social sciences are possible candidates for this role. Neither is easily characterized by the old realist or liberal labels.

The first, which places more of the explanatory burden on the system, is an evolutionary theory of change in which variation and selection are the dynamic. An evolutionary theory requires very little information about units and very few assumptions, if any, about their behavior. Waltz's structural realism, rationalized and individualized by others, explicitly adopts selection as one of the key links between system and unit, and the only link that can explain change.[96] Unfortunately, Waltz himself and other neorealists have not extended this critical (and briefly remarked) feature of structural realism. Gilpin's neorealist alternative, with far more attention paid to the motivations and calculus of states, does introduce a selective mechanism of sorts as an explanation of change. As Stephan Haggard has pointed out, Gilpin's attention to changing comparative costs suggests a mechanism for explaining greater predisposition for states to change the system. One could push such arguments further in an evolutionary direction as well by arguing that the shifts in comparative costs favor (in terms of capabilities or economic development) certain societies over others. This type of reformulation offers only one systemic selector that may have explanatory value.[97]

A valuable research agenda could be constructed around an evolutionary model of international change, directed to explaining the scale and characteristics of units in the system. Hendrik Spruyt and Charles Tilly have already offered quasi-evolutionary accounts of the emergence of the modern territorial state in the face of its institutional rivals. The question of scale of units is also an important one at a time when existing states are threatened with fragmentation: Does large or small scale carry with it particular selective advantages? Finally, the intensities themselves of selective pressures are an important subject for research. Since 1945 very few states have been selected out, despite the existence of microstates whose military and economic viability would have been in doubt in earlier systems. Identifying the selective pressures in earlier systems, their decline after 1945, and their apparent intensification in recent years (as many more states are threatened with disintegration) would constitute another line of investigation.

Evolutionary models of international change require few assumptions about state goals or strategies. Social learning models explain change by incorporating a much more active image of societies in relation to the international environment. The appeal of learning as a metaphor cannot disguise serious disagreements about the prerequisites of learning models and even the definition of learning itself.[98] Linking cognitive change or learning to particular changes in behavior (and eliminating alternative explanations for behavioral change) is only one empirical hurdle for models of learning. Models of social learning must also contend with the "level-of-learning" problem: If individual cognitive change is required for social learning to occur, individual change must be transferred to an organization; social and political learning requires embedding learning in more than one institution. This process of transfer is typically murky. Individual cognitive change may not be required; a process of political selection may choose one body of knowledge (and its bearers) "off the shelf," demoting its competitors. The dynamic then becomes one of political competition and influence, not cognitive change at the individual level. Finally, the depth and permanence of learning must be investigated. Peter Hall delineates first-order, second-order, and third-order learning to capture these differences.

The appeal of evolutionary or learning models may be enhanced by international events. Explanations for the end of the Cold War and the transformation and disintegration of the Soviet Union typically include both external competitive pressures and an internal process of learning.[99] Although social learning models are often associated with liberal approaches to international relations and evolutionary models with the selective and competitive images of realism, the association is neither necessary nor strong. These models may be compelling precisely because they lie outside the divide between liberal and realist. The end of the Cold War enhanced the security of most citizens of the world. If it produces a new surge of theoretical variation before the inevitable process of scientific selection, rather than another swing in the cyclical predominance of the hoary theoretical contenders from the past, it will have fulfilled another, not insignificant promise.

Notes

I wish to thank Hayward Alker, Brian C. Schmidt, participants in the Australian National Research School of Pacific Studies seminar, and two anonymous reviewers for their helpful comments on earlier versions of this chapter.

1. For a genealogical account of self-images in international relations that stakes out this position, see Steve Smith, "The Self-images of a Discipline: A Genealogy of International Relations Theory," in *International Relations Theory Today*, edited by Ken Booth and Steve Smith (University Park: Pennsylvania State University Press, 1995), pp. 1–37.

2. Among such studies are John G. Gunnell, *The Descent of Political Theory: The Genealogy of an American Vocation* (Chicago: University of Chicago Press, 1993); Peter Novick, *That Noble Dream: The 'Objectivity Question' and the American Historical Profession* (Cambridge: Cambridge University Press, 1988); Dorothy Ross, *The Origins of American Social Science* (Cambridge: Cambridge University Press, 1991); and Raymond Seidelman, *Disenchanted Realists: Political Science and the American Crisis, 1884–1984* (Albany: State University of New York Press, 1985).

3. An externalist account of the hegemony of certain fields within political science was offered by Theodore J. Lowi in his presidential address to the American Political Science Association. "The State in Political Science: How We Became What We Study," *American Political Science Review* 86, 1 (March 1992):1–7.

4. One intriguing example of the way in which invented traditions shape behavior is given by the Maoris, who accepted "inaccurate" readings of their past by early Western investigators, incorporated those misreadings, and made those "traditions" their own. See also Eric Hobsbawm and Terence Ranger, eds., *The Invention of Tradition* (Cambridge: Cambridge University Press, 1983).

5. See Stanley Hoffmann, "An American Social Science: International Relations," *Daedalus* 106, 3 (1977):41–60; K. J. Holsti, *The Dividing Discipline: Hegemony and Diversity in International Theory* (Boston: Unwin Hyman, 1985), chapter 6; Miles Kahler, "International Relations: Still an American Social Science?" in *Ideas and Ideals: Essays on Politics in Honor of Stanley Hoffmann*, edited by Linda B. Miller and Michael Joseph Smith (Boulder: Westview Press, 1993), pp. 395–414.

6. Even critics of realism often accept this stylized view of the field's development. See Michael Banks, "The Evolution of International Relations Theory," in *Conflict in World Society*, edited by Michael Banks (Brighton, UK: Wheatsheaf Books, 1984), pp. 3–21, and Jack Donnelly, "Realism and the Academic Study of International Relations," in *Political Science in History*, edited by James Farr, John S. Dryzek, and Stephen T. Leonard (Cambridge: Cambridge University Press, 1995), pp. 175–197.

7. Brian C. Schmidt argues forcefully for such an "internal discursive history" in "The Historiography of Academic International Relations," *Review of International Studies* 20, 4 (October 1994):349–367.

8. Schmidt, "Historiography," p. 362.

9. Schmidt contends that the "prehistory" of international relations (before World War I) is also important for understanding the interwar reaction against the juristic state as a central artifact of international relations. ("Lessons from the Past: A Reconsideration of the Great Debate Between Idealism and Realism" [paper presented at the Ninety-first Annual Meeting of the American Political Science Association, August 31–September 3, 1995]).

10. For a highly selective lampooning of the idealists along these lines, see Michael Joseph Smith, *Realist Thought from Weber to Kissinger* (Baton Rouge: Louisiana State University Press, 1986).

11. Norman Angell, *The Great Illusion* (1909; reprint of 1911 edition, with an introduction by S. J. Stearns, New York: Garland Publishing, 1972), p. 44. On Angell and other economists writing at this time on the issue of war, see William J. Barber, "British and American Economists and Attempts to Comprehend the Nature of War," in *Economics and National Security: A History of Their Interaction,* edited by Craufurd D. Goodwin (Durham, NC: Duke University Press, 1991), and Jaap de Wilde, "Norman Angell: Ancestor of Interdependence Theory," in *Interdependence and Conflict in World Politics,* edited by James N. Rosenau and Hylke Tromp (Aldershot, UK: Avebury, 1989), pp. 13–30. John Mueller rehabilitates some of Angell's arguments in *Retreat from Doomsday: The Obsolescence of Major War* (New York: Basic Books, 1989).

12. *The Autobiography of James T. Shotwell* (Indianapolis: Bobbs-Merrill, 1961), pp. 69–70.

13. "Blood and iron have been not only the historical instruments of every state for the assertion of its will among its neighbors, but they have been as well the instruments within the state by which political institutions have come into life and maintained themselves throughout the centuries." (James T. Shotwell, *War as an Instrument of National Policy* [New York: Garland Publishing, 1974], p. 9.)

14. Ibid., pp. 36–37. Shotwell's capsule summary of the significance of World War I as total war is excellent: "[I]t is not so significant that the war involved so many peoples as that it involved them so completely" (p. 34).

15. Ibid., pp. 27–28; James T. Shotwell, *On the Rim of the Abyss* (New York: Macmillan, 1937), p. 42.

16. For an early statement of hope on the power of public opinion, see James Bryce, *International Relations* (Port Washington, NY: Kennikat Press, 1966), p. 264.

17. Frederick L. Schuman, *International Politics* (New York: McGraw-Hill, 1933), p. viii.

18. William C. Olson and A.J.R. Groom, *International Relations Then and Now* (London: HarperCollins Academic, 1991), pp. 81, 69–70.

19. On this emigration and political theory, John G. Gunnell comments that the émigrés were "in sharp conflict with the values of American social science." (*The Descent of Political Theory,* p. 185.

20. Hans J. Morgenthau, "Fragment of an Intellectual Autobiography: 1904–1932," in *Truth and Tragedy: A Tribute to Hans Morgenthau,* edited by Kenneth Thompson and Robert J. Myers (Washington, DC: New Republic Book Company, 1977), pp. 1–17.

21. Morgenthau's antiliberal and antirational stance is clearest in *Scientific Man Versus Power Politics* (Chicago: University of Chicago Press, 1946): "Our civiliza-

tion assumes that the social world is susceptible to rational control conceived after the model of the natural sciences, while the experiences, domestic and international, of the age contradict this assumption" (p. 2).

22. Anders Stephanson, *Kennan and the Art of Foreign Policy* (Cambridge: Harvard University Press, 1989), pp. 180–181.

23. Ross, *Origins of American Social Science*, p. xiii.

24. On the importance of Merriam in efforts to construct a "science of politics" in the 1920s, see Albert Somit and Joseph Tanenhaus, *The Development of American Political Science: From Burgess to Behavioralism* (Boston: Allyn and Bacon, 1967), pp. 110–113.

25. William T.R. Fox, "Pluralism, the Science of Politics, and the World System," *World Politics* 27, 4 (July 1975):597–611. See also Joseph Kruzel and James N. Rosenau, *Journeys Through World Politics* (Lexington, MA: Lexington Books, 1989), p. 237. Brian C. Schmidt notes in "Lessons from the Past" the reaction of these protopluralists against the earlier concentration within political science on the juristic theory of the state.

26. Kenneth W. Thompson, "Philosophy and Politics: The Two Commitments of Hans J. Morgenthau," in *Truth and Tragedy*, ed. Thompson and Myers, p. 24. Thompson notes that although Quincy Wright did not oppose Morgenthau they were not close, and that Morgenthau's chief supporters were not to be found among his faculty colleagues in the department of political science (pp. 22–23).

27. Edith E. Ware, ed., *The Study of International Relations in the United States: Survey for 1934* (New York: Columbia University Press, 1934), pp. 12–13.

28. For an account of Shotwell's work with the Institute of Pacific Relations, the Social Science Research Council's Advisory Committee on International Relations, and the Carnegie Endowment for International Peace, see Harold Josephson, *James T. Shotwell and the Rise of Internationalism in America* (Rutherford, NJ: Fairleigh Dickinson University Press, 1975), pp. 99–115, 188–193.

29. The Yale Institute of International Studies was founded in 1935; similar research centers were founded around the same time at Princeton and Johns Hopkins Universities.

30. The emphasis on "intelligent planning" was pervasive in this era. John Foster Dulles, for example, argued (along lines strikingly parallel to E. H. Carr) that planning and accommodation with the "energy" of Japan, Germany, and Italy could have reduced the possibility of violence later. (*War, Peace, and Change* [1939; reprint with an introduction by Charles Chatfield, New York: Garland Publishing, 1971], pp. 143–147, 155).

31. Ross, *Origins of American Social Science*, pp. 463–467; Somit and Tanenhaus, *Development of American Political Science*, pp. 117–118.

32. Grayson Kirk, *The Study of International Relations* (New York: Council on Foreign Relations, 1947), pp. 4–5.

33. See Fox's harsh review, "Interwar International Relations: The American Experience," *World Politics* 2, 1 (October 1949):67–79. Fox's review is in turn cited by Dwight Waldo, *Political Science in the United States* (Paris: UNESCO, 1956), pp. 55–56. The loop was then closed when Fox misquoted Waldo, stating that "genuine 'anti-realists' are hard to find," in William T.R. Fox and Annette

Baker Fox, "The Teaching of International Relations Research in the United States," *World Politics* 13, 3 (April 1961):343.

34. Waldo, *Political Science*, p. 56.

35. Novick, *That Noble Dream*, p. 332.

36. William T.R. Fox, "E. H. Carr and Political Realism: Vision and Revision," *Review of International Studies* 11, 1 (January 1985):7.

37. Nicholas John Spykman, *America's Strategy in World Politics* (New York: Harcourt, Brace and Company, 1942), p. 470.

38. On American interpretations of Ranke, see Novick, *That Noble Dream*, pp. 27–29; on the Americanization of political science, see Somit and Tanenhaus, *Development of American Political Science*, pp. 87–88; on "pragmatic meliorism," see William T.R. Fox, "A Middle Western Isolationist-Internationalist's Journey Toward Relevance," in *Journeys Through World Politics*, ed. Kruzel and Rosenau, pp. 239–240.

39. John H. Herz, *Political Realism and Political Idealism: A Study in Theories and Realities* (Chicago: University of Chicago Press, 1951).

40. Quincy Wright, "Realism and Idealism in International Politics," *World Politics* 5, 1 (October 1952):116–128.

41. Harold Lasswell, "Introduction," in *Dynamics of International Relations,* edited by Ernst B. Haas and Allen S. Whiting (New York: McGraw-Hill, 1956), p. xix.

42. One example of postwar idealism is Thomas I. Cook and Malcolm Moos, *Power Through Purpose: The Realism of Idealism as a Basis for Foreign Policy* (Baltimore: Johns Hopkins University Press, 1954). On weariness with the great debate, see Waldo, *Political Science*, p. 61.

43. Ernst B. Haas, "The Balance of Power: Prescription, Concept, or Propoganda?" *World Politics*, 5, 4 (July 1953): 442–447.

44. On this issue, see Christopher Hill, "1939: The Origins of Liberal Realism," *Review of International Studies* 15, 4 (October 1989):319–328.

45. John Gange, *University Research on International Affairs* (Washington, DC: American Council on Education, 1958), p. 112; Claude E. Hawley and Lewis A. Dexter, "Recent Political Science Research in American Universities," *American Political Science Review* 46, 2 (June 1952):113.

46. Olson and Groom, *International Relations Then and Now*, pp. 96–97.

47. Stephen Krasner makes this point in "Fortune, Virtue, and Systematic Versus Scientific Inquiry," in *Journeys Through World Politics*, ed. Kruzel and Rosenau, pp. 417–428.

48. Novick, *That Noble Dream*, p. 332.

49. *Institutes and Their Publics* (New York: Carnegie Endowment for International Peace, 1953), p. 97.

50. Gabriel A. Almond, *The American People and Foreign Policy* (New York: Harcourt Brace, 1950).

51. According to John Gange: "[I]t seems that value-directed research focused on preserving peace and preventing war will be less than effective (and hence ought to have a lower priority) until the basic elements of international affairs and human conduct have been more adequately explored." (Gange, *University Research*, p. 128).

52. On the unwillingness of international relations theorists to discuss the range of choice, see Fox, "E. H. Carr and Political Realism," p. 10.

53. Ross, *Origins of American Social Science*, p. 388.

54. The principal exchange of arguments is included in Klaus Knorr and James N. Rosenau, eds., *Contending Approaches to International Politics* (Princeton: Princeton University Press, 1969). On the rise of behavioralism in political science, see Somit and Tanenhaus, *Development of American Political Science*, pp. 183–201.

55. Somit and Tanenhaus, *Development of American Political Science*, pp. 186–187.

56. Marion Levy, "'Does It Matter If He's Naked?' Bawled the Child," in *Contending Approaches*, ed. Knorr and Rosenau, pp. 87–109, quotation on p. 106.

57. On neo-Grotianism and the problems with Bull's rendition of it, see A. Claire Cutler, "The 'Grotian Tradition' in International Relations," *Review of International Studies* 17, 1 (January 1991):41–65; on connecting Bull to the study of "fundamental" international institutions, see Alexander Wendt and Raymond Duvall, "Institutions and International Order," in *Global Changes and Theoretical Challenges: Approaches to World Politics for the 1990s,* edited by Ernst-Otto Czempiel and James N. Rosenau (Lexington, MA: Lexington Books, 1989).

58. Hedley Bull, "International Relations Theory: The Case for a Classical Approach," in *Contending Approaches*, ed. Knorr and Rosenau, p. 37.

59. For an excellent critical account of the successive waves of deterrence theory, see Robert Jervis, "Deterrence Theory Revisited," *World Politics* 31, 2 (January 1979):289–324.

60. The methodology and assumptions of deterrence theory could point in different policy directions, of course, spawning alliances or divisions within the community of strategists. On this question, see Emanuel Adler, "The Emergence of Cooperation: National Epistemic Communities and the International Evolution of the Idea of Nuclear Arms Control," *International Organization* 46, 1 (Winter 1992):109–124.

61. On the peace research movement, see Peter Wallensteen, ed., *Peace Research: Achievements and Challenges* (Boulder: Westview Press, 1988).

62. Joseph S. Nye Jr. and Robert O. Keohane describe their own feeling that the field of international organization had failed to grapple with these changes, spurring the project that produced a seminal volume in international political economy, *Transnational Relations and World Politics* (Cambridge, MA: Harvard University Press, 1970). Other key early contributions included C. Fred Bergsten and Lawrence B. Krause, eds., *World Politics and International Economics* (Washington, DC: Brookings Institution, 1975); Richard Cooper, *The Economics of Interdependence* (New York: Council on Foreign Relations, 1968); and Raymond Vernon, *Sovereignty at Bay* (New York: Basic Books, 1971).

63. Edward Morse, *Modernization and the Transformation of International Relations* (New York: Free Press, 1976), especially chapter 5.

64. Robert O. Keohane and Joseph S. Nye, *Power and Interdependence: World Politics in Transition* (Boston: Little, Brown and Company, 1977).

65. Novick, *That Noble Dream*, pp. 445–455.

66. Robert Jervis explicitly calls into question assumptions of unmediated systemic compulsion on states as well as the "deterrence" model of the Cold War in

Perception and Misperception in International Relations (Princeton: Princeton University Press, 1976); Graham Allison introduced organizational process and bureaucratic politics models in *Essence of Decision* (Boston: Little, Brown and Company, 1972).

67. On the sources of developmental pessimism among dependency theorists, see Joseph L. Love, "The Origins of Dependency Analysis," *Journal of Latin American Studies* 22, 1 (February 1990):154–157.

68. Joseph A. Kahl, *Three Latin American Sociologists* (New Brunswick, NJ: Transaction Books, 1988), p. 136.

69. Love, "Origins of Dependency Analysis," p. 167.

70. Among the indicators of this wide acceptance was a special issue of *International Organization* [32, 1 (Winter 1978)] devoted to dependency theory.

71. Holsti, *The Dividing Discipline*, pp. 87–89, 100. It should be noted that Holsti's sample included only texts published before 1981.

72. Kenneth Waltz, *Theory of International Politics* (Boston: Little, Brown and Company, 1979). Surprisingly, Robert O. Keohane, a leading neoliberal, was one of those who endorsed a modified structural realist approach as the core for a research program in international relations. See "Theory of World Politics: Structural Realism and Beyond," in *Neorealism and Its Critics,* edited by Robert O. Keohane (New York: Columbia University Press, 1986), pp. 158–203.

73. See, for example, John A. Vasquez, *The Power of Power Politics: A Critique* (New Brunswick, NJ: Rutgers University Press, 1983).

74. Robert O. Keohane and Joseph S. Nye Jr., *"Power and Interdependence* Revisited," *International Organization* 41, 4 (Autumn 1987):737.

75. Peter Evans, a leading North American interpreter of dependency theory, has both contributed to and commented on these developments. See *Dependent Development* (Princeton: Princeton University Press, 1979); "After Dependency: Recent Studies of Class, State, and Industrialization," *Latin American Research Review* 20 (1985):149–160; and "Class, State, and Dependence in East Asia: Lessons for Latin Americanists," in *The Political Economy of the New Asian Industrialism,* edited by Frederick Deyo (Ithaca: Cornell University Press, 1987), pp. 203–226.

76. On the addition of rational-actor foundations, see Keohane, "Theory of World Politics," pp. 40, 46.

77. Joseph S. Nye Jr., "Neorealism and Neoliberalism," *World Politics,* 40, 2 (January 1988); Richard W. Mansbach, "The Realists Ride Again: Counterrevolution in International Relations," in *Interdependence and Conflict in World Politics,* ed. Rosenau and Tromp, p. 220.

78. Robert G. Gilpin, *U.S. Power and the Multinational Corporation* (New York: Basic Books, 1975); Charles Kindleberger, *The World in Depression, 1929–1939* (London: Allen Lane, 1973).

79. Ernst B. Haas, *The Obsolescence of Regional Integration Theory* (Berkeley: Institute of International Studies, 1975).

80. Ross, *Origins of American Social Science,* p. 473.

81. On the think tanks, see I. M. Destler, Leslie H. Gelb, and Anthony Lake, *Our Own Worst Enemy* (New York: Simon and Schuster, 1983), and R. Kent Weaver, "The Changing World of Think Tanks," *PS: Political Science and Politics* 22, 3 (September 1989):563–578.

82. An excellent summary of this debate is provided in David Baldwin, ed., *Neorealism and Neoliberalism: The Contemporary Debate* (New York: Columbia University Press, 1993).

83. The philosopher Michael Ruse has noted that "[t]oo frequently the term [paradigm] is used as a propaganda tool, bolstering the pretensions of some supposed major breakthrough. Paradigm founder today. Nobel Prize winner tomorrow. Burial at Westminster Abbey the day after that." "Is the Theory of Punctuated Equilibria a New Paradigm?" in *The Dynamics of Evolution,* edited by Albert Somit and Steven A. Peterson (Ithaca: Cornell University Press, 1992), p. 139.

84. Of course, some could find, even in the end of the Cold War, a likely return to older, realist patterns of international behavior; see, for example, John Mearsheimer, "Back to the Future: Instability in Europe After the Cold War," *International Security*, 15, 1 (Summer 1990):5–56. More typical were claims that the Cold War's end forced a rethinking of international relations theory.

85. For a more optimistic, though critical, assessment, see David Lake, "Leadership, Hegemony, and the International Economy: Naked Emperor or Tattered Monarch with Potential?" *International Studies Quarterly* 37, 4 (December 1993):459–489.

86. For example, Bruce Bueno de Mesquita and David Lalman, *War and Reason: Domestic and International Imperatives* (New Haven: Yale University Press, 1992).

87. For example, Stephen Walt, *The Origins of Alliances* (Ithaca: Cornell University Press, 1987).

88. Pauline Marie Rosenau, *Post-modernism and the Social Sciences: Insights, Inroads, and Intrusions* (Princeton: Princeton University Press, 1992).

89. Alexander Wendt and Raymond Duvall, "Institutions and International Order," in *Global Changes*, ed. Czempiel and Rosenau, p. 54.

90. For a summary of the institutionalist research program in sociology, see Walter W. Powell and Paul J. DiMaggio, *The New Institutionalism and Organizational Analysis* (Chicago: University of Chicago Press, 1991).

91. Holsti, *The Dividing Discipline*, pp. 130–131.

92. Ibid., p. 131.

93. Two examples of such questioning from a constructivist and a neorealist, respectively are: Alexander Wendt, "Anarchy is What States Make of It: The Social Construction of Power Politics," *International Organization* 46, 2 (Spring 1992):391–425; Stephen D. Krasner, "Compromising Westphalia," *International Security* 20, 3 (Winter 1995/1996):115–151.

94. One enterprise of this kind, based on a strategic-choice approach, is David Lake and Robert Powell, *Strategic Choice and International Relations* (Princeton: Princeton University Press, forthcoming).

95. One recent effort to revise structural realism and incorporate a broader notion of system is Barry Buzan, Charles Jones, and Richard Little, *The Logic of Anarchy* (New York: Columbia University Press, 1993).

96. The other link is socialization, which explains the persistence of behaviors, not their change.

97. A further elaboration of evolutionary models is provided in Miles Kahler, "Evolution, Choice, and International Change," in *Strategic Choice and International Relations,* ed. David Lake and Robert Powell, (forthcoming).

98. For recent examples of such models, see Ernst B. Haas, *When Knowledge Is Power: Three Models of Change in International Organizations* (Berkeley: University of California Press, 1990); George W. Breslauer and Philip E. Tetlock, eds., *Learning in U.S. and Soviet Foreign Policy* (Boulder: Westview Press, 1991); Joseph S. Nye Jr., "Nuclear Learning and U.S.-Soviet Security Regimes," *International Organization* 41, 3 (Summer 1987):371–402; Nancy Bermeo, "Democracy and the Lessons of Dictatorship," *Comparative Politics* 24, 3 (April 1992):273–292; and Peter Hall, "Policy Paradigms, Social Learning, and the State," *Comparative Politics* (forthcoming).

99. See, for example, Daniel Deudney and G. John Ikenberry, "Soviet Reform and the End of the Cold War: Explaining Large-Scale Historical Change," *Review of International Studies* 17, 3 (July 1991):225–250.

3

Post-Theory: The Eternal Return of Ethics in International Relations

JAMES DER DERIAN

Postmodernism: This word has no meaning. Use it as often as possible.
—Modern-day *Dictionary of Received Ideas*

This paper consists of little more than a list and a question, and nothing less than a provocation for International Relations (IR).

First, a list of all things post. Postmodernism, postmodernity, poststructuralism. Postphilosophy, *posthistoire,* post-Enlightenment, post-ideology. Postbehavioralism, postpositivism, postfeminism, post-analytical. Post-realism, post-idealism, postrationalism, post-Marxism, post–international relations. Post-Fordism, postindustrialism, postcapitalism, postdevelopment, postcolonialism. Post–Cold War, post-Yalta, postwar. Postmodern architecture, postmodern film, postmodern culture, postmodern science, postmodern sportswear. Postmodern parody, pastiche, and irony, Postmodernism *avant la lettre.* Post-postmodernism, Post-Toasties, pre(post)-erous. Post-theory. Postscript.

Second, the question, one that precedes all others about the topic, the approach, and yes, sometimes the fad, of postmodernism in International Relations. This is the question that surrounds and keeps one distant from it, the question that goes unasked in polite company: Why bother?

My answer can only be partial, in both senses of the word. The topic is too wide, too diverse, and in many ways too *out-of-date* to be recounted in one chapter. I am, as well, too closely self-identified with postmodernism to claim a neutral, impartial position. Yet there has been in IR a disposition to take the path of least intellectual resistance in dealing with postmodernism—to dismiss it by polemic or ignore it through arrogance. I intend only to scan the general question of *what* postmodernism is and to focus instead on *why* one should be bothered by postmodernism as a global phenomenon and on why one might consider poststructuralism as an appropriate theoretical response.

Let me enumerate the reasons why one should bother with and be bothered by poststructuralism, make my theoretical case, and then leave for last an empirico-postmodernist proof. First, I believe poststructuralism is a valuable—indeed an invaluable—intellectual tool for understanding the ways of postmodernity, or as I prefer, late modernity. Second, poststructuralism offers an ethical way of being in highly contingent, highly relativist times. Third, and most important for the discipline of IR, poststructuralism provides a reflexive method for constantly challenging and testing the validity of the first two claims.[1] Other current approaches in IR might be able to meet one or even two of these claims, but they fail to fulfill all three of them.

The Toolbox of Poststructuralism

I do not intend to provide here a primer on poststructuralism (which I have done elsewhere).[2] I wish to make the case that late modern times require poststructuralist, *among other*, critical pluralist approaches. However, to make sure that we are leaving from the same starting gate, it might be useful to review some of the conceptual distinctions that I presented in two earlier books, *International/Intertextual Relations* and *Antidiplomacy.*

My opening list of all things post does not prove anything. However, it should suggest, even to the epistemologically challenged, that we are witnessing some kind of an epochal rupture with modernity that signals the emergence of a different, perhaps even new social condition. The use of "postmodern" to designate this shift predates Lyotard, Habermas, Derrida, Foucault, and other "Frankfurters" (critical theorists) and "French Fries" (poststructuralists): It can be traced at least back to Beefeaters (non-Marxist, pre–Mad Cow materialists), like the historian Arnold Toynbee who in 1954 referred to the emergence of a "postmodern" period in volume nine of his *Study of History.* I prefer to use the term "late modernity" rather than "postmodernity" to describe this shift, not out of some semantic purism, but first, to better distinguish a historical, social condition ("late modernity," "postmodernity") from a theoretical response ("postmod-

ernism," "poststructuralism"); second, to avoid the kind of historical peri-
odization of a clean break that belies that the time-warp quality of late
modernity, where past, present, and future seem to meld in real-time representations and simulations; and third, because "postmodernism" in general
has begun to take on more meanings than it can sensibly carry, as suggested
by the semihumorous quote that opens this chapter.

Some years ago I voiced some trepidation about the use of "postmod- ·
ernism" in the preface to *On Diplomacy*[3] (which was only heightened
when I later heard Devo's song "Post-post-modern Man"). But one lesson I
learned upon my reentry into North American IR—which has always been
more a taxonomy than a subject matter—is that without a label, a box, or a
school, one does not exist. So I became a postmodernist, without meaning—or meaning to.

It is much easier, and less controversial, to say what I mean by the phenomenon of "late modernity/postmodernity." What I wrote in shorthand
back in 1989 holds up, I believe, fairly well today:

> [I]ncreasingly postmodern world politics is very much in need of poststructural
> readings. The basis for the claim, and our written response to its implications,
> can be traced to an overdetermined (yet underdocumented) "crisis" of moder-
> nity, where foundational unities (the autonomous subject, the sovereign state,
> grand theory) and synthetic oppositions (subject-object, self-other, inside-out-
> side) are undergoing serious and sustained challenges. We are witnessing
> changes in our international, intertextual, inter*human* relations, in which ob-
> jective reality is displaced by textuality (Dan Quayle cites Tom Clancy to de-
> fend anti-satellite weapons), modes of production are supplanted by modes of
> information (the assemblyline workplace shrinks, a computer and media-gen-
> erated cyberspace expands), representation blurs into simulation (Hollywood,
> and Mr. Smith, goes to Washington), imperialism gives way to the Empire of
> Signs (the spectacle of Grenada, the fantasy of Star Wars serve to deny imperial
> decline). With these tectonic shifts, new epistemological fault lines develop: the
> legitimacy of tradition is undermined, the unifying belief in progress frag-
> ments, and conventional wisdom is reduced to one of many competing rituals
> of power used to shore up a shaky (international) society.[4]

I make my case for the diverse approaches that make up poststructuralism in my book *Antidiplomacy*.[5] My toolbox for the task draws from the
works of Nietzsche, Bakhtin, Barthes, Bataille, Blanchot, Foucault,
Deleuze, Derrida, Lyotard, Rorty, Kristeva, Said, Jameson, Lacan, Irigaray,
Spivak, Baudrillard, Virilio, and other critical and postmodernist thinkers. I
provide some of the protocols that inform poststructuralism and distinguish it from the traditional approaches of IR. My goal was then and is
now to move the engagement with poststructuralism in IR from closed, defensive positions to an open, dialogical terrain. Not so long ago mental flak

jackets were de rigueur if one so much as uttered the "P-word" among IR scholars. To be sure, the poststructuralists were not blameless in this regard, but the ghost of Vince Lombardi—the best defense is a good offensive(ness)—haunted IR long before po-mo came on the scene. I like to believe that the era of mindless dismissal by one side and reflexive defensiveness by the other is on the wane, as IR as well as the other social sciences appropriate the key concepts (if not the more radical implications) of postmodernism.[6]

That said, I am not about to produce an easy target in the form of a pat definition of an intellectual approach that is, by definition (*pace* Nietzsche, "only that which has no history can be defined") the product of inversion, a going beyond, a calling into question of essentialist structures, not least among them definitions. So, by way of post-Hegelian negation, I offer a consideration of what poststructuralism is not by what critics have claimed that it is. I will limit myself to four of the most reasonable criticisms.

First, poststructuralism is not, as critics have claimed, inherently antiempirical. It does in my own work and in others contain a "research program," but not one that assumes that the object of research is immaculately reproduced by the program. Poststructuralism differs from rationalist approaches in that it does not hold that international theorists mirror the reality of world politics through their intellectual analysis. Both use and are used by language: Meaning endlessly differs and is deferred through the interpretive interaction of theorist and text. Rationalists cling to the faith that there is an objective reality out there that is waiting for the right method to come along and in the name of scientific progress make use of, make sense of, give order to it. However, the realities of world politics increasingly are generated, mediated, even simulated by successive technical means of reproduction, further distancing them from some original and ultimately mythical meaning. From diplomatic notes to popular postcards, from engravings to photographs, from radio to television, from textbooks to the internet, reality has shifted into the domain of virtual technologies. It also signals the arrival if not yet the acceptance of a broader range of plural realisms for a newly multipolar, multicultural International Relations.

Second, critics assert that not only is there no ethics to poststructuralism, but also that it advocates a relativist, even nihilist position. The poststructuralist response is that relativism is an historical response to the metaphysical desire for the last word and highest truth that long predates the arrival of Foucault, Derrida, Rorty, et al. on the late modern scene. It has taken many forms, from the "vulgar" relativism of Raskolnikov (where "all is permitted") to the "refined" relativism of Isaiah Berlin ("to realize the relative validity of one's convictions and yet stand for them unflinchingly, is what distinguishes a civilized man from a barbarian").[7] It has been interpreted by Nietzsche as proof of eternal recurrence ("There is no pre-established harmony between the furtherance of truth and the well-being of mankind"[8]) and promoted by John Stuart Mill as the stepchild of progress: "It is hardly possible to overrate the value, in the present low state of human improvement, of placing human beings in contact with persons dissimilar to themselves, and with modes of thought and action unlike those with which they are familiar. . . . Such communication has always been, and is peculiarly in the present age, one of the primary sources of progress."[9]

A poststructuralist response is not, then, for all its purported relativism, axiomatically apolitical or amoral: It is in fact an attempt to understand— *without* resort to external authorities or transcendental values—why one moral or political system attains a higher status and exercises more influence than another at a particular historical moment. If there is a practico-ethical injunction to poststructuralism, it is to identify and to assess the dangers of systems of thought (like universal rationalism) and systems of politics (like the Pax Americana) that deny the historical reality and pragmatic appeal of relativism. As political theorist William Connolly describes it, the current worry of academics about relativism is "untimely"; indeed, their acts of theoretical closure and nostalgia for lost certainties reveal an anxiety about the openness of late modernity:

> Nor is relativism the consummate danger in the late-modern world, where every culture intersects with most others in economies of interdependence, exchange, and competition. Relativism is an invention of academics who yearn for a type of unity that probably never existed, who worry about an alienation from established culture that seldom finds sufficient opportunity to get off the ground, and who insist that ethical discourse cannot proceed unless it locates its authority in a transcendental command.[10]

In contrast, the ethics of poststructuralism is located in and through the construction of subjectivity. It does not reside outside as a set of principles to guide individual behavior, but as a prior and necessary condition for identity formation.[11] Ethics begins with the recognition of the need for the other, of the need for the other's recognition. It proceeds, in other words, from an interdependency of caring and responsibility that cannot be separated from the pluralism and relativism of multiple identities. An ethical way of being emerges when we recognize the very *necessity* of heterogeneity for understanding ourselves and others.

Third, a poststructuralist approach does not seek to reduce IR to a linguistic practice; nor does it claim that there is *no* truth, *no* values, *no* reality. Rather, it aims to refute the claim that there is an external being, supreme epistemology, ultimate theory that can prove, adjudicate, verify an existence or truth independent of its representation. It is not, then, "all is permitted," but rather "all is questionable," in recognition that the most pernicious truths are the effects of unchallenged interpretations. A poststructuralist approach proceeds on this suspicion by investigating the interrelationship of power and representational practices that elevate one truth over another, that legitimate and subject one identity against another, that make, in short, one discourse matter more than the next.[12] Such an investigation requires a semio-critical approach, one that might dismantle and invert empirico-positivist categories by revealing their internal (conceptual and logical) contradictions and external (descriptive and interpretive) inadequacies.[13]

Let me second-guess one reaction to the last sentence—and perhaps even those before—and say, What? Which leads to the fourth criticism: Could this not all be said more simply? Just as we have begun to be familiar with Hegel's "mediation of mediation," Marx's "alienation of alienation," Sartre's "totalization of totality," along come Deleuze's "rhizomes," Foucault's "genealogy," Baudrillard's "precession of simulacra," Derrida's *"differance"* with a difference. Do we really need this level of linguistic difficulty, this rhetorical excess, this pastiche posing to understand the world? For many the reply has been, no, no, and once again, no to po-mo.[14]

At the disciplinary level, this question and others like it reflect the continuing domination of a philosophical realism in IR—from its logical positivist to rational choice forms—which holds that the purest, most parsimonious statement most accurately, usefully, authentically expresses a thought or reflects an event. At the level of common sense, they suggest a natural preference for conceptual rigor and clarity. After all, even Wittgenstein in his most radical linguistic assault on foundationalist philosophy—a challenge that anticipates poststructuralism—states unequivocally that "everything that can be put into words can be put clearly."[15]

These questions could be dismissed as parochial concerns or philistine conceits. They could be interpreted as the residue of a particularist sign system posing as a universal discourse. Or, as in the reaction to relativism, they reflect a longing for simpler times expressed in simpler terms. At times the debate has an uncomfortably familiar ring to it, reminiscent of conversations overheard at a gallery when someone declares—usually while standing in front of a cubist, an abstract expressionist, or some other avantgarde work of art—"I could do that." Of course, few can, and worse, many do not know why they cannot. Nevertheless these questions, if only for their repetition in IR, deserve a serious response.

One often-used justification is that new, sometimes difficult words must be coined for new phenomena. In his preface to an English translation of *Capital*, Engels felt compelled to apologize to his new audience: "There is, however, one difficulty we could not spare the reader: the use of certain terms in a sense different from what they have, not only in common life, but in ordinary Political Economy. But this was unavoidable. Every new aspect of a science involves a revolution in the technical terms of that science."[16]

But something else is going on. It is expressed more self-consciously by Hegel than Marx, when he stated that "the familiar, just because it is familiar, is not cognitively understood."[17] In *other* words (literally), we might be able to get closer to the constraints of meaning, to understand the *aporia*, or gap between rhetoric and rationality that invariably opens up when a critical language is applied to the various constructions of language. This "making strange" through language, then, is meant to disturb. Why its continental, rhetorical form should be more disturbing in IR than its positivist, modeled form is for the most part a matter of acceptable styles and disciplinary practices, although I suspect that a paradigmatic incommensurability might also be at work.[18]

The most effective (that is, most powerful) style in IR is (like power itself) the one that appears as most transparent and least visible. One poststructuralist might use style as a physics teacher uses iron filings, to *reveal* (and simultaneously to reinscribe) the rhetorical force fields that draw us to this statement, repel us from that one. Another might use it as a clown uses greasepaint, to *distort* (and simultaneously to parody) the "normal" face that cannot express the excess of meaning and the absurdities of life. For the poststructuralist, style is a sign, if not *the* sign, of the author's will in the text. It can be, as Derrida has artfully demonstrated, as light as a feather (*"stylo,"*) or as dangerous as a dagger (*"stylet"*).[19] But sometimes it takes an excess of poststructuralist style to understand how the neopositivist stylelessness of the North American journals *American Political Science Review, International Organization,* or *International Studies Quarterly* precedes inquiry, delimits debate, suppresses alternative modes of expression—and in the process preempts practical possibilities for change.[20]

Enmeshed in a similar debate in the 1960s about the "dangerous language" of the "new criticism," Roland Barthes launched an attack on the ideological assumptions implicit in the call for clarity. His response to his critics helps us to understand why traditional IR theory seems perennially predisposed to an epistemological status quo:

> When a word like dangerous is applied to ideas, language or art, it immediately signals a desire to return to the past. . . . Discourse reflecting upon discourse is the object of a special vigilance on the part of institutions, which normally contain it within the limits of a strict code: in the literary State, criticism must be controlled as much as a police force is: to free the one would be quite as "dangerous" as democratizing the other: it would be to threaten the power of power, the language of language.[21]

This important interrelationship of language, ethics, and identity, so long neglected in traditional IR, finds its seminal expression in the writings of the linguist and literary theorist Mikhail Bakhtin.

How our efforts to fix the meaning of what something is by establishing what it is not is always already warped by the space between the sender and receiver, sign and referent, *langue* (the social code) and *parole* (individual message), author and reader. The heteroglossia of language—the constant renegotiation of meaning and values that goes on with each utterance—bespeaks a heterodoxia in world politics, where radical alterity should be assumed and asserted rather than subsumed and repressed.[22] This shifts if not obliterates the positivist fact-value dichotomy in which the anguished social scientist seeks to expunge subjective factors from objective analysis.

In this context, consider first Bakhtin's critique of monologism:

> Ultimately, *monologism* denies that there exists outside of it another consciousness, with the same rights, and capable of responding on an equal footing, another and equal I *(thou)*. The monologue is accomplished and deaf to the other's response; it does not await it and does not grant it any *decisive* force. Monologue makes do without the other; that is why to some extent it objectivizes all reality. Monologue pretends to be the *last word*.[23]

And then, from the last writings of Bakhtin in 1974:

> There is no first or last discourse, and dialogical context knows no limits (it disappears into an unlimited past and in our unlimited future). Even *past* meanings, that is, those that have arisen in the dialogue of past centuries, can never be stable (completed once and for all, finished), they will always change (renewing themselves) in the course of the dialogue's subsequent development, and yet to come. At every moment of the dialogue, there are immense and unlimited masses of forgotten meanings, but, in some subsequent moments, as the dialogue moves forward, they will return to memory and live in renewed form (in a new context). Nothing is absolutely dead: every meaning will celebrate its rebirth.[24]

This is a distillation of Mikhail Bakhtin's intertextual theory of *dialogism*, which shows how all understanding, like language itself, is a responsive act that depends upon prior as well as anticipates future discourses.[25] Since it is through the communicative acts of negotiating meaning and values with others that the self is constituted, identity *requires* difference: "The psyche," says Bakhtin, "enjoys extraterritorial status."[26]

Yet in world politics the self clearly "enjoys" territorial and sovereign protection. This can partially be explained by the heightened sense of insecurity and long history of estrangement that have created "deep identities" and a rationalist faith in the state to keep the contingencies of life at bay. These artesian sources of monological, sovereign reasoning in IR, which bubble up just when global dangers threaten to overcome the abilities of the nation-state to control them, induce a self-fulfilling dread and denial of an extraterritorial identity.[27]

A dialogical reading of traditional approaches in IR might raise several questions. Is it possible to imagine and construct a new dialogue in IR, one in which identities are not predetermined or fixed by national, class, or chronological origins external to the dialogue but rather are constantly interacting and shifting in the interlocutionary space between the self and the other? Informed by this psychic interdependency, would they be less willing, perhaps even unable, to declare the other persona non grata in this extraterritorial land? In this move from a metalinguistic concept to an interdiscursive relationship, does dialogism exceed its function as a metaphor or formal model and point the way toward not just a "rethinking" but a reformation of IR? Ultimately, it probably depends most on just how jealous each is of the right to the last word.

In sum, poststructuralism helps to disturb the convention upheld with such vigor in IR that theory and practice are distinct phenomena, or more fundamentally, that reality is independent of any language used to describe it. At a time when almost every other social as well as physical science has begun to consider how theory, practice, and language are inextricably linked through social constructions and representational practices, there is an added imperative for a poststructuralist approach (yes, among others) to IR. More specifically, the strange and estranging ways of writing and thinking by poststructuralists provide an intellectual method to reverse the acts of theoretical enclosure and political neutralization that have been instituted in North American IR theory, that assume rational choice, game theoretic, or formal modeling are sufficient representations of world politics. Finally, it is my belief that the accelerating, transparent, hypermediated practices of late modernity *exceed* the representational capabilities of traditional IR theory, and *require* new poststructuralist approaches.

Yet there remains a lingering criticism of poststructuralism, a criticism of criticism. However, poststructuralism is not simply a negative critique—although it has, by its more modish uses, been confused as such. In most cases—and certainly in the case of thinkers such as Michel Foucault—it clears but does not destroy or deny the existence of the ground for a constructive theory. Even in the more radical applications of deconstruction it takes aim at totalist, transcendentalist, closed theory—not *all* theory. If one ignores the disciplinary imprecations and drops the epistemological blinders of IR's modernist mandarins, a host of "constructive" or "applied" poststructuralist and critical theoretical research projects have been published and more can be spotted on the horizon. To name just a few:[28] books like Rob Walker's *Inside/Outside*, David Campbell's *Writing Security*, Bill Chaloupka's *Knowing Nukes*, Chris Hables Gray's *Postmodern War*, V. Spike Peterson's *Gendered States*, Christine Sylvester's *Feminist Theory and International Relations*, Cindy Weber's *Simulated Sovereignty*, and Roxanne Doty's *Imperial Encounters* as well as recent articles by Simon

Dalby, G. M. Dillon, Jerry Everard, Kate Manzo, Mark Neufeldt, Nicholas Rengger, Sandra Whitworth, and Michael Williams.

Semiology, Genealogy, and Dromology

What might the elements of a constructive poststructuralist theory look like? Here I can offer only the skeleton of three that have come to inform my work: genealogy, semiology, and dromology.

First, to reinterpret IR theory is to step backward, look wider, and dig deeper, not to excavate some reality that has been lost or lurks beneath the surface of things, but to lay bare persistent myths of a reality that can be transcribed by a school of thought and yet still claim to speak for itself. As I argued in my inquiry into the beginnings of diplomacy, a *genealogy* is the most appropriate way to begin such a task.[29] A genealogy calls into question the immaculate origins, essential identities, and deep structures of IR theory.

This is particularly true in the case of the strongest and most persistent form of IR theory, realism. A genealogy can reveal the metaphorical and mythical beginnings of a uniform realism while producing through interpretation several realisms that never "figure" in the IR official story. What Bertolt Brecht said of the study of realism in literature equally applies to our own field of inquiry: "Realism is an issue not only for literature: it is a major political, philosophical and practical issue and must be handled and explained as such—as a matter of general human interest."[30]

Second, a *semiology* is needed, in the sense of a study of IR theory as a symptom of a more general condition of late modernity, in which an old order is dying and a new one not yet constituted. To the ear of the other, this might have the sound of a Marxian dialectic, a linguistic structuralism, or a metaphysical eschatology. In intent if not in fact a semiology is an *anti*-metaphysical, pragmatic investigation of the reliance of realism in IR theory on an archaic sign-system in which words mirror objects and theory is independent of the reality it represents. The subsidiary purpose is to show how this paraphilosophical conceit has disabled IR theory's power to interpret as well as to manage the current disorder of things.[31]

A semiology, then, provides a method for a study of the interdependent mix of power, meaning and morality that makes up IR theory. In *The Twilight of the Idols*, Nietzsche exposes this link with a harsh clarity: "To this extent moral judgment is never to be taken literally: as such it never contains anything but nonsense. But as *semeiotics* it remains of incalculable value: it reveals, to the informed man at least, the most precious realities of cultures and inner worlds which did not *know* enough to 'understand' themselves. Morality is merely 'sign' language, merely symptomatology; one must already know *what* it is about to derive profit from it."[32]

He is equally blunt about the potentially radical effects of a semiological inquiry: "I fear we are not getting rid of God because we still believe in grammar."[33] His fear applies as well to poststructuralist theory: Disturbing the apodictic link between a positivist theory of IR and a correspondence philosophy of language, it cannot be construed as merely an academic exercise—which perhaps is one more reason why the IR academy has kept poststructuralism at a distance.[34] The dual imperative of securing a sovereign center for the state and IR theory, and protecting it from anything more threatening than incremental change, has placed a premium on "traditional" approaches. A semiology disturbs this naturalized order, not out of a faddish desire for innovation but out of a suspicion that there are high moral costs attached to the kinds of inertial systems of thought that become institutionalized in high politics and higher learning.[35]

Third, a *dromology* of IR is required, in Paul Virilio's sense of a study of the science or logic of speed, because the representational principle described earlier that underpins realism has itself increasingly become undermined by the ascendancy of temporality over spatiality in world politics.[36] Elsewhere I have identified this as the "(s)pace problematic" of IR, where the displacement of geopolitics by chronopolitics makes a nation-state security founded on the stasis of a fixed identity and impermeable territory increasingly difficult to maintain.[37] In turn, the multifarious effects of speed compound the need for a semiology of IR: The instantaneity of communication, the ubiquity of the image, the flow of capital, the videographic speed of war have made the reality of world politics a transitory, technologically contingent phenomenon.[38]

In a world in which speed is not just the measure but the end of progress, tendencies and flows, arrivals and departures, all forms of moment come to govern and devalue both the immobile object and objectivity itself. *Real* estate, in the dual sense of transparent and immovable property, loses out to *irreal* representations, which are infinitely transferable. In short, the dromocratic machine colonizes reality and its "reflective" mediation, realism. With a casual hyperbole Virilio freeze-frames this imperialism of movement: "It's clear that we are currently in a period of substitutions. One generation of reality is in the process of substituting itself for another and is still uncertain about how to represent itself. And we have to understand that it is very much connected to real-time images. It's not a problem of the configuration or the semiotics of the image, but a problem of the temporality of the image."[39]

In the current age of speed, surveillance, and simulation, genealogy, semiology, and dromology provide new deconstructive tools *and* antidiplomatic strategies to reinterpret IR.[40] Poststructuralism, then, is doubly prodomal for IR, a sign of both the heightened anxiety and trammeled hope that appear when the mirror of an old order cracks and we must remember, reimagine, and if possible, reconstruct a new image of our own self-identity.

A Pre(post)erous Provocation

Some years ago, when first invited to present this paper at Princeton, the speakers were asked to include an "empirical" account of how our first, stumbling efforts to rethink IR theory might yield new insights about world politics; in so many words, we were asked to "strut our stuff." Forgoing the easy out—declaiming this arbitrary separation of theory and practice—I spoke on the Gulf War as the first and certainly not our last hyperreal war of simulation, surveillance, and speed, and of how the poststructuralist writings of Baudrillard, Foucault, and Virilio should be gleaned for insights into these developments.[41] Five years on, while I do believe that my initial assessment still holds, I doubt whether the interest of the reader does. Hence, I would like to introduce a different event, one that might allow me to "strut" the theoretical, ethical, critical values of the poststructuralist approach that I have enumerated, without denying the importance of the "stuff" of world politics which so preoccupies IR today. I will do this *in extremis*, turning some of the criticisms of the critics back on them, to offer a reevaluation of the ethics and pragmatics of poststructuralism.

To be honest, I tire of this tactic. I look forward to pointed critiques of poststructuralism from both within and outside its ranks. But more often than not the range of criticisms have gone from simple to crude. Someone thumps on a table, and says, does this table not exist? Or worse, beats on their chest, and says, did the Holocaust not happen? I have become used to the caricature and vilification of relativism (of course the table exists—but that existence is conveyed by interpretive and discursive fields as well as perspectival action), but the ahistorical trivialization of genocide still stuns me. Of course the Holocaust happened, as did other genocides in the past, and as will others, I fear, in the future—especially if one thinks facts speak for themselves rather than through and for powerful discourses of memory and forgetting. Caught in this either/or logic—either a vulgar empirico-materialism or nothingness, either Enlightenment (i.e., rationalism, progressivism, foundationalism) or Barbarism—such inquisitors of postmodernism ignore or just cannot comprehend some of the most powerful "variables" of IR, like irony and contingency, accident and synchronicity, resentment and caring, alienation and recognition, ambiguity and paradox.

My response is to offer an empirico-postmodernist proof (more in the sense of a trial impression than the establishment of a truth) that poststructuralism can provide both pragmatic ways of thinking and ethical ways of being. Thinking and being are sundered when we "other" history, whether it takes the form of objective detachment, psychological denial, or political triumphalism. The very enjoinder "to rethink IR" reinforces this separation, presuming that history—especially a radical break in history—is something that happened, and that our task is merely to record what actually happened (*wie es eigentilich gewesen*), rather than to understand history as something perpetually under construction and reinterpretation. Where some find relativism, even nihilism in this perspective, Friedrich Nietzsche, nemesis of the Enlightenment project and one of the forefathers of postmodernist thought, locates the ethical imperative of the eternal return:

> Behold, we know what you teach: that all things recur eternally, and we ourselves too; and that we have already existed an eternal number of times, and all things with us. You teach that there is a great year of becoming, a monster of a great year, which must, like an hourglass, turn over again and again so that it may run down and run out again; and all of these years are alike in what is greatest as in what is smallest; and we ourselves are like every great year, in what is greatest as in what is smallest.[42]

Nineteen eighty-nine was such a monster year, unleashing great changes, great hopes, and not a few conferences to rethink what it all meant. Yet there was no lingering sense of a great becoming. Too quickly the euphoria inspired by the twilight of totalitarianism faded in the morning-after of resurgent nationalisms. To be sure, decades of an intellectual inertia weighed heavily on a freshly minted idealism, which, once weakened by uncertainty and self-doubt, was soon invirallated in the West by an epidemic of endism, usually taking the graceless forms of triumphalist gloatings about what had been won (the Cold War) or nostalgic musings about what had been lost (again, the Cold War), rather than imaginative, globalist ideas about what now might be built. Before one could say "Henry Kissinger," realism, posing as superego comfort for a new global disorder, returned as the repressed. "Post's" and "pre's" proliferated—were we in a post–cold war, pre–cold peace, or post-imperial space?—attesting to the insecurity of living in flux-times, where accelerating flows of capital, goods, and information were force-multiplied by real-time media representations of spillover ethnic and civil conflicts that seemed beyond management by a balance or even a hegemony of power.

By now this story as well as the criticism has become overly familiar, too banal for serious scrutiny—one more reason, therefore, to defamiliarize it, to avoid the clichés of a folkloric common sense (*plus ça change . . .*) but, more important, to reinterpret and possibly undermine the resurgence of yet another wave of realism in IR. This does not mean that we must refute realism's historical foundations (recurrence and repetition) but its pharmacological prescription (in the original Greek sense of *pharmakon* as both cure and poison, that is, power as the only antidote for the drug of power) posing as a philosophical conceit (that theory is independent of the reality it represents).

Nietzsche's genealogical approach and his idea of eternal return provides one way to go beyond rethinking and move toward a reliving of IR. As I stated earlier, a genealogy can be used to call into question the realist portrayal of immaculate origins, essential identities, and deep structures in IR, revealing, I believe, the metaphorical and mythical beginnings of a supposedly uniform statecraft while producing through interpretation dissident practices that never "figure" in the official story. Nietzsche's controversial idea of eternal return would then be seen not as some cosmological truth but as a practical guide for political practice in ambiguous and uncertain times. Both entail ethical considerations as well, for we live in conditions under which the Other is hard upon us and yet justice, in the sense of a mediated recognition for the Other, is hard to come by.

In my own work I have focused on this general and persistent condition of estrangement as it has been manifested and produced by diplomatic and antidiplomatic practices.[43] But it is a personal moment of synchronicity that prompts this particular deconstructive response: the invitation to write something new on IR, but also the discovery of a document that seemed to represent the eternal return of the old in the new, and the ethical obligation to respond in a critical way to this recurrence.

Writing of another "monster year," 1919, and eyeing only the "high politics" of diplomacy, participant and historian Harold Nicolson provided wise counsel for those who might think that the whole picture can be captured by traditional methods alone:

> Of all branches of human endeavor, diplomacy is the most protean. The historian and the jurist, relying upon the *procès verbal*, may seek to confine its lineaments within the strict outlines of a science. The essayist may hope to capture its colours in the vignettes of an art. The experts—and there have been many experts from Callières to Jusserand, from Machiavelli to Jules Cambon—may endeavour to record their own experience in manuals for the guidance of those that come after. The journalist may give to the picture the flashes and interpretation of the picturesque. Yet always there is some element in such accounts which escapes reality, always there is some aspect which refuses to be recorded or defined.[44]

From a somewhat lower perspective than the Paris peace conference, I found his view confirmed when I found a document referring to the same event. The document is yellowed-into-brown, well thumbed, and well traveled, having survived the journey from my grandfather's attic through the family archives maintained in a variety of basements by my father, and now to me. It is simply, if not naïvely titled in bold letters, "The Treaty." Reprinted from the *Boston Evening Transcript*, the forty-eight-page pamphlet contains the "Complete Text of the Treaty of Peace as Drawn by the Paris Conference and Issued by the United States Senate." It is signed and dated by my grandfather, June 20, 1919, less than a year after he had emigrated to America from Armenia.

A close reading reveals the reason why a straw boss of the coke ovens at Ford Motor Company would cherish "The Treaty." It was the first to give a legal, if provisional, standing to a country he had spent four years fighting for. Article 22 gave birth to the mandate system and, in the process, provided for the first, if brief, moment of the independence of Armenia. It reads:

> To those colonies and territories which as a consequence of the late war have ceased to be under the sovereignty of the states which formerly governed them and which are inhabited by peoples not yet able to stand by themselves under the strenuous conditions of the modern world, there should be applied the principle that the well-being and development of such peoples form a sacred trust of civilization and that securities for the performance of this trust should be embodied in this Covenant. . . . Certain communities formerly belonging to the Turkish Empire have reached a stage of development where their existence as independent nations can be provisionally recognized subject to the rendering of administrative advice and assistance by a mandatory until such time as they are able to stand alone.

The subsequent "treaties of the Paris suburbs" diplomatically inscribed the short life of Armenia as well as Kurdistan. The 1920 Treaty of Sèvres, in Articles 88–93, enshrined the independence of Armenia. However, the decline in Wilson's political and personal fortunes, differing views among the allies on what might assure security in conditions often described in the proceedings as "strenuous times," and, finally but not exhaustively, the need to enlist new allies from the associated powers against bolshevism in the Caucasus, all were key factors in the removal of the "self" from the determination of nationhood. Not three years later, in the 1923 Treaty of Lausanne, Armenia and Kurdistan simply disappear, unmentioned except as abstract "minorities" that Turkey committed itself to "protect" (Articles 37–45).

This is only one brief vignette from a recurring story of a nation's destiny determined by great-power diplomacy: 1648, 1815, 1871, 1919–1923, 1945–1948, and, still subject to debate, 1989 stand out as the "monster years." To be sure, and to a varying degree and duration, peace and order were secured in the aftermath of war and chaos. But for how long, and to what extent does injustice for the defeated or small powers come at the expense of a durable order? The dialogue between order and justice, most profoundly charted by Hedley Bull, is eternally renewed, and diplomacy seems eternally to get it wrong. I believe the most important question is not whether IR can be rethought or global politics renewed. It is whether IR can learn from the "monster years" and accept their eternal return not as bane or boon, but as Nietzsche did, as an ethical challenge to accept that one will relive the consequences of one's actions, in "greatness or smallness."

Will 1989, then, be what Nietzsche described as "a great year of becoming . . . which must, like an hourglass, turn over again and again so that it may run down and run out again"? Much depends on the philosophical as well as the practico-ethical response to great historic moments: Can we opt out of the either/or logic of Enlightenment or barbarism, idealism or realism, millenarianism or fatalism, and reinterpret the eternal return of history as an obligation to take every encounter with the Other as Nietzsche counsels, in the knowledge that in such encounters "we ourselves are like every great year, in what is greatest as in what is smallest."

If such questions are not to deteriorate into grand metaphysical musings, some historical sense is needed of *how* traditional interpretations of what is old, what is new, and what is recurrent in IR act to delimit the range of options not only for contemporary statecraft but also for individual ethical action. It is this constructive nature of theorizing that poststructuralism seeks to chart, reconstruct, and yes, deconstruct when violence, as it so often is, becomes naturalized in IR. Nowhere is this truer than in the motivation and justification of the genocidal act, whether it is considered necessitous to keep public order as the Ottoman Empire decays, to cleanse the body politic as the Hitlerite empire grows, or to define a Serbian identity out of a collapsing Yugoslavian one.[45]

> *The greatest Weight.* What if some day or night a demon were to steal after you into your loneliest of loneliness and say to you: "This life as you now live it and have lived it, you will have to live once more and innumerable times more; and there will be nothing new in it, but every pain and every joy and every thought and everything unutterably small and great in your life will return to you, all in the same succession and sequence. . . . "[46]

Between Nietzsche and Nicolson there can be found some common ground. Indeed, pararealist assumptions about the nature of humankind and the repetition of its errors are both on display. But where Nicolson (and traditional realists) would find in such a condition cause for the elevation of what he called the principle of *"sauve qui peut . . . or security,"* Nietzsche would find one more reason for a transvaluation of all values.[47] Under such antidiplomatic conditions, in which no border is impermeable, no sovereignty absolute, no "people" without their internal Other, then security itself is predicated upon the insecurity of all values. Here Nietzsche is at home, and when he completes his thoughts on the "greatest weight" of the eternal return, we find an ethical imperative to revalue IR:

> If this thought [of the eternal return] were to gain possession of you, it would change you as you are, or perhaps crush you. The question in each and every thing: "Do you want this once more and innumerable times more?" would lie upon your actions as the greatest weight. Or how well-disposed would you have to become to yourself and life *to crave nothing more fervently* than this ultimate confirmation and seal?[48]

Post-Script (Not the Last Word)

The eternal return never stops. At a recent meeting on apocalyptic violence, I was asked to help organize and to sign a petition that was to appear in the

New York Times and the *Chronicle of Higher Education;* it was to appear under the title, "Taking a Stand Against the Turkish Government's Denial of the Armenian Genocide and Scholarly Corruption in the Academy." It was prompted by a letter that Robert Jay Lifton had received in October 1990 from the Turkish ambassador, Nuzhet Kandemir, in which the ambassador criticizes references in Lifton's book, *The Nazi Doctors: Medical Killing and the Psychology of Genocide,* to the "so-called 'Armenian genocide,' allegedly perpetrated by the Ottoman Turk."[49] After dismissing Lifton's references because they were based on "questionable secondary sources," the ambassador applied the disciplinary whip: "It is particularly disturbing to see a major scholar on the Holocaust, a tragedy whose enormity and barbarity must never be forgotten, so careless in his reference to a field outside his area of expertise." Whence did the ambassador acquire his own scholarly expertise in the manner? By accident, or perhaps through a subversive act of solidarity, a memorandum and a draft letter had accompanied the official letter sent by the ambassador to Lifton. The memorandum is addressed to the ambassador. It includes excerpts and citations for each of Lifton's references to the Armenian genocide (there are seven in the 561 pages of the book). The memorandum ends with an offer from the author: "On the chance that you still wish to respond in writing to Lifton, I have drafted the following letter, which, due to the absence of an address for Lifton will have to be sent to him care of his publisher." The draft letter is virtually identical to the official letter.

The memorandum and letter are from "Dr. Heath W. Lowry." At the time that he wrote the letter and memorandum he was the head of the Institute of Turkish Studies in Washington, D.C., funded by grants from the Republic of Turkey. And from 1994 on, he has been the first incumbent of the Ataturk Chair in Turkish Studies at Princeton University, also funded by the Republic of Turkey.

Understandably, most studies on genocide have been undertaken to comprehend the act rather than the denial of genocide. Ideology, racism, and careerism are usually common to both. However, one study finds that scholars who deny the existence of genocide usually resort to "scientificism" (a lack of sufficient empirical evidence to prove genocide took place) and "definitionalism" (deaths are acknowledged but not as a result of "genocide" per se).[50]

One scholar's questionable actions do not besmirch a whole institution; nor does the dubious invocation of scientific method repudiate all positivist methodologies. Scholars and diplomats alike make choices and justify actions according to a given discursive field in which power is omnipresent. The denial of this relationship between power and knowledge is probably the surest sign of a pure congruence of the two at work. This means that when the stakes are high—and few come higher than the end of totalitarianism and the memory of genocide—one must do more than thump tables and evoke the Holocaust to have the last word. One must have recourse to a philosophical, reflexive, critical approach that helps us to understand how one's own identity is implicated in the study of the killing of others—for this remains the "greatest weight" of IR.

Notes

1. Hedley Bull endorsed the classical approach for similar reasons in his essay "International Theory: The Case for a Classical Approach," *World Politics,* vol. 18, no. 3 (April 1966):361–377. His criticism, leveled against the rise of behavioralism in IR theory, still holds for the wave of behavioralism by other means (such as rational-choice theory and game theory) that continues to dominate North American IR: "My seventh and final proposition is that the practitioners of the scientific approach, by cutting themselves off from history and philosophy, have deprived themselves of the means of self-criticism, and in consequence have a view of their subject and its possibilities that is callow and brash."

2. See J. Der Derian, "Introducing Philosophical Traditions in International Relations," *Millennium Journal of International Studies,* vol. 17, no. 2 (Summer 1988):189–194; "Preface" and "The Boundaries of Knowledge and Power in International Relations," in *International/Intertextual Relations: Postmodern Readings of World Politics*, edited by J. Der Derian and M. Shapiro (Lexington, MA: Lexington Books, 1989), pp. ix–xi and 3–10; and J. Der Derian, "Introduction: A Case for a Poststructuralist Approach," in *Antidiplomacy: Spies, Terror, Speed, and War* (Oxford: Blackwell Publishers, 1992), pp. 1–15.

3. J. Der Derian, *On Diplomacy: A Genealogy of Western Estrangement* (Oxford: Blackwell, 1987).

4. See J. Der Derian, "Preface" in *International/Intertextual Relations,* pp. ix–x.

5. See *Antidiplomacy*, pp. 1–15.

6. John Ruggie, "Territoriality and Beyond: Problematizing Modernity in International Relations," *International Organization,* vol. 47, no. 1 (1993):139–174.

7. See Isaiah Berlin, *Four Essays on Liberty* (Oxford: Oxford University Press, 1969), p. 46; and Berlin, "Alleged Relativism in Eighteenth-Century European Thought," in *The Crooked Timber of Humanity* (New York: Vintage, 1992), pp. 70–90.

8. F. Nietzsche, *Human, All Too Human* excerpted in *A Nietzsche Reader,* selected and translated by R. J. Hollingdale (Middlesex, UK: Penguin, 1977), p. 198.

9. J. S. Mill, *Principles of Political Economy*, in *Collected Works of John Stuart Mill* (London: 1981), p. 594, quoted by Berlin, *Crooked Timber of Humanity*, p. 90.

10. See William Connolly, *Identity/Difference: Democratic Negotiations of Political Paradox* (Ithaca: Cornell University Press, 1991), p. 174.

11. See Emmanuel Levinas, *Face to Face with Levinas*, edited by Richard A. Cohen (Albany: State University of New York Press, 1986). For an excellent elucidation and application of Levinas's ethical views, see David Campbell, *Politics Without Principle: Sovereignty, Ethics, and the Narratives of the Gulf War* (Boulder: Lynne Rienner, 1993).

12. A good example of how interpretation precedes facts with a political effect can be seen in the recent accusations that the journalist I. F. Stone was an agent of the KGB. When the original accuser, espionage "expert" Herbert Romerstein, was asked why he would now believe claims made by an unnamed source in the KGB (which were contradicted by another KGB agent, Oleg Kalugin), he replied: "I disbelieved them when they said what I knew to be false. I believe those things that either can be confirmed or cannot be proved to be lies." See Andrew Brown, "The Attack on I. F. Stone," *New York Review of Books,* October 8, 1992, p. 21.

13. On semio-criticism, see R. Barthes, "To Write: An Intransitive Verb?" in *The Rustle of Language,* translated by R. Howard (New York: Hill and Wang, 1986), pp. 11–12. On the *"problématiques"* approach, see M. Foucault, "On the Genealogy of Ethics: An Overview of Work in Progress," *Foucault Reader,* ed. Paul Rabinow (New York: Pantheon, 1984), p. 343.

14. An infrequently noted pedigree of "postmodern" might temper this response. The writer credited by the Merriam-Webster dictionary with coining the term postmodern in 1947 (to describe the period of history since 1875) is Arnold Toynbee, the highly respected historian who influenced "classical realism" most notably through his collaboration with Martin Wight on parts of his multivolume *A Study of History* (Oxford: Oxford University Press, 1935–1959).

15. L. Wittgenstein, *Tractatus Logico-Philosophicus* (1922), 4.116.

16. F. Engels, "Preface to the English Edition," in K. Marx, *Capital,* vol. 1 (Moscow: Progress Publishers, 1974), p. 14.

17. G. Hegel, *Phenomenology of Spirit* (Oxford: Oxford University Press, 1977), p. 18.

18. An Anglo-Saxon intolerance for new words, which I witnessed firsthand at a British International Studies Association conference, might also be at work. At a panel organized by John Vincent on Hedley Bull's influence in IR theory, a voice from the audience cried out "Shame!" when I used the word "heterologue" to describe Bull's style—to which I felt compelled to reply that probably some of Bentham's peers took offense when he coined the word "international" in 1789.

19. See J. Derrida, "Spurs: Nietzsche's Styles," *A Derrida Reader,* edited by P. Kamuf (New York: Columbia University Press, 1991), pp. 355–377.

20. On the political implications of "plainspeak," see R. Barthes, *Criticism and Truth* (Minneapolis: University of Minnesota Press, 1987), and Henry Giroux and Stanley Aronowitz, "The Politics of Clarity," *Afterimage,* October 1991, pp. 4–5.

21. R. Barthes, *Criticism and Truth,* translated by K. Keuneman (Minneapolis: University of Minnesota Press, 1987), pp. 32–33.

22. Writing about Bakhtin, Paul de Man makes this point with more sophistication than I can muster: "On the other hand, dialogism also functions . . . as a principle of radical otherness. . . . [F]ar from aspiring to the telos of a synthesis or a resolution, as could be said to be the case in dialectical systems, the function of dialogism is to sustain and think through the radical exteriority or heterogeneity of one voice with regard to any other. . . . The self-reflexive, autotelic or, if you wish, narcissistic structure of form, as a definitional description enclosed with specific borderlines, is hereby replaced by an *assertion* of the otherness of the other, preliminary to even the possibility of a *recognition* of his otherness." ("Dialogue and Dialogism," in *The Resistance to Theory* [Minneapolis: University of Minnesota Press, 1986], p. 109).

23. M. Bakhtin, *Problems of Dostoevsky's Poetics*, translated by Caryl Emerson (Minneapolis: University of Minnesota Press, 1984), p. 318.

24. M. Bakhtin, "Concerning Methodology in the Human Sciences," quoted by Tzvetan Todorov, *Mikhail Bakhtin: The Dialogical Principle* (Minneapolis: University of Minnesota Press, 1984), p. 110.

25. For a fuller understanding of how identity is not internally but rather dialogically constructed in a verbal community, see Mikhail Bakhtin, *The Dialogic Imagination: Four Essays by M. M. Bakhtin*, edited by Michael Holquist (Austin: University of Texas Press, 1981); Todorov, *Mikhail Bakhtin: The Dialogical Principle*; and Paul de Man, "Dialogue and Dialogism."

26. M. Bakhtin, *Marxism and the Philosophy of Language* (New York: Seminar Press, 1973), p. 39.

27. See William Connolly, "Global Political Discourse," in *Identity/Difference*, pp. 36–63, for an incisive study of the impact of the "globalization of contingency" on public identities.

28. For the first wave, see: David Campbell, *Writing Security: United States Foreign Policy and the Politics of Identity* (Minneapolis: University of Minnesota Press, 1992); James Der Derian, *Antidiplomacy*; Jim George, *Discourses of Global Politics: A Critical (Re)Introduction to International Relations* (Boulder: Lynne Rienner, 1993); Bradley Klein, *Strategic Studies and World Order* (Cambridge: Cambridge University Press, 1994); Christine Sylvester, *Feminist Theory and International Relations in a Postmodern Era* (Cambridge: Cambridge University Press, 1994); R.B.J. Walker, *Inside/Outside: International Relations as Political Theory* (Cambridge: Cambridge University Press, 1993). Of the IR journals, *Millennium, Alternatives, Review of International Studies,* and *European Journal of International Relations* are most likely to have articles on or applying poststructuralist approaches.

29. See J. Der Derian, *On Diplomacy: A Genealogy of Western Estrangement* (Oxford: Blackwell, 1987), and "A Genealogy of Security," in *The Political Subject of Violence*, edited by D. Campbell and M. Dillon (Manchester, UK: Manchester University Press, 1993).

30. Bertolt Brecht, quoted by Sandy Petrey, *Realism and Revolution: Balzac, Stendhal, Zola, and the Performances of History* (Ithaca: Cornell University Press, 1988), p. xii.

31. I characterize the current assumptions of realism in IR as "paraphilosophical" because they take on the dress (say, as Serbian paramilitary forces pose as a legitimate army) of a uniform realism without any intellectual engagement with the debates (especially of the last two decades) that have surrounded a mitotic body of thought. My particular point of purchase against the tradition is extrinsic and poststructuralist and can be tracked from Wittgenstein and Austin to Barthes and Derrida (see later). But there has been another tributary (among others) of thought closer to the mainstream of philosophical realism that poses just as serious an internal challenge to many of the positivist as well as political assumptions of IR realism—one, I might add, that has suffered just as serious neglect in the field. I refer to post-Marxist theorizing about the relationship of realism to idealism, materialism, and empiricism. For instance, the interwar period produced a series of rich, aesthetic antinomies, most notably between Bertolt Brecht's agitprop expressionism

and Georg Lukács's essentialist formalism, and Walter Benjamin's romantic subjectivism and Theodor Adorno's psychoanalytic modernism, all of which in one form or another held up realism as a means to cut through false consciousness, "defetishize" a reified reality, and provide a commonality of purpose and action. The emergence of the Frankfurt School as well as the post-Marxist phenomenological and structuralist critiques of Jean-Paul Sartre and Louis Althusser attest to a diversity of realisms that have been ignored until quite recently by IR theory. For a review of how some of these thinkers influenced debates over realism, see Frederic Jameson, *Marxism and Form: Twentieth-Century Dialectical Theories of Literature* (Princeton: Princeton University Press, 1971), and Roy Bashkar, *Reclaiming Reality: A Critical Introduction to Contemporary Philosophy* (London: Verso, 1989). For arguments endorsing their significance for IR, see V. Kubalkova and A. A. Cruickshank, *Marxism and International Relations* (London: Routledge, 1985); Mark Hoffman, "Critical Theory and the Inter-paradigm Debate," *Millennium,* vol. 16, no. 2 (Summer 1987):231–250; John Maclean, "Marxism and International Relations: A Strange Case of Mutual Neglect," *Millennium,* vol. 17, no. 2 (Summer 1988):295–320; and Jim George and David Campbell, "Patterns of Dissent and the Celebration of Difference: Critical Social Theory and International Relations, *International Studies Quarterly,* vol. 34 (1990):269–293.

32. F. Nietzsche, *Twilight of the Idols,* translated by R. J. Hollingdale (Middlesex, UK: Penguin, 1968), pp. 55.

33. Ibid., p. 38.

34. I cite Nietzsche and use the term "semiology" here to provide a broad description of the "linguistic turn," that is, the various theoretical reactions to the loss of a pivotal center of meaning that has taken the form of structuralism, structurationism, or poststructuralism. Although they remain in the shadows (largely because their visage—not to mention verbiage—is not overly appreciated in IR discourse), two thinkers along with Nietzsche guide this semiology: Roland Barthes and Jacques Derrida. Particularly useful are two essays that engage historical and linguistic forms of realism: Barthes's *S/Z* (New York: Farrar, Straus and Giroux, 1974), which takes apart line by line Balzac's *Sarrasine*—and many of the tenets of representational realism with it; and Derrida's *Limited, Inc a b c . . .* (Baltimore: Johns Hopkins University Press, 1977), which pushes beyond the limit the radical implications of J. L. Austin's speech-act theory through a critical, often polemical engagement with the philosopher of language, John Searle. An especially useful bridging text between speech-act theory and later applications of structuralist and poststructuralist theories of representation is Petrey's *Realism and Revolution.*

35. Semiology may be more resistant than other approaches to this inertia, but it is not immune, as Roland Barthes, whose own career moved from a structural semiotics to an artful semiology, makes amply clear in an interview: "[I] could say, however, that the present problem consists in disengaging semiology from the repetition to which it is has already fallen prey. We must produce something *new* in semiology, not merely to be original, but because it is necessary to consider the theoretical problem of repetition . . . to pursue a general and systematic enterprise, polyvalent, multidimensional, the fissuration of the symbolic and its discourse in the West." See "Interview: A Conversation with Roland Barthes," *Signs of the Times* (1971), reprinted in *The Grain of the Voice* (New York: Hill and Wang, 1985), p. 129.

36. See Paul Virilio, *Pure War* (New York: Semiotext(e), 1983); *Speed and Politics* (New York: Semiotext(e), 1986); *War and Cinema: The Logistics of Perception* (New York: Verso, 1989). A trivial but telling recent example of the primacy of time over space (and what fills that space) is the lead-in commentary on President Bill Clinton's 1993 inaugural address: The three major networks and PBS put the emphasis on its fourteen-minute brevity.

37. See J. Der Derian, "The (S)pace of International Relations: Speed, Simulation, and Surveillance," *International Studies Quarterly* 34 (1990), pp. 295–310.

38. This mood and need was captured in a remark by Tom Brokaw, quoted in Michael Kelly, "Being Whatever It Takes to Win Election," *New York Times*, August 23, 1992: "The news cycle has become a 24-hour-a-day thing, and it moves very fast all the time now. What happens is that a fragment of information, true or false, gets sucked into the cycle early in the morning, and once it gets into the cycle it gets whipped around to the point that it has gravitas by the end of the day. And, unfortunately, people are so busy chasing that fragment of information that they treat it as a fact, forgetting about whether it is true or not."

39. Virilio, interview, from *Art and Philosophy* (Milan: Giancarlo Politi Editore, 1991), p. 142.

40. For an explanation of the dangers and opportunities presented by the new "antidiplomacy," see Der Derian, *Antidiplomacy*.

41. For a full account, see Der Derian, "Cyberwar, Videogames, and the Gulf War Syndrome," in *Antidiplomacy*, pp. 173–202.

42. F. Nietzsche, *Thus Spoke Zarathustra*, translated by R. J. Hollingdale (Harmondsworth, UK: Penguin, 1969), p. 237.

43. See *On Diplomacy; Antidiplomacy;* and the entry "Diplomacy" in *The Oxford Companion to the Politics of the World,* ed. Joel Krieger (New York: Oxford University Press, 1993).

44. Harold Nicolson, *Peacemaking* (London: 1933), p. 3.

45. In spite of a contrary opinion in IR—often based on secondary accounts—postmodernism from Nietzsche to Derrida and after has been informed and compelled by ethical questions about violence and genocide. See Emmanuel Levinas, *The Levinas Reader,* edited by Sean Hand (Oxford: Blackwell Publishers, 1989); Zygmunt Bauman, *Modernity and the Holocaust* (Ithaca: Cornell University Press, 1990); and Jacques Derrida, *The Other Heading: Reflections on Today's Europe*, translated by Pascale-Anne Brault and Michael B. Naas (Bloomington: Indiana University Press, 1992).

46. Friedrich Nietzsche, *The Gay Science*, translated by Walter Kaufmann (New York: Vintage, 1974), p. 273.

47. Nicolson, *Peacemaking*, p. 70. With the meaning of 1989 at stake, the entire quote is worth repeating: "Paris was something very different from Delphi, and when pressed to explain himself our Oracle ended all too frequently by explaining himself away. It is no exaggeration to attribute the sudden 'slump in idealism,' which overwhelmed the Conference towards the middle of March, to the horror-struck suspicion that Wilsonism was leaking badly, that the vessel upon which we had all embarked so confidently was foundering by the head. Our eyes shifted uneasily in the direction of the most contiguous life-belt. The end of the Conference became a *sauve qui peut*: we called it '*security*': it was almost with a panic rush that

we scrambled for the boats; and when we reached them we found our colleagues of the Italian Delegation already comfortably installed. They made us very welcome."

48. Nietzsche, *The Gay Science*, p. 274.

49. See Roger W. Smith, Eric Markusen, and Robert Jay Lifton, "Professional Ethics and the Denial of the Armenian Genocide," *Holocaust and Genocide Studies,* vol. 9, no. 1 (Spring 1995):1–22.

50. Israel Charny and Daphna Fromer, "A Follow-up of the Sixty-nine Scholars Who Signed an Advertisement Questioning the Armenian Genocide," *Internet on the Holocaust and Genocide*, special double issue, no. 25/26 (April 1990):6–7, quoted in Smith, Markusen, and Lifton, "Professional Ethics," p. 15.

4

Feminist Inquiry and International Relations

JEAN BETHKE ELSHTAIN

There are many creatures with many names inhabiting the universe of international relations theory: realism, neorealism, world-systems theory, neoliberal institutionalism, dependency theory, game theory, rational-choice theory, structuralism, neostructuralism, and poststructuralism. Feminist discourse, too, appears in a bewildering number of varieties. There are, for example, feminist variants on many of these familiar approaches to international relations.[1] Often feminist scholars set about correcting for exclusions of gender categories in the study of international relations by "putting gender back in." This is construed as correcting for a systematic male or masculine "bias" in international relations.

My approach in this essay is somewhat different. A focus on "bias" may not be the most fruitful way to go. Why? First, because to speak of "bias" is to place oneself inside an epistemology in which one's conceptual and ethical evaluations depend upon one's "biases" or "emotive preferences." This is not the sturdiest base from which to launch a strong set of normative claims. Matters are far more complex.[2] Second, the claim of bias tends to generate a counterbias in which gender threatens to become all-determinative, functioning as the key to any and all questions and problems, serving a conceptual and political purpose rather like "class" does in Marxist discourse. Absolutizing gender is a temptation to be resisted, despite the fact that scholars of many persuasions find the prospect of a privileged epistemic ground seductive. Why should those laboring in the vineyard of feminist theory be an exception?

The problem of point of view is central to debates among feminist thinkers. Here at the outset it is worth offering several examples drawn from another important arena of social science, anthropology, but applicable to the matter at hand. Assessing the contention of a group of feminist anthropologists that as members of a "universal category" they are somehow "free from bias," anthropologist Marilyn Strathern notes the self-confirming nature of such claims. The argument is that one validates one's anthropological study by taking up and speaking from the "women's point of view," under the presumption that a woman has a "specific, non-replicable insight" into any given culture that is in principle unavailable to a male researcher.[3]

The self-consciously feminist point of view, the argument continues, is not subject to the charge of bias that can and must be leveled against a male point of view. Moreover, an identity is said to exist between the "author and subject of study," a "naturally grounded" congruity. The result is a position of epistemological privilege that enables the feminist researcher to negate or undermine male knowledge claims or interpretations. But this privileged position can also derail challenges from other female anthropologists. Disagreement may be put aside as a form of "false consciousness." Thus Judith Shapiro questions the claim that a double standard is legitimate for assessing male bias, on the one hand, and a privileged female "double consciousness," on the other.[4] Too often claims to a privileged standpoint are self-insulating and promote a refusal to engage the aims and claims of others.

An alternative approach that is critically interpretive, theoretically modest, empirically grounded, aware of the need for an appropriate distance between the subject matter of one's inquiry and one's own world and identity, and flexible yet sturdy enough to sustain strong knowledge claims and to adjudicate between better and worse arguments, helps to keep alive debates by refusing to move to definitive closure. Such an approach to international relations insists that interpretive dilemmas cannot be evaded. Though knowledge and understanding may in some interesting ways be embodied—and this may help to account for why men and women, at least some of the time, and to culturally specific ends and purposes, experience the world in different ways—no embodied being, male or female, has access to the whole, or to anything like "the totality." This being the case, the scholar is free to explore gender differences without presuming the superiority of a gendered narrative that closes out contesting interpretations.

Not being hobbled in advance by the conceptual claims of gender as *prison*, the critic is open to the intimations and possibilities of gender as *prism*. This essay, then, is an invitation to an engagement, one already under way, between feminist scholars and those laboring in the vineyards of international relations theory and the ethics of war and peace. Because I traverse the territory marked by these areas of scholarly commitment, what follows should be taken as an extended prolegomenon, an adumbration of fruitful points of contact between and among gender scholars, political theory, and international relations.

One final preliminary point must be made. It is no doubt a banal point, but it surfaces frequently. Scholars looking at gender in international relations are not *primarily* lobbying for an increase in the number of women in the ranks of international relations scholars or as heads of states. (Of course, one can hope that this will happen as a matter of equity.) Rather, they are pondering what difference it might make to the study of international relations if questions of gender were centrally and routinely included rather than being peripheral, to the extent they appear at all. By gender questions or gender representations, I do not have in mind the much-debated notion that, were women to gain control over states, wars would be resorted to less frequently and less relentlessly. Those of us who have done work in this area recognize that women as leaders and women as mothers and women as workers have sustained and supported the wars of their states in far greater numbers than women in any capacity have acted in opposition to wars, militarism, and nationalistic excess.

If these are not the most salient issues, what emerges as exigent if one claims that concerns with gender are important to theorizing about the study of politics, including international relations? My working assumption is that tending to the inclusion of feminist themes—and none that I will take up is narrowly or exclusively feminist—makes a contribution to more robust thinking across the board about the complex world of women, men, the state, and war.

There are four general areas of theoretical demarcation and conceptual contestation in international relations that feminist inquiry necessarily touches on. I will take up each in turn.

The Reading and Use of Classic Texts

We have heard much in recent years about the discursive terrain that helps to constitute the study of international politics as the complex practice that it is. It is not surprising that a number of feminist scholars have been drawn to a rereading and rethinking of foundational texts, including Thucydides, Machiavelli, Hobbes, Clausewitz, and others. They do this because these and other historic thinkers continue to set the framework for dominant approaches to the study of international relations.

The contemporary realist, for example, locates himself inside a well-honed tradition, exuding the confidence of one whose narrative long ago "won the war."[5] Many of the texts central to the construction of realist and neorealist discourse are richer and more problematic than received understandings indicate. For example, Daniel Garst presents, in his 1989 piece "Thucydides and Neorealism," a "sharply different" interpretation of *The Peloponnesian War* than that which dominates in the work of Kenneth Waltz, Robert Gilpin, and Robert Keohane. One of Garst's most telling points is that the generalizations Thucydides offers should *not* be taken as causal laws of politics; rather, they correspond to what Peter Winch (following the later Wittgenstein) calls "rule-governed behavior." To understand *The Peloponnesian War*, one must unravel a complex rhetorical universe that consists of those conventions of argument in action by which the Greek city-states "maintain and regulate their relations with one another"—Garst here cites Martin Wight.[6]

If we pay close attention, we notice that Thucydides does not begin by talking about the distribution of power in a system or the behavior of states, but about forms of political knowledge and civic identity that propel states into particular relations with one another *given* their "habits, customs, and political institutions: and the activities and forms of power that flow from, or are contingent upon, well-defined and accepted social conventions and institutions."[7] Garst draws out the implications for contemporary neorealist theory of his alternative reading by claiming that his approach undermines the views of political power that prevail in realist and neorealist argument. One can move on from the points Garst makes to insist upon the importance of *strategic cultures*, noting that states qua states do not behave as they do simply by virtue of their "stateness" or statehood. There is a repertoire of civic concepts available to states that locates them in the agonistic arena of international affairs in a variety of different ways. This effort to create a countertradition pries open received arenas of discourse to fresh critical scrutiny. Such contextual readings are not just the endless interplay of "intertextualities" but pose a more fundamental challenge. To the extent that alternative readings of central works prevail, theoretical approaches and models that depend upon received readings will be altered, as will the presuppositions, frameworks, and predictions they have helped to generate.

Going back over classical texts is by no means an uncontroversial enterprise within the world of feminism and international relations. There are scholars who question the exercise as yet another attempt to "defeat the master with his own weapons." But those of us with a political theory background work continually with texts from the past. What makes many of these works great is that one can return to them again and again without exhausting what they have to say. Moreover, it surely matters whether, for example, Machiavelli belongs within a school that assumes that *political behavior* can be predicted, in contrast to an alternative, namely, that rules for *political action* can be explored. This is a big difference. It means, as a close reading shows, that Machiavelli, far from being a constructor of causal laws, was something of a fabulist, inventing dialogue and deploying mythical modes of understanding. Machiavelli was attuned to multiple and often antithetical points of view. He offers not so much a form of *scientific reason* as a mode of *practical reason*, an exploration of the grounds for action in a world in which half of human affairs is governed by fortune.

Criticizing classic and inescapable texts is but one feature of a more general attempt to open received arenas of discourse to critical scrutiny. The importance of such contestation spills out of the text and into the world, so to speak. Readings themselves are constitutive of practices. There are, in other words, performative implications to the concepts we embrace. They invite us to act or to refrain from acting. They offer up a justificatory code to guide and to assess action. Sorting out those performative implications that flow from theories is a "utility" that has to be assessed, to be sure. We are, then, further obliged to explore criteria for what is to count as success or failure by looking at the ways in which competing theoretical understandings locate us in the political world. The strong claim would be that *which Machiavelli* and *whose realism* one embraces positions actors in the world in quite different ways that touch on, shape, and in turn are shaped by real world events. I mention this in order to urge the reader to see this sort of activity as one not at all removed from the world of men, women, and states but very much a part of it.

Take, for example, the fact that Machiavelli's understanding of politics and political power revolves around a particular sort of divide in which women are separated from what Joan Scott has called "the high politics of wars and states."[8] I refer, of course, to the way in which Machiavelli celebrates *virtù*, a particular *manly* virtue, as well as collective armed *esprit*, in contrast to soft "feminized" inefficacy in the tough world of men and states. Following on the heels of this observation, one notes that, despite Machiavelli's insistence on the exclusion of women from the manly arts of war and politics as the defining public activity, he nevertheless analogizes from private to public insistently in his work. In other words, he breaches the divide he himself has set up. This has implications that were ignored until feminist scholars suggested that there are political implications to be teased out of Machiavelli's public-private distinction.

The way "Machiavellian" men act in public, including mastery in the arts of deception and realpolitik, is also available to women in private. Here Machiavelli's play, *Mandragola*, unread by international relations theorists, is instructive. It indicates that the ethics of action appropriate to a world of conflict is not "gendered" all the way down, in Machiavelli's view, although the spheres within which men and women operate are sharply distinguished: Women occupy only one, the private.

One might go on to note that the prince's relationship to his people is shaped by Machiavelli's distinction between a formless female principle (*materia*) and a male principle (*forma*) that shapes what would otherwise be an inchoate mass. In sum, there is a conceptual barrier between public and private in the Machiavellian world that is consistently breached with his analogizing between public and private imperatives and principles. What would change in international relations theory if we asked the "real Machiavelli" to please stand up by routinely displaying the ways in which much of what he says turns on nuances of gender and categories forged on the anvil of what is "masculine" and what is "feminine"? Do these categories *require* one another? If our assumptions about one or the other changes, how is the overall perspective affected?

Varieties of Gendered Identities

Contemporary feminist theory may be understood as coming to grips with the creation of gendered identities in historically concrete and specific times and places; indeed, this has been a focus of feminist theorizing since the early 1970s.[9] It is scarcely open to dispute that war and civic life are productive of male and female identities and that war especially has shaped men and women as civic subjects of a particular kind.[10] Historically constructed and continually reinscribed exemplars come into play when we consider war and warmaking in the West. Feminist scholarship has brought into bold relief the prototypical emblems and identities that emerge when the subject matter is men, women, and war. A few words of summary may be helpful here. Men have fought as avatars of nation-state-sanctioned violence; women have worked and wept and sometimes protested within the frame of practices that turn them out, militant Spartan mother and pacifist protester alike, as collective alternatives to the male warrior. These female identities served as underpinnings for decision and action. The "Just Warrior" and the "Beautiful Soul," as I tag them, help to secure women's locations as noncombatants and men's as soldiers; moreover, these paradigmatic figures have overshadowed other voices and stories—of bellicose women, pacific males, of cruelty incompatible with just-war fighting and of martial fervor at odds, or so we choose to believe, with maternalism in women. My point is that the imagery of war and the collective identities called forth by war capture features of what men and women have become, or are capable of becoming, in civic life.

Why mention this in a discussion of feminist themes in the study of international relations? For this reason: To speak of identities in a rich sociocultural or collective sense is to transgress the classic "levels of analysis" or "three images model" deeded to us by Kenneth Waltz, among others. Readers are familiar with the model—the individual (especially psychological characteristics or presumably universal motivation), the state, and the anarchic international arena itself comprise three levels of explanation and causation. According to Waltz, the scholar must opt for one level in order to maintain coherence. Waltz, of course, opts for the level of structural determination, the third level. But consideration of politics and identity compels the scholar to move in and through all three levels of analysis as he or she examines the ways in which individual, group, and national identities are constituted. Presuppositions about gender figure at each point, moving in and through each category.

Let me offer a hint of what is at stake by returning to the theme of war. In my book *Women and War*, I argue that rather than obedience or disobedience to an abstract set of stipulative requirements, in time of war what makes the difference in how a nation-state as a collective entity behaves is the structure of that nation's history and experience—its strategic culture. The latter is by far more salient in assessing how decisionmakers act than are finely honed theoretical assumptions about international anarchy and the pursuit of self-interest narrowly defined. This means that we must look at the repertoire of possibilities available in particular societies at particular times. What terms define the dominant political rhetoric? How do citizens of *this* society construe themselves domestically and in their relations with others? How does *this* collective identity have determinative force when it comes to relations between one state and another? For example, the strong claim often made on U.S. action, in contrast with claims made on others, is couched currently in the language of human rights, noting the particular responsibility the United States has for upholding a normative vision of decent political relationships. For obvious reasons, the United States can be called upon in this way. There is no way to get at this sort of complexity unless you put the "domestic" and the "international" into a complex relationship with one another. Once you have done that, gender relations and identities take on greater conceptual weight.

In addition, by looking at identities that transgress levels of analysis, the scholar is afforded critical distance from the presupposition that the identity of sovereign states is simply given by a stipulative definition of what a state is and therefore how a state must act. Taking up complex identity questions means that one cannot presume that all states work to maximize or secure their own power (with power understood in an unproblematic way, either as capabilities or as force one can bring to bear, and so on). Such inquiry opens up challenges to the received notions of state sovereignty. When we talk about those modes of argumentation that have prevailed in the academic study of international relations, we are talking about a set of assumptions that adds up to a predetermined identity for states qua states, as well as for men and women and the parts they play in the great stories of war and politics. Challenging fixed assumptions helps us to rethink "what we are doing," in the words of political philosopher Hannah Arendt. It also helps to open up new arenas for political action because we are invited to go beyond Waltzian levels and to look at the ways in which women as political subjects play a variety of complex roles in actual political life.

The State and the Question of Sovereignty

A third primary area of inquiry, one already alluded to, is a rethinking of the state from a variety of feminist perspectives. What I have in mind here is nothing grandiose. Rather, I am building on the question of the politics of cultural and strategic identities, including the presumption that much of what international relations scholars have taken for granted must be scrutinized. This includes the assumption that the state is a unitary rational actor (with rationality understood as "reckoning consequences," in Hobbes's words). This view rests on an analogous view of the individual as a rational, autonomous, and independent actor propelling himself forward unless checked by counterpressure of some sort—an unlikely fusion of Kantian and Hobbesian imperatives. An enormous body of feminist scholarship challenges the view of the ideal moral agent as a being who is disembodied, ageless, sexless, and transcendent of all historical particularity. I will not rehearse these arguments here. My point is to note that the rational-actor model, whether of individuals or of states, offered us a kind of "pastiche-person," particularly in models of analysis dominated by a view of maximization of utilities as what drives both individuals and collectives. Feminist questions concerning this particular model of the state come to us from many directions. Of course, there is no single outcome once this dominant view of the state is challenged. Marxist feminists have a very different understanding of the state from that of pacifist feminists, or postmodern feminists, or liberal feminists. Questioning received categories is not so much an end in itself as it is an inducement to further thought and to work of a sort that touches on complex questions of political obligation and action.

One way in which this matter is currently being approached is through the study of sovereignty.[11] Classical formulations hold that sovereignty is indivisible and inalienable. Those endorsing the classic definition insist, with great self-assurance, that even as sovereignty shifts over time from king to state, the state "can no more alienate its sovereignty than a man can alienate his will and remain a man."[12] The state and sovereignty are united. Each sovereign country is free to regulate its own domestic affairs without outside interference. The state is an independent territorial monopoly of political power. We all know this story. But how secure is it? Is it really the case that the modern body politic would grind to a halt if the assumption that there was a final and absolute authority within it were to be abandoned? Is not sovereignty constrained in all sorts of ways that the classical theory represses? There are, after all, other entities that make rival claims

on us—churches, families, political parties, regional and linguistic forma-
tions; is not the international arena itself a *society*—in Hedley Bull's
terms—comprising *many* actors, not just states? And these entities, moreover, engage one another in a variety of ways, including reciprocal rule-
following. The possessiveness and the exclusiveness of the classical concept
of sovereignty is open to challenge from many directions. The feminist direction points to a multiplicity of powers and loyalties moving us away
from the unitariness of sovereign willing, required in a classical account as
the only way to stave off cacophony and chaos. Feminist concern with this
matter is traceable, in part, to analogies drawn by sovereign theorists between the power of the absolute *dominus* in the Roman household and the
power of the absolute king or parliament in the polity. These came to be
analogized in the urging that within the family and within the common-
wealth final authority must be singular.

To those who insist that final authority within a political regime and the
sovereignty of instrumental reason must reign supreme, one modulated response might be to defend the notion of territorial or political entities but
to argue that they need not be sovereign in the classical sense of dominion,
including the laying down of the law in a command-obedience structure.
Perhaps a chastened notion of homeland and of sovereignty as a limited
concept might come to prevail. Like the franchise, sovereignty offers political standing and enables people to defend the integrity of particular ways of
life. This poses a heavy theoretical and political challenge to feminist
thinkers. Put starkly: Can one "desovereignize" political entities even as
one endorses a notion of political independence? These are concerns not
unique to feminism, of course, but they have been put on the table in particular ways by feminist thinkers.

Power as Plural, Not Singular

A fourth arena of conceptual contestation is a rethinking of power itself.
Feminist thinkers who have challenged neorealist assumptions and the ahistorical abstractions of game theory, formal modeling, and so on, call upon
us to reexamine all our key concepts, especially power. If politics is about
power, what is power about? The hard-line answer is domination, control,
compulsion, bringing force to bear to best advantage. One can see power in
operation—and it can be both posited and tested. This is, one can assess
power empirically by contrasting the moves of one entity in comparison to
another. This very mechanical definition of power once reigned in
American political science.

Of course nearly everyone is now more sophisticated than this formula allows. But the reductive quality of many views of power continues to haunt
the projects of those dedicated to political prediction. Interestingly, the tradi-

tion of Western political thought challenges the notion of power as the compulsion of one unitary actor or agent upon another. This tradition offers multiple understandings of power, its meaning, its range of application, its legitimate and its illegitimate uses, and its relation to authority, justice, and order. Something intriguing happens if one recalls the two Latin terms for power: *potestas* and *potentia*. The former denotes control, supremacy, dominion; the latter is power understood as might or ability, efficacy, potency, especially unofficial and possibly threatening anarchy and disorder. Fascinatingly, these contrasting usages demarcate roughly the boundaries of gendered representations of power historically. Men have been the official wielders of institutional power and dominion; women the unofficial and hence potentially uncontrollable repositories of nonpolitical power. *Potentia* conjures up the threatening, because it occupies a boundary that falls outside the reign of official power; hence is potentially disordered and disordering.

Potestas has taken the form of highly institutionalized and centralized entities, including states with their sovereign power. Much more work needs to be done in order to unravel the thread that appears to run through a vast tangle of historical and ethnographic evidence featuring formal male power balanced or even undermined by informal female power. The point, once again, is that power is not a singular or unitary concept. By spelling out its diverse meanings, one comes to grips with contrasting political, economic, and social realities.

Working with nuanced understandings of power might, for example, help one to make sense of the irony of women's participation in struggles for statehood. Such struggles involve creating or sustaining a collective identity as a people and searching for the means to protect and defend that identity. But once statehood is secured, women tend to be absent in the councils of state. An historical reconstruction of the drive toward state systems, focusing on the elimination of competing forms of social organization and power, is surely a preeminent and important enterprise for feminist scholars. What is at work here is the possibility of opening up political space by pushing back the sway of *potestas* in favor of modes of social organization less dominated by fear of multiple sources of power and action than the "state-centric" model presumes. These forces, feminist scholars have argued, should be nurtured, not swamped. In the process of centralization and codification of state power, women have tended to get lost and to be excluded. It appears that centralization itself relegates women to particular sites that are essential to the social order but seen as marginal within it. This, surely, is a matter open to empirical adjudication, including case studies assessing who wins and who loses when things change.

One final point about power. Many feminist scholars now draw upon Hannah Arendt, given her attempt to rescue politics from war by separating violence from power. I have noted Arendt's argument that by conflating the instrumentalism of violence with power, one eclipses public space within which citizens act in civically robust ways. Arendt's argument is powerful, as is her use of the metaphor of natality to characterize new and fragile political beginnings in a dangerous world. But Arendt's analysis is by no means unproblematic when it comes to relations between states. In this matter, she simply opts for the Hobbesian war of all against all because she sees no alternative.[13] To be sure, she decries the sovereignty of the state as the source of this "Hobbesian rule." But that is as far as she goes, despite the fact that she declares "the identification of freedom with sovereignty" to be "perhaps the most pernicious and dangerous consequence of the political equation of freedom and free will." She further adds that the "famous sovereignty of political bodies has always been an illusion which, moreover, can be maintained only by instruments of violence, i.e., with essentially nonpolitical means."[14] This is a terribly untheorized feature to Arendt's political thought. Simply reincorporating it into feminist discourse as a preferred alternative to older notions of power and dominion does not push us very far toward believable theoretical and political alternatives. One common theme in feminist analysis is to endorse a vision of power as a form of connection and care that is in contrast to "harsher" alternatives. But connection may as easily breed conflict as anything else, and care may turn "maternalistic" and controlling.

Conclusion: The Politics of Peace

Finally, a few words on the oft-noted connection between feminism and the politics of peace. Because international relations has opened up in recent years to peace and world security studies and to questions of conflict management and arbitration, feminist resurgence in international relations would seem to be a spin-off. A vast literature on these general themes is now available, and it is growing in historical sophistication and conceptual robustness. As the scholarly work blossoms, it seems likely that the concept of peace that dominated much early feminist reflection on "the war system" will falter. In such formulations war was seen as threatening disorder and peace as healing order; war was aggressivity and peace was nonviolence, primarily if not exclusively "female." Such assumptions were among the dubious outgrowths of early gender theorizing, and serious feminist scholarship puts pressure on such simplistic distinctions. The feminists who once dominated debates about war and peace were all too often ideologists who called for a free-flow from a supposedly benevolent and feminized private world to a peaceful, once feminized, public world. This variant on feminist universalism contrasted itself with masculinism, patriarchy, violence, and disorder.

Feminist peace discourse of this sort recreated the character I call "the Beautiful Soul" by giving her a feminist gloss. Challenging such ideological constructions in the name of a critical feminism is an important and ongoing project. One might try the following thought experiment: Suppose the current war/state system were to pass. What sort of conflicts would occur? What alternative conceptualizations of political struggle and action might we imagine? Is there a specifically *feminist* way to conceptualize politics as an activity that tames the conflicts that have led historically to war? One quickly recognizes that simply calling for an end to states does not suffice: One must come up with plausible alternative ways to organize political life. Perhaps, as Michael Howard has suggested, a world without states would be a more, not less, violent world.[15]

No single standpoint or perspective, feminist or nonfeminist, gives us transparent pictures of reality. Many perspectives and ways of seeing expand the horizons of international relations discourse and make more supple our thinking about the world of men, women, and states. The most robust feminist projects in international relations are those that embrace an attitude of constraint and moderation even as feminist scholars challenge dominant presuppositions, frameworks, and models. A final feminist theme is the vital importance of theoretical debate as itself a political and conceptual imperative of the first rank.

Notes

1. For an interesting sorting out of the field of feminist discourse in international relations, see Christine Sylvester, "The Emperor's Theories and Transformations: Looking at the Field Through Feminist Lenses," in *Transformations in the Global Political Economy,* edited by Dennis Pirages and Christine Sylvester (London: Macmillan, 1988). See also Cynthia Enloe, *Does Khaki Become You? The Militarism of Women's Lives* (London: Pluto Press, 1983); J. Ann Tickner, *Gender in International Relations: Feminist Perspectives on Delivering Global Security* (New York: Columbia University Press, 1992); and V. Spike Peterson's introduction to her edited volume, *Gendered States* (Boulder: Westview Press, 1992). In the Peterson volume, R.B.J. Walker, "On the Discourses of Sovereignty: Gender and Critique in the Theory of International Relations," sees the value of feminist theory in rather an ascetic way: It can help us to answer questions about who we are, given the "fragility of historically constituted certainties"; hence a "more active intersection between feminism and international relations" is called for. Other general treatments worth consulting include Peter R. Beckman and Francine D'Amico, eds., *Women, Gender, and World Politics* (Westport, Conn.: Bergin and Harvey, 1994); Rebecca Grant and Kathleen Newland, *Gender and International Relations* (Bloomington: Indiana University Press, 1991); and James Rosenau, ed., *Global Voices: Dialogues in International Relations* (Boulder: Westview Press, 1993). Essays in the Grant and Newland volume include such titles as "The Sources of

Gender Bias," "Women in I.R.?", "Gender Planning in the Third World," "Feminism and the Claim to Know," and "Hidden from I.R.: Women and the International Arena." Some feminist theorists are universalist in claim and aim; others eschew universalistic aspirations, a repudiation tethered frequently to the insistence that to reach for the universal is by definition to do damage to the culturally specific by seeking to appropriate and to tame difference—often cast as the other, the silenced denizen of a realm of suppressed knowledge and the like. For most feminist scholars working in IR, all *prefeminist* international relations thinking is considered suspect because of its systematic "gender bias." See, for example, the discussion by Rebecca Grant, "The Sources of Bias in International Relations," in *Gender and International Relations*, ed. Grant and Newland, pp. 8–26.

2. For a fuller epistemological discussion, see Jean Bethke Elshtain, "Methodological Sophistication and Conceptual Confusion: A Critique of Mainstream Political Science," in *The Prism of Sex*, edited by Julia A. Sherman and Evelyn Torton Beck (Madison: University of Wisconsin Press, 1979), pp. 229–252.

3. See Marilyn Strathern, "Culture in a Netbag: The Manufacture of a Subdiscipline in Anthropology," *Man*, vol. 16 (1981):665–688.

4. Judith Shapiro, "Anthropology and the Study of Gender," in *A Feminist Perspective in the Academy: The Difference It Makes*, edited by Walter Langland and Elizabeth Gove (Chicago: University of Chicago Press, 1981), pp. 110–129.

5. See Jean Bethke Elshtain, "Realism, Just War, and Feminism in a Nuclear Age," *Political Theory*, vol. 13, no. 1 (February 1985):39–57. Let me add that to emphasize the importance of texts is not to deny the importance of social structures, economic forces, and so on. To claim that texts are authoritative in constituting a practice of scholarly inquiry is not to insist on the pristine autonomy of ideas. Thus a new reading of a complex thinker such as Thucydides helps us to determine whether or not we can draw usefully upon Thucydides today. Does he continue to teach us about matters on which we need the very best possible instruction? For those who are convinced, as I am, that the answer to this question is "yes," new readings are vital, not to eliminate any text from the canon but to look at the ways in which texts have been used and perhaps misused.

6. Daniel Garst, "Thucydides and Neorealism," *International Studies Quarterly*, vol. 33, no. 1 (March 1989):3–28 (quotation on p. 7). See also James H. Nolt, "Social Order and War: Thucydides, Aristotle, and the Critique of Modern Realism" (paper presented at the annual meeting of the American Political Science Association, 1989).

7. Garst, "Thucydides and Neorealism," p. 11.

8. Joan Scott, *Gender and the Politics of History* (New York: Columbia University Press, 1988), pp. 7, 48–49.

9. Christine Sylvester, in her *Feminist Theory in International Relations in a Post-Modern Era* (Cambridge: Cambridge University Press, 1994), sorts out the intricacies of gender and IR's pretheoretical and theoretical understandings in a complex manner by surveying the terrain that moves through what she calls the early field and the second and third debates in IR. Sylvester's book also includes a quite comprehensive bibliography.

10. See, for example, Jean Bethke Elshtain, *Women and War*, 2d ed. (Chicago: University of Chicago Press, 1994).

11. See, for example, R.B.J. Walker, *Inside/Outside: International Relations as Political Theory* (Cambridge: Cambridge University Press, 1993); Cynthia Weber, *Simulating Sovereignty* (Cambridge: Cambridge University Press, 1995); Hendrik Spruyt, *The Sovereign State and Its Competitors* (Princeton: Princeton University Press, 1994).

12. Charles Merriam, *History of Sovereignty Since Rousseau: Studies in History, Economics, and Public Law* (New York: Columbia University Press, 1900), Vol. 12, No. 4, p. 33.

13. Hannah Arendt, *On Violence* (New York: Harcourt, Brace, Jovanovich, 1969), p. 6.

14. Hannah Arendt, *Between Past and Future* (Baltimore: Penguin Books, 1968), p. 164.

15. See Michael Howard, *The Causes of War* (Cambridge, Mass.: Harvard University Press, 1994).

5

Geopolitics and Change

DANIEL DEUDNEY

Grasping geopolitical theory's understanding of the nature of change in world politics is particularly difficult because of the atrophy of geopolitical theory in the contemporary study of international relations. Among the traditions of international relations theory, geopolitics is among the most ancient and extensive. In one of the earliest extant Western works on politics the Greek geographer Strabo observed that "the greater part of geography subserves the needs of states."[1] Despite its antiquity, geopolitics has largely disappeared as a distinct theoretical position in contemporary international relations theory.

The decay and eclipse of geopolitical theory is puzzling because of the close relationship between geopolitics and realism, the currently dominant school of international relations theory. Most forms of geopolitics are types of realism, and many of the insights of realism were articulated by geopolitical theorists before the term "realpolitik" was coined in the nineteenth century. But within the classic realist accounts of the origins and evolution of realist and international relations theory, the early literature of geopolitics is almost invisible. Martin Wight, widely regarded as a founder of the English school of realism, made no mention of this geopolitics in his essay "Why Is There No International Theory?"[2] Similarly, E. H. Carr's complaint in *The Twenty Years' Crisis* that the study of international affairs had been dominated by idealistic approaches completely ignored the vast outpouring of literature produced by German writers associated with the Institute for Geopolitics in Munich, by far the single largest body of theoretical and scholarly writing on international affairs produced during the first forty years of the twentieth century.[3] Hans Morgenthau's vision of an

epic struggle between realism and idealism also effectively wrote geopolitical theory into oblivion.[4] And Kenneth Waltz's widely employed "three-
image" typology of international relations theories made no reference to
these approaches.[5]

Change is one of the major topics in international relations theory about
which there is a widespread sense of inadequacy for theorists of all
schools.[6] Neorealism, which has occupied center stage in American international relations theory during the 1980s, has been criticized for its inadequate ability to conceptualize and explain change. In particular, the widely
influential theories of structural or neorealism of Kenneth Waltz have come
under vigorous attack by John Ruggie, Friedrich Kratochwil, Richard
Ashley, R.B.J. Walker, and others.[7] The main criticism leveled against Waltz
is that he only has a theory of the consequences of structure and has no
means to explain the origins or the causes of structure. Neorealism thus
lacks a generative dimension: It can explain the reproduction of structures
but not their initial production. Waltz and neorealists take the state and the
state system as givens and from there analyze the system's operation, but
they do not attempt to explain its origins and thus the possible circumstances of its demise or fundamental transformation.

Robert Gilpin, another neorealist whose major work is focused on
change, does not attempt to provide much insight into the origins of the
state and state system. Gilpin's analysis of change focuses upon *systemic*
change (changes of relative power and position within a given system)
rather than *system* changes (changes in the fundamental units and nature of
the system).[8] The failure of neorealism with regard to fundamental change
is one of omission rather than of commission; it is not that neorealists have
sought to understand fundamental change and failed but rather that they
have not tried. Insofar as theorists find fundamental or system change to be
of central interest, they cannot be satisfied with neorealist international relations theory. Much of the animosity toward neorealism on the part of its
critics derives from this refusal of neorealism to deal with system change
while at the same time it magisterially purports to be a largely complete or
routinized science. Not surprisingly, the silence of neorealism on the issue
of system change has been a central theme in the recent debate over the
causes of the end of the Cold War.[9]

Geopolitics contains the realist tradition's main theories of fundamental
change. Neorealism has refined one set of important realist arguments, without exhausting realism's conceptual resources. It is not by accident that as
geopolitics has decayed, realism has come to be focused on statics and secondary systemic change. Recovering geopolitical approaches offers a realist
theory of fundamental or system change. In this chapter I seek to contribute
to that goal by exploring geopolitical concepts of change. I begin by mapping
the main theoretical claims of the five main clusters of geopolitical theory, in

order to acquaint the reader with its distinct varieties. I then sketch the main features of a geopolitics reformulated as a theoretically disciplined social science model, which I refer to as structural-functional security materialism, or neoclassical geopolitics, for short. After these preliminaries, I explore both how this theory understands the nature and sources of change in security systems, and its treatment of transitions and contradiction.

The Varieties of Geopolitical Theory

Few words in the study of world politics are as widely used and vaguely defined as the term "geopolitics." As Robert Harkavy has observed, "the term 'geopolitics' has come to be used in such a variety of contexts that it is no longer clear just what it means . . . it has come to mean almost everything, and therefore perhaps almost nothing."[10] In short, the word "geopolitics" is overdetermined: It stands for several quite distinct theories or understandings of world politics.[11] There are five[12] overlapping but distinct clusters of ideas that have been advanced as geopolitical: (1) a primitive political naturalism; (2) an extreme realism couched in organic and Darwinian metaphors; (3) a realist theory of interstate conflict that emphasizes geographical features; (4) political geography; and most important, (5) analyses written in the late nineteenth and early twentieth centuries of the global power system created by the technologies of the industrial revolution interacting with the largest geographical features of the earth.

Naturalist Social Science: Physiopolitics

By far the oldest and most heterogeneous cluster of geopolitical arguments concerns the impacts of nonhuman physical nature upon human affairs. Naturalist political science begins with the ancient Greeks, extends through Jean Bodin and Montesquieu in the early modern era, and then takes new directions in the nineteenth century.[13] The basic claim of naturalist social and political theory is that fundamental differences among human societies are the product of the different natural environments (particularly climate, topography, arable land, and access to the sea) in which these societies live and to which they must adapt. The appeal of this naturalism is the simple notion that the physical constraints and opportunities provided by nature significantly affect the performance of very basic functional tasks that are universal to human groups (most notably economic production and protection from violence). Naturalist theory is not confined to international or world politics but includes broad aspects of culture, economics, and politics; it produces hypotheses that belong as much to anthropology,[14] sociology, psychology, and economics as to political science. Natural facts are seen shaping the character of individual humans, the customs and structures of societies, and societies' sizes and relations with others. In some cases political interactions between large groups were seen as indirectly shaped by environmental and geographical factors. But with some factors, such as topography, the causal relations were seen as quite close and direct.

Thus the term geopolitics is too narrow to capture the breadth of naturalist political and social science. The independent or causative variable in such arguments is nature rather than geography, and the dependent variables encompass more than international or even political phenomena. The term "physiocracy"—literally "the rule of nature"—would be most suitable, but it has been associated with the eighteenth-century school of French economists who believed that natural endowments were the decisive factors in production—a school that more accurately could be called "physioeconomics."[15] The branch of physiocratic science concerning political outcomes might thus be "physiopolitics"—the study of the impacts of nature upon politics. Thus we can say that physiopolitics and physioeconomics are branches of physiocratic science.

In the human sciences, explanations from nature come in two broad streams. Theories of biological determinism emphasize human physical nature (race, intelligence, etc.).[16] Theories of environmental determinism emphasize nonhuman physical nature as determining variables. Although racial and eugenic biological theories share in common with environmental theories a strong materialism, the two are otherwise near opposites, for they focus on entirely different aspects of material reality.

In looking for the natural causes of social and political outcomes, physiocratic science is different from the main body of twentieth-century social-science theory. The main tendency of social science is to look for the causes of social and political outcomes in social and political factors, whereas physiocratic science looks for the causes of social and political outcomes in natural factors. Although arguments of the natural causation of social outcomes have not disappeared in social science, social science has marked its break with natural history by downplaying the impact of nature upon human affairs.[17]

German Geopolitik

The second important cluster of geopolitical theoretical argument is the extreme statist realism cast in Darwinian metaphors of the German school of *geopolitik*. Since the term was coined by Rudolf Kjellen in the early years of this century, most self-described "geopolitics" has been written by Germans.[18] Although there are differences in emphasis among different theorists, there are six main ideas characteristic of German *geopolitik*. First, the primary political entities are states, and states are organisms. Second, the life of these state organisms is heavily dependent upon territory, thus making geography of paramount concern to statesmen and political scientists. Third, the interaction of state organisms is heavily competitive, making war a normal condition of world politics. Fourth, in the economic sphere state organisms strive toward autarky. Fifth, because states are natural beings, their actions are beyond right and wrong, subject only to the judgment of success and not the standards of abstract law or morality. Sixth, in the industrial era the optimum size of states is expanding, stimulating sharp competition and the creation of new empires. German *geopolitik* was thus extreme statism combined with an interstate social Darwinism emphasizing competition, material forces (particularly territory), and organic metaphors.

German *geopolitik* was an intellectual movement with wide influence on German politics.[19] The three most important figures in German *geopolitik,* Friedrich Ratzel (1846–1911), Rudolf Kjellen (1846–1922), and Karl Haushofer (1869–1946), were all prolific and widely read advocates of German expansion. Haushofer, introduced to Adolf Hitler by one of his students, Rudolf Hess, extensively tutored Hitler while he was in prison for the Beer Hall Putsch. *Mein Kampf,* written during this period, contains extensive passages about *lebensraum* and other themes of *geopolitik.* Under Haushofer's leadership, a group of German scholars established the *Journal of Geopolitik* and the Institute for Geopolitics in Munich after World War I. During the 1920s and 1930s *geopolitik* was a flourishing intellectual enterprise with scholarly and popular organs, well-funded institute and academic supporters, and a critical mass of practitioners sharing a common set of assumptions. During this period there were far more self-described "geopolitical" analysts of world politics writing in Germany than there were "international relations" scholars in Britain, the United States, and France.

In sum, German *geopolitik* was a highly conflictual statist realism formulated in the metaphors of vitalistic metaphysics. As a school or approach to the study of world politics, German *geopolitik* is now dead, in the sense that it has no living practitioners, and few scholars in the field of international relations study its works or make reference to its concepts. In part this is because of Germany's crushing defeat in World War II and the world's revulsion at Nazi barbarism. But aside from these dubious associations, the vitalism and the organic metaphors of German *geopolitik* seem more quaint than compelling, more suggestive than scientific.

But stripped of its heavy baggage of organic vitalism and social Darwinian analogies, German *geopolitik* bears a striking resemblance to the more extreme and simplistic versions of realism that give almost complete paramountcy to the state and conceptualize the interaction of states in starkly conflictual terms. Seen in this light, German *geopolitik* is a dead branch of a broader Germanic and continental tradition of statism and realpolitik that stretches back through Trietschke and Hegel to the seventeenth-century theorists of the absolute state. Although dead, German *geopolitik* played an important role in the formation of the realist school in the United States, and the term itself lives on as a dimension of this newer and still lively intellectual tradition.

Realism Plus Geography

The third distinctive way in which geopolitics is used is as a synonym for realism generally, and for realism with an emphasis upon geographical factors. This version of geopolitics is perhaps the most prevalent today, particularly in the United States. In contemporary American discussions, the term geopolitics has both a broad and a narrow meaning. In its broad usage, geopolitics is employed to mean "power politics between states." In a narrower meaning, it indicates "power competition between major states in peripheral areas." As a synonym for power politics, the term geopolitics is used by realists and non-realists alike. In its broader meaning geopolitics seems to embrace the most important issues separating the leading states in the interstate system. Perhaps the most authoritative employer of geopolitics in this broad sense is Henry Kissinger. In his earlier theoretical writings Kissinger never used the term in an important context, but in recent writings he has used it frequently, more or less synonymously with "power politics."[20] Kissinger's power politics is rooted in the largely unchanging world of territoriality. It embodies a suspicion of both the simplicities of social-scientific modeling and ideological extremism, attitudes he shares with other postwar American realists like Hans Morgenthau and George Kennan.

The term geopolitics is also frequently used more narrowly to refer to great-power competition in geographically remote regions of the world. An authoritative instance of this more circumscribed usage occurred in 1984, when Secretary of State George P. Shultz, introducing his testimony on the overall condition of U.S. foreign policy before the Senate Foreign Relations Committee, divided his remarks into two parts, "strategic affairs" and "geopolitics."[21] The former encompassed relations with the Soviet Union, with a heavy emphasis on nuclear forces and arms control; the latter concerned regional conflicts in the Middle East, in Central America, and in the Persian Gulf. Here "geopolitics" is employed to describe spheres of influence, client states, and limited wars, which have little in common except that they do not touch upon the paramount survival issues of the leading states in the international system.

The most ambitious recent claim for geopolitics has been made by Colin Gray: "[G]eopolitics is not simply one set of ideas among many competing sets that might help illuminate the structure of the policy problems. Rather it is a meta- or master framework. . . . "[22] But Gray does not actually formulate anything approximating a social-scientific version of geopolitics as a theory. In Gray's analysis geopolitics amounts to the claim that states are inevitably in competition and that the geopolitical analysts of the late nineteenth and early twentieth centuries provide the best guide for understanding Soviet-American strategic antagonism. In short, most of the contemporary public discourse of "geopolitics" is more a thematic and rhetorical dimension of American state-centered realism and strategic studies than a distinctive or articulated theory.

Political Geography

The fourth cluster of ideas often referred to as geopolitics is political geography, the branch of the academic discipline of geography that concerns the spatial aspects of politics. Like physiocratic science, political geography encompasses more than claims about world politics. The attempt to establish a separate subfield of "political geography" either in the academic disciplines of political science or in geography has been unsuccessful.[23] During the interwar years, when German *geopolitik* was at its peak, but before the Nazi aggressions had begun, the few self-described realists in American academic life sought to distinguish "geopolitics" from "political geography." Several American writers suggested that "political geography" was scientific and value-neutral, whereas "geopolitics" implied a political commitment.[24] As late as the 1950s and 1960s Harold Sprout was arguing that political geography was a name for the scientific insights contained within the literature of "geopolitics."[25] Also recoiling from the excessive ambitions and unsavory associations of German *geopolitik*, geographers have eschewed developing a "political geography" that grapples with the major issues of world security politics.[26] Nor was "political geography" consolidated as a subfield of political science, as Sprout hoped. In attempting to escape the larger theoretical questions, political geography became a flat and theoretically unfocused enterprise.

Classical Global Geopolitics

Finally, the most important and most well-known body of geopolitics is the extensive literature produced in the late nineteenth and early twentieth centuries on the relationship between world politics and the material forces unleashed by the industrial revolution. Alfred Thayer Mahan, Halford Mackinder, John Seeley, Karl Haushofer, Friedrich Ratzel, H. G. Wells, Nicholas Spykman, Homer Lea, Frederick Teggart, Frederick Jackson Turner, James Burnham, E. H. Carr, Vidal de la Blanche, and many less well-known figures employed a common set of general assumptions and approaches and grappled with a common set of contemporary problems.[27] The theoretical orientation of these writers was often muddled and undisciplined, their works tended to mix analysis with policy advocacy, and they exhibited many of the most pernicious racial and class prejudices of the era.[28] The global geopoliticans were deeply divided in their political and national loyalties. They spent more effort attempting to influence policy and sway public opinion than attempting to establish geopolitics as a disciplined and institutionalized intellectual or academic enterprise. But taken as whole, their analyses constitute the most sophisticated and insightful body of geopolitical analysis thus far produced.

The main goal of the global geopoliticans was to understand how the material capabilities of transportation, communication, and destruction produced by the industrial revolution (most notably railroads, steamships, telegraphy, chemical high explosives, and airplanes) interacting with the largest-scale geographic features of the earth would shape the character, number, and location of viable security units in the emergent global-scale security system. They brought into their analyses a bewildering range of variables, from political culture and strategic leadership to natural resource endowments and population growth rates, but their overarching organizing framework was essentially materialist in character.

Most global geopolitical theorists thought that the new global era would be characterized by a closed system, units of increased size, and intense competition. Most also believed that a great upheaval in world politics was imminent, that the balance of power system was obsolete as an ordering mechanism for Europe, that the British empire (the superpower of the nineteenth century) was ill suited to the new material environment and would probably be dismembered, and that the United States and Russia were the two states best situated in size and location to survive in the new era. They vigorously disagreed about the character, number, and location of the entities that would prove most viable in the new material context.

From this brief group portrait it is obvious that the problem of change was central to global geopolitics. In conceptualizing the sources of change, the global geopoliticans departed from earlier naturalist theorists by emphasizing technological change as the driving element in world political change. The term "geopolitics" suggests an exclusive focus on geography, but all the global geopolitical theorists incorporated, implicitly or explicitly, claims about technology in their arguments.[29] Before the onset of the industrial revolution, technological assumptions were mainly implicit in geopolitical theory, but technology occupied a central role in the analyses of the global geopoliticans. The inclusion of an explicit role for technology in geopolitical theory helped to explain change but is problematic because it is not obvious how much technology and geography have in common. Global geopolitical theorists also tended to conceptualize the process of change in terms of Darwinian analogies of adaptation and natural selection.

It is often assumed that global geopolitical theory was, like German *geopolitik* and more recent American geopolitics, entirely realist in character. There are important similarities between realism and global geopolitics, but important differences as well. Two main themes—the role of power (particularly material capabilities) in shaping world politics, and the primacy attached to security—are common to both. But global geopolitical theory differs from contemporary American realism, particularly neorealism, in several important ways. The global geopoliticans did not take the state as an inevitable feature of world politics, and many of them thought that the anarchic state system would be extinguished by the creation of a world state.

The most significant way in which global geopolitics differs from contemporary realism concerns the importance that some global geopoliticans attached to nonstatist political forms in world politics. It is often overlooked that Halford Mackinder's main geopolitical work, *Democratic Ideals and Reality*, which expounds the "heartland thesis" that is generally recognized as the single most important concept in global geopolitics, advocates a peculiar version of a League of Nations organization. The liberal and antistatist strain in global geopolitics is most visible in the analyses of the autodidact polymath H. G. Wells, who argued that the anarchic state system in the most materially developed North Atlantic region would be replaced by what he termed a "greater synthesis" analogous to the Swiss Confederation and the United States.[30] Like their more competition-oriented contemporaries, liberal geopolitical theorists employed Darwinian analogies of natural cooperation and symbiosis.[31] Liberal geopolitical theory was not entirely novel but rather extends insights about the relationship between material contexts and liberal political forms that were developed by Montesquieu in the eighteenth century.[32] These neglected liberal strands in the global geopolitical debates challenge the common notion that liberalism is idealistic and realism is materialist. In short, global geopolitical theory contains a powerful set of arguments asserting that liberal political forms are better suited to the material conditions created by the interaction of industrial technologies and global geography.

Neoclassical Geopolitics:
Structural-Functional Security Materialism

The atrophy of geopolitical theory since the 1960s has left international relations theory, particularly realism, without a robust theory of system change. In order to fill this theoretical lacuna, I have refurbished and reformulated the inchoate notions of earlier geopolitical theory into a social-science model containing testable propositions about the functional fit between different material contexts and different security practices and structures. To avoid confusion with the other varieties of geopolitics, I label this model neoclassical geopolitics. In more technical language, the model is appropriately labeled structural-functional security materialism. A full exposition of the model is beyond the scope of this essay, but a brief sketch of its main features is necessary in order to frame and to situate its distinctive arguments about the nature of change. This section outlines the model and summarizes its main propositions.

The Simple Model

The simple model incorporates several main elements and posits several relationships between them (see Figure 5.1). The model posits that human security institutions are practical mediations between the unchanging natural human need for security and the changing constraints and opportunities of the material environment. The model assumes that security goals animate security practices and structures because the human need for physical security from violence is natural. Human nature is of course more complex than this, and other aspects of human nature impede and enable the achievement of the goal of security, but this goal is the measure against which security practices are judged functional or not. Security practices and structures are not part of nature but rather are created by humans engaged in practical problem solving. The characterization of human social agency as pragmatic means that social practices and structures are practical and instrumental solutions to fundamental and recurring problems. This characterization incorporates the notion that individuals are by and large self-interested and capable of instrumental rationality. But in assuming specific, naturally endowed sets of security ends, the model posits a set of interests that are recurring and fundamental. The need for security is natural, and in pursuit of this goal human practices and structures must adapt to powerful constraints and opportunities of the material context within which they must function. This material environment is composed of the interaction of geography and technology, which are for human practical purposes effectively revelations of natural possibility beyond human control. These material contexts change, sometimes in very fundamental ways, as new natural possibilities are revealed and discovered. Such changes pose new security problems while eliminating or ameliorating others. When this occurs the institutions that provide security must be reconstructed if they are to be able to continue to provide security.

Functional-structural materialist theories of security orders can be conveniently schematized using the conceptual apparatus of Marxian historical

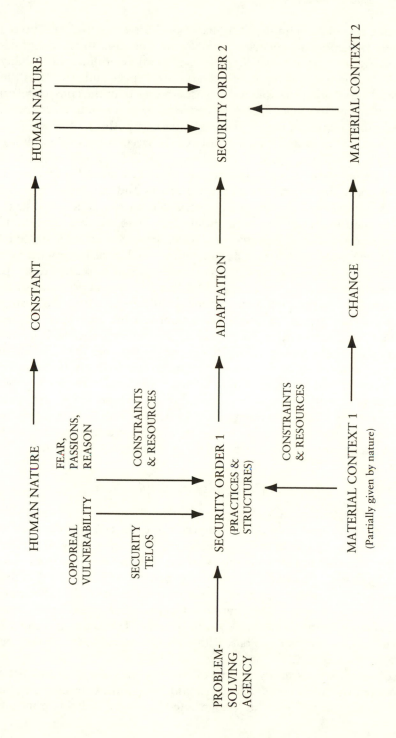

FIGURE 5.1   Structural-functional security materialism: A simple model

production materialism, in which a "base" or "infrastructure" constituted by largely exogenous independent variables (in this case, the forces of destruction and protection rather than of production) determines the viability of a "superstructure" (in this case, protection practices and structures). In addition to attempting to explain the causes (rather than the consequences) of particular distributions of power, functional security materialist theory also seeks to understand how variations in the composition of power (i.e., the intrinsic strengths and limits of different power assets) shape political outcomes.

The essential nature of the causal relationship in the model is functional, and its propositions assert that different practices and structures fit or fail to fit fixed security ends in particular material contexts. Practices and structures are solution sets to particular problems, and so which practices and structures are functional depends upon which problems exist. As material forces change, problems change, and therefore which security practices are functional also changes. The model's central propositions on functional fit are subject to empirical validation and falsification. If practices and structures identified in the model as dysfunctional persist without a system breakdown, or a "crash," then the propositions of the model are falsified (see Figure 5.2). But whether the practices and structures specified as functional in a particular context actually emerge, or whether the outcome of dysfunction and crash occurs, cannot be ascertained simply by knowing which practices and structures are functional. Agency determines whether particular practices and structures arise, but not whether they are functional or dysfunctional. But the model does provide ancillary propositions on transitions, lags, and crashes that offer insight into the probability of functional adjustment or dysfunctional crash in particular situations.

Outline of Main Propositions

Although a full articulation of the model's taxonomic apparatus and substantive propositions would be inappropriate here, the essential thrust of its main arguments should be briefly summarized in order to prevent the discussion of change from becoming too abstract and disconnected from practical and historical problems. The overall proposition of the model is that as constraints on violent power have eroded as a result of the advance of science and technology, viable security orders are characterized by increasing social constraints on the employment of force. The material context is schematized in several dimensions, with violence interaction capability being the most important.[33]

In conceptualizing security structures, both at the unit level and at the system level, the neorealist dyadic conception of political structures as being either anarchic or hierarchic is augmented by a third ordering principle,

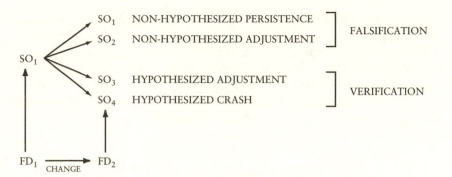

FIGURE 5.2   Falsification and verification in functional theories

negarchy, which is present when both anarchy and hierarchy are constrained.[34] This third ordering principle incorporates into the model the notion found in republican, democratic, federal, and constitutional theory about how practices of co-binding generate nonhierarchic and nonanarchic structures. Key historical examples of political systems ordered by this third principle include the early United States and the European Union. The nuclear arms control regime exemplifies it in a less fully developed form. With this conceptual apparatus the model incorporates both statist and nonstatist forms of political order and offers propositions on their viability of providers of security in different material contexts.

The unconstrained violent power historically associated with anarchy and hierarchy has been compatible with security in the past because of constraints provided by the material context. Over the past several centuries, as the advance of science and technology has produced a material environment of increasingly abundant violence capability, anarchy and hierarchy as well as the anarchy-hierarchy combination of the state system (islands of hierarchy in a sea of anarchy) have become increasingly dysfunctional.

In order to apply this model to historical cases, four broad historical periods (premodern, early modern, global-industrial, and planetary-nuclear) are delineated on the basis of the material capabilities dominant in each. In the global-industrial era (approximately from 1850 to 1950), the model hypothesizes that the anarchic state system was dysfunctional on a regional scale but viable on a global scale. The collapse of the European state system in the twentieth century vindicates the expectations of the model, as does the emergence of the global state system with continent-sized great powers. In the planetary-nuclear era, the model hypothesizes that the anarchic state system is dysfunctional and that only a system-level negarchy is functional.[35] The gradual emergence of the nuclear arms control regimes provides a partial vindication of this hypothesis.

This proposition does not challenge the core claim of realism about anarchy but rather sets it in a historically dynamic material context. Full anarchy—the "state of nature"—has always been recognized by realists to be a security dysfunctional situation. What neoclassical geopolitics adds is that the size of the area in which anarchy is security dysfunctional has been successively increasing, and with the advent of nuclear explosives and ballistic missiles, it has come to encompass the entire planet.

The Nature and Sources of Change

With the essentials of the neoclassical geopolitical argument now sketched, it is possible to turn to the more specific question of how this understanding of world politics conceptualizes change in world security politics.

Change and the Crisis of Naturalist Theory

If the forgotten functional-structural materialist strand of geopolitical theory offers a theory of unit and system genesis, then its understanding of change is central to its appeal. Before turning to an explication of the specific ways in which functional security materialism deals with change, it is useful to review briefly the issue of change in the evolution of naturalist and materialist social theory. The greatest limitation of the early naturalistic theories of politics was their limited ability to explain historical change. Nature and society were conceptualized in either static or cyclical terms, and as a result such theories had great difficulty in explaining noncyclical change. Because nonhuman nature changed rarely and slowly—if at all—naturalist theories were at a loss to explain historical differences between institutions located in the same place. As Hegel, with uncharacteristic directness, noted, "Nature gives the Greeks, but history gives the Turks."[36] Naturalist theories could make plausible explanations for variations across space but not time.

Beginning in the late eighteenth and unfolding in the nineteenth century, there began in the West a broad intellectual effort to explain noncyclical change in nature and human life. This tendency is visible in the geologists' efforts to explain the changes in the newly discovered "deep time," Hegel's dynamic idealistic historicism, Darwinian and other theories of biological change, the political economists' theories of economic growth, and the sociologists' efforts to understand change in social structures and revolutions.[37] As is so often the case, the way was led by natural scientists who conceptualized noncyclical patterns of natural change. Geologists and biologists, who obviously could not explain aeons of change in the earth and its life forms as the result of human development, began to uncover a broad range of processes of natural change. Nature was found to have a history.

In the human sciences the dominant tendency was to look for the source of change outside of physical nature and in the development of human institutions and culture. The most pronounced such nonmaterialist was probably Hegel, who attempted to explain all human change in essentially idealistic terms as the dialectical unfolding of "spirit" (*Geist*) becoming progressively more conscious of itself. The main tendency within modern social science is to discern patterns and laws that are intrinsic to human institutions.

But not all social theorists abandoned naturalism. Many theorists, inspired by Darwin, sought to modify naturalist theory rather than to discard it. They took a different approach from the main tendency within Western social science in attempting to advance beyond the impasses of naturalist theory. Their response to the limits of static and cyclical naturalist theories was to incorporate technology—which changes—into their concept of the base or physical environment. They present an image of a *mutating* nature as the source of change in human arrangements. Or, to put the same point somewhat differently, the nature exogenous to human control changes via technological development. This idea of "nature changing through technology" is at the heart of the historical-materialist project of explaining historically variable political outcomes by reference to changing material forces.

Technology as a Source of Change in Materialist Theory

The realization that technology constitutes a change in nature as it presents itself for human purposes helped to deal with the problem of change, but in doing so it seems to have undermined the basic thrust of naturalism that a reality exterior to human intent and design intrudes into human affairs and decisively shapes them. How useful is it to speak of technology as "natural" or "like nature," when humans seem to have such a major role in creating and directing technology? The prevalent view among contemporary international relations theorists is that technology is primarily derivative of human and political choice and that technology is socially determined rather than socially determining. Thus the key to restoring the plausibility of geopolitical theory rests upon a modified version of technological determination.[38]

One solution to this puzzle is simply to attribute a reciprocal or "dialectical" relation between technology and humans. Obviously without humans there would be no technology, and human institutions shape many aspects of technology. This is to say that the base or infrastructure is at least in part determined by the superstructure, that the relationship of causality runs both ways. However, it is the hallmark of all historical materialism that the base determines the superstructure more than the superstructure determines the base. If in fact the relationship between the base and the superstructure is essentially reciprocal, then the basic assumption of the materialist approach is wrong.

The plausibility of the materialist characterization of technology in naturalist terms can be greatly strengthened by distinguishing several quite distinct phenomena that are often conflated as "technology." It is useful to distinguish between *scientific research, scientific knowledge, technology,* and *technics.* Broadly speaking, scientific research is a process of seeking and validating claims about nature. Scientific knowledge is the set of truths about nature discovered by scientific research.[39] Technology, strictly speaking, is engineering "know-how," a practical knowledge of how natural principles can be put to work or harnessed to perform certain tasks. Technics are the actual tangible machines, apparatuses, and devices that are the product of labor and technology applied to natural resources. Scientific knowledge and technological know-how are intangible systems of symbols, whereas technics have materiality and can directly interact with nature. Another important difference is that scientific and technological knowledge diffuses, whereas technics have (or, in some cases, lack) mobility. Many of the effects commonly attributed to "technology" are really the effects of "technics."

Given these distinctions, there are three main ways in which scientific-technological phenomena may accurately be thought of as standing, like nonhuman physical nature, as significantly outside of human control and as a material structure to which humans must adapt. First and most important, the features of nature that science apprehends are not of human creation or subject to human alteration. Thus the discovery of some new feature of nature is in reality a change in the human environment, much like the discovery of a new ocean or mountain range. Recent scholarship in the history of science has emphasized how social context determines scientific activity. Which questions are posed, which research projects get funded, and even which conceptual frameworks natural scientists employ in framing their investigations are heavily influenced by the social and cultural milieux.[40] And with the expansion of corporate and governmental support—and direction—in scientific research, the haphazard influence of the social milieu has been replaced by conscious policy. There is, however, an inescapable limit to the social determination of science. Humans may control, with increasingly conscious awareness, the rate and direction of scientific research, but they do not choose and cannot change the features of nature discovered by science. For example, the decision to equip Columbus's expedition into the Western ocean was, like all acts of statecraft, the product of human factors and choices. However, what he found—a "new world" rather than islands off the coast of Asia—was not shaped by his milieu, and it would have been the same regardless of the human milieu from which the explorers came. Scientific research finds natural realities that may or may not fulfill social priorities.

Second, the human environment, once changed by the advent of scientific knowledge and technical know-how, cannot easily be returned to its previous state. Because scientific knowledge and technological know-how are both information, it is very difficult to reverse or eradicate them. New realities of nature and know-how rarely disappear, unless they are supplanted by some newer version of scientific knowledge or technological know-how. History does provide examples of forgetting, such as the loss of knowledge about siege machines in Western Europe after the fall of the Roman Empire, or the loss of the formula for the Byzantines' "Greek Fire." Loss of knowledge was much more likely to occur in premodern times, when it often was a craft secret held by a few individuals and was unconnected to systematic science. In contrast, modern scientific knowledge and technology is widely disseminated and capable of being regenerated due to its systematic character. Barring a massive civilizational collapse or regression, there is little prospect that any substantial body of modern scientific or technical knowledge will cease to exist.

Third, technics, once built, are for human purposes like objects of nature. Their scope of potential consequence is set by their physical features and their interaction with their environment rather than by the intent or purpose of their makers or users. Technics do not *have* to be built, and once they are built they can be destroyed. But while in existence, technics are part of the physical world, and their consequences are bound by natural physical laws as well as human choices as to how to employ them. An example of this is provided by Arnold Toynbee, who noted that the Roman system of roads, which were built to expand military mobility, were as useful to the invading Germanic tribes as they were to their builders.[41] Because of the material characteristics of technics, the theoretical apparatus of geographical materialism may be extended to encompass them.

The range of human institutional choice for technics is different from that for scientific and technical knowledge. Humans have more choice about whether there will be a particular technic than whether there will be a unit of scientific or technical information. Technics are produced by humans and can most assuredly be completely destroyed by humans if they so desire. In contrast, technology in the sense of knowledge about the ways in which the physical world can be manipulated is much harder to eradicate or control. Particularly when based upon science, technological know-how presents itself to humans more as a fact of the natural world than of the social world. Thus, for example, the discoveries of scientists and the inventions of technologists that make nuclear explosives possible are similar to a discovery of geography: Once revealed, knowledge of such features of nature permanently changes the opportunities and constraints of human groups.

Because functional security materialism posits that technological possibilities have a great impact upon human institutions, it is essentially an argument for "technological determinism." Recent works on international relations and technology by Barry Posen, Matthew Evangelista, and others have argued against "technological determinism," by which they mean that if a technical capability is possible or feasible, then it will be developed and/or used.[42] This image of technological determinism is something of a straw man, however, for despite occasional rhetorical proclamations of this sentiment,[43] it is hard to suppose seriously that any device that can be built will be built. In contrast, the functional-structural materialist model posits that the emergence of a significant new violence capability will either cause a system change or a crash—a system breakdown.[44] If a violence technology significant for security emerges and does not generate either an institutional adjustment or a crash, then the security materialist model would be falsified.

To sum up on the question of nature and technology, the security materialist model posits that natural forces—particularly geography and technology—have an objective reality outside human intent or desire. These material forces present obstacles and opportunities for human institutions as they pursue the long-standing and basic goal of providing physical security. As these material circumstances change, the nature of functionally viable security practices and structures changes. Whether functional practices and structures emerge or whether the system suffers a dysfunctional security crash is not determined by the main propositions of the model.

Functionalism, Punctuation, and Path Dependency

Functionalist theories that hold that structures are adaptations to changing environments recently have been challenged by theorists of "path dependency" and "punctuated equilibrium."[45] The essential notion of rapid change was noted by the geopolitical theorist Frederick Teggart[46] early in the twentieth century but has reentered social theory from evolutionary biologists, who developed these concepts to supplement the gradualist models of change in Linnaeus, Lyell, and Darwin with one in which rapid changes are driven more by random and contingent factors than by actual variations in the adaptability of different organisms. These modifications in evolutionary theory were introduced to explain the results of catastrophic perturbation of ecosystems by exogenous geophysical intrusions (e.g., asteroidal collision or intense volcanism) that wiped out numerous forms of life, clearing the way for other, previously marginal species that were not intrinsically more adaptive than those they succeeded but were simply fortunate to be at the right place at the right time.[47] If the exogenous material forces shaping world security orders make themselves felt in a similarly punctuated pattern, then the resulting institutional forms may have little or no real adaptive or functional advantage over those they replace, and the functionalist logic of security materialism is compromised.

The pattern by which changes in the forces of destruction affect security-providing institutions is significantly unlike the punctuation in evolutionary biology in two major ways. First, a new technological possibility or geographical discovery may arrive upon the political scene quite suddenly, but it remains a permanent part of the material environment to which security institutions must adapt. In contrast, geological or cosmological intrusions in ecosystems inflict their damage and then in relatively short order the geophysical environment returns approximately to its previous state (see Figure 5.3). Institutions are confronted with multiple occasions on which to respond to the imperatives of a new material environment, and this ensures that random and contingent factors play less of a role than the intrinsic adaptability of different institutional forms. Second, the adaptive potential of biological organisms is governed by their genetically based morphology, and organisms do not, contrary to Lamarckian theories, pass new behaviors to their offspring. In contrast, the adaptive potential of human societies is, except in very broad ways, not dictated by genetic endowment and can be transmitted to other humans without alterations in physical human morphology.

There is, however, another way in which temporal factors may deflect the impact of material forces. When technological succession is rapid, new security problems may crowd out previous ones before they have fully shaped practices and structures. Once introduced, new technologies persist, but they may be superseded by other technologies. Thus it may occur that institutions have not completed their adaptation to a new material environment before they are pulled and pushed in altogether different directions. Rapid succession and truncated adaptation occurred, for example, when the development of nuclear explosives and the other associated technologies that define the planetary era appeared on the world scene before the effects of the previous global industrial technologies had been fully registered.

Progressive, Sequential, and Developmental Change

As thus sketched, it is clear that neoclassical geopolitics has a conception of historical progress and repetition quite different from that of most realists. Like liberalism and Marxism, neoclassical geopolitics holds that history has a progressive or cumulative character. The far more typical view among realists such as Thucydides, Morgenthau, Wight, Gilpin, and others is one of history as cycles, a pattern thought to reflect human nature and institutional patterns derived from it.

The geopolitical approach sees progress, not cycles, but does not fully reject the pessimistic or tragic sense of realism. History does not repeat itself, but it is not necessarily getting better. History has direction simply because there is a cumulative increase in scientific knowledge and technological capability. Neoclassical geopolitics denies that history is coming closer to a

110

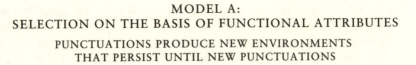

MODEL A:
SELECTION ON THE BASIS OF FUNCTIONAL ATTRIBUTES

PUNCTUATIONS PRODUCE NEW ENVIRONMENTS
THAT PERSIST UNTIL NEW PUNCTUATIONS

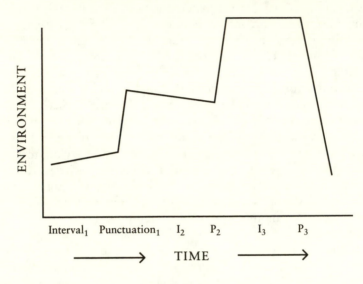

ENVIRONMENT

Interval$_1$ Punctuation$_1$ I$_2$ P$_2$ I$_3$ P$_3$

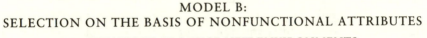   TIME

MODEL B:
SELECTION ON THE BASIS OF NONFUNCTIONAL ATTRIBUTES

PUNCTUATIONS PRODUCE NEW ENVIRONMENTS,
BUT THESE QUICKLY RETURN TO THEIR PREVIOUS STATE

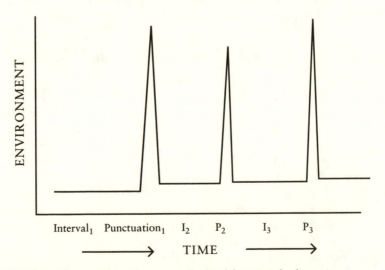

ENVIRONMENT

Interval$_1$ Punctuation$_1$ I$_2$ P$_2$ I$_3$ P$_3$

   TIME

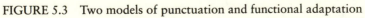

FIGURE 5.3   Two models of punctuation and functional adaptation

realization of mankind's "ideal" or "true" nature, as it is for many liberals and Marxists. For neoclassical geopolitics, historical change occurs because science and technology alter nature, but nothing guarantees that these new constraints and opportunities will improve the human condition, or that humans will be competent enough to seize the opportunities and compensate for constraints. The agnostic stance of neoclassical geopolitics toward Enlightenment meliorism separates it from the mainstream of modern liberalism and Marxism. Marx's claim that mankind "inevitably sets itself only such tasks as it is able to solve" betrays an unfounded Enlightenment optimism not shared by neoclassical geopolitics.[48] It is perfectly possible that further human exploration of nature will reveal potential capabilities of destruction so extreme as to defy plausible institutional control. Scientific and industrial advances have altered the human situation by increasing available power capabilities but have not guaranteed a corresponding increase in human self-control.

Although neoclassical geopolitics posits that history is driven by a cumulative alteration of the forces of destruction, the relationship between the different stages is sequential, not developmental: The security institutions of one epoch are not necessarily developed or unfolded out of prior ones in any tight or essential fashion.[49] Rather, the institutions of one stage stand or fall in relationship to the material context of that age. In seeing the relations between subsequent stages as sequential rather than developmental, security materialism is closer to the theorists of the Scottish Enlightenment than to Hegel and Marx. Hegel's concept of succession is completely developmental, with internal contradictions and tensions in one phase giving character to subsequent ones, and Marx usually characterizes successive economic modes in a similar fashion, with resolutions of contradictions in earlier phases defining subsequent ones. More consistent with materialist approaches, Adam Smith, John Millar, and Adam Ferguson suggested that successive stages had little developmental relationship with one another.[50]

Although the relationship between successive security modes is not developmental, history does not begin anew with a tabula rasa when material contexts change. Important continuities between stages may exist because anomalous and marginal practices and structures from one stage may prove to be viable in a subsequent context, and parts of the dominant mode of one era may be preserved and reused as part of a quite different mode. Also, the rate and ease of adaptation of security practices to a major change in material context may be significantly affected by the presence of such marginal and anomalous practices inherited from previous eras.

Transitions and Contradiction

The primary propositions of the neoclassical geopolitical model concern the functional fit between material environments and security orders. These propositions are verified either by the emergence of security orders hypothesized as functional or by the occurrence of a crash. But the difference between an adaptive transition and a maladaptive crash is of great practical importance. To provide insight into this important aspect of change, a set of ancillary propositions is advanced. The ancillary propositions concern the probability of particular societies' successfully adjusting by producing practices and structures fitted to particular new material environments. The primary and ancillary propositions of the model are thus very different in kind. The primary propositions specify what must be done to be secure in a particular material environment, whereas the secondary propositions specify the factors shaping the likelihood of successful or unsuccessful adaptation. In presenting these propositions I will illustrate them with reference to developments during the planetary-nuclear era.

Transitions: Crashes, Lags, and Adjustment

When new material forces emerge, an existing set of security practices and structures may either *persist, crash, lag in adjustment,* or *adjust.* The determinants of crashes, lags, and adjustments are varied, calling into play aspects of a social system directly related to security, more general societal capacities to solve problems, as well as the features of the new material forces themselves. When a new set of material forces of destruction emerges, it is logically possible that the practices and structures congruent with its requirements will already exist (in effect prefitted), in which case adjustment requires no change and crash is highly unlikely.[51] Of much greater concern are situations in which the practices and structures functionally viable in a new material context are significantly unlike those viable in the preceding period.

Eight factors determine whether a particular set of security practices and structures is prone to crashes, lags, or adjustment: (1) *inheritance diversity* (the character of the practices and structures produced in the preceding era that form the starting point from which adjustment must proceed); (2) *embeddedness* (how interconnected security practices and structures are with nonsecurity practices and structures); (3) *militarization* (when the military arm has subordinated the entire polity or achieved subsector autonomy, or when the populace at large has been militarized); (4) *democratization* (the extent to which security policy is accountable to the public); (5) *learning and innovation capacity* (ability to interpret and correctly understand new situations to develop new practices and structures); (6) *social memory capacity* (the ability to formulate, preserve, and widely inculcate authoritative social understandings); (7) *distinctiveness* (how different violence capabilities are from those prevalent in civilian society) and *potential for reclusion* (how easy is it to keep violence capabilities hidden from civil society); and (8) *dysfunction acuity* (acuteness with which dysfunction is experienced).

The first factor shaping proneness to crash or adjust is the diversity of in-herited security practices and structures. An inheritance that is highly ho-mogeneous will be much more prone to crash or lag than a diverse one. A diverse inheritance greatly increases the likelihood that some existing prac-tice or structure will be at least partially fitted to the new material environ-ment. Inheritance diversity can vary widely, but it is likely to be lower when the inherited security order has existed for long periods, and so a set of ma-terial forces that lasts a relatively short period of time before being super-seded by another will yield an inheritance of practices and structures with components that had survived from a preceding period. The inheritance of the global-industrial era to the planetary-nuclear era was diverse because of the shortness of the global era. The partially negarchical structure of the United States was dysfunctional and declining in the global-industrial era but has contributed to adjustment in the planetary era.

The second factor shaping the likelihood of a successful and rapid transi-tion of security practices and structures to a new material context is the ex-tent of the embeddedness of inherited security practices and structures. Highly embedded security practices and structures have greater staying power and lesser adaptability than those less heavily embedded. All else be-ing equal, embeddedness is likely to be greater in a superstructure that has had a long time to take shape, but embeddedness can vary greatly regard-less of duration, and its extent hinges more directly on whether the security practices and structures of a particular era lend themselves to integration with other factors. Throughout the Cold War, the embeddedness of military organizations in both the United States and the Soviet Union was high, and this impeded successful adjustment to the new material environment of the planetary-nuclear era.

The third factor is the extent of militarization. Militarized polities are prone to crash and lag. Autonomous militaries are likely to be slow to ad-just because the power of dominant social actors hinges on particular ori-entations to violence capability. Both the United States and the Soviet Union had strong traditions of civil control of the military, but because of their sheer size and complexity, superpower militaries had some autonomy. The militarization of the civilian population was high in both countries during World War II but faded rapidly after the war, and neither country glorified violence, as did fascist states. Taken together, these features made successful adjustment more likely.

Fourth, the extent of political and social democratization also helps to define probable outcomes. In more democratic political orders adjustment is likely to be more rapid. Democracy is linked to adjustment through legit-imacy. All else being equal, dysfunctional security practices are likely to be perceived as illegitimate by the general body politic because they undermine the fundamental security interests of the consumers of security services.

Democratization was highly asymmetrical in the nuclear era, but at key junctures, such as during the early 1980s, Western publics were an important constituency for arms control.

The fifth factor shaping capacities to adjust are social capacities to learn and innovate, which are correlated with modernity.[52] The best simple index of these capacities is modernity, characterized by the prevalence of scientific, rationalistic, and instrumental approaches to problem solving. The scientific orientation encourages testing and experimentation; rationalism encourages actors to weigh evidence and better assess causes and consequences; instrumentalism helps adjustment because of its problem-solving focus. Highly modern polities have "learned to learn." Converting new knowledge into new practices and structures requires reforms and innovations, and modern societies are engaged in ceaseless efforts to adjust practices and governmental capacities to solve problems.[53] Because both the United States and the Soviet Union were highly modern, they had high learning and innovation capacities, and this made successful adaptation to the security imperatives of the nuclear era more probable.

The sixth factor shaping the adaptability of societies to changes in material contexts is social memory capacity.[54] Social memory, like learning and innovation, involves social cognition—information, knowledge, and symbols—but societies adept at one are typically poor at the other. Highly modern polities have very high capacities for cognitive memory, with immense capacities for preserving information (particularly scientific and technological knowledge that is logically integrated and situated in specialized organizations). But highly modern societies have very low social memory capacities because they lack authoritative mechanisms for encoding and transmitting social knowledge from one generation to another through rituals, ceremonies, narratives, initiations, and venerated elders.[55] In highly modern societies undergoing rapid technological and institutional change, the experience of one generation seems irrelevant to the next, the old is suspect, and novelty is prized. The institutionalization and professionalization of history provide the basis for sounder lessons from the past to be drawn, but the sheer volume and range of accumulated historical information induces informational overload and historical relativism and impedes the simplifications and elisions necessary for authoritative social knowledge to emerge. In contrast, premodern or partially modern societies change more slowly and maintain abilities to encode and transmit authoritative knowledge between generations. They learn little, but they forget little that they do learn.[56] The weak social memory capacities of highly modern societies means that nuclear learning is less likely to become part of social memory. What might be termed "nuclear forgetting" is thus an important factor impeding adjustment.

The seventh factor affecting probability of adjustment is the distinctiveness of the new forces of destruction and the possibilities for reclusion created by high distinctiveness. Distinctiveness shapes not only the kind of security practices and structures that are functional but also the probability that functional forms will emerge. Highly distinctive forces of destruction impede rapid and successful adjustment because they are subject to reclusion—that is, they can readily be kept "out of sight" and thus "out of mind." When capabilities are highly distinctive and reclusion is practiced, their dysfunctional character remains hidden until the actual dysfunction of a crash or near-crash occurs or until their reclusion has been explicitly countered. Nuclear and space capabilities are highly distinctive and lend themselves to reclusion, thus making successful adjustment less probable.[57]

Eighth and finally, dysfunction acuity shapes proneness to crash, lag, and adjustment. Dysfunctions may exhibit themselves in either a chronic or an incremental fashion. When dysfunctions are chronic they pose continuous costs and are highly visible to wide segments of a society, and so they are likely to stimulate incremental change. Conversely, dysfunction manifesting itself in infrequent and acute forms is likely to stimulate more episodic and sudden adjustments, or—if the dysfunction is acute enough—crashes. Dysfunction acuity is very high in the nuclear era, and this makes successful adjustment less probable.

This brief analysis of the salient factors shaping the probability that a society will successfully adjust to major changes in the material environment demonstrates the diversity and complexity of the forces at play. Applied to the case of the planetary-nuclear era, these factors point toward sharply conflicting outcomes, with some of them facilitating and some impeding the probability of a successful transition.

Lagging Adjustment and Contradiction

Established security practices and structures tend to persist, and adjustments to new material environments are never instantaneous. For the core propositions of the security materialist model, what matters is what eventually happens and whether the model postulates the outcome. However, in the nuclear era the long term is not yet here, raising the crucial epistemological and methodological question of how dysfunction short of a crash can be identified today. The neoclassical geopolitical model posits that practices and structures that are not in adjustment to their material context are in a state of misfit, or fundamental contradiction. The four main empirical indicators of such an important contradiction are *disproportionality, superstructural incoherence, disengagement,* and *reversal.*

Disproportionality occurs when a small cause produces a large consequence. In security orders, the most telling sign of disproportionality is when a small crisis triggers a major upheaval. In Gilpin's analysis of lagging adjustment and contradiction in hegemonic systems, the ability of a small crisis to trigger a hegemonic war[58] signals the existence of a contradiction between the role of a hegemon as the source of systemic order and the material capacities of the hegemon to sustain its role. Similarly, in the security materialist model, the existence of a fundamental contradiction is indicated when crises over minor matters trigger major changes in practices and structures.

Superstructural incoherence occurs when the components of a security order, particularly practices and structures, cease fitting or working together. Some incoherence is an inevitable part of all human affairs, but when the major elements in a security order that previously operated as a functional system cease to do so, a contradiction is indicated. Such incoherence manifests itself in several ways: Actors find themselves increasingly compelled by circumstances to say one thing while doing another; established behavior patterns begin to yield counterproductive consequences; anomalous behavioral patterns and structural components begin to take on a more important practical role, but are discordant in juxtaposition with more established components; and traditional political coalitions are disrupted and disintegrated.

The experience of incoherence can be an important stimulus to change—both functional and dysfunctional—in institutions and patterns of behavior. Incoherence produces tensions as components come under stress. A small cause can produce large consequences as pent-up tension is released. The behavior of actors can become deroutinized and more volatile. Incoherence also imposes psychic burdens upon the actors, and in order to make sense out of contradictory situations actors may embrace schizoid beliefs and doctrines or irrational doctrines that rationalize discordance. Actors may also respond to incoherence by intensifying their obsolete behavior patterns. Such intensification occurs when actors conclude that failures and problems should be met with more forceful application of the old approaches rather than change in them. This may take the form of the hypertrophic expansion of the capabilities that are implicated in the maladjustment.

A third indicator of fundamental contradiction is disengagement, which occurs when actors suspend old practices and instead rely upon ad hoc solutions to problems. Although signaling contradiction, disengagement also entails an element of adaptive behavior, as the actors have learned enough about the new circumstances to cease relying upon the old practices, even if they have not yet fully replaced them with more suitable ones. Previously functioning structures take on a façade-like character as they become disengaged from the functional demands that gave rise to them. Disengagement may also occur within ideologies and their associated theories. Theoretical discourse reflects disengagement when idealistic theories become more prevalent and when theories emphasizing functional and generative processes decline. Dissociation of structures from their functional roles is reflected in and legitimated by theories that take particular structures as inevitable or desirable in themselves. Such theoretical discourses accompanying disengagement have the tendency to retard adaptation by inducing actors to discount performance factors, to the degree that is possible.

The fourth indicator of fundamental contradiction, reversal, occurs when the components of a system that previously functioned in one way come to serve completely different, perhaps even opposite, roles. In its simplest form, reversal occurs when governments find themselves doing the opposite of what they formerly did for the old reasons and goals, or doing new things for old reasons. The previously taboo is embraced, at least in practice, as necessary, while previous necessities become passé. Reversal also is present when substantive and symbolic roles are transposed, and when previously marginal or anomalous structural features are relied upon to serve central functional roles, while the previously central structures, roles, and procedures lose their relevance without disappearing. Reversal is also in evidence when political coalitions begin to take fundamentally new forms, particularly when vanguard coalitions crystallize across previously stark divides.

Reversals are strong evidence for the existence of a fundamental contradiction, but they also indicate substantial movement toward the resolution of the contradiction through the emergence of new practices and structures. New security orders are rarely built de novo but instead often take components of the old system, reconfigure them, and combine them in new ways. Like the stones of an old city, serving in one era as columns to a temple and in the next as pieces of a wall or road, social-structural components are reemployed and reshaped for new purposes in new contexts. Reversals indicate the recasting and rehabilitation of previous components into a new security order, and they make it possible to discern empirically, rather than only deductively, the contours of a newly viable security order. Every contradiction points toward a resolution (even if it is one beyond the ability of the actors to achieve). Reversals indicate more clearly than incoherence and disengagement evidence not simply of maladjustment but coalescing patterns of adjustment.

Conclusions

In order to contribute to an improved theoretical understanding of change in world politics, this essay has sketched the approach to change found in geopolitical theory. The refined and reformulated version of geopolitics outlined here offers to fill an important gap in realist theory left by the incompleteness of neorealist structural theory. Neoclassical geopolitics differs from neorealist theory in that it seeks to explain what neorealist assumes—

the existence of states in anarchy. This recast version of geopolitics gains greater purchase on the phenomenon of fundamental change by recovering the functionalist and materialist dimensions of earlier geopolitical theorizing that neorealist theory had dropped. The neoclassical geopolitical model also complements the neorealist variable of distribution of power, with an analysis of the consequences of variations in the composition of power. The neoclassical geopolitical model also advances beyond the division of international relations theory into competing realist and liberal schools. By recovering and rehabilitating the notion found in Montesquieu and other early naturalist and geopolitical theorists that liberal security practices and structures are—like statist ones—functional in some material contexts but not others, realist and liberal insights are combined into one model.

Early geopolitical theory offered many particular insights, but for a variety of sociological and conceptual reasons it never coalesced into a disciplined and social-scientific set of propositions. Early geopolitical theory also tended to have a highly reductionistic and deterministic view of politics. Reformulated geopolitics redresses these failings by placing human agency back at the center of security politics while still insisting that material contexts constrain in very significant ways the ability of human agents to fulfill their fundamental natural need for security from physical violence. Neoclassical geopolitics thus restores the practical value of international relations theory. In setting forth what must be done to be secure in given material context, geopolitics sets forth clear practical goals while leaving the question of whether what must be done is in fact done to the free play of political choice.

Notes

1. Strabo, *Geography*, Book I, Section I.16, translated by H. L. Jones (Cambridge, MA: Loeb Classical Library, 1968).

2. Martin Wight, "Why Is There No International Theory?" in *Diplomatic Investigations*, edited by Herbert Butterfield and Martin Wight (Cambridge, MA: Harvard University Press, 1968).

3. E. H. Carr, *The Twenty Years' Crisis: An Introduction to the Study of International Relations* (London: Macmillan, 1939).

4. Hans J. Morgenthau, *Scientific Man vs. Power Politics* (Chicago: University of Chicago Press, 1946).

5. Kenneth Waltz, *Man, the State, and War* (New York: Columbia University Press, 1954). None of the leading global materialist thinkers appear in Waltz's index. The recent effort by Robert North and others to conceptualize a "fourth image" of global-level analysis is an attempt to respond to this theoretical lacuna. See Robert North, *War, Peace, Survival* (Boulder: Westview Press, 1990).

6. Barry Buzan and R.J. Barry Jones, eds., *Change and the Study of International Relations: The Evaded Dimension* (New York: St. Martin's Press, 1981).

7. John Ruggie, "Continuity and Transformation in the World Polity: Toward a Neorealist Synthesis," *World Politics*, vol. 35, no. 2 (1983):261–285.

8. It is notable, however, that Gilpin's brief consideration of system change points extensively to geographic and technological factors. See his *War and Change in World Politics* (Cambridge: Cambridge University Press, 1981), pp. 56–66.

9. Friedrich Kratochwil, "The Embarrassment of Changes: Neo-realism as the Science of Realpolitik Without Politics," *Review of International Studies*, vol. 19 (1993):63–80; Richard Ned Lebow, "The Long Peace, the End of the Cold War, and the Failures of Realism," *International Organization*, vol. 48, no. 2 (Spring 1994):249–277.

10. Robert Harkavy, *Great Power Competition for Overseas Bases: The Geopolitics of Access Diplomacy* (New York: Pergamon, 1983), p. 271.

11. Many other commentators as well have noted the confused status of the term "geopolitics." Ladis Kristof has summed it up accurately in lamenting that "it is very difficult to give a definition of today's geopolitics." Kristof, "The Origin and Evolution of Geopolitics," *Journal of Conflict Resolution*, vol. 4 (March 1960):20. Somewhat more charitably, another writer has found diversity in this confusion: "Geopolitical analysis is a manifold phenomenon, ranging on scales from reductionist and determinist 'theory' to awareness of the geographical factor in strategy, and from highly politicized partisanship to a fairly noncommitted mode of analysis." Oyvind Osterud, "The Uses and Abuses of Geopolitics," *Journal of Peace Research*, vol. 25, no. 2 (1988):198.

12. I have omitted the new literature of "critical geopolitics" and "most-modern geopolitics" because the main thrust of this literature is critical of geopolitics and is radically antimaterialistic. A major theme of this literature is that the constructs of geopolitical writers are not to be taken seriously as claims about reality, but rather as power-serving ideologies. For example, see Gearoid O Tuathail, *Critical Geopolitics* (Minneapolis: University of Minnesota Press, 1996).

13. The single best reconstruction of this tradition is provided by Clarence Glacken, *Traces on the Rhodian Shore: Nature and Culture in Western Thought from Ancient Times to the End of the Eighteenth Century* (Berkeley: University of California Press, 1967). However, Glacken focuses most on theories of climate as a shaping influence, and says little about early theories of nature emphasizing topography, land-sea interactions, and arable land.

14. Although such theories have been neglected by political scientists, anthropologists have continued to develop them. See Marvin Harris, *Cultural Materialism: The Struggle for a Science of Culture* (New York: Random House, 1979), and Martin F. Murphy and Maxine L. Margolis, eds., *Science, Materialism, and the Study of Culture* (Gainesville: University Press of Florida, 1995).

15. Ronald L. Meek, *The Economics of Physiocracy* (Cambridge, MA: Harvard University Press, 1963).

16. For overviews of theories of biological determinism in the human sciences and their impacts upon society and politics, see, for example, Stephen Jay Gould, *The Mismeasure of Man* (New York: Norton, 1981).

17. "In part, social science has asserted its independence as a discipline by demonstrating the limited explanatory power of physical concepts of human behav-

ior." Samuel Z. Klausner, "Thinking Social-Scientifically about Environmental Quality," *The Annals*, May 1970, p. 4.

18. For overviews of German *geopolitik* in English, see Strausz-Hupé, *Geopolitics* (New York: Putnam's Sons, 1942); Andreas Dorpalan, *The World of General Haushofer* (New York: Farrar and Reinhardt, 1942); and Geoffrey Parker, "German *Geopolitik* and Its Antecedents," chapter 5 in *Western Geopolitical Thought in the Twentieth Century* (New York: St. Martin's Press, 1986).

19. Woodruff D. Smith, *The Ideological Origins of Nazi Imperialism* (New York: Oxford University Press, 1986), and H. W. Koch, "Social Darwinism as a Factor in the New Imperialism," in *The Origins of the First World War,* edited by H. W. Koch (New York: Taplinger, 1972), pp. 329–354.

20. "[Kissinger's] ideas on power, prestige, and the importance of the great powers all belong, I shall argue, in the realist tradition, even if Kissinger himself prefers the term 'geopolitics.'" Michael Joseph Smith, *Realist Thought from Weber to Kissinger* (Baton Rouge: Louisiana State University Press, 1986), p. 19. See also Henry Kissinger, *Diplomacy* (New York: Simon and Schuster, 1994).

21. "Statement of Secretary of State George Shultz," in U.S. Congress, Senate, Committee on Foreign Relations, *United States Foreign Policy*, January 1984.

22. Colin S. Gray, *The Geopolitics of the Nuclear Era: Heartlands, Rimlands, and the Technological Revolution* (New York: Crane Russak, 1977), p. 11; Colin S. Gray, *The Geopolitics of Super Power* (Lexington: University Press of Kentucky, 1988).

23. The geographer R. D. Dikshit has observed: "The reasons for the neglect of research in political geography and the resultant retardation of the sub-field during the post-war period, are not difficult to understand. With its blanket ban on generalization, theory and model-building in general, political geography became a much too dull subject. It was rendered a field of study that seemed to be devoid of any real academic challenge." R. D. Dikshit, "The Retreat from Political Geography," *Geography*, vol. 17 (1981):238.

24. Johannes Mattern also makes this distinction between "geopolitics" and "political geography": "[W]here and when geographers extend their sphere of investigation to include the configuration of land and sea, and the relationship of both as factors of nation- and state-building and of practical politics, but confine their endeavor to a purely analytical and descriptive treatment of the subject, they may be classed as political geographers. . . . [W]here they [geographers] proceed, ex cathedra, and on the authority of Science, to develop and propose rules of conduct and means of procedure for application by the state and by those conducting the affairs of the state, internal and external, then they are to be classed as geopoliticans." Johannes Mattern, *Geopolitik: Doctrine of National Self-sufficiency and Empire* (Baltimore: Johns Hopkins University Studies in Historical and Political Science, 1942), p. 45.

25. See Harold Sprout, "Political Geography," in *International Encyclopedia of the Social Science*, vol. 6 (New York: Crowell Collier & Macmillan, 1968).

26. Yves Lacoste, "The Geographical and the Geopolitical," in *International Geopolitical Analysis: A Selection from Herodote*, translated and edited by Pascal Girot and Eleonore Kofman (London: Croom Helm, 1987), p. 20.

27. The seminal texts are: Alfred Thayer Mahan, *The Influence of Sea Power upon History, 1660–1783* (Boston: Little, Brown and Company, 1890); Halford J.

Mackinder, *Democratic Ideals and Reality* (New York: Henry Holt, 1919); Vidal de la Blanche, *Principles of Human Geography* (Constable: London, 1936, 1962); Frederick Teggart, *Theory of History* (New Haven: Yale University Press, 1925); Frederick Jackson Turner, *The Frontier in American History* (New York: Holt, Rinehart, and Winston, 1920); H. G. Wells, *The Idea of a League of Nations* (Boston: Atlantic Monthly Press, 1919); James Burnham, *The Managerial Revolution* (New York: John Day, 1941); Nicholas J. Spykman, *America's Strategy in World Politics* (New York: Harcourt, Brace and Co., 1942); J. R. Seeley, *The Expansion of England* (Chicago: University of Chicago Press, 1971).

28. See David N. Livingstone, "Should the History of Geography Be X-Rated?" and "A 'Sternly Practical' Pursuit: Geography, Race, and Empire," chapters 1 and 7, respectively, in *The Geographical Tradition: Episodes in the History of a Contested Enterprise* (Cambridge, MA: Blackwell, 1992).

29. Harold H. Sprout, "Geopolitical Hypotheses in Technological Perspective," *World Politics*, vol. 15, no. 2 (January 1963):187–212.

30. H.G. Wells, *Anticipations of the Reaction of Mechanical and Scientific Progress upon Human Life and Thought* (New York: Harper & Brothers, 1902).

31. For an analysis of the full range of ways that Darwinian analogies were used to make arguments about international politics, see Paul Crook, *Darwinism, War, and History: The Debate over the Biology of War from* The Origin of Species *to the First World War* (Cambridge: Cambridge University Press, 1994).

32. Montesquieu, *The Spirit of the Laws* (Cambridge: Cambridge University Press, 1989 [original 1748]).

33. For earlier treatments of violence interaction capability, see Kenneth Boulding, *Conflict and Defense* (New York: Harper & Row, 1963); Patrick O'Sullivan, *Geopolitics* (New York: St. Martin's Press, 1986); and Barry Buzan, Charles Jones, and Richard Little, *The Logic of Anarchy: Neorealism to Structural Realism* (New York: Columbia University Press, 1993).

34. For discussion, see Daniel H. Deudney, "The Philadelphian System: Sovereignty, Arms Control, and Balance of Power in the American States-Union, ca. 1787–1861," *International Organization*, vol. 49, no. 2 (Spring 1995):191–228.

35. For further discussion, see Daniel Deudney, "Nuclear Weapons and the End of the Real-State," *Daedalus*, vol. 124, no. 2 (Spring 1995):209–231; and Daniel Deudney, "Dividing Realism: Security Materialism Versus Structural Realism on Nuclear Security and Proliferation," *Security Studies*, vol. 2, no. 3/4 (Spring/Summer 1993):7–37.

36. Hegel, quoted in Edward Whiting Fox, *History in Geographic Perspective* (New York: Norton, 1971), p. 19. See also Georg Wilhelm Friedrich Hegel, *Lectures on the Philosophy of World History*, translated by H. B. Nisbet (Cambridge: Cambridge University Press, 1975).

37. For an overview of nineteenth-century efforts to understand change, see Peter Bowler, *Evolution: The History of an Idea* (Berkeley: University of California Press, 1983).

38. The view most prevalent among contemporary international relations scholars is stated by Robert Gilpin: "[W]hereas environmental factors such as climate and geography lie outside of state control, the technological environment is man-made, and a society will develop technological capabilities in order to gain an ad-

vantage over other states." *War and Change in World Politics*, p.55. For further elaboration on this view of technology, see also Robert Art, *The Influence of Foreign Policy upon Seapower* (Beverly Hills, CA: Sage, 1973), and Robert Art and Kenneth Waltz, "Technology, Strategy, and the Uses of Force," in *The Use of Force*, edited by Art and Waltz (Boston: Little, Brown and Company, 1971).

39. For further discussion, see James K. Feibleman, "Pure Science, Applied Science, and Technology: An Attempt at Definitions," *Technology and Culture*, vol. 2 (1961):305–317, and Derek de Solla Price, "The Difference Between Science and Technology," *Science Since Babylon* (New Haven: Yale University Press, 1961; enlarged edition, 1975).

40. Arnold Pacey, *The Maze of Ingenuity, Ideas, and Idealism in the Development of Technology* (Cambridge, MA: MIT Press, 1976).

41. Toynbee later elevated this pattern to a principle of history: "Our survey has brought to light so many cases in which a brilliantly planned and magnificently executed system of public communications has ultimately been turned to account by unexpected and unintended beneficiaries that we may tentatively regard this tendency as illustrating an historical law." Arnold Toynbee, *A Study of History*, vol. 7A, *Universal States* (Oxford: Oxford University Press, 1947), pp. 91, 703.

42. Barry Posen, *The Sources of Military Doctrine* (Ithaca: Cornell University Press, 1984), and Matthew Evangelista, *Innovation and the Arms Race: How the United States and the Soviet Union Develop New Military Technologies* (Ithaca: Cornell University Press, 1988).

43. A rare example is Ralph Lapp's claim that "the unremitting buildup of the atomic arsenal represents another example of the technological imperative—when technology beckons, men are helpless." Ralph E. Lapp, *Arms Beyond Doubt: The Tyranny of Weapons Technology* (New York: Cowles, 1970) p. 173.

44. The distinction between technics and technology (science-based technical know-how) is key to understanding the logic of deep nuclear control regimes: All nuclear explosive devices can be dismantled, but the possibility of fashioning nature into nuclear explosives is effectively a permanent feature of the natural world in which humans live. Thus massively constraining nuclear explosive devices does not mark the end of the nuclear era but rather the emergence of practices and structures adapted to its actual imperatives.

45. See, for example, Stephen Krasner, "Sovereignty: An Institutionalist Perspective," *Comparative Political Studies*, A, vol. 21, no. 1 (April 1988):66–94.

46. "This alternative model, then, envisages the course of evolution consisting in (1) antecedent long periods of relative inactivity, stagnation, and fixity (during which slight, continuous modifications may occur without, however, leading to 'new' forms), followed by (2) short critical periods during which forms undergo abrupt change in which they make sudden fundamental advances or submit to extinction." Frederick Teggart, *Processes of History* (New Haven: Yale University Press, 1918), p. 149.

47. Stephen Jay Gould, "Toward a Vindication of Punctuational Change," in *Catastrophes and Earth History: The New Uniformitarianism*, edited by W. A Berggren and John A. Van Couvering (Princeton: Princeton University Press, 1984), pp. 9–34. See also Stephen Jay Gould, *Wonderful Life: The Burgess Shale and the Nature of History* (New York: W. W. Norton, 1989). Gould notes that nongradual-

ist images of change in biology and geology were derived from social theory, particularly from the thought of Karl Marx and Frederick Teggart.

48. Karl Marx, "Preface," in *A Contribution to the Critique of Political Economy,* translated by S. W. Ryazanskaya (New York: International Publishers, 1970), p. 21.

49. For further discussion of these distinctions, see Stephen K. Sanderson, *Social Evolutionism: A Critical History* (Cambridge, MA: Blackwell, 1990).

50. Security materialism's image of the relation of successive stages thus may be likened to that of grass growing between the cracks of the old order, rather than of a new order maturing in the womb of the old, and the type and relative plenitude of the grasses in the cracks of previous orders bears heavily upon the speed with which new forms will take root.

51. Although the security materialist model offers categories to schematize different material contexts, it offers no insight into whether one material context will be superseded by another, how rapid this sequencing will be, or how alike the problems posed by the new and old material contexts will be.

52. For concepts of modernity, see N. J. Rengger, *Political Theory, Modernity, and Postmodernity* (Oxford: Blackwell, 1995), pp. 39–76.

53. Here I use "learning" in the ordinary-language sense to refer to acquired knowledge, in contrast to Ernst Haas's use, in which learning refers to adaptation based on a new knowledge that reality is different. See Ernst Haas, *When Knowledge Is Power: Three Models of Change in International Organizations* (Berkeley: University of California Press, 1990), pp. 1–50.

54. For social memory and its relationship to history, see Jack Le Goff, *History and Memory,* translated by Steven Rendall and Elizabeth Claman (New York: Columbia University Press, 1992).

55. For the importance of ritual and ceremony in the constitution and preservation of social memory, see Paul Connerton, *How Societies Remember* (Cambridge: Cambridge University Press, 1989).

56. The existence of highly developed social memory capacity means that harms inflicted in the distant past have a long afterlife, providing fuel for conflicts to burn long after their actual causes have disappeared. Social forgetfulness contributes to peace by erasing memories of past grievances and struggles.

57. For further analysis, see Daniel Deudney, "Political Fission: State Structure, Civil Society, and Nuclear Security Politics in the United States," *On Security,* edited by Ronnie Lipschutz (New York: Columbia University Press, 1995), pp. 87–123.

58. Robert Gilpin, "The Theory of Hegemonic War," in *The Origin and Prevention of Major Wars,* edited by Robert I. Rotberg and Theodore K. Rabb (Cambridge: Cambridge University Press, 1989), pp. 15–38.

6

Complexity, Formal Methods, and Ideology in International Studies

JAMES DeNardo

In this chapter I address the promise of formal methods in international studies, an interesting though slippery problem. One might approach such questions by surveying the development of formal work in international relations with a critical eye to the major debates, the outstanding questions, and the record of accomplishment. That job is probably better left to specialists who know the local byways and back alleys better than I do. Instead, I shall explore a single case in closer detail—how mathematical modelers attempted to understand the impact of Ronald Reagan's Strategic Defense Initiative (SDI) on the nuclear arms race and deterrent stability.

I realize that the world has changed a lot since the Reagan years and that the nuclear arms race has abated remarkably. That SDI is no longer a "hot topic" is all the better for my purposes, because we can reexamine it without falling prey to the intense partisan passions that generated the heat. The passions that drove the debate about SDI are nevertheless important to think about, for they go to the heart of the question addressed in this chapter. The appeal of formal scientific methods in the social sciences is largely rooted in their promise to displace partisan prejudice with rational judgment. Understanding why they often fail to do so—why important policy debates remain highly ideological—is therefore critical for judging that promise.

The spectacular success of mathematical methods in the natural sciences drives the ongoing movement to formalize the social sciences. By harnessing the logical, conceptual, and computational power of mathematics and statistics, one hopes that dubious notions about political and social dilemmas might be replaced with carefully reasoned and dispassionately tested scientific inferences. But even though the technical sophistication of social scientists has increased dramatically over the years, many social policy debates remain openly partisan. Neither highly refined mathematical models, nor careful experimentation, nor painstaking quantitative measurements—all hallmarks of high science—have substantially diminished the ideological character of debates about affirmative action, environmental protection, the "energy crisis," the federal budget deficit, welfare reform, gun control, educational philosophy, trade policy, capital punishment, health care reform, or arms control.[1]

Why haven't sophisticated scientific methodologies curtailed the influence of partisan prejudices about, say, SDI or immigration policy in the same way that they conquered religious prejudices about cosmology, evolution, and disease control? Trying to find out is an interesting way to consider the intellectual payoff and potential of formal methods in international studies.

Critics, of course, harbor no expectation that public policy might ever be reduced to rational scientific judgments. They argue that mathematical methods are largely irrelevant in the social domain because basic aspects of human affairs cannot be quantified. Social science models, they say, are grossly unrealistic reductions of complex phenomena, achieved by ignoring considerations that cannot readily be counted or measured. A related argument is that social questions, unlike questions about physical laws of nature, inevitably turn on basic conflicts of value that cannot be resolved by scientific reasoning or evidence. The importation of scientific methods to social studies rests, in this view, on a misguided understanding of the questions at issue.

In my opinion, neither of these arguments explains why scientific inference has yet to displace ideological inference in the social sciences or provides a useful understanding of formal methodological work. By failing to specify what can and cannot be described quantitatively or what aspects of human affairs are basic, the first argument remains evasive and self-contradictory. Surely performance in school, casualties in war, levels of trade, the incidence of disease, characteristics of missiles, sizes of deficits, and rates of immigration can be counted or measured. Are these aspects of human affairs somehow less interesting than others? More basically, the strong claim about the infeasibility of quantification presupposes a sophisticated theory of scaling and measurement—an enterprise whose existence would already belie the larger argument. The second argument similarly supposes that conflicts of interest, tradeoffs in values, and normative dilemmas cannot be understood formally. But why not? Welfare economists and moral philosophers rely on such reasoning all the time, not necessarily to produce value judgments but to reveal their structure and to clarify the choices before us. No one would (or should) argue that formal methods can settle every question in international studies. But by dismissing the formal enterprise out of hand, its strident critics both underestimate its potential and misconstrue serious problems that deserve wider scrutiny.

This chapter reflects on the potential of formal methods in international relations by exploring the recent acrimonious debate about SDI. The debate makes an instructive case study for several reasons. Formal mathematical methods appeared first in international studies, and evolved furthest there, in applications to arms races and military strategy. The controversy about SDI involved many sophisticated modelers, including physicists, operations researchers, strategists, and mathematical economists. Its shrill partisan tone cannot be attributed to a lack of technical finesse or proper scientific training. At the same time, the substantive issues raised in the debate bear a strong resemblance to others in political economy, international relations, and public affairs. Like many large-scale problems in the social sciences, arms races involve diverse mechanisms operating on several levels, including elements from psychology, strategy, technology, economics, and politics. And finally, as so often occurs, we observe stubborn political dogma and sophisticated technical analysis locked in apparent stalemate. By exploring the debate in considerable detail, from the modeler's point of view, I hope to convey both the promise and the limitations of a formal approach, to develop a concrete feeling for the craft, and to offer some thoughts about the poorly understood interactions between scientific analysis and ideological inference.

Three Models of Strategic Stability Under SDI

The formal literature about SDI, like the wider political debate, focused on a fundamental strategic question: Is the stability of nuclear deterrence enhanced or diminished when the nuclear powers deploy strategic defenses like that envisioned in Ronald Reagan's "Star Wars" missile shield? Of course if each side deployed a perfect, permanent, inexhaustible nuclear defense (and everyone knew it) there would be no problem to analyze. Nuclear weapons would be rendered impotent and obsolete, and deterrence would be replaced by "mutual assured survival." The difficult questions arise when the defenses are less than perfect (as any practical system surely would be). Then the adversaries remain exposed to nuclear attack, and security still requires deterrence in the usual sense.[2] The big question was whether or not deterrence would be compromised by incomplete missile defenses.

When mutual assured survival is out of reach, the analysts I consider here all agreed that stable deterrence resides in the capability to retaliate lethally after a nuclear attack. What deters a nuclear *first strike*, they assumed, is the compelling prospect of a retaliatory *second strike*. When both sides can marshal a devastating second strike, neither has any incentive to strike first—even in a crisis. Moreover, neither requires more or different nuclear forces to deter the other side. In this way, secure second strikes provide both *crisis stability* and *arms race stability*.

Deterrent stability is jeopardized when a first striker can neutralize the victim's capability to retaliate. This dangerous situation might arise in two ways. The aggressor could successfully mount a *counterforce attack* on the victim's retaliatory forces, destroying them preemptively before they "get off the ground." The attacker could also devise a *nuclear defense* to absorb the retaliatory second strike before it does any damage. The key to stable deterrence is to ensure that neither generic threat to the retaliatory forces materializes. To deter a first strike, each side needs enough nuclear forces to weather a determined counterforce attack, and then to penetrate a nuclear defense with a devastating number of warheads.

These well-rehearsed classical arguments may be summed up in what might be called the *Fundamental Equation Of Stable Deterrence*. In the special case in which nuclear weapons are housed on ballistic missiles, the fundamental equation prescribes that the following number of missiles be deployed:

$$Missiles = Min + F + D \tag{1}$$

where

Min   is the MINIMUM number of missiles required to inflict devastating retaliation on the opponent (when no defense exists);

F is the number of missiles that the opponent could destroy in an all-out FIRST STRIKE;

D is the number of retaliatory missiles that the opponent's DEFENSE can intercept or negate.

The equation requires, in addition to the minimums needed to inflict forbidding punishment, a surplus, $F + D$, sufficient to negate the two destabilizing threats. Strategic theorists typically study the outcome of nuclear exchanges with and without defenses, asking which configurations of forces create an incentive to strike first (or to arms race) by leaving either side with an inadequate surplus. One should notice that the concern here is not with how to fight nuclear wars but with how to avoid them. To disparage such work as morally deficient, as many people do, misses this basic point. Whether disarmament or deterrence is a better strategy in a nuclear environment can be debated, but deciding the answer surely requires careful thinking about how deterrence works.[3]

On the face of things, none of the central elements in the problem appears to be unquantifiable. The arrangements of offense and defense, the idea of second-strike stability, the perceptions of decisionmakers, and the costs of the nuclear forces all can be readily described in a quantitative framework. Nor does the controversy about strategic stability appear to rest on normative disagreements, since everyone accepts that undermining nuclear deterrence would be a bad thing. Finally, it is hard to see how the complex interactions that determine *Min*, *F*, and *D* could be fathomed without some formal multivariate apparatus. In this problem, as in many others, simple intuition seems to be a weak substitute for careful quantitative analysis. But if the problem is so well suited to a quantitative approach, one might wonder, why did the modelers not provide a straightforward solution sufficient to dispel the partisan controversy? Would SDI be destabilizing or not?

Radner's Model of Defense-Protected Build-Down

The first analysis I would like to consider portrays strategic defenses in their most positive light, as a mechanism that allows both sides to reduce dramatically their nuclear arsenals. By substituting defense for offense, the economist Roy Radner and others argued, a "defense-protected build-down" could eliminate nuclear weapons without jeopardizing deterrent stability along the way.[4]

The methodological focus of Radner's analysis is to measure the size of the arsenals required for stable deterrence when there is stochastic uncertainty about the effectiveness of nuclear attacks. Radner recognizes that when each attacking warhead has a (fixed and independent) probability p of destroying its target, the number of targets destroyed by an n warhead counterforce first strike will vary randomly from attack to attack (just as the number of heads will vary randomly when n coins are tossed over and over again). The deterrer's goal is to remain highly confident that an adequate second-strike reserve will survive a counterforce attack, even when chance variation favors the attacker.

To justify such confidence, Radner proceeds conservatively, designing a missile force that will yield a sufficient reserve even when everything goes the attacker's way. His model requires the defender to ride out a counterforce attack that deploys the first striker's arsenal with maximum efficiency. In particular, the first striker attacks one surviving missile at a time, with one warhead per target, if necessary until all n warheads are used up. (This "shoot-look-shoot" strategy would not be possible if the defender "launched under attack.") Radner shows how to calculate the number of missiles required to preserve an adequate second-strike reserve (what I have called *Min* in the fundamental equation, he labels *s*), even when the attacker does not waste warheads on targets that have already been destroyed.

The kind of attack Radner describes may be modeled as a simple Bernoulli process, familiar from elementary probability theory, with n independent trials, each resulting in a "success" or "failure," and with fixed probability of success, p, on each trial (here a "trial" means launching one warhead against a missile site, and a "success" means destroying the target). The number of successes in n Bernoulli trials, call it S_n, is a random variable that takes on values 0, 1, 2, . . . up to n with probabilities given by the binomial distribution. Specifically, the probability of hitting exactly f missile silos in an attack with n warheads is:

$$\Pr(S_n = f) = \frac{n!}{f! \, (n - f!)} \; p^f (1 - p)^{(n - f)} \; for \; f=0 \; to \; n \qquad (2)$$

The probability of achieving no more than r successes in n trials (i.e., of r successes or less) is the cumulative binomial probability:

$$\Pr(S_n \leq r) = \sum_{f = 0}^{r} \; \Pr(S_n = f) \qquad (3)$$

If the attacker's force has the potential to destroy f missiles in a first strike, then the defender wants enough missiles, m, so that the number of survivors, $(m - f)$, will be at least s, where s is the minimum required for devastating retaliation. (Notice that to make $(m - f) \geq s$ entails that $f \leq (m - s)$. Here $(m - s)$ is the first-strike surplus, F, in the fundamental Equation 1). Thus stable deterrence occurs when the defender builds enough missiles to ensure that

$$Pr(S_n \leq (m - s)) \approx 1 \qquad (4)$$

In words, the defender needs enough missiles, m, to make it virtually certain that the first-strike surplus will not be exhausted in a counterforce attack by n warheads.

The great virtue of the probability model is that we can now calculate how many missiles will assure an adequate deterrent reserve, given the opponent's arsenal (characterized by the parameters n and p). By formalizing the concept of stable deterrence, Radner's model provides the kind of useful calculation that national security policy makers presumably want and need. A practical difficulty is that the binomial model is computationally extremely awkward. When the attacker's arsenal becomes realistically large,

Equations 2–4 require summing thousands of binomial probability terms, each containing several explosively large factorial expressions.[5]

To overcome the computational obstacle, Radner exploits the well-known DeMoivre-Laplace limit theorem from probability theory. As n grows large (and p is not too close to zero or one), it turns out that the binomial random variable S_n is distributed approximately normally with expected value (mean) = np, and standard deviation = $\sqrt{np(1-p)}$. Figure 6.1 illustrates the situation. The distribution shows the probability with which different numbers of successes occur in an attack with n warheads. To be, say, 99.9 percent certain that the first-strike surplus will be adequate, we must make the probability that $(S_n > (m-s)) \leq .001$. Referring to the standard normal probability table, it turns out that the critical value $(m-s)$ must lie at least 3.1 standard deviations beyond the expected number of successes in the distribution to make a successful counterforce attack extremely unlikely. To be confident in *deterrence at level* $\delta = .999$, we choose m so that $(m-s) = np + 3.1\sqrt{np(1-p)}$. Doing so defines the following security function (Radner's version of the fundamental Equation 1 when $\delta = .999$):

$$m = s + np + 3.1\sqrt{n\,p(1-p)} \tag{5}$$

The example in Figure 6.1 shows how the calculation works. For some purposes, it is useful to reexpress the opponent's warheads n as the number of missiles m times the number of warheads per missile w (the MIRV factor—multiple independently targetable reentry vehicles). Using subscripts keeps the two sides straight:

$$m_1 = s + (pw)m_2 + 3.1\sqrt{(wm_2)\,p(1-p)} \tag{5.1}$$

We now have a simple formula that tells us how many missiles are required to ensure devastating retaliation, given the number of missiles in the opponent's arsenal, their MIRV factor, and counterforce effectiveness. But for a stable nuclear relationship to exist, both sides' security functions must be satisfied simultaneously. The complete model of stable deterrence therefore involves a pair of simultaneous equations, quadratic in $\sqrt{m}$. Here, the nonlinearity of the system is an unwelcome complication. To simplify matters (more so than does Radner), I shall take the liberty of neglecting the third term on the right-hand side of Equation 5.1. Doing so *linearizes* the system. As the example in Figure 6.1 shows, the linear approximation is very close to Radner's formula because the quantity $3.1\sqrt{(wm_2)\,p\,(1-p)}$ typically contributes only 2–4 percent of the prescribed arsenal (if we wish, an adjustment can be added to the term s, which is somewhat arbitrary in the first place). It will also be useful to rewrite the security functions in a more transparent notation (one that recalls the Cold War context of the problem):

$$SOV = Min_{sov} + \beta_{us}US \qquad\qquad (6a)$$

$$US = Min_{us} + \beta_{sov}SOV \qquad\qquad (6b)$$

where

SOV, US — are the number of missiles deployed by the Soviet Union and the United States, respectively;

Min_{sov}, Min_{us} — are the minimum number of missiles required by each side, respectively, to inflict unacceptable damage on the other (Radner's s);

β_{us}, β_{sov} — are the EXCHANGE RATIOS of the two missile forces—that is, the expected number of missiles destroyed for each missile launched by a first striker. Equation 5.1 shows that the exchange ratios are the product of the single-shot kill probability for each warhead and the MIRV factor ($\beta = p * w$).[6]

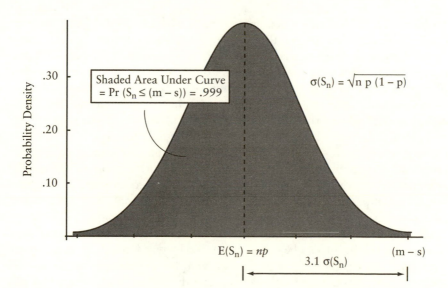

FIGURE 6.1 Probabilities of S_n successes in an n warhead missile attack (normal approximation to the binomial probability distribution)

The Geometry of the Strategic Arms Competition

Figure 6.2 illustrates the geometry of a missile competition between two nuclear powers who follow the prescriptions of Equations 6a,b. The security functions describe two straight lines with intercepts equal to *Min* and slopes equal to β (to keep the discussion simple, we make the arsenals symmetrical). Notice that the domain of the U.S. security function is described by the SOV axis, and the domain of the Soviet function by the US axis. To see how many missiles the United States needs for stable deterrence, one locates the number of Soviet missiles along the SOV scale and then reads the associated value of the U.S. security function (and vice versa). For both adversaries to achieve a reliable deterrent at once, the two security functions must intersect. At the point of intersection (the solution of the simultaneous equations), and in the shaded region beyond, the number of missiles deployed by each side is consistent with the security of the other. Neither one can muster a disarming first strike.

Suppose for a moment that the nuclear powers deploy missiles with single warheads in hardened missile silos that are invulnerable to attack (so that $w = 1$, $p = 0 \Rightarrow \beta = 0$). The upper left panel in Figure 6.2 describes the security problem in this ideal case when missiles have exchange ratios equal to zero (i.e., no counterforce potential). The slopes of the security functions then equal zero, and stable deterrence requires no more than *Min* missiles on each side, however large the opponent's offense may be. Notice that any deployment in the shaded *region of mutual security* above the point (Min_{us}, Min_{sov}) would also satisfy the adversaries' security requirements, though at a higher cost. When the discussion requires a definite prediction about which of these viable deployments will transpire, one might assume—naïvely perhaps—that the security seekers select the least expensive arsenal consistent with national security (i.e., the point of intersection itself). If both sides are so motivated, the intersection represents an equilibrium solution to the arms competition, such that neither side has any incentive unilaterally to add or remove missiles, given the deployment of the other side.

Experience shows that relatively palatable situations like the minimal deployment equilibrium can be disturbed by the forward march of technology. The lower left panel of Figure 6.2 shows what happens when the missile arsenals become a counterforce threat to each other (after being equipped with warheads of higher yield and accuracy, rapid delivery systems, penetration aids, or other technical "improvements"). The exchange ratios then increase from zero toward one, and the threat of a first strike drives both countries to deploy a surplus of missiles beyond the minimums (in Equations 6a,b the United States requires a first-strike surplus ($\beta_{sov} SOV$) > 0, while the Soviets need ($\beta_{us} US$) > 0). But as one side adds missiles to neutralize the new threat, it compounds the threat faced by the other side—which must then

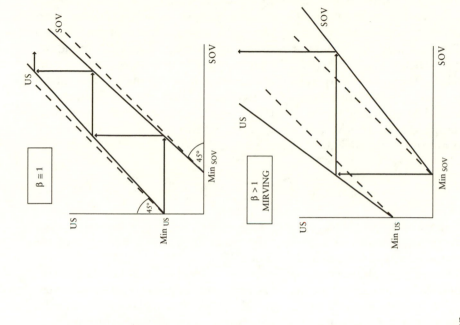

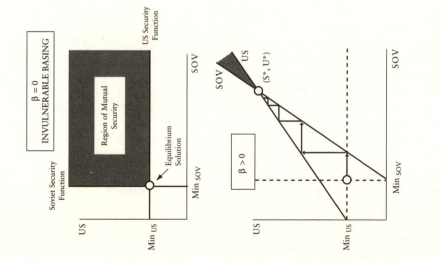

FIGURE 6.2   Geometry of the missile competition

add a greater surplus still. There ensues an arms buildup that eventually results in a new equilibrium at the point (S^*, U^*).

Geometrically speaking, the rising exchange ratios make the slopes of the security functions steeper, displacing them as in the lower left panel of Figure 6.2. When $\beta > 0$, the original deployment of missiles, (Min_{us}, Min_{sov}), no longer satisfies either side's security requirements, and a sequence of actions and reactions (along the path indicated by the arrows) leads to a new equilibrium at a higher level of armaments. In the upper right panel of Figure 6.2, we see what happens as technology enhances the counterforce lethality of each new generation of missiles. If the single-warhead missile forces remain in vulnerable silos, the exchange ratios themselves approach 1 (as $p \to 1$ then $\beta \to 1$), and the nuclear arsenals expand. To calculate how fast, the reader may verify that the equilibrium solutions to Equations 6a,b are given by:

$$S^* = \frac{Min_{sov} + \beta_{us}\,Min_{us}}{(1 - \beta_{us}\beta_{sov})}, \quad U^* = \frac{Min_{us} + \beta_{sov}\,Min_{sov}}{(1 - \beta_{us}\beta_{sov})} \tag{7}$$

If we take $Min_{us} = Min_{sov} = 100$ (a baseline that makes it easy to appreciate the implications of a rising exchange ratio) and $\beta_{us} = \beta_{sov}$, then the arms race will proceed as indicated in Table 6.1.

To many people, the buildup to levels of nuclear overkill fantastically beyond the minimums needed for devastation might appear reckless and crazy. But to these nuclear powers, the crucial consideration is how many missiles survive a first strike, not the arsenal's absolute size. This arms race is driven by the desire to maintain a viable deterrent (and, just as critically, by an inability to control the advance of missile technology). As counterforce threats arise, the two sides add missiles to preserve their secure second strikes.

If there is any solace to be found in this story, it lies in the observation that arms races never become truly intractable in the era of single-warhead missiles. Because no engineering system ever achieves perfection, the exchange ratios of such missiles must always remain below 1 (because p is necessarily < 1, if $w = 1$ then $\beta < 1$). It follows that the security functions of the two adversaries must always intersect, and that an equilibrium balance of terror can always be restored after each wave of technological innovation. If we take single-shot kill probabilities of .95 as a reasonable upper bound on the advance of weapons technology, the two sides will deploy 2,000 single-warhead missiles apiece—a large but hardly ruinous number.

Suppose, however, that someone comes up with the clever idea of putting more than one warhead on each missile, in multiple independently targetable reentry vehicles (MIRVs). Then the story changes fundamentally. MIRVing the forces allows one missile of a first striker to destroy several missiles of the victim, even when the accuracy and reliability of each war-

TABLE 6.1   Missile Equilibriums as the Exchange Ratio Increases (*Min* = 100)

β	S*, U*
0	100
.25	133
.50	200
.75	400
.90	1000
.95	2000
.98	5000
.99	10000
1	∞

head remain less than perfect. (When $w > 1$ and $p > 0$, the exchange ratio $β = wp$ can itself become greater than 1). The lower right panel of Figure 6.2 shows what happens when the slopes of the security functions become greater than 1 (steeper than the 45° lines). In this case no equilibrium solution to the security functions exists (the curves do not intersect whatever number of missiles the two sides build). MIRVing can make deterrent stability unattainable in principle, creating a "window of vulnerability" like the one that dismayed U.S. strategic thinkers after the Soviet Union and the United States deployed MIRVs in the early 1970s. As a result of studying models like these, de-MIRVing remained a basic objective of arms controllers throughout the Cold War period and beyond. The lessons we have just learned inform the recent START II treaty, which largely eliminated land-based MIRVed intercontinental ballistic missiles (ICBMs).

Finally, what about missile defenses? Radner addresses the problem by defining defenses in a disarmingly simple way: "*An increase in defense is anything that decreases the probability that an attack against a given site will be successful.* . . . If each attacking missile has a probability p of destroying its target, then I shall say that $q = (1 - p)$ is the *effectiveness of defense.*"[7] A review of the security functions in Equations 6a,b will now reveal why strategic defenses are an untarnished good thing in Radner's analysis. By diminishing the counterforce effectiveness of missiles, a defense in this sense directly reduces the exchange ratio β. As the defense becomes more and more effective, $β → 0$, and the equilibrium deployment of missiles steadily diminishes toward the ideal minimum. The magnitude of the gain can be seen by reading Table 6.1 from the bottom up. Geometrically, a better defense moves us from the lower right toward the upper left panel in Figure 6.2. Formally, the effect of the defenses is equivalent to de-MIRVing the nuclear arsenals or to hardening the missile silos—both of which, experts agree, clearly enhance stability. These considerations support Radner's basic conclusion that "increased defense is not destabilizing." In this model, arms-race stability steadily improves as the defenses get better, just as the defenders of SDI claimed.

Remarks

Radner's reasoning is conceptually explicit, logically rigorous, technically adroit, and replicable—qualities that are often advertised as the special virtues of scientific methods. And though the model ultimately can be reduced to very simple pictures, it supports many nontrivial deductions. Nothing about the analysis appears partisan or ideological except its conclusions, which fly directly in the face of the conventional wisdom that underlies the ABM Treaty of 1972.

No one, including Radner, would describe his model as "realistic," however. Like all models, it relies on a battery of simplifying assumptions that come in several varieties. The first might be called *unquestioned substantive assumptions*—for example, that stable deterrence rests on secure second strikes, that there are only two nuclear adversaries, that both sides perceive the world the same way, and that all political actors share common strategic preferences. Such assumptions define the intellectual framework in which the analysis proceeds and often receive only cursory acknowledgment. They are accepted by the modeler before the analysis begins, and they reflect a larger disciplinary point of view.

A second category includes the *working substantive assumptions*—for example, that the warheads are placed on missiles in vulnerable silos, that the missiles are MIRVed or not, that the defender plans to survive a "shoot-look-shoot" attack, or that the arsenals have similar technology and only one kind of missile. The way these assumptions are configured defines the alternative scenarios that the modeler considers. Working substantive assumptions are the part of the problem that one investigates explicitly during the analysis.

Technical assumptions form a third major category. Some of these might be described as purely *technical assumptions of convenience*. The Gaussian (normal) approximation to the binomial probabilities and the linear approximation to the Gaussian security functions make the model much easier to handle (i.e., to compute, display, or discuss) and introduce only minor quantitative errors. It is in this category that the modeler's technical skill often comes to the fore. In this case, a series of technical finesses rescues a problem that verges on computational infeasibility.

The assumption that each warhead launched is an independent trial with fixed probability of success seems to have a different, less innocuous, character. It might be called a *technical assumption of necessity* since the mathematical framework of the analysis (here probability theory) more or less imposes it on us, whether we like it or not. In this case, the assumption of independence leads to the binomial distribution, which is the cornerstone of Radner's development. In many problems, technical assumptions of necessity involve some form of symmetry (equivalence or alikeness). They arise because symmetry can happen in a single well-defined way, whereas the lack of it can occur in any number of ways. Symmetry makes the problem tractable and well behaved, whereas its absence opens a Pandora's box (of limitless, ill-specified scenarios).

The trouble with technical assumptions of necessity is that they often carry hidden substantive implications or *technical baggage.* Evidently, the dangers will be greatest when methods invented for other purposes are imported into a new discipline. The question always is whether new problems have been crammed into old baggage where they do not fit. Unfortunately, the interaction between technical baggage and substantive conclusions can be very hard to recognize and diagnose. In this case, nobody knows whether a missile attack will proceed as independent trials do or not. The answer depends on the performance of command-and-control systems that are mind-bogglingly complex and virtually untested under conditions of nuclear war (not a bad thing!). As a result, one can object to the arbitrariness of the independence assumption, but there is little to be done about it. Other alternatives are no less arbitrary, and much less straightforward.[8]

Another interesting interaction between technical and substantive considerations appears in Radner's definition of a missile defense. Though hardly a technical necessity, defining the defense as anything that reduces the missile site kill probability p is a natural and inviting formalization, given the analytical apparatus. The lurking trouble is that such defenses seem very unlike Reagan's SDI, even though SDI would "decrease the probability that an attack against a given site will be successful," as the definition requires. If we return to the fundamental equation of stable deterrence, we can see that Radner's security function omits the term D—the surplus required to overcome the adversary's missile defense in a retaliatory strike. By defining the defense as he does, Radner tacitly assumes that the victim's retaliatory strike will proceed to its targets unscathed. This might be true if the first striker's defense protected silos only, and not the cities or military facilities that would be the logical target of a retaliatory attack (why fire back at empty silos?). But Reagan proposed a space-based defense of the whole country—a territorial or *national-area defense*, not a *point defense* of silos. If such a defense materialized, it would necessarily interfere with a countervalue second strike against the urban industrial base or other-than-nuclear targets, and thereby compromise the deterrent threat to retaliate. The *antideterrent effect* of area defenses is the principal reason that critics opposed SDI as destabilizing. As far as I know, no one has argued that a pure missile site defense (including, under Radner's definition, measures such as silo hardening, placing warheads on mobile launchers, or submarine basing) would be anything but stabilizing. By confining his analysis to site defenses, Radner's conclusions do not obviously address the central issues of the SDI debate.[9]

The Kent, Wilkening and Watman, O'Neill, and Bracken Defensive Transition Models

In this section I describe a second kind of model that redresses two suspect features of Radner's analysis. These models proceed by superimposing a full-blown national area defense on the existing strategic arsenals of the nuclear superpowers. By doing so, they remove the assumption that the arsenals contain only one kind of missile. More important, they describe a defense that can intercept both first and second strikes. To convey how they work, I will follow the line of development in Jerome Bracken's version.[10]

The object in the defensive transition models is to see whether building area defenses of increasing effectiveness would destabilize the existing nuclear environment. The point of departure is an index of stability called the "first-strike payoff." In the simplest case, the index compares the fraction of the aggressor's and the victim's "value targets" or "societal resources" that survive a nuclear exchange. When a first striker can substantially damage the victim's society or military forces and suffer little harm in return, the first-strike payoff is high. Bracken defines the first-strike payoff to the "Blue" side in a Red versus Blue scenario as follows:

F^B = [(Fraction Blue Value Surviving)$^\alpha$ –
(Fraction Red Value Surviving)]

When $\alpha = 1$, Blue attaches equal weight to preserving its own assets and to destroying those of the Red side. If α is much greater than 1, then Blue attaches much greater weight to its own resources. In the language of international relations theorists, the parameter α adjusts the measure of stability from "relative gains" toward "absolute gains." To keep things simple, let us agree for now that $\alpha = 1$.

When Blue can destroy all of the Red value targets without suffering any damage in return, $F^B = 1 - 0 = 1$, and the incentive to strike first is maximized. If Red can retaliate in equal measure, then $F^B = 0 - 0 = 0$, and there exists mutual assured destruction (MAD). If both sides have perfect nuclear defenses, there exists "mutual assured survival" (MAS). Neither can destroy any of the other's societal assets, and $F^B = 1 - 1 = 0$. Under MAD or MAS, or whenever $F^B < 0$, there is no incentive to strike first since the status quo already provides $F^B = 1 - 1 = 0$. Once defenses enter the picture, the question is whether we can get from mutual assured destruction to mutual assured survival without creating instabilities in between.

As in the first model, the measure of instability reflects the idea that stable deterrence can be sustained by a capability for damaging retaliation (which drives the attacker's value assets toward zero). The new formula also admits the possibility of deterring by "denial," using an area defense to thwart a countervalue attack. Notice too that the focus shifts from arms-race instability to crisis instability as the description of the nuclear forces becomes more elaborate. Now the arsenals contain many different components, including ICBMs and SLBMs (submarine-launched ballistic missiles) that can be used either in counterforce or countervalue attacks, cruise missiles and bombers that can attack value targets (but are too slow to attack missile sites), ballistic missile defenses, and air defenses. In addition, each side has a specified number of value targets (cities, military bases, seaports, and so on.) To characterize all these forces requires at least twenty parameters, including for each side the number of each weapon, the MIRV factor of missiles, the counterforce kill probabilities of the ICBMs and SLBMs (one against ICBMs and another for bomber bases; submarines and cruise missiles are considered invulnerable), the number of bomber bases, the exhaustion thresholds of the air and missile defenses, their leakage rates below the threshold, and the number of value targets. Some versions allow the defenses to become vulnerable to attack. With so many extra parameters in play, one can describe the existing nuclear arsenals much more realistically than Radner did. At the same time, the number of possible scenarios increases dramatically. For example, a first striker can now design many different kinds of attack, depending on which weapons are allocated to which targets (recall that Radner's model involved only one attack scenario).

Exchange Calculations

The nuclear exchange model involves two steps:

1. The first striker attacks a combination of weapon sites and value targets, allocating warheads over targets to maximize the first-strike payoff.
2. The second striker retaliates by directing all surviving warheads against the first striker's value targets.

In the first stage the attacker fires all of the warheads at once, allocating them over weapon sites (using ICBMs and SLBMs) and value targets (using missiles, bombers, and cruise missiles). The counterforce element of the attack contributes to the first striker's payoff by blunting the victim's retaliatory strike. The countervalue component contributes by destroying the enemy's assets directly. When defenses are present, both components of the first strike pass through a sieve that *randomly subtracts* warheads—that is to say, removes them without regard to their characteristics or targets. (Radner's *preferential defense* of missile sites, in contrast, selectively removes counterforce warheads). In the simplest case, no warheads leak through the defense until it reaches an *exhaustion threshold*, after which everything gets through. One can also make the defenses leaky below the threshold and vulnerable to preemptive attack, complications that I shall not discuss here.[11]

To compute the outcome of the first strike, one has to calculate how many of the victim's weapon sites and valued assets survive. After the surviving warheads are fired back through the attacker's defenses, the first-strike index then compares the damage to each society and whether the first striker "comes out ahead" or "wins" the exchange. Doing so suggests which configuration of forces creates an incentive for preemptive attack.

Making these calculations involves two major tasks. The first problem is to figure out how many of the victim's nuclear forces survive the counterforce attack. Unlike the "shoot-look-shoot" scenario of Radner, the attacker here launches everything at once, possibly including several warheads of different kinds at each weapon site. The basic probabilistic structure of the model remains unchanged, however; each launch remains an independent trial, and the probability of destroying targets cumulates by the multiplication rule for independent events. How many warheads arrive at each target site depends on the design of the attack (the fraction of warheads allocated to counterforce and countervalue) and the size of the defense (how many warheads it can subtract). The *building-block formula* describes the expected number of weapon sites that survive when there are N identical attackers (i.e., penetrators of the defense), M identical sites, and single-shot kill probability p:

$$E_{survivors} = M * <N/M> (1-p)^{[N/M]+1} + M * (1 - <N/M>)(1-p)^{[N/M]}$$

where $<N/M>$ represents the fractional part of the ratio N/M, and $[N/M]$ is the integer part. For example, if 5,200 warheads attack 2,700 silos, so that $N/M = 1.93$, then 93 percent of the silos get two warheads and 7 percent get one. The expected number of silos that survive the two-warhead attack is $5,200 \times .93 \times (1-p)^2$. The expected number that survive the one-warhead attack is $5,200 \times .07 \times (1-p)^1$. The formula allocates warheads as evenly as possible over targets to minimize the number of survivors. When there are ICBM and SLBM warheads with different kill probabilities, and several kinds of targets, the formula becomes quite a bit messier, but the underlying principle remains the same.

The missile site survivor calculation can be repeated for any possible allocation of the first strike to counterforce and countervalue targets. The next step in the problem is to figure out the optimal allocation of the attack, from the first striker's point of view. Doing so requires repeating the building-block calculation over a large grid of possible allocations and then calculating the outcome of each exchange. The attack allocation that maximizes the first-strike index determines the design of the (optimized) first strike. Finally the whole process is reversed, placing the original victim in the role of the first striker. In this way an optimized first-strike index is computed for both sides. Bracken's ultimate index of crisis or first-strike instability is the sum of the two sides' first-strike incentives:

$$G = \text{Crisis Instability} = F^B + F^R$$

where $-2 \leq G \leq 2$. When the index approaches 2, both sides have a strong incentive to strike first, and crisis instability becomes intense.[12]

The calculations I have just described require so many parameters to define each scenario and involve such complex optimizations that no simple formula exists anymore to describe the relationship between stability and the design of the arsenals. Necessarily, then, computation plays a much bigger role than it did with Radner's approach. The same tendency appears in many other fields. Theoretical analysis often begins with simple models that provide explicit analytical results. Attention then shifts toward more complex problems that can be addressed only with intensive numerical simulations. The general pattern seems to be this: When computing is very expensive, strong technical assumptions are used to avoid it. As it becomes cheaper, the strong assumptions are replaced with computations.[13]

An essential element of the computational program is finding ways to summarize and visualize the huge quantities of numerical output that modern computers can produce. In this case, the first-strike instability indices are displayed in what is called the "joint-defense domain," a two-dimensional space whose coordinate axes describe the size (or interception rate) of each side's defense. (It is common to fix the parameters of the air and missile shields in some fixed proportion. Then one dimension can describe both components of the defense at once.) Figure 6.3 illustrates this useful graphical display. Here the joint defense domain on the floor of the picture contains possible combinations of the U.S. and Soviet defenses. The defensive transition from a world without defenses (at the origin in the lower corner) to mutual assured survival (upper corner) will follow some trajectory through the domain. For example, if the two sides match each other's efforts, the defensive transition will proceed across the center of the floor. Taking the offensive arsenals as given (as in the notional scenario below the picture), one can use the model of nuclear exchanges to calculate first-strike incentives throughout the entire domain. A set of three-dimensional elevations makes it possible to see whether any particular transition path will

	Blue	Red
ICBMs	1000	1200
MIRV	2.75	3.0
RVs	2750	3600
Silo KP	.80	.80
SLBMs	600	800
MIRV	4.0	2.0
RVs	2400	1600
Silo KP	.10	.10
Value	1750	1500

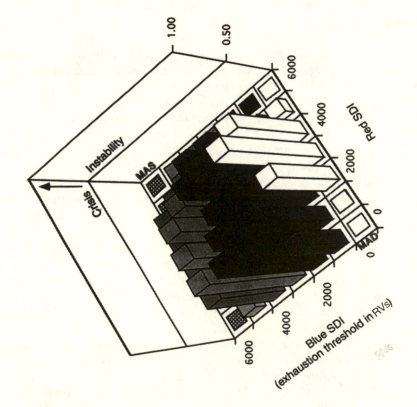

FIGURE 6.3   An unstable defensive transition

produce instabilities, whether a stable path exists, and which path is most stable. In this way some very complicated calculations can be summarized in a simple picture.

The elevations in Figure 6.3 display some calculations I made using a simplified version of Bracken's model. To avoid lots of complications, I deleted the bombers, cruise missiles, and air defenses so that the arsenals contain only vulnerable ICBMs, invulnerable SLBMs, and an SDI-like defense against ballistic missiles (the chains of formulas still fill up a spreadsheet that would cover your kitchen floor). Despite these simplifications, the simulations produce results that are characteristic of the entire genre. The regions with no defenses (MAD) and with heavy defenses (MAS) are highly stable, and those with middling defenses generate incentives for both sides to strike first. Echoing the dominant theme of SDI's critics, these models demonstrate how the defensive transition can destabilize the nuclear environment. When there are middling defenses, a coordinated first strike can still do significant damage, after which the attacker's defense "mops up" the victim's "ragged retaliation."

Remarks

The defensive-transition modelers place much greater emphasis than Radner does on portraying both the nuclear arsenals and the strategic defenses realistically. The added realism comes at a price, however. The new models involve so many extra parameters and such complicated exchange dynamics that their implications can no longer be expressed in simple analytical formulas. One may try to reduce the complex simulations to simple pictures and diagrams, but their internal workings become much more difficult to comprehend or explain.

The new models also sacrifice an important political element of the problem. In an action-reaction approach (like Radner's and many others'), the offensive arsenals are not fixed in advance but respond dynamically to changes in the strategic environment. The plausible idea is that the two sides continually adjust their offensive arsenals to preserve a secure second strike. A problem with the defensive transition models is that they fix the offensive arsenals in place (usually at current levels) and then superimpose the defenses. Doing so demonstrates that the defensive transition might be unstable if the two sides do not adjust their offenses, but why would the nuclear powers only adjust one element of their forces—the defenses—without touching the others?[14]

Because they lack arms-race dynamics based on an explicit strategic objective function, the new models describe the defensive transition in a highly restricted way. The reason is easy to appreciate. When the nuclear arsenals become realistically complex, action-reaction adjustments will be very difficult to anticipate. Will a destabilizing defensive deployment produce adjustments in the land, sea, or air components of the triad, in the defenses, in antidefensive countermeasures, or across the board? The possibilities seem open-ended, to say the least. The answers depend on the two sides' attitudes toward risk, their domestic politics, their economic capabilities, their geographic circumstances, and more—new parameters that would be very difficult to specify with conviction, that are not in the strategist's realm of expertise, and that would complicate the defensive transition models enormously (again by proliferating scenarios).[15]

DeNardo's Security Seeker Model

The last model I shall discuss is one that I devised during the Star Wars debate. Although many people told me they liked the model, I should confess that its rendering of the players' motivations leaves me cold.[16] All the same, it does provide an interesting complement to the two models I have just presented, since it combines an action-reaction logic with a realistic treatment of national area defenses. This combination of elements produces intriguing patterns that defy the conventional wisdom on all sides of the debate.

The point of departure in the "security seeker model" is the linear security functions described in Equations 6a,b. The equations describe two silo-based missile arsenals before defenses are deployed. (Radner's model provides a probabilistic rationalization for these functions.) If we add (unsaturated) area defenses with an interception rate γ to the problem, the security functions take the following form:

$$SOV = \frac{(Min_{sov}/w)}{(1 - \gamma)_{us}} + \beta_{us}(1 - \gamma)_{sov} US \qquad (8a)$$

$$US = \frac{(Min_{us}/w)}{(1 - \gamma)_{sov}} + \beta_{sov}(1 - \gamma)_{us} SOV \qquad (8b)$$

To understand why area defenses entail these formulas, it will be useful first to verify that the equations satisfy the fundamental equation for stable deterrence:

Missiles = Min + D + F

The final terms in each equation represent the number of surplus missiles needed to neutralize the opponent's threat of a first strike (the quantity F). In the Soviets' security function, for example, $(1 - \gamma)_{sov}$ is the fraction of U.S. missiles that would leak through the Soviet shield. $[(1 - \gamma)_{sov}US]$ is the number of missiles that would penetrate in an unconstrained U.S. first strike, and $[\beta_{us}(1 - \gamma)_{sov}US]$ is the expected number of Soviet missile sites that the U.S. penetrators could then destroy. Notice that this expression embodies the de-MIRVing effect of the defender's shield (the only aspect of defenses that Radner considers). Because the leakage rate, $(1 - \gamma)$, lies between zero and one, the effect of the shield is to diminish the exchange ratio of the first striker's missiles. The de-MIRVing effect creates the potentiality for missile reductions (the so-called defense-protected build-down) by reducing the surplus deployments, F, required to neutralize the threat of a first strike. Supporters of strategic defenses frequently invoked the effect to defend SDI (their arguments all have to do with disrupting a Soviet first strike).

At the same time, however, the opponent's shield will force each side to expand its deterrent reserves, because some fraction of any second strike will now be absorbed by the defense. $[(Min_{sov}/w)/(1 - \gamma)_{us}]$ measures the Soviet adjustment to the U.S. defense and embodies the antideterrent effect of the shield. The term (Min_{sov}/w) is simply the minimum reserve needed to deter adjusted for the number of warheads, w, on each missile (as the missiles are MIRVed, fewer are needed to inflict devastating retaliation). The term $(1 - \gamma)_{us}$ in the denominator requires the Soviets to enlarge their reserves as the U.S. defense gets better. The antideterrent effect has the potential to drive a vigorous offensive buildup since the expression explodes as the leakage rate in the denominator approaches zero.

It remains to show that the terms $[(Min_{sov}/w)/(1 - \gamma)_{us}]$ represent together the minimum needed for assured destruction plus a surplus sufficient to neutralize the defense (the remaining quantities $Min + D$ in Equation 1). Formally speaking, the problem is to find an adequate surplus, D, so that at least (Min/w) missiles will penetrate the defense:

$$(1 - \gamma)[(Min/w) + D] = (Min/w)$$

Here the quantity in square brackets represents the total second-strike force available to be delivered against the shield (the remainder in Equation 1 after the first strike has destroyed F missiles). When multiplied by the shield's leakage rate, $(1 - \gamma)$, the result is the number of retaliatory missiles that will penetrate the shield. Stable deterrence requires that this number of penetrators equal the minimum needed to inflict devastating retaliation. Dividing both sides by $(1 - \gamma)$, we get

$$[(Min / w) + D] = \frac{(Min / w)}{(1 - \gamma)}$$

with

$$D = (Min / w) \frac{\gamma}{(1 - \gamma)}$$

Thus the first terms in Equations 8a,b do correspond to the quantities ($Min + D$) in Equation 1, and the security functions as a whole satisfy the fundamental equation.

In this model the defense produces two competing effects. Partisans of SDI argued that the *de-MIRVing effect* would dominate behavior, and opponents emphasized the *antideterrent effect*. To understand their joint impact, we must study how the solutions of the new security functions behave, both as the effectiveness of the shield and the exchange ratio vary. When the two sides build similar technology, the equilibrium arms-race solutions are given by:

$$S^*, U^* = \frac{\dfrac{(Min/w)}{(1-\gamma)} + \beta(Min/w)}{[1-\beta^2(1-\gamma)^2]} \quad w \geq 1 \tag{9}$$

Missile Defenses Before MIRVs
(The ABM Problem)

The upper panel in Figure 6.4 portrays the solutions of the security functions when both sides have single-warhead missiles deployed in partially vulnerable silos (so that $w = 1$, and $\beta < 1$). In these ways the situation resembles the one debated during the ABM controversy of the late 1960s. The solutions to the security functions describe a slowly accelerating offensive arms race, whatever the value of β. As long as the two sides remain committed to preserving a secure second strike, they deploy more and more offense to neutralize the other's defense. For a long while, the arms-race instability is moderate. It becomes pathological after the interception rate reaches 90 percent or so, when many more missiles are required to neutralize each new increment in the shields' effectiveness. It follows that a ballistic missile defense contributes nothing to either side's security during this era and, on the contrary, propels an arms race that makes security increasingly difficult to maintain.

These conclusions are reflected in the ABM Treaty of 1972, which essentially outlawed the deployment of missile defenses. The preamble of the agreement states: "[E]ffective measures to limit anti–ballistic missile systems would be a substantial factor in curbing the race in strategic offensive arms and would lead to a decrease in the risk of outbreak of war involving nuclear weapons." The same action-reaction logic persuaded Secretary of Defense Robert S. McNamara to disparage ABM systems in his famous San Francisco speech of 1967: "Were we to deploy a heavy ABM system throughout the United States, the Soviets would clearly be motivated to so increase their offensive capability as to cancel out our defensive advantage. . . . We do not want a nuclear arms race with the Soviet Union—primarily because the action-reaction phenomenon makes it foolish and futile" (ad-

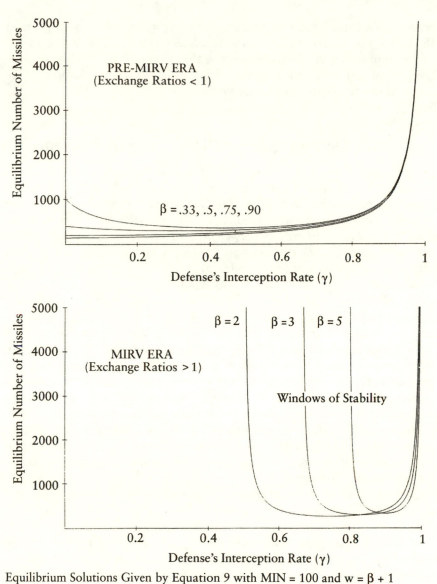

Equilibrium Solutions Given by Equation 9 with MIN = 100 and w = β + 1

FIGURE 6.4   Effectiveness of defense and equilibrium missile forces: security seeker model

dress before United Press International Editors and Publishers, September 18, 1967). In this scenario, then, the antideterrent effect does dominate behavior, supporting the critics who argue that area defenses will be destabilizing (by undermining the deterrent threat to retaliate) and futile (by provoking offensive expansions to negate them).

Missile Defenses After MIRVs (The SDI Problem)

The recent debate about SDI so closely paralleled the earlier debate about the ABM—not only in the strategic arguments presented but in the people presenting them—that there seemed to be a virtual consensus that the two situations were analogous. The lower panel of Figure 6.4 suggests otherwise. The dramatic differences between the two pictures result from setting the exchange ratios of the silo-based missiles above 1 as required after MIRVing opens the "window of vulnerability."

Notice that each of the new curves has the same general form—essentially a bowl with a rounded bottom that is bounded by two asymptotes—and that each curve tells a qualitatively similar story. For rates of interception below the lower asymptote, no positive solution to the security functions exists. In this range of SDI technology, the de-MIRVing effect of the defenses is insufficient to restore a strategic-weapons equilibrium and the shield provides no tangible security benefits at all. Instead, the "window of vulnerability" remains wide open, and neither side enjoys a secure second strike. The lower asymptote therefore sets a minimum standard of performance below which no shield can be said to "enhance deterrence." (Notice that the lower asymptote shifts to higher levels of performance as the exchange ratio increases. Heavier MIRVing requires a better defense to stabilize the environment.)

Once the shields' interception rate surpasses the lower asymptote, however, stable deterrence is restored to the system—even in the presence of MIRVs. As the performance of the shield improves a bit further, the equilibrium missile deployments diminish rapidly, allowing both sides to build down their arsenals from many thousands of missiles to only hundreds. And these benefits occur at rates of interception far less than "near perfection." In the middle range between the asymptotes, the de-MIRVing effect dominates behavior and the shield performs like an arms controller's dream—restoring equilibrium to the unstable MIRVed environment and allowing both sides to reduce their arsenals dramatically. For these reasons, this range of interception rates can aptly be called the *window of stability*.

If technology could be frozen in the window of stability (best of all where the shields allow the smallest missile deployments), the strategic benefits of the defenses would be significant. But as the defensive technology improves further, we enter a region of renewed strategic insecurity. Both sides find their deterrent forces in growing jeopardy, and both must resume building offensive weapons at an accelerating pace. The difficulties occur because the antideterrent effect eventually overwhelms the de-MIRVing effect, causing a renewed arms race that turns pathological when the shields become highly effective (after $\gamma > .95$ or so).

In the MIRVed era, then, the implications of the security seeker model cut against the grain of expert opinion on both sides of the SDI debate. On the one hand, the model belies the argument of SDI partisans who claim that any SDI is better than none and that stability improves continuously as the defenses get better (as in Radner's model).[17] On the other hand, the model suggests that even leaky shields can provide important strategic benefits. Indeed, the optimal shields are grossly leaky, and the very good shields are highly destabilizing. It is interesting to compare the following opinions drawn from both sides of the Star Wars debate:

Because of its obvious expense and complexity, a space-based defense will probably not be deployed unless it is a low-leakage system.[18]

President Reagan's "Star Wars" program seems unlikely ever to protect the entire nation against a nuclear attack. It would nevertheless trigger a major expansion of the arms race. . . . To be useful, a nationwide defense would have to intercept and eliminate virtually all the 10,000 or so nuclear warheads that each side is currently capable of committing to a major strategic attack.[19]

[D]efense at much lower levels of effectiveness [than 99–99.9 percent] would not be very interesting even if feasible and if not offset by the adversary's improving offensive capabilities. Given the present and projected levels of offensive forces, the United States and the Soviet Union could each be destroyed as a going society even if each could intercept 50–90 percent of the adversary's offensive warheads. . . . And, if there could be no assurance that defense could reduce damage significantly, would it be politically or militarily useful? Could either side feel more secure—would either behave differently in crises—if it had such a defense than if it did not? It seems unlikely.[20]

The common assumption underlying these remarks is that the strategic value of a ballistic missile defense resides entirely in its ability to limit damage after a nuclear attack occurs. Overlooked is the benefit of enhancing deterrence before an attack. The lost irony is that a positive rationale for a national area defense can be generated from the same strategic premises that motivated the ban in the ABM Treaty.

I shall leave it to the reader to criticize my model. There are many others as well in the literature, but we have seen enough already to appreciate a fundamental problem. The three models considered here suggest strikingly different conclusions about the effect of missile defenses on strategic stability. In the first model, stability increases continuously as the defenses improve in quality. In the second, deterrence is stable with very bad and very good defenses, and it deteriorates in the middling range. In the third, middling defenses produce the most stability, and very good and very bad defenses produce unstable outcomes.

I believe that similar analytical inconsistencies drive many of our major policy debates and go a long way toward explaining the coexistence of formal scientific methods and partisan inferences in modern social science. It is important, then, to reflect carefully about when such inconsistencies arise and why they are so difficult to resolve.

Why Was the SDI Debate Ideological?

If we reflect on our three examples, it becomes evident that each modeler has confronted the same fundamental obstacle in a somewhat different way. Let us call the set of variables or factors that operate systematically in a problem, and their functional relationships, a metamodel (a metamodel could also be called the "true structure" of the problem). Sometimes, of course, it is hard to perceive lurking variables in the metamodel. But I do not believe that hidden causes are the basic obstacle in many social science problems. I do not believe, as a result, that the problem of ideology originates in "false consciousness" or the remoteness of political causation. Here the SDI issue is a good example. True, it takes some training to write the models I have reviewed; not everybody could do it. But it is not as though they include impalpable, mysterious things like quarks or antimatter. All of the factors I have described are concrete and intuitively plausible. Indeed, most readers could readily extend the list of factors discussed above without a lot of study or effort (the models have not considered budgetary constraints, bureaucratic politics, electoral influences, intelligence-gathering methods, and much more).

The more common trouble, and the basic difficulty here, is that we do not know what values many clearly relevant variables assume. To describe the metamodel, then, becomes a cumbersome enterprise. For each variable that cannot be assigned some known value, we must devote an entire dimension to describe its potential values. In the SDI problem, for example, who knows what kind of sieve the defenses will present, how they will be perceived or misperceived, what they will cost, how vulnerable they will be to suppression, what configuration the offensive forces will assume, what economic and technological capabilities the nuclear powers will have in the future, or what the value of the relative gains parameter might be? Representing the metamodel of deterrent stability therefore requires a high-dimensional surface, describing a huge set of potential scenarios that can be generated by the relevant considerations. Located somewhere along that surface is the true path that strategic stability will eventually follow, if and when the defenses materialize. Understanding this path, which might be called *the true scenario*, is the modeler's objective.

The fundamental obstacle I referred to a moment ago is that multivariate surfaces of high dimensionality are impossibly complicated to comprehend, to visualize, and to explain. Even in modestly complicated problems (like this one), we cannot gain direct access to the metamodel because it is both too complicated to picture in our minds and analytically intractable. The difficulty continually reappears in our examples, which constantly verge on careening "out of control" (i.e., of becoming computationally or mathematically unmanageable) whenever one tries to make the models more realistic. Nobody finds it difficult at all to think of considerations that might be added to these models. The struggle is finding a way to bring them in without creating "a mess."[21]

Of course, the "inaccessibility of the metamodel" is merely one way to describe the complexity of the world and our ignorance about it. Modeling does not create that complexity; it is rather, like all methodologies, a strategy for addressing it. When methodologies compete for a discipline's soul, as they surely do in international studies, one must ask which strategy most effectively confronts the complexity that arises in typical problems.

To gain insight about the true scenario, the analytical strategy in formal modeling is to *project* the very high-dimensional structure of the metamodel onto a lower-dimensional space (just as architects project three-dimensional buildings onto two-dimensional blueprints and cartographers project the Earth's spherical surface onto flat maps). The goal is to obtain an *image* of the true scenario that is both comprehensible *and* undistorted. The art of the modeler, one often hears, lies in finding a simple representation of the problem that contains its essential features. This is a less formal way to describe the projection operation. Figures 6.2, 6.3, and 6.4, and Table 6.1 are all examples of such projections. The pictures contain an image, in two or three dimensions, of the path that strategic stability will travel as defenses improve (they are low-dimensional pictures of the path along which, it is claimed, the true scenario lies).

In practice, producing such projections is accomplished in several ways. Sometimes we constrain certain parameters to a fixed value, thereby reducing a whole dimension to a single point. (In the defensive transition models, the nuclear arsenals are set at current values. In the action-reaction models, the number of submarines and bombers is set at zero.) Constraining several parameters to be proportional (or equal) reduces several dimensions to one. (In the action-reaction calculations, the exchange ratios of each missile force are made equal. In the defensive-transition models, the air and ballistic missile defenses are made equally effective.) Sometimes whole dimensions are deleted altogether (all the models ignore economic variables). Usually this means that some parameter has been set implicitly at a particular value (for example, military budgets are assumed to be sufficiently large that expenditures to secure second strikes will not be constrained). All of these restrictions on parameters in the metamodel (or "assumptions") reduce the dimensionality of the problem, making it simple enough to analyze and represent in a comprehensible way.

Critics invariably point to the unrealism (or the ahistoricism, the simple-mindedness, the incompleteness, or the artificiality) of social-science models to impugn the modeling enterprise. But how else could one possibly gain understanding about a fifty-plus-dimensional surface (the demonstrable complexity of problems like SDI) except by projecting it into a lower-dimensional space? The modeler would argue that such simplifications are unavoidable if we are to make the world comprehensible, and that it is better to select them in an explicit, controlled, and self-conscious way than to pretend that "realism" is possible or desirable (under the complex circumstances). The modeler's quest for simplicity is not driven by merely aesthetic considerations, nor by a simple-minded ignorance of the world's complexities. It is rather undertaken as the only feasible strategy in an otherwise intractable situation.

By studying shadows on the wall (i.e., projected images), the modeler hopes to understand the more complicated and inaccessible object that cast them. Naturally the shadows are not as fully featured as the object itself, but they can nevertheless provide lots of useful information about it (like the information provided by a good blueprint). For this reason, modelers are rarely impressed by objections that their creations are "unrealistic." Of course they are unrealistic. But just because a projection suppresses some dimensions of the problem (rests on unrealistic assumptions) does not mean that it produces a distorted image of the true scenario. Good maps eliminate a myriad of features from the "real world" without necessarily distorting those essential to the user's purpose (such as the configuration of roads or the location of water sources). To impugn a model, then, one must show that it creates a distorted image—not merely that it is unrealistic.

But there is the rub: How do we tell whether a projected image is distorted or not? As everyone knows, shadows on the wall may or may not convey the true shape of the object that casts them. Or to put the problem differently, the direction in which we project the light can have a dramatic effect on the shadow we get. Since there are many different ways to configure the assumptions in a model—and the more so as the metamodel becomes increasingly elaborate—there are many different projections to choose from. Our models of SDI are a case in point. How, then, does one develop confidence that any particular view is undistorted?

The first and most important approach is to test the predictions of the model against experience. If we have several maps that provide different estimates of the distance between A and B, then we can measure the distance to decide which map is correct. In the social sciences, this paradigm often takes the form of fitting mathematical models to statistical evidence and testing their performance. Unfortunately, the outcome is rarely as straightforward as the map example suggests. In fact, testing formal models against experience is typically very difficult, and sometimes even impossible. Explaining why could easily fill another chapter (or volume), but here are sketches of several important reasons:

1. Specification drives estimation. In most problems, the inferences one draws from multivariate social science data depend on which statistical model the researcher fits to the evidence. Unless the correct specification of the statistical model is already known (virtually never true), or unless the explanatory variables happen to be unconfounded (virtually never true except in experiments), then the estimated effect of each variable depends on which other variables appear in the analysis. In this way, beliefs about the correct specification of the statistical model often influence the inferences drawn from the data (and not necessarily the other way around, as we would like).[22]

2. Extrapolation is treacherous when experience is narrow. Competing models often fit the observed data equally well (because they have enough free parameters to tailor the fit) even though their predictions diverge sharply outside the observed range of experience.

3. Statistical models with many parameters often produce unstable estimates. When data are highly confounded or contain lots of "noise," then complicated statistical models tend to "capitalize on chance," producing estimates that are stable neither across samples nor across specifications. Unfortunately, social science data are frequently very noisy, or highly collinear, and interesting problems often contain many parameters.

4. Often there are no data. In the SDI problem, no one can compare the predicted to the actual effect of defenses on stability because no SDI systems have been built. Likewise for (early) predictions about the course of the AIDS epidemic, global warming, ozone depletion, and European monetary integration. In all of these problems the value of the models lies precisely in their ability to prescribe good policies before the events they describe actually unfold.

I should emphasize that these conditions are neither inevitable nor exhaustive, and that data sometimes forcefully support one model in preference to others. It is precisely when experience provides strong and direct feedback (as in the map example) that formal models tend to converge the most rapidly, to evolve the most, and to provide highly fruitful information that could not be obtained otherwise.

Suppose, however, that some or all of these conditions do apply, so that data place weak constraints on models. Is there any way, then, to develop confidence that a particular image is undistorted? Here the prospects are dimmer, though reassurance may be gained when the predictions derived from many different models all converge on a single image. Here is how one well-known modeler of SDI, Barry O'Neill, put the argument:

> A study like ours is part of a growing body of quantitative models of BMD [ballistic missile defense] and stability. Each of these projects made slightly different assumptions about the components of the stability model—definition of stability, details of the nuclear exchange, dynamics of space defenses—but there is often the common result that middle levels of BMD are less stable, even with defense invulnerability. ... This type of convergence gives us confidence in the findings despite each model's specific assumptions.[23]

In fact, our survey suggests that O'Neill's conclusions may have been premature. Far from converging on a single image, the models of SDI considered here diverge sharply. I believe the divergent pattern is actually more typical of modeling work on large-scale policy problems in politics and economics.

These observations bring us at last to the heart of our problem—why was the debate about SDI ideological? The main elements of the puzzle, I believe, are these:

- When we have complex, high-dimensional metamodels, comprehension requires a projection into lower-dimensional spaces. Sometimes different projections all produce the same image, but often they do not. It is usually possible to obtain diverse images.
- Without experimental control over parameters, and with very great uncertainty about correct specification, it becomes difficult to evaluate the truth value of competing images. (The data rarely decide the issue on their own.)
- Many people fail to appreciate the complexity of big questions in the social sciences. The result is a misguided enthusiasm for "realism" and a failure to understand that realism and comprehension stand at odds with each other.
- Decisions often have to be made before a scientific consensus emerges.

Under these conditions, we have a climate that is ripe for partisan inference and ideological controversy, notwithstanding the best efforts of scientific analysts. People of every ideological persuasion can find a model (or a scientist) to suit them. The three models considered here produce enough images of SDI to sustain every conceivable political prejudice. Radner's model suggests that stability will continuously improve as the defenses become more effective. In the defensive-transition models, stability is lost and then regained. In DeNardo's ABM model, stability erodes continuously as the defenses improve, whereas in the SDI version stability is regained and then lost. Given the weak control over inferences exercised by evidence and experience, nobody's model produces an obviously truer image than the rest. None is obviously distorted either. At the same time, all the models manifestly rely on unrealistic assumptions (so as to reduce the dimensionality of the metamodel). Doing so is inherent in producing a projection and therefore necessary for comprehension. But for people who do not appreciate the modeling approach, it becomes all too easy to dismiss any model one does not like as "oversimplified." Even the modelers themselves, who are supposed to know better, seem to live by the same double standard. They accept the unrealism in their own models as artful simplification, while the other guy's unrealism leaves them cold.

I believe this general pattern arises over and over again, throughout the social sciences. It also sustains the methodological controversies that continue to rage in political science and elsewhere. Critics of mathematical methods invariably return to the unrealism of models to dismiss the formal enterprise. Modelers, they say, do not know enough history, they do not go to Washington and talk to the politicians, they do not understand the subtleties of politics. Modelers, in contrast, find little substance in claims that immersion per se produces superior comprehension. The core of their case is that rigorous mathematical techniques provide a demonstrably better grasp of complex multivariate interactions than human intuition alone can provide. The proof of the pudding lies in examples like those I have presented here. Even in highly simplified models like these, the mathematical analysis reveals things that most people would never see. The modelers do not understand how immersing oneself in the lore of politics can reveal the structure of, say, a fifty-dimensional surface. Moreover, when they look at more mature disciplines, they do not see any field that has gone down the formal road and then turned back.

Conclusions

It would be pretentious to predict how this unsettled state of affairs will be resolved and what the ultimate payoff of formal methods will be in international studies. Can the complexity that drives our puzzle be conquered in the future? Without sophisticated mathematical methodologies, I would say no. With them, who knows? It would be more useful, I think, to remark on possible strategies for enhancing the payoff of formal methods in the face of such complexity. Three strike me as particularly salient.

Temper Conclusions with
Honest Estimates of Uncertainty

At the height of the Cold War, Albert Wohlstetter cautioned technologists about abusing the "authority of science" in pressing their opinions on questions of nuclear strategy and national security.

> Passionate assurance on these intrinsically uncertain matters is not justifiable on logical grounds. Some technologists who are most articulate on matters of public policy in the defense and arms control field should worry us the most in their moments of boundless conviction, when they assume the role of seers. . . . No one has the gift of foresight on these cardinal choices. The primary thing, then, is not to be positive. The basic failure of the physical scientists and engineers in their turbulent history during the cold war is not their lack of prescience but their acting frequently as if they had it.[24]

Twenty-five years later, Charles Kupchan admonished conventional force planners with a reprise of Wohlstetter's advice:

> [T]he pervasive and seemingly irreducible uncertainty that characterizes the assessment process is not sufficiently recognized, and the claims made for the models are far too ambitious. . . . Information of uncertain quality is plugged into equations that are based upon questionable assumptions. The models thus contain numerous layers of uncertainty and the outcomes produced may fall within very wide margins of error. . . . Although it is frustrating for politicians and force planners that it is impossible to arrive at a precise measure of "how much is enough," the uncertainty surrounding net assessment raises the question of whether such precision is desirable.[25]

Kupchan's prescription, like Wohlstetter's, is for more truth in advertising. "Making explicit the full range of political and strategic assumptions that produce a given output does not obviate the need to improve confidence levels and to include error terms with all assessments."

This is all well and good. No careful scientist would argue against the idea of reporting honest confidence interval estimates. One could even turn the argument around, I suppose, and recognize that the possibility of careful sensitivity analysis and explicit descriptions of analytical uncertainty do not arise until formal methods appear on the scene. One of the first payoffs that a modeling approach can deliver in a new field is a realistic understanding of complexity and uncertainty.

The trouble with these well-meaning pleas for temperance is not their scientific cogency but their extreme psychological unrealism, both for the producers and the consumers. Politicians already know the world is complicated, that their decisions involve risks, and that nothing is certain. They nevertheless have to make hard, consequential choices today—not when all the evidence is in—and they understandably gravitate toward advisers who are confident in their opinions. However scientifically appropriate, it simply does the decisionmaker no good to be told: "If there is a 'bottom line' to our analysis, it must be that there is no single and concise answer to the question, 'Are defenses destabilizing?' other than, 'It depends.' . . . We hope this volume will have helped the conscientious reader sort through the arguments . . . and reach his own conclusions."[26]

At the same time, can we expect the modeler to invest months and years of hard effort trying to achieve a comprehensible reduction of a difficult problem, and then to proceed as though nothing was learned? Should the modeler stand by while casual argument carries the day in a political debate and decisions are taken that the model refutes? How much certainty is required to sound the alarm on global warming or ozone depletion, if one has a model that predicts it?

Gain Better Control over the Choice of Projections

Whereas the first strategy merely attempts to characterize analytical uncertainties, a second would be to reduce them. If we accept the necessity of a modeling approach, a basic concern becomes the mysterious process that controls the process of projection (the choice of simplifying assumptions, approximations, and the selection of variables). As we have seen in the SDI problem, a great deal of latitude arises in these choices. While the econometrician Radner concentrates on specifying the probabilistic elements of the problem, for example, the Rand modelers focus on force structure. There is certainly nothing wrong with an eclectic approach, which helps to reveal what parameters in the metamodel have a critical effect on the projected image (and what the competing images are). But I think everyone would feel better if there existed good data to constrain the parameters that define each projection. With empirical evidence to guide the choice of analytical scenarios, an important element of arbitrariness would be eliminated from the modeling process.

A critical problem in international studies is that the disciplinary commitment to data acquisition and to systematic data analysis remains very low. When modelers have to decide whether the adversaries play by relative or absolute gains, for example, or whether perceptual biases are conservative or not, they will find very little empirical evidence for guidance. The remedy is not simply gathering more data or historical case studies but collecting data that pin down the parameters that theory suggests are important, that discriminate between alternative scenarios, and that permit careful tests of theoretical predictions. I believe this undertaking, more than any other, would accelerate progress in the field.

Bounded Rationality and the Factional Structure
of International Politics

The two strategies discussed so far attempt, respectively, to characterize the uncertainties in our problems, and to reduce them. A third strategy would be to embrace them. If we concede that major uncertainties are inescapable in politics, that scientific methods will never produce unambiguous answers to the cardinal questions, and that decisionmakers will nevertheless continue to face hard choices, then it follows that the politicians' intuitive models of strategic problems and their "ideological" choices should themselves become a focus of scientific attention. Such a program would make the bounded rationality of political actors, the heterogeneity of their strategic preferences, and the factional politics driven by them the central elements in models of international behavior and change.[27]

Notes

I would like to thank Michael Doyle, Dean Wilkening, George Nolfi, John Londregan, Susanne Lohmann, George Tsebelis, Andrew Lister, Steve Newhouse, and Michael Wallerstein for their thoughtful comments on the arguments presented in this chapter.

1. The term "ideological" is notoriously difficult to specify precisely, and I shall not attempt to do so here. Loosely speaking, an ideological debate is one driven by partisan political beliefs rather than scientific inference. Such debates display the following features: nonconvergence among experts, imperviousness to evidence, alignment with wider political cleavages, and irresoluteness. For an extensive study of intuitive ideological thinking about nuclear strategy, among both experts and novices, see James DeNardo, *The Amateur Strategist: Intuitive Deterrence Theories and the Politics of the Nuclear Arms Race* (New York: Cambridge University Press, 1995).

2. Whether deterrence is relevant or necessary after the adversary collapses is another interesting question. No one considered it during the SDI debate, and I shall not address it here. In general, theories of deterrence take the existence of hostile powers for granted. In this chapter I refer to Russia as the Soviet Union, as it was called during late Cold War, when it still played the villain's role in U.S. thinking.

3. For an argument that nuclear disarmament would be less stable than deterrence in a hostile international setting, see Thomas Schelling, *The Strategy of Conflict* (New York: Oxford University Press, 1960). Schelling's book, a masterpiece of social science, is the most influential application of formal thinking to international affairs ever written.

4. See Roy Radner, "Attrition, Deterrence, and the Value of Ballistic Missile Defense," working paper, AT&T Bell Laboratories, 1985, and Radner, "A Model of Defense-Protected Build-Down," working paper, AT&T Bell Laboratories, 1987. The latter paper is reprinted in Alvin M. Weinberg and Jack N. Barkenbus, eds., *Strategic Defenses and Arms Control* (New York: Paragon House Press, 1988). It

also appears in Jack N. Barkenbus and Alvin M. Weinberg, eds., *Stability and Strategic Defenses* (Washington, D.C.: Washington Institute Press, 1989). See also Alvin M. Weinberg and Jack N. Barkenbus, "Stabilizing Star Wars," *Foreign Policy*, vol. 54 (Spring 1984):164–170, and "Moving to Defense Through Defense-Protected Build-Down," in Weinberg and Barkenbus, *Strategic Defenses and Arms Control*.

5. When n = 500, a rather small counterforce attack, the term n! = n × (n – 1) × (n – 2) × . . . × 1 in Equations 2–4 is already a seriously big number: 500! ≈ 1.22 × 10^{1134}.

6. The simultaneous Equations 6a,b are a close mathematical relative of the famous Richardsonian model of the arms race, which also includes linear reaction functions for two military adversaries. These models have been widely studied with respect to defense spending and military buildups of all kinds. For further information and a sense of the diverse forms the Richardsonian models can assume, the reader might wish to consult Peter A. Busch, "Mathematical Models of Arms Races," Appendix in Bruce M. Russett, *What Price Vigilance?* (New Haven: Yale University Press, 1970), or Walter Isaard, *Arms Races, Arms Control, and Conflict Analysis* (New York: Cambridge University Press, 1988). An influential application to the nuclear arms race is Michael D. Intriligator, "Strategic Considerations in Richardson Models of Arms Races," *Journal of Political Economy*, vol. 83, no. 2 (1975). The scheme of motivation and criteria of stability used here qualify the superpowers' security functions as an action-reaction model of the classical type in national security studies. For interesting discussions of the action-reaction model, see George Rathjens, "The Dynamics of the Arms Race," *Scientific American*, April 1969; and Graham T. Allison, "What Fuels the Arms Race," in *American Defense Policy*, 5th ed., edited by John F. Reichart and Steven R. Sturm (Baltimore: Johns Hopkins University Press, 1982).

7. "A Model of Defense-Protected Build-Down," pp. 3, 5.

8. Radner's discussion of the independence assumption is unusually frank: "Regarding this . . . 'independence assumption,' it is not clear to me whether more realistic assumptions would lead to a higher or lower estimate of deterrence. More complicated assumptions . . . would lead to a more complicated Markov-chain model. . . . In principle, the mathematical problem of calculating a lower bound on the probability that the attacker loses can be solved by the method of dynamic programming." (Radner, "Attrition, Deterrence, and the Value of Ballistic Missile Defense," p. 11). Given Radner's evident hesitation to travel down the complicated path he describes, a reasonable translation seems to be: Without the independence assumption, we're in trouble.

9. Radner is open enough about his assumptions and cautious in his conclusions (without, however, dismissing them): "I want to emphasize that my analysis is not restricted to, or even particularly appropriate for, space-based defense of the 'Star Wars' type. . . . For more generalized defenses such as those envisaged in the SDI effort, a significantly different analysis might be required; in particular the above conclusions about the stabilizing effects of defense might no longer be valid." Radner, "A Model of Defense-Protected Build-Down," in *Stability and Strategic Defenses*, pp. 267, 278. Radner's defense of his critical assumption seems, however, to beg the question: "Given the currently available defense technology, the first assumption—

that neither side's defenses are good enough to prevent unacceptable damage by a retaliatory strike against cities—is reasonable for a reserve force of a few hundred missiles" (p. 278). To answer the critics of SDI, this conclusion should be demonstrated in a model that includes area defenses, not used as a justification to ignore them.

10. Several of these papers are collected in Barkenbus and Weinberg, eds., *Stability and Strategic Defenses,* including Glenn A. Kent and Randall J. DeValk, "Strategic Defenses and the Transition to Assured Survival," and Dean Wilkening and Kenneth Watman, "Strategic Defenses and First Strike Stability." See also Barry O'Neill, "A Measure for Crisis Instability with an Application to Space-Based Antimissile Systems," *Journal of Conflict Resolution,* vol. 31, no. 4 (December 1987), and Jerome Bracken, "Stable Transitions from Mutual Assured Destruction to Mutual Assured Survival" (mimeographed paper, March 1989).

11. The discussion here oversimplifies the complete typology of defenses that modelers consider. More details may be found in the appendix in Kent and DeValk, "Strategic Defenses and the Transition to Assured Survival."

12. Notice that the crisis instability index produces the same result when neither side can profit by striking first ($F^B = F^R = 0$) as it does when one side has a strong incentive to strike and the other a strong incentive not to ($F^B = 1$, and $F^R = -1$, for example). The formula assumes that crisis instability occurs only when both sides have a first-strike advantage. Wilkening and Watman, "Strategic Defenses and First Strike Stability," and Barry O'Neill, "A Measure for Crisis Instability," devise more elaborate indices that make each side's first-strike incentives dependent on the other side's. Doing so does not seem to affect the qualitative behavior of the models, however.

13. Robert Axelrod's famous Prisoner's Dilemma tournament is a familiar example of the trend toward computation in international studies, which is also developing rapidly in cognitive science, statistics, computational economics, and many other fields. For another highly imaginative application with extensive references to recent developments, see Joshua M. Epstein and Robert Axtell, *Growing Artificial Societies: Social Science from the Bottom Up* (Cambridge, Mass.: MIT Press, 1996).

14. Some of these modelers discuss how stabilizing offensive adjustments could be made during the transition. Their goal is to show that a stable transition is at least a logical possibility. Nothing in the model defends the stable paths as a prediction about behavior, however.

15. Wilkening and Watman describe the dilemma as follows: "Arms race stability is not considered here. No one should doubt that deploying strategic defenses will stimulate some form of arms race. . . . Whether one side's strategic defenses stimulates like deployments, countermeasures designed to reduce the effectiveness of these defenses, or offensive force proliferation depends in large part on the relative cost effectiveness of each option. Since both the cost and the effectiveness of projected strategic defenses are extremely difficult to calculate at this point, predicting responses to defense deployments is equally problematical. Thus, it is not possible to predict with confidence whether the resulting arms competition will be unstable, and in particular, whether proliferation of the nuclear arsenals will be a likely result." Wilkening and Watman, "Strategic Defenses and First-Strike Stability" (Santa Monica: Rand Corporation, November 1986), R-3412-FF/RC.

16. See James DeNardo, "Are Strategic Defenses Strategically Defensible?" Center for International and Strategic Affairs (CISA) Working Paper, University of

California, Los Angeles. My recent book, *The Amateur Strategist*, presents much evidence that casts doubt on the core assumptions of the security seeker model (and, by extension, many other theories in international relations that treat states as unitary rational actors).

17. Partisans of an "evolutionary" strategy of deployment claimed that "even U.S. defenses of limited capability can deny Soviet planners confidence in their ability to . . . satisfy attack objectives, thereby strengthening deterrence. Intermediate defenses can also reduce damage if conflict occurs" ("Ballistic Missile Defenses and U.S. National Security ['Hoffman Report'], p. 280). Their arguments rested on an implicit assumption of continuity: "[T]he more effective the defenses, the greater the protection, but there is no reason to expect a threshold of required effectiveness" (Fred S. Hoffman, "The SDI in U.S. Nuclear Strategy," p. 3). Both Hoffman pieces are reprinted in S. Miller and S. Van Evera, eds., *The Star Wars Controversy: An International Security Reader* (Princeton: Princeton University Press, 1986).

18. John C. Toomay, "The Case for Ballistic Missile Defense," in *Weapons in Space*, ed. Franklin A. Long, Donald Hafner, and Jeffrey Boutwell (New York: W. W. Norton, 1986), p. 233.

19. Hans Bethe, Richard L. Garwin, Kurt Gottfried, and Henry W. Kendall, "Space-Based Ballistic-Missile Defense," *Scientific American*, vol. 251, no. 4 (October 1984):41.

20. George Rathjens, "Reactions and Perspectives," in *Ballistic Missile Defense*, edited by Ashton B. Carter and David N. Schwartz (Washington, D.C.: Brookings Institution, 1984), p. 424.

21. Jerome Bracken describes the dilemma as follows: "The relatively straightforward analysis presented here is very difficult to fully comprehend, particularly as one begins to change assumptions. There are on the order of 50 dimensions in the analysis. . . . There is of necessity a tradeoff between understandable analysis and more and more detailed analysis." (Bracken, "Stable Transitions from Mutual Assured Destruction to Mutual Assured Survival," p. 38.) Roy Radner raises similar concerns in a discussion about diversity: "The discussion in the previous sections has proceeded as if all of the attacking warheads were identical, and all of the targets were identical. In reality, of course, there is a great diversity. . . . [The approach] required for realistic planning would be to develop a more elaborate mathematical model, incorporating a more realistic representation of the actual situation. Such models are well within the capabilities of modern techniques of analysis, especially with present-day computational resources. . . . Unfortunately, the analysis of such a model would not be as transparent as the [one presented here], and some intermediate approximations would be useful to reinforce the credibility of the results of the more complex analysis" (Radner, "A Model of Defense-Protected Build-Down," in Weinberg and Barkenbus, p. 289). K. C. Li ("Uncertainty Analysis for Mathematical Models with SIR," UCLA Technical Report) explains why it is very difficult to understand the shape of a function that has more than several arguments, even when we know a formula that links input and output. In a problem with ten variables, for example, picturing the relationships among them requires forty-five bivariate plots at a minimum, assuming we know what values to choose for the suppressed variables. If we do not, and we allow three choices for each of them, there are suddenly $3^8 \times 45 = 295{,}245$ plots to consider.

22. For an excellent discussion of these problems, see E. Leamer, *Specification Searches: Ad Hoc Inferences with Nonexperimental Data* (New York: John Wiley and Sons, 1978); E. Leamer, "Let's Take the Con out of Econometrics," *American Economic Review*, vol. 73 (1983):31–43; or Frederick Mosteller and John W. Tukey, *Data Analysis and Regression* (Reading, Mass.: Addison-Wesley, 1977), especially chapter 13, "Woes of Regression Coefficients."

23. O'Neill, "A Measure for Crisis Instability," p. 662.

24. Albert Wohlstetter, "Scientists, Seers, and Strategy," *Foreign Affairs*, April 1963.

25. Charles Kupchan, "Setting Conventional Force Requirements: Roughly Right or Precisely Wrong," *World Politics*, vol. 61, no. 4 (1989).

26. Barkenbus and Weinberg, introduction in *Stability and Strategic Defenses*, ed. Barkenbus and Weinberg, p. 6.

27. An application of this approach to the nuclear arms race may be found in James DeNardo, *The Amateur Strategist*. The book explores the connection between cognitive foundations of strategic preferences and the factional structure of arms control politics. For recent developments in the burgeoning fields of complexity theory, bounded rationality, behavior game theory, and cognitive psychology, the reader might consult Epstein and Axtell, *Growing Artificial Societies;* John H. Hagel and Alvin E. Roth, eds., *Handbook of Experimental Economics* (Princeton: Princeton University Press, 1995); George Lakoff, *Moral Politics* (Chicago: University of Chicago Press, 1996); Ariel Rubinstein, *Lectures on Modeling Bounded Rationality* (CORE Lecture Series, 1995); and John H. Holland, Keith J. Holyoak, Richard Nisbett, and Paul Thagard, *Induction: Processes of Inference, Learning, and Discovery* (Cambridge, Mass.: MIT Press, 1986).

7

Realist International Theory and the Study of World Politics

JOSEPH M. GRIECO

For almost half a century—since the publication in 1948 of the first edition of Hans Morgenthau's *Politics Among Nations*—realist international theory has been at the heart of the study of world politics in the United States.[1] Many scholars have found realist theory to be a useful framework within which to investigate world politics. This is because realist theory addresses the key questions in international relations: What are the causes of conflict and war among nations, and what are the conditions for cooperation and peace among them?[2] Precisely because it engages these fundamental international problems, other scholars, seeking to develop alternative analytical approaches to international affairs—for example, different types of liberal institutionalism, domestic structural analysis, group decisionmaking theory, individual cognition and personality theory, and most recently, postmodern constructivism—have often defined their theoretical perspectives and research programs in large measure through their opposition to one or more elements of realist theory. Hence if we wish to understand the development and current status of academic discourse in the United States on international relations, we need to understand realist international theory and confront its analysis of world politics.

In this chapter I present a critical appreciation of realist international theory. The first main section provides an outline of realism's main assumptions about states, and the central propositions that realists derive from these core assumptions about the preferences and behavior of states in world affairs. In the second section I examine a sampling of realist-informed scholarship in the fields of international political economy and international security studies in order to assess the degree to which realist theory has contributed to our understanding of international relations. The view put forward in that section is that realism does in fact provide substantial leverage on many aspects of world politics. However, in the third and final main section of the chapter I identify two serious conceptual ambiguities and tensions in realist theory and offer a discussion of possible lines of analysis that might address these problems and thus allow realist theory to provide a more effective understanding of politics among nations.

The Core of Realist International Theory

Assumptions

About the Actors in World Politics: Centrality of the State

For realists, as Robert Gilpin suggests, "the essence of social reality is the group," and in particular, "in a world of scarce resources and conflict over the distribution of those resources, human beings confront one another ultimately as members of groups, and not as isolated individuals."[3] For realists, the fundamental unit of political organization for the past several centuries has been, and at present it is, the nation-state. Realists recognize that other actors such as international institutions, multinational enterprises, and transnational bodies such as the International Committee of the Red Cross operate in the international system, but, as Kenneth Waltz suggests, "states set the scene in which they, along with nonstate actors, stage their dramas or carry on their humdrum affairs. Though they may choose to interfere little in the affairs of nonstate actors for long periods of time, states nevertheless set the terms of the intercourse. . . . When the crunch comes, states remake the rules by which other actors operate."[4] Similarly, Gilpin observes that "the state is the principal actor in that the nature of the state and the pattern of relations among states are the most important determinants of the character of international relations at any given moment."[5] Finally, Stephen Krasner justifies his assumption that states are the "basic actors in the international system" by arguing that "the behavior of other actors, including multinational corporations and international organizations, is conditioned and delimited by state decisions and state power."[6]

About the Context of Action: The Anarchy Assumption

Realism's second core assumption is that states coexist in a context of international anarchy, that is, the absence of a reliable central authority to which they can appeal for protection or the redress of grievances.[7] The assumption of international anarchy has at least two main realist-posited implications for states. First, in light of the absence of a reliable central authority, states know that others may renege on promises, use force or the threat of force as a way of exerting pressure on them, or even try to hurt or destroy them. Raymond Aron, for example, observes that international relations "present one original feature which distinguishes them from all other social relations: they take place in the shadow of war, or, to use a more rigorous expression, relations among states involve, in essence, the alternatives of peace and war."[8] E. H. Carr makes a similar point: War "lurks in the background of international politics just as revolution lurks in the background of domestic politics."[9] Similarly, Waltz argues that "if force is used by one state or its use is expected, the recourse of other states is to use force or be prepared to use it singly or in combination. No appeal can be made to a higher entity clothed with the authority and equipped with the ability to act on its own initiative. Under such conditions the possibility that force will be used by one or another of the parties looms always as a threat in the background."[10] For realists, then, states recognize that they coexist in a dangerous environment.

Second, and related to the first implication, the absence of a centralized authority means that states are by definition self-help agents. As Waltz puts the matter, "to achieve their objectives and maintain their security, units in a condition of anarchy—be they people, corporations, states, or whatever—must rely on the means they can generate and the arrangements they can make for themselves. Self-help is necessarily the principle of action in an anarchic order."[11] As I will show later, realists argue that it is the violence-permissive anarchical context of the international system, together with its associated implication that states recognize that they are self-help agents, that profoundly constrains and shapes both the goals states choose to pursue (their substantive rationality) and the means they elect to pursue in order to achieve those goals (their instrumental rationality).

About the Actors: States as Rational, Autonomous, and Unitary Agents

Realists work with a cluster of three interrelated assumptions about states. The first part of this cluster is the assumption that states are rational actors.[12] State rationality, from a realist viewpoint, has at least three elements. First, realists assume that states are goal-oriented. Although realists diverge in certain important respects with regard to the primary ends they ascribe to states (see the discussion later in the third main section of the chapter), they assume that states have such goals and devise strategies specifically aimed at their achievement. Second, realists assume that states have consistent goals. That is, state preferences are ordered and transitive in the sense that if outcome A is preferred to B, and B is preferred to C, then A is preferred to C. Third, states are assumed by realists to devise strategies to achieve their goals. These strategies take into account the rank-ordering by states of these goals. As an extension, realists assume that states are "sensitive to costs" and thus can change their strategies in the face of changes in external constraints and opportunities, negative experiences of their own, and observation of both the successes and the failures of other states.[13]

The second part of the cluster of realist assumptions about the nature of states is that they have sufficient autonomy from their national societies to recognize and pursue the interests of the nation as a whole, and not just those of particular powerful groups within the community, and they might actually establish goals and strategies that run counter to the preferences of important parts of society. This is a vitally important assumption for realists, for it enables them to posit the view that decisionmakers respond on behalf of the nation-state as a whole to the opportunities and dangers engendered by the international system.[14]

The third and final part of the realist cluster of assumptions about states is that states possess the capacity for unity of action. This means that states have the capacity to act in a coherent manner with regard to other countries.[15] Coherence in turn means that central decisionmakers maintain sufficient control over different organizational elements of their governments to allow them to direct and coordinate government actions in such a way as to implement the decisionmakers' strategies, and to do so in a way that reflects their rank-ordering of goals. Thus endowed with the capacity for coherent action in support of a centrally established and consistent hierarchy of goals, states, according to realists, are able not just to perceive systemic-level constraints but also to formulate and to execute measures in response to them.

Propositions

State Interest in Security: States as Defensive Actors

On the basis of its three core assumptions, realism has developed a number of propositions about the essential character of states and their basic preferences as they interact with other states. First, for realist theory the key result of the recognition by states of the possibility that force can be used against them is that they have security as their principal interest. Gilpin, for example, suggests that although individuals or groups may seek truth, beauty, and goodness, "all these more noble goals will be lost unless one makes provision for one's security in the power struggle among social groups."[16] Similarly, Waltz notes that "in anarchy, security is the highest end. Only if survival is assured can states safely seek such other goals as tranquility, profit, and power."[17] In the same vein, Krasner observes that "all states share the same minimalist objectives of preserving territorial and political integrity."[18] In addition, Aron argues that "politics, insofar as it concerns relations among states, seems to signify—in both ideal and objective terms—simply the survival of states confronting the potential threat created by the existence of other states." "What then," he asks, "is the first objective the political unit [i.e., the state] may logically seek?" His response, following Hobbes, is that "each political unit aspires to survive. Leaders and led are interested in and eager to maintain the collectivity they constitute together by virtue of history, race, or fortune."[19] In realist theory, anarchy causes states to be agents concerned first and foremost with their survival and security, and therefore we may say that, to the extent that they are responding to and are being shaped by their external environment, states, according to realist theory, are profoundly *defensive* actors.

The Relativity of Power: States as Defensive Positionalists

Because realists argue that states recognize that their security depends on their own efforts, they also argue that states tend to be concerned about their *relative* capabilities, for it is these that determine whether states are able to meet actual or potential threats posed by other states. State power, then, is by definition relative—indeed, Morgenthau points out that "the concept of power is always a relative one."[20] The relativity of power in turn causes states to be positional actors. That is, states, from a realist viewpoint, typically compare themselves to others and assess their own actions, the actions of others, and their relationships and interactions from the viewpoint of their effect on relative capabilities. Tying this realist argument to the realist view that anarchy causes states to be concerned about their security and survival, realist theory argues that anarchy causes states to be *defensive positionalists.*[21]

It should be noted that many realists assert that states seek not just to minimize gaps in power that favor others but also to maximize gaps to their own advantage. This ambiguity creates a number of problems for realist theory, which are discussed more fully in the third major section of this chapter. However, for the moment I would only suggest that in my view, although there is nothing in realist theory that would preclude us from observing that *some* states may seek to maximize their relative power (perhaps because of the particularities of national leaders or domestic structures), the theory's emphasis on anarchy itself probably does not predict more than that *most* states (and certainly *all major* states) will seek the minimum level of power that is needed to attain and to maintain their security and survival. Indeed, and as is discussed more fully later, given realism's emphasis on state defensiveness, it would follow that if a state had an opportunity to increase its power, but this conflicted with its goal of security maximization, then the state—to the extent that it is responding to systemic constraints—would forgo the former in favor of the latter.

State Interest in Independence and Autonomy

Realists also argue that because they are defensive positionalists and are concerned about their relative power, states seek to be free to choose strategies that are most likely to promote their security and to try to undertake those actions both internally and externally that they believe are most likely to maintain their relative power position and thereby to help ensure their safety. Hence anarchy causes states to value autonomy of decision and independence of action. In addition, states, according to realist theory, seek in the self-help context of anarchy to retain a capacity to carry out those functions that are conducive to security, survival, and maintenance of relative position: They seek, for example, to have an independent capacity for diplomacy, for the gathering of intelligence, and, ultimately, for the credible threat or actual employment of force. Since these functions in turn require national control over certain resources—most important, a diversified economy able to support military power—states are wary, according to realist theory, of becoming dependent on others (for example, as a result of specialization on the basis of comparative advantage) to the extent that they can no longer act autonomously.[22] Of course, not all states may be able actually to perform all of those functions, but most—and certainly all of the major states—will have as an interest the retention of the capacity to carry them out to the greatest degree possible.

In sum, realist theory assumes that states are the key actors in world affairs; that they are rational, autonomous, and unitary actors; and that their goals and strategies are shaped by their anarchical context. On the basis of these assumptions, realists argue that states are fundamentally concerned about their security and in consequence are defensively positional in character; that as such they are anxious about their relative capabilities; and as a result they are attentive to their capacity for autonomous choice and independent action. These assumptions and propositions form the core of realist international relations theory.

The Utility of Realist Theory

The previous section provided a brief outline of the main elements of realist theory. The question, of course, is whether they can be used to shed significant light on the actual behavior of states and the outcomes of that behavior in the international system. The present section addresses that question.

Evaluation of the State-as-Unitary-Actor Assumption

Most applications of realist theory test propositions that are derived from realism's core assumptions and general propositions. However, it should be noted that many realist-informed scholars have investigated directly the feasibility and usefulness of what is perhaps realism's most controversial assumption, namely, that states can act as unitary actors relatively unconstrained by the character of domestic institutions or the content of the preferences of particularistic societal segments.[23] For example, Stephen Krasner finds that substantial governmental autonomy can be observed even in the seemingly hard case of a generally "weak" U.S. state interacting with a "strong" American society. In particular, in his study of postwar U.S. monetary and commercial policy (in which he suggests that the state has had greater autonomy in the former than the latter) and in his investigation of U.S. foreign policy in the natural-resources issue area during most of the twentieth century, Krasner demonstrates that the key foreign policy–making sectors of the U.S. government—that is, the executive branch in general and the office of the president in particular—have been able to attain the autonomy and coherence of action needed to meet to an important degree the unitary-actor assumption.[24]

Krasner's key finding—that the U.S. executive can act with substantial autonomy and coherence—is supported by John Ikenberry's study of U.S. oil-price decontrol policy during the 1970s. As in the Krasner studies, Ikenberry argues that the U.S. government came to specify its goals and to devise a policy to move toward the decontrol of oil prices not in response to domestic interests—which were divided among themselves or argued in favor of continued controls—but instead as a part of a U.S. bargain made with the other major industrialized countries at the Bonn summit meeting of 1978.[25] Similarly, David Lake demonstrates that even in the hardest of hard cases—that is, commercial policy in the United States, in which a particularistic Congress is constitutionally entitled to share in policymaking—the U.S. executive was able from 1887 through 1939 to respond to a surprising degree to systemic opportunities and constraints.[26] Hence studies that directly address the utility of the assumptions of state autonomy and coherence—the assumptions without which realists could not argue that states respond to external stimuli—appear to have solid empirical grounding, and beyond that they shed light on the actual foreign policies of even a highly pluralistic political system such as that of the United States.

Realist Empirical Propositions: Tests and Extensions

Balancing

In addition to undertaking studies that address core realist assumptions, realist-informed scholars have developed and investigated three major clusters of expectations about actual state behavior and international outcomes. The first specifies what is perhaps the major realist expectation regarding the behavioral manifestation of the interest of states to ensure their survival in the face of anarchy. That expectation concerns the tendency of states to engage in *balancing* behavior; that is, if the security and independence of some states are threatened by the growth in power of one state or a group of states, the threatened states, according to realist theory, will respond to that challenge by seeking to take actions that mitigate or offset the growth in power of the rising side. They will not, by way of contrast, engage in *bandwagoning* behavior, that is, they will not rush to join the stronger side in the hope of making the best arrangements possible and of exploiting those that are the (immediate) target of the rising side.

Balancing efforts may include individual attempts by the threatened states to accumulate additional national capabilities sufficient to match those of the challenger.[27] Alternatively, balancing may take the form of states seeking to establish informal or formal alliances aimed against the rising state or group of states. Aron calls this tendency to undertake balancing through alliances a "policy of equilibrium" and defines it most generally as "maneuvering in order to prevent a state from accumulating forces superior to those of its allied rivals." He notes further that "every state, if it wishes to safeguard the equilibrium, will take a position against the state or coalition that seems capable of achieving such a superiority."[28] Aron emphasizes that balancing is systemically induced. He observes, for example, that "hateful or admirable, baneful or precious, the diplomacy of equilibrium does not result from a deliberate choice on the part of statesmen—it results from circumstances."[29] He also stresses that balancing is usually defensive in motivation, arguing that it "issues from the prudence necessary to the states concerned to preserve their independence and not be at the mercy of another state possessing irresistible strength"; he returns to this defensive motive in balancing when he notes that "the concern for equilibrium inspires diplomacy to the same extent that men—both governed and governing—cling to the independence of their political unit."[30]

For realist theory the tendency of states to balance against challengers through the formation of defensive alliances is a strong behavioral expectation about the effects of anarchy on states. It is also a key sign, according to realism as it has been articulated by Waltz, that states are more interested in security than in power. Waltz argues that "if states wished to maximize power, they would join the stronger side, and we would see not balances forming but a world hegemony forged. This does not happen because balancing, not bandwagoning, is the behavior induced by the system. The first concern of states is not to maximize power but to maintain their positions in the system." He goes on to note that "secondary states, if they are free to choose, flock to the weaker side; for it is the stronger side that threatens them. On the weaker side, they are both more appreciated and safer, provided, of course, that the coalition they join achieves enough defensive or deterrent strength to dissuade adversaries from attacking."[31]

In recent years Stephen Walt has modified the basic realist argument that states will balance against and not bandwagon toward a rising challenger. Realist theory, Walt argues, has too readily equated physical power with external challenges, and therefore it has too readily predicted that states will determine against which country they should balance solely on the basis of which is rising in sheer material power. Walt argues that power is indeed a key factor on which states focus in making their balancing decisions, but in addition to power they are sensitive to the level of political threat that a state may pose against them. In other words, states balance against those that are most *threatening* to them. Walt illustrates the efficacy of this argument by demonstrating that threat-balancing has prevailed over bandwagoning in the Middle East and in Southwest Asia since World War II, and that the threat-balancing thesis provides a better grasp on alliance decisions in the region than do such alternative explanatory factors as ideology, foreign aid, or foreign interventions in local politics.[32]

The realist proposition on balancing has recently been subjected to an important critique by noted historian Paul Schroeder.[33] Schroeder says that instead of self-help and especially balancing, states historically have often pursued alternative strategies in the face of threats from others. They have, he suggests, often turned to "hiding" (avoidance of the threat posed by other countries) or to "transcending" (seeking to solve the problem that brought the countries into conflict). Most interestingly, Schroeder indicates that in contrast to the views of Waltz and Walt, "I see bandwagoning as historically more common than balancing, especially by smaller powers."[34]

In addition, Michael Barnett and Jack Levy, in their study of shifts in Egyptian military alliances from the early 1960s to the early 1970s, find that Egypt's movement from hostility to progressively closer coordination with the conservative oil-rich Arab countries such as Saudi Arabia over the course of that period, and its decision to move first from partial engagement in the early 1960s to close alliance with the Soviet Union between 1967 and 1970, followed by disengagement from 1971 until 1973, cannot be readily attributed simply to changes in Egypt's diplomatic position with respect to Israel. Instead they emphasize and persuasively argue that these shifts were the result both of international factors *and* the domestic political situation and the struggles of Egypt's leaders, Gamal Abdel Nasser and Anwar Sadat.[35] This finding about the impact of domestic factors is important because, as they note, the particular case of Egyptian alliances has been cited by realists as confirming their approach to the subject.[36] Their study is also important because it presents disconfirming evidence for realist expectations precisely in circumstances (international security affairs) that otherwise would be thought to be most likely to yield a confirming case for realism. At the same time, the case offers supporting evidence for a theory (domestic-structuralism, loosely defined) in circumstances in which such confirmation might be expected to be least likely to occur.[37]

In the same vein, Steven David argues that in addition to—and sometimes, if necessary, instead of—responding to external threats, national state elites, acting to protect their personal as opposed to state interests, make alliance choices on the basis of internal threats to their domestic political control. He refers to this as "omnibalancing." He finds that Mengistu Haile Mariam's decision in the mid-to-late 1970s to switch Ethiopia from a pro-U.S. to a pro-Soviet alignment is puzzling from a balance-of-power viewpoint but makes sense when one takes into account the fact that although the United States was not prepared to support Mengistu in his efforts to suppress the secessionist movement in Eritrea, the Soviet Union was willing to provide such support. In contrast, Anwar Sadat's move away from the Soviet Union and toward the United States in the late 1970s, David suggests, was driven by Sadat's concerns and calculations about which patron would help him contain challenges to his personal power from within Egypt.[38] As in the Barnett and Levy study, domestic dynamics, and not just international imperatives, appear to drive exactly the form of behavior that is presumably at the center of the realist understanding of world politics, namely, state choices and strategies regarding political-military alliances. This argument about the domestic sources of state alignment choices (discussed more fully later) is a challenge not only to realist ideas about balancing but also to the entire realist orientation to world politics.

System Polarity and Stability

Realists, while emphasizing that the international system is conducive to competition and conflict among states, also argue that the stability of the international environment can be affected by systemic factors and particularly by system polarity, that is, the number of major states in the system. Most significant is Waltz's thesis that multipolar systems tend to be more prone than bipolar systems to instability and possibly severe military conflict.[39] He suggests, for example, that balancing is relatively more difficult in multipolar than in bipolar systems; that the risk of miscalculation is higher in multipolar than in bipolar systems; and that alliance leaders are more likely to be drawn into conflicts by their weaker partners in multipolar than in bipolar contexts. He also argues that bipolar systems are by definition ones in which there is less economic interdependence (defined as mutual vulnerability) than in multipolar systems, and this too causes bipolar systems to be more stable and less conflict-prone than multipolar systems.

Waltz's polarity thesis has been subjected to a number of useful criticisms. For example, Thomas Christensen and Jack Snyder point out that there is a troubling indeterminacy in Waltz's arguments about the manner in which alliance dynamics in multipolar international systems might result in unintended war. That is, they note that according to Waltz such wars in multipolar systems might arise from "chain-ganging" (allies are dragged into war by reckless partners) or "buck-passing" (each ally hopes that its partners will stand up against a rising challenger, and thus none do so until it is too late). They show with substantial persuasiveness that an understanding of the "pathologies" of multipolarity prior to World War I (chainganging) and World War II (buck-passing) requires the addition of a factor not included in Waltz's structural analysis, namely, perceptions of national decisionmakers about the likely efficacy of offensive military strategies.[40]

Another interesting critique of Waltz's polarity thesis is provided by Ted Hopf. He suggests in a study of European international politics from 1495 to 1559 that there was no significant change in the level of stability of the system in spite of a shift from multipolarity (which characterized the 1495–1521 subperiod) to bipolarity (1521–1559). He claims, as do Christensen and Snyder, that an argument focusing on decisionmaker perceptions about the advantages of offensive as opposed to defensive military strategies provides greater insight into the continuities in conflict across the two time periods than does a focus solely on the structure of the international system.[41]

Yet, in spite of its problems, the polarity thesis retains a remarkable degree of vitality. Joanne Gowa, for example, while not addressing specifically Waltz's arguments about system structure and stability, shows that the international trading order is likely to be more liberal and more stable if it is embedded in alliances that are formed under conditions of bipolarity than of multipolarity.[42] The salience of realism's polarity thesis is also evidenced by the debate that John Mearsheimer has sparked about the future of Europe. Mearsheimer argues that the bipolar structure of the international system from 1945 until 1989 was the main cause of the security and stability that obtained in Western Europe during that period and was also the main factor facilitating the cooperation that evolved among the nations in that region. He argues further that in the wake of the collapse of the Soviet Union and the end of the Cold War, it is likely that Europe will return to multipolarity and that this will possibly mean a return to instability and conflict on the continent.[43] Only time will determine the degree to which Mearsheimer's argument about multipolarity is correct, but at the very least it may be predicted with confidence that his realist-informed analysis will set the terms of debate in much of the literature on intra-European relations for many years to come. In addition, Aaron Friedberg and Richard Betts, though not writing from a realist perspective, both focus in their respective studies of the future of East Asia on the impact of growing multipolarization in that region, and both suggest that this trend—especially in light of the low presence or even the absence of the domestic-political and regional-economic characteristics that may be promoting peace and inhibiting conflict in Western Europe—has the potential to produce serious instability in that part of the world, including arms races and perhaps even war.[44]

Realism and the Problem of International Cooperation

Hypothesized Constraints on Cooperation.   Realism holds that states may cooperate by forming defensive alliances aimed against external challengers. More generally, it should be emphasized that realist-informed scholars have long recognized that cooperation is an important feature of world politics. However, they have argued—and in doing so have produced a second set of empirical expectations—that cooperation is harder to achieve and more difficult to maintain than is suggested, for example, by the liberal-institutionalist tradition. In particular, realists have identified at least three systemically induced constraints on the willingness of states to cooperate even when they share common interests.

The first constraint (and the one most typically emphasized by realism's liberal challengers) is the problem of cheating. Without a centralized authority capable of enforcing promises, and in the face of common but also mixed interests, states both will be tempted to cheat and will fear being the victim of such cheating by their partners.[45]

Second, as noted earlier, realists argue that states as self-help agents prefer to be able to perform as many functions (especially those having an effect on their security and autonomy) as possible. The preference of states, then, is to maintain a low level of functional differentiation between themselves and others. However, cooperation usually entails some degree of specialization of function: In the military realm, for example, an alliance is strengthened as a collective if the sea powers within it concentrate resources on their naval strength at the expense of their ground forces while the ground powers do the reverse. Similarly, in the economic realm the gains arising from trade liberalization are maximized if such liberalization permits specialization on the basis of comparative advantage. Yet it is precisely this specialization in function that states resist, according to realists. As Waltz puts the matter, although "the domestic imperative is 'specialize'!," one finds that "the international imperative is 'take care of yourself'!"[46] In other words, to ensure their security states prefer to have a "robust" military force structure; if and to the extent that it is possible, they would like to have formidable naval *and* ground *and* air forces. States also prefer a "balanced" economic structure—that is, to possess, if and to the extent possible, advanced-technology industry *and* basic heavy industry *and* agricultural self-sufficiency *and* a diversified service sector. In sum, to the extent that cooperation entails functional differentiation, states, according to realist theory, will be wary about such cooperation as a result of anarchy-induced concerns about their security and independence.[47]

The third constraint operating on the willingness of states to cooperate, realists suggest, is the matter of relative gains. Waltz defines the issue in these terms: "When faced with the possibility of cooperating for mutual gain, states that feel insecure must ask how the gain will be divided. They are compelled to ask not 'Will both of us gain?' but 'Who will gain more?' If an expected gain is to be divided, say, in the ratio of two to one, one state may use its disproportionate gain to implement a policy intended to damage or destroy the other. Even the prospect of large absolute gains for both parties does not elicit their cooperation so long as each fears how the other will use its increased capabilities."[48] Drawing from this argument, it may be suggested that defensive state positionalism fosters a relative-gains problem for international cooperation: Given its defensive concerns about relative capabilities, a state will decline to join, will leave, or will sharply limit its commitment to a cooperative arrangement if it believes that gaps in gains will substantially favor partners.[49]

Several analytical critiques have been offered recently of the realist expectation that states will tend to exhibit defensively oriented concerns about the distribution of gains arising from cooperation with others. For example, several authors suggest that state concerns about relative gains may dissipate in the face of large numbers of actors or when the possibility of war is low.[50] Yet recent works by Michael Mastanduno and Stephen Krasner support the realist view that the relative-gains problem may hinder efforts by states to achieve otherwise mutually beneficial forms of cooperation. In a study of U.S.-Japanese state interactions affecting cooperation between corporations based in their respective countries, Mastanduno finds that important elements of the U.S. government became more concerned about the distribution of gains between the United States and Japan in the fields of fighter aircraft, civilian satellites, and high-definition television (HDTV) as Japan went from a position of clear subordination in these areas prior to the 1980s to one of substantial competitiveness during that decade. He demonstrates that organizational politics determined whether the U.S. government actually acted on the basis of such relative-gains concerns, and he shows that the U.S. government, though deciding not to intervene in the HDTV area, did seek to reduce what it viewed to be unfavorable distributions of gains in the cases of satellites and to some degree aircraft.[51]

Stephen Krasner presents similar findings in his study of international cooperation in the field of global communications.[52] He demonstrates that in instances in which states have had to coordinate their policies so that global communications could grow and provide important absolute benefits to all—the allocation of the electromagnetic spectrum for radio transmissions, telecommunications, and satellite communications—much of the negotiations revolved around the precise distribution of gains. The states in these negotiations all agreed that coordination would allow each to enjoy an improvement in its absolute welfare. However, they disagreed as to the distribution of rewards to be generated by their cooperation. According to Krasner, what then determined whether cooperation would occur, and what form it would take, was the relative power of the United States, the European countries, and the developing countries in the particular field of communications in which they were trying to coordinate policies.

In sum, realists have argued that cooperation among states is difficult to achieve because of fears about cheating, dependency, and relative gains. Yet realist-informed scholars have also argued that cooperation can be achieved and have tried to specify the conditions necessary for it.

Conditions for Cooperation: Hegemonic Leadership. As noted earlier, a long-standing realist argument is that states will cooperate through alliances in order to balance against external challengers. In addition, realist-informed scholars have sought to develop an explanation for cooperation in the international political economy: the theory of hegemonic leadership.[53] Drawing from the theory of collective goods, Robert Gilpin and Stephen Krasner argue that a necessary condition for the formation and maintenance of a liberal (i.e., market-based) international economy is that a single state be available that is both able and willing to invest the resources and to bear the burdens associated with the operation of such an economic order.[54] According to Gilpin, the worldwide spread of British foreign direct investment during the nineteenth century was a manifestation and a key element of a liberal world economy that in turn was made possible by British power, and the similar spread of U.S.-based firms around the globe in the 1950s and 1960s was the result of the liberal international order established by the United States immediately after World War II.[55] Similarly, Krasner suggests that changes in relative national power—in particular, the rise and decline first of Britain and then of the United States—explain many of the changes in the degree of openness that can be observed in the international-trade order from the early nineteenth century through the latter third of the twentieth century.

The Gilpin/Krasner argument about hegemonic leadership has been subjected to sustained critical examination. For example, John Conybeare, Timothy McKeown, Arthur Stein, and Duncan Snidal identify important problems with its theoretical logic. McKeown and Stein also question the historical interpretation offered by Gilpin and Krasner regarding the degree to which Britain played a key role in bringing about freer trade during the nineteenth century, and Stein criticizes Krasner's argument that protectionism increased in the late nineteenth century in the way and to the degree suggested by Krasner.[56] Further, Robert Keohane suggests that what he terms the hegemonic stability thesis, although helpful in accounting for changes in the post–World War II international petroleum regime, does less well with regard to money and especially trade.[57] He also suggests that the hegemonic stability thesis is unable to account for the continuance of what he takes to be moderately high levels of economic cooperation among the advanced democracies in the 1970s and 1980s in spite of the apparent decline of the U.S. hegemon.[58] Moreover, Bruce Russett and Susan Strange raise important questions about the Gilpin/Krasner view that there has been a deterioration in the economic order to the degree they suggested, about their thesis that U.S. material power has declined since the 1970s, and about their use of sheer economic-physical capabilities as a measure of U.S. hegemonic ascendancy and decline as opposed to (potentially still very great) U.S. military, technological, intellectual, and cultural capabilities and status in the world.[59]

Yet the realist-informed hegemonic leadership thesis still has life in it. For example, Joanne Gowa offers thoughtful realist-informed responses to two of the main criticisms often made of the hegemonic leadership approach, namely, that hegemons would be irrational to pursue free trade rather than an optimum-tariff strategy, and that hegemons are not really needed insofar as a small "k group" (a small number of system-critical countries) can by itself maintain a liberal economic trading order.[60] Further, John Ikenberry and Charles Kupchan show that one aspect of U.S. hegemonic leadership after World War II took the form of the United States using its power to socialize the Western European states to be more oriented to international economic openness.[61] In addition, David Lake demonstrates that the basic trajectory of U.S. trade policy from the latter quarter of the nineteenth century to the first third of the twentieth conforms to the basic expectations of the hegemonic leadership approach. For example, Lake argues that what might be called U.S. predatory protectionism at the end of the nineteenth century is consistent with the approach's thesis that in the face of (in this case, British) hegemony, some states will free-ride and use protectionism to advance national economic interests. Lake demonstrates further that, the 1930 Smoot-Hawley Tariff notwithstanding, as the United States became more economically developed it began to show limited leadership and sought to move its trading partners in a more liberal direction during the 1920s and the second half of the 1930s.[62]

Realist International Theory: Standard Criticisms, New Problems, and Prospects for Future Research

Many students have found realist theory to be helpful in their investigations of international relations. Other scholars, however, argue that realist theory is severely flawed and that there are sharp limits on its ability to shed light on international affairs. Many of the particular criticisms that scholars offer of realist theory have already been noted in the discussions of balancing, hegemonic leadership, system polarity and stability, and the relative-gains problem for international cooperation. In this section I discuss my own concerns about realist theory after assessing some of the standard criticisms in the international relations literature.

Standard Criticisms

The Issue of International Change

Criticism.   A major line of criticism that is pursued in regard to realist theory is that the approach does not recognize and cannot account for international change, including, very significantly, the end of the Cold War. For example, Friedrich Kratochwil provides a powerful critique of modern realist theory in the light of the peaceful end of the Cold War. His major theme is that realism could not anticipate and may not now readily explain the end of the Cold War because it pays too much attention to structural constants and not enough to domestic change and the evolution of norms that are commonly held among nations.[63] Of course this criticism regarding the momentous events of 1988–1991 is not being directed only at realist theory: John Lewis Gaddis argues that virtually every major behavioral and structural approach to international relations is fatally flawed because all failed to forecast the end of the Cold War.[64]

Speaking in more general terms, Robert Keohane argues that "realism is particularly weak in accounting for change, especially where the sources of that change lie in the world political economy or in the domestic structures of states."[65] Keohane acknowledges that Gilpin, for example, tries to explain the rise and decline of hegemons and the effect of this on war and peace among states, but he argues that Gilpin's theory is flawed insofar as its explanation of the decline of hegemons is partly based on domestic factors. Overall, according to Keohane, "this Thucydides-Gilpin theory is a systemic theory of change only in a limited sense. It explains the *reaction* to change systematically, in a rationalistic, equilibrium model. Yet at a more fundamental level, it does not account fully for the sources of change." Keohane goes on to suggest that "although it is insightful about systemic factors leading to hegemonic decline, it also has to rely on internal processes to explain the observed effects."[66]

Similarly, John Ruggie argues in his critique of Waltz's *Theory of International Politics* that Waltz fails to tackle the key question of how the modern interstate system evolved out of feudalism. Ruggie argues that Waltz is unable to explain such a momentous development because he ignores progressive increases in domestic integration—what Ruggie, following Emile Durkheim, calls increases in the "dynamic density" of societies. Today such increases, according to Ruggie, might be taking the form of "demographic trends, quantitative and qualitative changes in industrial production and location as well as in technologies, ecological and resource constraints, and shifts in the international balance of forces."[67] Ruggie suggests that he "would be surprised to learn that some of the changes alluded to above do not adversely affect the managerial capacity of bipolarity and, thereby, alter systemic outcomes."[68] Yet these factors, Ruggie stresses, are left out of Waltz's model, making the latter underdetermining; as Ruggie emphasizes, "the problem with Waltz's posture is that, in any social system, structural change itself ultimately has no source *other than* unit-level processes. By banishing these from the domain of systemic theory, Waltz also exogenizes the ultimate source of systemic change."[69] In a similar vein, Alexander Wendt suggests that the very ideas of "states" and "anarchy" are socially constructed—that is, they exist because individuals and human collectivities think they exist—and states could escape both anarchy and the dangers it engenders through new ideas and new, more cooperative practices.[70]

Response. One response by realist-informed scholars to this first general line of criticism might be to question its premise, namely, that what is most important "out there" is international change. Realists in fact have offered the counterclaim that continuities are more important than changes in interstate (and before that, intercity; and before that, intertribe) politics. Robert Gilpin, for example, although noting that there have been changes in statecraft, nevertheless makes it clear that, in his view, "the fundamental nature of international relations has not changed over the millennia." He goes on to suggest that as a result of such continuities in the nature of world politics, "the classic history of Thucydides is as meaningful a guide to the behavior of states today as when it was written in the fifth century B.C."[71]

Similarly, Waltz notes that "although changes abound, continuities are as impressive, or more so, a proposition that can be illustrated in a number of ways." One such illustration is that "one who reads the apocryphal book of First Maccabees with events in and after World War I in mind will gain a sense of the continuity that characterizes international politics"; another is that "whether in the second century before Christ or in the twentieth century after, Arabs and Jews fought among themselves and over the residues of northern empire, while states outside of the arena warily watched or actively intervened." For Waltz, then, "the texture of international politics remains highly constant, patterns recur, and events repeat themselves endlessly. The relations that prevail internationally seldom shift in type or in quality. They are marked instead by dismaying persistence, a persistence that one must expect so long as none of the competing units is able to convert the anarchic international realm into a hierarchic one."[72] Waltz also says more specifically with regard to unit-level forces that although they might in principle yield international changes, nevertheless "the structure of a system acts as a constraining and disposing force, and because it does so systems theories explain and predict continuity within a system. A systems theory shows why changes at the unit level produce less change of outcomes than one would expect in the absence of systemic constraints."[73] More recently Waltz assigns importance to one major unit-level factor—nuclear weapons—in bringing about a "troubled peace" among the major powers since 1945. Nevertheless, while there has not been war among the major powers, Waltz stresses that "states have continued to compete in economic, military, and other ways. The use of force has been threatened, and numerous wars have been fought on the peripheries."[74]

In sum, realists might first respond to the claim that they pay insufficient attention to change by suggesting that this relative neglect is warranted insofar as it allows them to concentrate their attention on what for them are the more important aspects of international affairs, namely, the continuities in state preferences in the face of the continuing absence of centralized international authority, and the resulting regularities in state behavior and international outcomes. Yet realists can go on to offer a second argument, namely, that while they find that there are important continuities in certain basic features of world politics, they nevertheless observe and can account for some very important shifts in national policies and in international outcomes.

It will be recalled, for example, that the goal of Gilpin and Krasner is to formulate a structural theory that explains the rise *and* the decline of world liberal economic orders. It will also be recalled that Keohane accepts their point that change in the sense of the movement toward a more liberal order requires a hegemon, and restricts his critique to trying to show that such an order might endure for some period of time without the *continued* support of a hegemonic leader.[75] Similarly, it may be recalled that Lake's study sought to explain *changes* in U.S. trade policy over half a century by focusing on *changes* in the world trading position of the United States. In the same vein, one of the main conclusions that Barry Posen draws from his study of British, French, and German military doctrine during the interwar period is that a focus on *changes* in systemic constraints and opportunities provides a firmer grip on understanding *changes* in such doctrines than might be provided by a focus on such factors as organizational politics or technological change. For example, Posen finds that given Hitler's interest in aggression, Germany's geographic position in the center of Europe made it structurally more predisposed than France or Britain to take note of the potential efficacy of armored warfare and to develop the appropriate doctrine for the offensive use of tanks—the Blitzkrieg strategy. Similarly, the rise in German power, according to Posen, caused Britain, with some slippage, to shift from an air-deterrent to an air-defense-oriented strategy.[76] Thus, notwithstanding their claim that continuity in the basic elements of international politics is high and consequential, realists might claim that their theory actually does explain quite a bit of the change that we observe in the international system.

The Issue of Unit-Level Variables

Criticism. The second standard criticism that is frequently leveled against realism—and the line of analysis that largely undergirds the criticism that realism is unsatisfactory in its understanding of the question of international change—is that it does not take into account the impact of *domestic factors* (political, economic, and social processes) on the foreign behavior of states.[77]

Response. Realists might claim in the first place that it is not true that they pay insufficient attention to domestic forces in world affairs. For example, as noted earlier, Waltz has adapted his structuralist argument to suggest that it was nuclear weapons, together with bipolarity, that mitigated (but did not terminate) U.S.-Soviet competition during the Cold War. He also suggests that in the future nuclear weapons will probably restrain (but, again, they will not wholly prevent) big-power competition (especially in the technological-economic domain) if and as the international system moves toward a multipolar structure including the United States, Russia, Japan, China, and either Germany or a united Europe.[78]

Similarly, it may be recalled that Stephen Walt has modified realist theory to suggest that states do not balance only on the basis of power calculations, although this is a major factor in their calculations, but that they balance against threats. One important element of such threat calculations, according to Walt, is whether a particular state is *perceived by others* to have *aggressive intentions*.[79] In the same vein, Christensen and Snyder, in their discussion noted earlier of chain-ganging and buck-passing, do not argue that a focus on decisionmaker perceptions about the efficacy of offensive strategies can by itself account for international conflict—that is, that it can replace structural theory—but rather that a focus on perceptions helps to account for the particular way in which multipolarity breeds such conflict.[80]

Displaying a similar sensitivity to unit-level factors but placing them in a context of a systemic explanation, Posen notes that institutional dynamics—and in particular the availability of individual "mavericks" such as General Heinz Guderian in Germany and Fighter Command chief Sir Hugh Caswell Dowding in Britain—play an important facilitating role in allowing systemic constraints and opportunities to make themselves felt and thus to yield doctrinal innovations.[81] Along the same lines, I suggest in *Cooperation Among Nations* that one reason a state might be concerned about relative gains arising from a cooperative agreement to liberalize trade might be its concern that the partners possess domestic structures better suited to take advantage of the new commercial opportunities produced by such an arrangement. In particular, that Economic Community (EC) members were concerned that their regulatory frameworks and overall capacity to compete internationally would allow the United States to achieve dispro-portionate gains from an aggressive implementation of the Tokyo Round government procurement and technical standards codes, and this concern led the EC to resist the United States (and the Nordic countries) in pressing for such an aggressive administration of those two codes.[82] Finally, Walt finds that a state that experiences a revolution is particularly likely to view the international environment as being hostile, and others are especially likely to view that state as being dangerous, and the resulting "spiraling" of mutual suspicion, fear, and perceived threat may ultimately propel all to-ward war.[83]

Hence realist-informed scholars have demonstrated an acute awareness of unit-level factors, and they have moved to incorporate such factors into their systemic-level arguments. But realists might even go further in re-sponding to the criticism that realism ought to focus on unit-level variables and say that in addition to, or perhaps instead of, such domestic structures affecting outcomes in the international system, it is the former that are ac-tually shaped by the latter. For example, Posen suggests that Franco-Prussian/German military conflict from the mid-1800s to the outbreak of World War I was itself an important (but by no means the only) cause for many of the military and, more interestingly, the educational reforms that took place in each of the two countries during that period. France and Prussia/Germany, Posen argues, sought to have available a pool of disci-plined, motivated, and above all *nationalistic* soldiers willing to work to-gether as effective military units and to accept the enormous hazards asso-ciated with large-scale land warfare as it was then developing in Europe. Therefore, each state moved to institute educational programs for progres-sively larger portions of their respective populations in order to increase military efficiency and, more important, to transmit to young men a na-tional "high culture" to which they would assign their loyalty and in the defense of which they would, if necessary, willingly give their lives.[84]

This argument about the impact of interstate dynamics on the specific characteristics of domestic political, social, and perhaps even cultural structures is anticipated and supported by the work of such historians as Otto Hintze.[85] It is also a major theme proposed by students of compara-tive government and sociology. Aristide Zolberg, for example, discussing the political development of the European states between 1450 and 1750, suggests that the simultaneous emergence of a number of such entities both created a system of states and that this system "developed its own particular dynamism whose repercussions may be regarded as specific vari-ables having retroactive effects upon each unit of the whole."[86] Similarly, Charles Tilly notes that one of Gabriel Ardant's most controversial in-sights is that "the pressure to extend the suffrage, increase national con-sciousness, give representation to the working classes, and generally draw the bulk of the national population into political life, which so marked the nineteenth century in Europe, came to an important degree from the fiscal demands of the great military and administrative machines brought into being by the Napoleonic Wars."[87] In addition, Theda Skocpol demonstrates that the French, Russian, and Chinese revolutions were in great measure triggered by, and followed a particular path as a result of, the interstate strategic situation in which these countries found themselves prior to the onset of domestic sociopolitical turbulence.[88] Finally, Brian Downing shows that variance in the geostrategic situation of European countries led to different national reactions to the military revolution of the sixteenth and seventeenth centuries—that is, the development of expensive modes of warfare requiring large land armies and therefore vast increases in state revenues. Downing also finds that this difference in state responses to the need for resources to meet the requirements of the military revolution was an important contributing factor leading, for example, to the long-run development of a hard form of militaristic absolutism in Brandenburg-Prussia on the one hand and, on the other, constitutional government and ultimately democracy in a more favorably positioned England.[89]

Hence it is highly possible that important features of the domestic institutions of states, aspects of the ways in which those institutions work, and the manner in which they emerged and developed historically—that is, the way in which social mobilization occurs or "dynamic density" increases—may be the result of interstate competitive forces and dynamics.[90] Realist theory, it should also be noted, has at its disposal an explanation for such an observation of external influences on internal development. That is, Waltz suggests that states are socialized over time into acceptance of interests and policies required by their anarchical environment as a result of experiences in that environment, and, as noted earlier, they have the ability to learn not just from those direct experiences but from observation and imitation of others as well.[91] This argument, as Posen suggests, can be readily applied not just to external influences on national interests and policies, but also to the development of national institutions. If this is so, then in fact Ruggie's important challenge to realism can be addressed effectively: The international system may be "generative" not just in the sense of inducing and constraining national behavior in the international system but also in the sense of shaping the timing and manner of the emergence of that system and even the character of the entities—that is, the internal structures of nation-states—constituting that system. Indeed, as Markus Fischer suggests, the (mostly conflictual) relationships of the various political entities that existed during the feudal period themselves appear to have emerged and evolved without effective and legitimate centralized authority, and were driven instead by the exercise of raw power, and therefore the character of those relationships appears to be readily explained by realist-informed concepts and arguments.[92]

Additional Puzzles and Problems for Realism

Realism may be quite successful in responding to the general criticisms discussed thus far. However, there are at least two other problems in realism that may leave realists with less reason to be sanguine.

The European Union and the Continuing Puzzle of International Institutions

The Issue.   Realist theory, as made clear by an important essay by John Mearsheimer, heavily discounts the salience of international institutions as objects of state policy or as autonomous actors in world politics.[93] Yet states (especially in the post–World War II era) seem to have a persistent habit of investing time and resources in the construction of institutions. An important example of state attention to and investment in institutions is the recent and quite remarkable resurgence of the European Community, now renamed the European Union (EU), beginning in the mid-1980s and carrying over into the early 1990s: the Single Market Program, such technology programs as ESPRIT and EUREKA, and especially the attempt (now seriously off-track) to attain Economic and Monetary Union (EMU) by the end of the 1990s. The interest displayed by the European countries in the EU creates a problem for realist theory.[94] That is, it may bring into conflict some of the major assumptions that realist theory makes about states and its major proposition about international institutions.[95]

Realism's core assumptions, it will be recalled, include the ideas that states are rational in their specification of goals and in their selection among alternative policy instruments, and that the substantive and the instrumental rationality of states is influenced heavily by international anarchy. Its major proposition about international organizations is that states, as a result of the danger-laden context of international anarchy, are extremely unwilling to assign importance to international institutions or to allow them to constrain their freedom of action. The problem for these key aspects of realist theory is that the EU's resurgence in the late 1980s and early 1990s entails the assignment by member states of greater responsibilities to EU institutions, and several elements of the union's proposed institutional program in monetary policy could lead to a fundamental shift in policymaking authority from the national to the union level. Hence the EU's revitalization puts realists in an awkward position: Either they must say that the EU member states have been behaving irrationally in assigning such greater authority to the union, or they must acknowledge that their understanding of international institutions is defective.

The best realist-informed response that is now available to the challenge of the EU attempts at reform and revitalization is to argue that its member states are increasing their cooperation in order to balance against Japan. This is a powerful argument. Yet the balancing argument raises a problem that realists would themselves pinpoint. It is quite possible that the EU members fortified their commitment to work together in the late 1980s in part to balance against Japan; however, this increased cooperation took place precisely as Germany was hegemonic in the area in which the EU renaissance was most ambitious—monetary affairs—and has continued (albeit with great unevenness) even though Germany might be poised to achieve relatively greater power in Europe. This is possible because of German unification (after a costly and difficult transition period) as well as the integration of the East European states into the West European economy, which will probably benefit Germany disproportionately, and because countries that are relatively more tightly connected to Germany, such as Austria and Sweden, have joined the EU. Hence, on the basis of realist theory, one might expect balancing against Germany by the other Europeans. Yet not only are these partners failing to balance against a potentially more powerful Germany, but they also appear to be "bandwagoning" toward Germany by way of integrating more closely with it in the context of the institutions of the EU. This would appear to be in contradiction to what one would expect of them on the basis of realist theory.

Possible Paths: Voice Opportunities and Dominance Rationalization. Scholars who find realism to be a helpful starting point for analyzing international politics may wish to review the realist perspective on international organizations. In particular, efforts need to be made to develop a realist-informed argument as to why the EU countries have been seeking to bring about a significant development of European institutions, and, more generally, why international institution-building may be a rational strategy for states.

One possible line of analysis in this respect might be to suggest that relatively weaker states may choose to cooperate through an institution in order both to pursue balancing against an external challenger *and* to mitigate their domination by the strongest partner in the balancing coalition by ensuring that the institution is composed of rules and practices that provide the weaker partners effective "voice opportunities."[96] This thesis could account for aspects of the EU's efforts at revitalization and particularly the efforts by the member states to achieve EMU.[97]

The voice-opportunities thesis could allow realism to retain its core rationality and anarchy assumptions as well as its key argument that states fear domination by others, while shedding light on the tendency of states to structure their collaborative relationships through formal institutions. But what about Germany? Why would it accept institutionalization if it is precisely the objective of its neighbors to employ such institutionalization to limit and contain German influence?

In response to this question it might be suggested by realists that European integration has yielded Germany tremendous economic benefits. It has also permitted German reentry into European and world affairs. Finally, the diplomacy of the European Community and now the European Union makes it clear that no important European initiative can occur without German support, and the case of EMU shows clearly that Germany is now coming to dominate—in a tactful, diplomatic, but unambiguous way—the key characteristics of important union initiatives.[98] Earlier institutional arrangements—the European Coal and Steel Community, the European Economic Community, and the European Community—gave Germany ways by which it could again be a civilized element of Europe; the EU may now provide it with a vehicle by which it may exercise its great and possibly growing power discretely and legitimately and thereby dominate its neighbors without arousing substantial resistance on their part or even very much resentment.

The Problem of Security vs. Power Maximization

The Issue.   The second—and possibly more challenging—theoretical problem for realism can be phrased as a question: Does anarchy lead "normal" states to be security or power maximizers, and is there an observable difference between the two goals?[99] I suggested in the first main section of this chapter that states, from the realist viewpoint, are "defensive positionalists." That is, by virtue of being in an anarchical environment in which self-help is the principle of action and relative capabilities constitute the basis for such self-help efforts, states will seek to attain that level of capabilities and retain that margin of autonomy that are needed to maintain their relative power position. It is not expected, according to this view, that states will respond to their anarchical environment either by seeking to achieve the maximum absolute power that might be generated by their internal resources and external efforts, or, more pointedly, by trying to maximize the gap in power between themselves and others to their advantage.

However, there is an alternative view that has been put forward with great vigor from within the general realist perspective. Randall Schweller suggests that modern realist theory as presented by Waltz and Walt has a problem, namely, that "it views the world solely through the lens of a satisfied, status-quo state."[100] In contrast to their view that states are primarily interested in maintaining their position and thus their relative power standing in the international system, Schweller, drawing upon earlier realist writings, points out that at least some states want to change their status in the system and therefore will want to advance their relative power position.[101] Thus Schweller suggests that in an anarchical environment in which some states are dissatisfied, at least some of the latter will seek to be offensively positional—they will seek to maximize gaps in power to their advantage and will take big risks to achieve those gaps in relative power.

But it is not necessarily the case that only revisionist states will be power maximizers. John Mearsheimer suggests that, as a general matter, "states in the international system aim to maximize their relative power position over other states."[102] He seeks to fix this view in the same basic structure of assumptions presented in the first section: specifically, that interstate anarchy shapes state preferences, and one key result is that "the most basic motive driving states is survival."[103] There is no question that Mearsheimer grounds his power-maximization thesis about states in the realist (including the modern realist) tradition and its focus on state defensiveness: For any given state, "the greater the military advantage one has over other states, the more secure it is."[104]

This question of whether states seek to maximize power for its own sake or attempt to maximize security *and therefore* are power maximizers is an important one for realism for at least two reasons. First, if realists think that states value power *even more* than security, then they would need to expect states to bandwagon rather than balance in those instances in which the former yielded greater power than the latter. This is a point that is made to great effect by Schweller in his analysis of revisionist states.[105] Moreover, if states seek to maximize power and therefore bandwagoning may sometimes prevail over balancing, then realists would need to predict that we will see world hegemony from time to time. Yet realists want to argue that states balance and that balancing explains why the state system remains characterized over time by a multiplicity of independent states.

The second reason for the importance of the security-power issue is that an assumption that states value power above all else would require realists to change their current specification of the problem of international cooperation. That is, they would need to argue that states seek not to avoid gaps in gains favoring partners, but instead to maximize gaps in their favor. This would imply a vastly more aggressive specification of the interests of states in circumstances in which they are considering cooperation with others: It would mean acceptance by realists of what Arthur Stein correctly calls a mercantilist understanding of such interests.[106] Operationally, a strong desire to maximize gaps in gains would make cheating much more attractive to states, and therefore the fear of cheating would be much greater. States would also have a much more aggressive set of interests regarding the distribution of gains from cooperation. They would not be interested only in making sure that they obtained absolute gains, and they would not be satisfied if they received absolute gains and if partners did not achieve relatively greater gains; instead, they would seek to enjoy a gap in gains to their advantage. In specifying such a world, realists would be driven to argue that cooperation among states is essentially impossible to achieve. Yet this would cause them to face the unbearable burden of explaining why there is in fact a substantial degree of cooperation among states.[107]

The question of whether states seek maximum power or maximum security is, therefore, of major importance to realist theory. In the second section of this chapter I suggest that realism argues that the anarchical structure of the international system causes states to be defensive positionalists that are interested in security, not power. Yet Hans Morgenthau viewed states precisely as power maximizers. For example, he argued that "whatever the ultimate aims of international politics, power is always the immediate aim," and that "the aspiration for power being the distinguishing element of international politics, as of all politics, international politics is of necessity power politics."[108] With regard to how much power states want, Morgenthau argued "all nations actively engaged in the struggle for power must actually aim not at a balance of power, that is, an equality of power, but at superiority in their own behalf. And since no nation can foresee how large its miscalculations will turn out to be, all nations must ultimately seek the maximum of power available to them."[109]

One possible realist response to such citations from Morgenthau is to argue that he is not representative of realist thinking about the particular matter of state preferences for security versus power. It could be suggested, on the one hand, that he locates the ultimate source of state behavior not in the environment of states but rather in the nature of human beings, and on the other, that he attributes to the latter a deep, unchanging desire to dominate others for no other reason than to do so.[110] Yet other realists who seek to be more explicitly systemic in their analyses also ascribe a power-maximization preference to states. More awkwardly (in terms of opening realism to the difficulties noted earlier), *they suggest that states seek maximum power because they want security.* For example, Nicholas Spykman suggests that although states in the international system have many goals, as do individuals in domestic society, "international society is, however, a society without a central authority to preserve law and order, and without an official agency to protect its members in its enjoyment of their rights. *The result* is that individual states must make the preservation *and improvement* of their power position a primary objective of their foreign policy."[111]

This same attribution of a power-maximization preference to otherwise security-oriented states can be observed in John Herz's specification of what he calls the "security dilemma." Herz argues that "where groups live alongside each other without being organized into a higher unity"—that is, "whenever such anarchic society has existed"—one finds that "groups or individuals living in such a constellation must be, and usually are, concerned about their security from being attacked, subjected, dominated, or annihilated by other groups and individuals." Herz argues that states respond to this concern for security in the following manner: "Striving to attain security from such attack, they are driven to acquire more and more power in order to escape the impact of the powers of others. This, in turn, renders the others more insecure and compels them to prepare for the worst. Since none can ever feel entirely secure in such a world of competing units, power competition ensues, and the vicious circle of security and power accumulation is on."[112]

It might be suggested that regardless of whether early realist writers argued that states sought to maximize power, this problem no longer obtains with regard to modern realists and their focus on the defensive orientation of states. Yet there are at least two points in Waltz's *Theory of International Politics* in which he appears to suggest that states are power maximizers. First, in a discussion of the intellectual background to his own balance-of-power theory, Waltz notes that the latter is deeply grounded in realpolitik thinking. He summarizes the main elements of realpolitik as follows: "The ruler's, and later the state's, interest provides the spring of action; the necessities of policy arise from the unregulated competition of states; calculation based on these necessities can discover the policies that will best serve a state's interests; success is the ultimate test of policy; and success is defined as preserving *and strengthening* the state."[113] Here it appears that states are both security and power maximizers, and that there is no difference between the two goals. This same line of discussion is presented a second time in *Theory of International Politics* when Waltz suggests in discussing the bases of his balance-of-power theory that "the theory requires no assumptions of rationality or of constancy of will on the part of all the actors," and that "nor need it be assumed that all of the competing states are striving relentlessly to increase their power. *The possibility that force may be used by some states to weaken or destroy others does, however, make it difficult for them to break out of the competitive system.*"[114] Again, and in contrast to views on his part cited earlier regarding the primary interest of states in security as opposed to power, it appears that Waltz is saying that the competitive nature of the international system tends to foster in states a defensively oriented interest "relentlessly to increase their power."

A certain tension may also be discerned in Robert Gilpin's work on the question of the goals of states. On the one hand, Gilpin chides political realists for suggesting that states seek to maximize power by observing that "there have been many cases throughout history in which states have forgone apparent opportunities to increase their power because they judged the costs to be too high."[115] On the other hand, Gilpin himself seems to attribute offensive positionalism to states. Stressing the importance of economic issues in world affairs, for example, he suggests that "in a world of scarcity the fundamental issue in domestic and international politics is the distribution of the available 'economic surplus,' that is, the goods and services produced in excess of the subsistence needs of society. Groups and states seek to control and organize economic relations and activities in ways *that will increase their own relative shares of this surplus.*"[116] Similarly, and as part of his critique of the "new economic history" that posits the view that social and political arrangements are adapted to maximize social welfare, Gilpin suggests that "this liberal assumption regarding sociopolitical change takes insufficient account of the fact than an equal, if not greater, motivation for political change is the desire of groups, social classes, or states to increase their individual welfare at the expense of others and at the expense of economic efficiency itself."[117] Finally, in seeking to locate a restraint on the interest of states to increase their power, Gilpin finds it not in the international system but within states: "The strong tendency of interstate oligopolistic competition to stimulate states to expand their power is offset by the fact that power and its exercise entail costs to the society; the society must divert human and material resources from other social objectives."[118]

Possible Path Forward. Perhaps one way that realist theory may be able to avoid the power-security maximization trap is to restrict, in the manner suggested in general by Waltz, its expectations about the impact of anarchy on the interests of states regarding relative power. The argument would be that realism's focus on anarchy cannot readily lead it to expect more than that states are concerned primarily about their survival and security and that they seek to ensure both not by maximizing power to their advantage but by minimizing gaps in power that are likely to favor rivals or adversaries. This restricted understanding of the effects of anarchy on state preferences regarding power may itself be rather far-reaching, for it yields such important expectations as those regarding the tendency of states to choose balancing over bandwagoning, the tendency of states to fear functional differentiation, and the likely prevalence of the relative-gains problem for cooperation.

Of course there are states that seek to maximize their power, and some do so to enhance their security. Yet realists may wish to acknowledge that a systemic theory may not be able to account for these instances of state behavior by itself. They may wish instead to argue that the factors leading states to define their security problem in terms of the need for a favorable imbalance of power may be driven by such nonsystemic factors as military technology or the perceptions of national decisionmakers, although they could still argue that international anarchy exacerbates tensions or "tightens" the security dilemma.[119] At the same time, realists would be able to argue that realism's expectations and analyses become highly relevant as soon as a power-maximizing state comes into being and begins to operate in the international system—for example, that one would expect to see balancing against that highly assertive state.

Conclusion

Two conclusions may be drawn from the discussion in this chapter. First, realism provides a well-developed perspective on world politics. It has a clearly delineated set of assumptions, basic propositions, and empirical expectations regarding politics among nations across a wide range of international issue areas. It provides substantial (although certainly not complete) leverage on many aspects of international politics. Realism's particular strength lies in its pointing out and explaining important continuities in world politics. Yet it is also true that realism can be used to understand such vitally important dynamic aspects of international history as the emergence of the nation-state, the rise and decline of major powers, and the oscillation in history between international conflict and cooperation. Given its tight analytical parsimony and wide empirical reach, it is likely that realism will continue to play a key role in setting the terms of debate in the field of international relations.

Yet the second conclusion that may be drawn from this chapter's discussion is that there are important unresolved questions within the core of realist international theory. Among the most important of these are whether states are security or power maximizers, and whether this makes a difference for their behavior toward one another. There are also important empirical puzzles for realist theory regarding state balancing and state interests in international institutions. Realism may be a helpful approach to the study of world politics, but it has several problems, and it has certainly not yet reached intellectual closure. There are contributions yet to be made by realism to our understanding of world politics.

Notes

I thank Robert Art, Ajin Choi, Peter Feaver, and David Priess for their comments on this paper. I also received helpful comments when I delivered earlier drafts to a session of the Peter B. Lewis Series on "New Thinking in International Relations Theory," sponsored by the Center of International Studies, Princeton University, April 30, 1992, and to a panel at the "Workshop on International Relations Theory: At the Crossroads of the Post–Cold War Era," sponsored by the Institute of International Relations, Panteion University, Athens, May 27, 1994.

1. Hans J. Morgenthau, *Politics Among Nations: The Struggle for Power and Peace* (New York: Alfred A. Knopf, 1948).

2. This is the purpose Quincy Wright posits for the field of international relations in his *Causes of War and Conditions of Peace* (London: Longmans, Green, 1935).

3. Robert G. Gilpin, "The Richness of the Tradition of Political Realism," in *Neorealism and Its Critics,* edited by Robert O. Keohane (New York: Columbia University Press, 1986), pp. 304–305.

4. Kenneth N. Waltz, *Theory of International Politics* (Reading, MA: Addison-Wesley, 1979), p. 94.

5. Robert Gilpin, *War and Change in World Politics* (New York: Cambridge University Press, 1981), p. 18; also see p. 17.

6. Stephen Krasner, *Structural Conflict: The Third World Against Global Liberalism* (Berkeley: University of California Press, 1985), p. 28.

7. Anarchy, according to Waltz, means that among states, "formally, each is the equal of all the others. None is entitled to command; none is required to obey." *Theory of International Politics*, p. 88.

8. Raymond Aron, *Peace and War: A Theory of International Relations,* abridged edition, translated by Richard Howard and Annette Baker Fox (Garden City, NY: Anchor Press/Doubleday, 1973), p. 6.

9. Edward Hallett Carr, *The Twenty Years' Crisis, 1919–1939: An Introduction to the Study of International Relations* (New York: Harper Torchbooks, 1964), p. 109.

10. Waltz, *Theory of International Politics*, p. 113; and Waltz, *Man, the State, and War: A Theoretical Analysis* (New York: Columbia University Press, 1959), p. 232.

11. Waltz, *Theory of International Politics*, p. 111.

12. I thank David Priess for his help in formulating this paragraph on the meaning of state rationality.

13. On state sensitivity to costs as an element of rationality, see Kenneth N. Waltz, "Reflections on *Theory of International Politics*: A Response to My Critics," in *Neorealism and Its Critics*, ed. Keohane, p. 331.

14. A very helpful discussion of the question of realist theory and the problem of state autonomy is provided by Stephen D. Krasner in *Defending the National Interest: Raw Materials Investments and U.S. Foreign Policy* (Princeton: Princeton University Press, 1978). Also see David A. Lake, *Power, Protection, and Free Trade* (Ithaca: Cornell University Press, 1988), pp. 67–74.

15. I thank Ajin Choi for emphasizing to me that there is a distinction in realist theory between its assumptions of state consistency of the formulation of policy goals and coherence of state implementation of strategies in pursuit of those goals.

16. Gilpin, "The Richness of the Tradition of Political Realism," p. 305.

17. Waltz, *Theory of International Politics*, p. 126; also see pp. 91–92. Waltz (pp. 91–92, 111) treats the survival/security preference as an assumption and not a proposition derived from realist premises. However, I would suggest that it is the dangers that result from international anarchy that cause states to focus so heavily on survival and security.

18. Krasner, *Structural Conflict*, p. 28.

19. Aron, *Peace and War*, pp. 7, 64.

20. Morgenthau, *Politics Among Nations*, p. 112.

21. This term resulted from a telephone conversation I had with Robert Jervis in the fall of 1987.

22. On this point, see Waltz, *Theory of International Politics*, p. 106.

23. For examples of scholarship that criticizes the assumption that states can be autonomous from their respective societies, see Peter A. Gourevitch, "International Trade, Domestic Coalitions, and Liberty: Comparative Responses to the Crisis of 1873–1896," *Journal of Interdisciplinary History* 8 (Autumn 1977):281–313; Peter J. Katzenstein, "Introduction" and "Conclusion" in *Between Power and Plenty: Foreign Economic Policies of Advanced Industrial States,* edited by Peter J. Katzenstein (Madison: University of Wisconsin Press), pp. 3–22, 295–336; Jeffry A. Frieden, "Sectoral Conflict and U.S. Foreign Economic Policy, 1914–1940," in *The State and American Foreign Economic Policy,* edited by G. John Ikenberry, David A. Lake, and Michael Mastanduno (Ithaca: Cornell University Press, 1988), pp. 59–90; and Beth A. Simmons, *Who Adjusts? Domestic Sources of Foreign Economic Policy During the Interwar Years* (Princeton: Princeton University Press, 1994). Key examples of scholarship on how intragovernmental politics prevents states from acting coherently include Graham T. Allison, *Essence of Decision: Explaining the Cuban Missile Crisis* (Boston: Little, Brown and Company, 1971); and John Steinbruner, *The Cybernetic Theory of Decision* (Princeton: Princeton University Press, 1974). Finally, for important examples of scholarship that argues that individual-level psychological and cognitive factors prevent national leaders from making decisions rationally in the way expected by a systemic perspective, see Ole R. Holsti, *Crisis Escalation War* (Montreal: McGill University Press, 1970); Robert Jervis, *Perception and Misperception in International Politics* (Princeton: Princeton University Press, 1976); Irving L. Janis, *Groupthink* (Boston: Houghton Mifflin, 1980); Richard Ned Lebow, *Between Peace and War: The Nature of International Crises* (Baltimore: Johns Hopkins University Press, 1981); Deborah Welch Larson, *Origins of Containment: A Psychological Explanation* (Princeton: Princeton University Press, 1985); and Robert Jervis, Richard Ned Lebow, and Janice Gross Stein, *Psychology and Deterrence* (Baltimore: Johns Hopkins University Press, 1988).

24. See Krasner, *Defending the National Interest*; and Stephen D. Krasner, "United States Commercial Policy: Unravelling the Paradox of External Strength and Internal Weakness," *Between Power and Plenty*, ed. Katzenstein, pp. 51–87. Joanne Gowa offers a useful critique of Krasner's trade-monetary and congressional-executive dichotomies as a basis for specifying the conditions under which the state may be more or less insulated from societal pressures; she argues that a more parsimonious and accurate analysis can be gleaned through the use of the theory of collective action. See Joanne Gowa, "Public Goods and Political Institutions: Trade and Monetary Policy Processes in the United States," in *The State and American Foreign Economic Policy*, ed. Ikenberry, Lake, and Mastanduno, pp. 15–32.

25. G. John Ikenberry, "Market Solutions for State Problems: The International and Domestic Politics of American Oil Decontrol," in *The State and American Foreign Economic Policy*, ed. Ikenberry, Lake, and Mastanduno, pp. 151–178.

26. Lake, *Power, Protection, and Free Trade*; also see Lake, "The State and American Trade Strategy in the Pre-hegemonic Era," in *The State and American Foreign Economic Policy*, ed. Ikenberry, Lake, and Mastanduno, pp. 33–58.

27. See, for example, Morgenthau, *Politics Among Nations*, p. 136, and Waltz, *Theory of International Politics*, p. 168.

28. Aron, *Peace and War*, pp. 118–119.

29. Aron, *Peace and War*, p. 121.

30. Ibid., pp. 118–119, 121. Similarly, Morgenthau argues that "the struggle between an alliance of nations defending their independence against one potential conqueror is the most spectacular of the constellations to which the balance of power gives rise"; he suggests further that "the opposition of two alliances, one or both pursuing imperialistic goals and defending the independence of their members against the imperialistic aspirations of the other coalition, is the most frequent constellation within the system of the balance of power." Morgenthau, *Politics Among Nations*, pp. 138–139. One can see from the Morgenthau quotation that at least one coalition may have imperialistic goals; but note also that he does not say that it is inevitable that both will, and that he does say that only one might.

31. Waltz, *Theory of International Politics*, pp. 126–127.

32. See Stephen M. Walt, *The Origins of Alliances* (Ithaca: Cornell University Press, 1987); and Walt, "Testing Theories of Alliance Formation: The Case of Southwest Asia," *International Organization* 42 (Spring 1988):275–316. Another realist-informed analysis of Egypt's alliance choices through the late 1970s is provided by Shibley Telhami, *Power and Leadership in International Bargaining: The Path to the Camp David Accords* (New York: Columbia University Press, 1990).

33. Paul W. Schroeder, "Historical Reality vs. Neo-realist Theory," *International Security* 19 (Summer 1994):108–148. For an interesting response to Schroeder's critique, and Schroeder's rejoinder, see Colin Elman and Miriam Fendius Elman, and Paul W. Schroeder, "Correspondence: History vs. Neo-realism: A Second Look," *International Security* 20 (Summer 1995):182–195.

34. Schroeder, "Historical Reality vs. Neo-realist Theory," p. 117.

35. Michael N. Barnett and Jack S. Levy, "Domestic Sources of Alliances and Alignments," *International Organization* 45 (Summer 1991):369–395.

36. Ibid., p. 379. Barnett and Levy specifically refer to Walt's *Origins of Alliances* and Telhami's *Power and Leadership*.

37. For a discussion of the capacity of such carefully chosen case studies to permit highly suggestive tests of competitive theories, see Harry Eckstein, "Case Study and Theory in Political Science," in *Strategies of Inquiry*, edited by Fred I. Greenstein and Nelson W. Polsby, volume 7 of *Handbook of Political Science* (Reading, MA: Addison-Wesley, 1975), pp. 118–120; and Arthur Stinchcombe, *Constructing Social Theories* (New York: Harcourt Brace, 1968), pp. 19–20.

38. Steven R. David, "Explaining Third World Alignment," *World Politics* 43 (January 1991):233–256.

39. Waltz, *Theory of International Politics*, pp. 138, 158–159, 163–176. For the alternative argument—that multipolar systems are more stable than bipolar systems—see Karl W. Deutsch and J. David Singer, "Multipolar Power Systems and International Stability," in *International Politics and Foreign Policy: A Reader in Theory and Research*, revised edition, edited by James N. Rosenau (New York: Free Press, 1969), pp. 315–324.

40. Thomas J. Christensen and Jack Snyder, "Chain Gangs and Passed Bucks: Predicting Alliance Patterns in Multipolarity," *International Organization* 44 (Spring 1990):137–168.

41. Ted Hopf, "Polarity, the Offense-Defense Balance, and War," *American Political Science Review* 85 (June 1991):475–493.

42. Joanne S. Gowa, *Allies, Adversaries, and International Trade* (Princeton: Princeton University Press, 1994).

43. John J. Mearsheimer, "Back to the Future: Instability in Europe After the Cold War," in *The Cold War and After: Prospects for Peace,* edited by Sean M. Lynn-Jones (Cambridge, MA: MIT Press, 1991), pp. 141–192. For arguments that Europe has the potential to remain stable in spite of multipolarity, see Jack Snyder, "Averting Anarchy in the New Europe," in *The Cold War and After,* ed. Lynn-Jones, pp. 104–140, in which Snyder emphasizes that domestic institutional factors will play a much more important role in determining the future trajectory of European affairs than the structure of the international system; and Stephen Van Evera, "Primed for Peace: Europe After the Cold War," in *The Cold War and After,* ed. Lynn-Jones, pp. 193–243, in which Van Evera suggests that changes both in military technology (nuclear weapons) and in the sociopolitical structure of European countries resulting from World War II will likely yield a more peaceful European future than that envisioned by Mearsheimer.

44. Aaron L. Friedberg, "Ripe for Rivalry: Prospects for Peace in a Multipolar Asia," *International Security* 18 (Winter 1993/1994):5–33; and Richard K. Betts, "Wealth, Power, and Instability: East Asia and the United States After the Cold War," *International Security* 18 (Winter 1993/1994):34–77.

45. See Robert Jervis, "Cooperation Under the Security Dilemma," *World Politics* 30 (January 1978):167–214.

46. Waltz, *Theory of International Politics,* p. 106.

47. It may be argued, then, that one reason that trade increased during the postwar period was that the trade regime encouraged the growth of *intraindustry* as opposed to *interindustry* trade. For an assessment of the postwar trade regime that argues that it promoted intraindustry commerce—without, however, attributing this to realist-specified concerns about security and independence—see Charles Lipson, "The Transformation of Trade: The Sources and Effects of Regime Change," in *International Regimes,* edited by Stephen D. Krasner (Ithaca: Cornell University Press, 1983), pp. 233–272.

48. Waltz, *Theory of International Politics,* p. 105. Important discussions of the possible inhibitory effects of relative-gains concerns on the willingness of states to cooperate are also provided by Joanne Gowa, "Anarchy, Egoism, and Third Images: *The Evolution of Cooperation* and International Relations," *International Organization* 40 (Winter 1986):175–179; and Robert Jervis, "Realism, Game Theory, and Cooperation," *World Politics* 40 (April 1988), especially pp. 334–336.

49. Joseph M. Grieco, *Cooperation Among Nations: Europe, America, and Nontariff Barriers to Trade* (Ithaca: Cornell University Press, 1990), pp. 10, 44.

50. See Duncan Snidal, "Relative Gains and the Pattern of International Cooperation," *American Political Science Review* 85 (September 1991):701–726; Robert Powell, "Absolute and Relative Gains in International Relations Theory," *American Political Science Review* 85 (December 1991):1303–1320; and Helen Milner, "International Theories of Cooperation Among Nations: Strengths and Weaknesses," *World Politics* 44 (April 1992):466–496. The essays by Snidal and Powell, together with a critical essay by Robert Keohane, "Institutionalist Theory and the Realist Challenge After the Cold War," are also in *Neorealism and Neoliberalism: The Contemporary Debate,* edited by David A. Baldwin (New York: Columbia University Press, 1993). In addition, see Emerson M.S. Niou and Peter C. Ordeshook, "'Less Filling, Tastes Great'": The Realist-Neoliberal Debate," *World Politics* 46 (January 1994):209–234. I try to respond to the arguments put forward

by Snidal, Powell, and Keohane and offer some additional thoughts on the subject of relative gains in my essay for the Baldwin volume, "Understanding the Problem of International Cooperation: The Limits of Neoliberal Institutionalism and the Future of Realist Theory," pp. 301–338. I respond to Snidal and Powell more fully, and they provide rejoinders, in "The Relative Gains Problem for International Cooperation," *American Political Science Review* 87 (September 1993):729–743. David Baldwin provides a superior assessment of the entire debate in his own contribution to *Neorealism and Neoliberalism,* "Neoliberalism, Neorealism, and World Politics," pp. 3–25. For additional insightful commentary, see Helen Milner, "International Theories of Cooperation Among States: Strengths and Weaknesses," *World Politics* 44 (April 1992):466–496; and Robert Powell, "Anarchy in International Relations Theory: The Neorealist-Neoliberal Debate," *International Organization* 48 (Spring 1994):313–344.

51. Michael Mastanduno, "Do Relative Gains Matter? America's Response to Japanese Industrial Policy," *International Security* 16 (Summer 1991):73–113 (reprinted in abridged form in *Neorealism and Neoliberalism,* ed. Baldwin, pp. 250–266).

52. Stephen D. Krasner, "Global Communications and National Power: Life on the Pareto Frontier," *World Politics* 43 (April 1992):351–360 (reprinted in abridged form in *Neorealism and Neoliberalism,* ed. Baldwin, pp. 234–249).

53. I have previously brought together many of the essays noted in this discussion of the hegemonic leadership literature and provide a brief introduction to its development. See Joseph M. Grieco, ed., *The International System and the International Political Economy,* vol. 1, *Hegemony and Cooperation in the International System* (Aldershot, UK: Edward Elgar Publishing, 1993). For a comprehensive review and a thoughtful assessment of the hegemonic-leadership literature, see David A. Lake, "Leadership, Hegemony, and the International Economy: Naked Emperor or Tattered Monarch with Potential?" *International Studies Quarterly* 37 (December 1993):459–489.

54. Gilpin's key works on this subject are "The Politics of Transnational Relations," in *Transnational Relations and World Politics,* edited by Robert O. Keohane and Joseph S. Nye Jr. (Cambridge, MA: Harvard University Press, 1972), pp. 48–69; *U.S. Power and the Multinational Corporation: The Political Economy of Foreign Direct Investment* (New York: Basic Books, 1975); and *The Political Economy of International Relations* (Princeton: Princeton University Press, 1987), especially pp. 72–80, 85–97. In his thinking about collective goods and the role of a hegemon in providing them in the international economy, Gilpin draws from the key work of Charles P. Kindleberger, *The World in Depression, 1929–1939* (Berkeley: University of California Press, 1973). Krasner's important works on this subject include "State Power and the Structure of International Trade," *World Politics* 28 (April 1976):317–347; and "Power Structures and Regional Development Banks," *International Organization* 35 (Spring 1981):303–328.

55. In a later work, Gilpin stresses two points: (1) that his formulation of a hegemonic leadership/stability argument was directed toward developing an explanation not just for any form of international economic interaction but specifically a market-based economy, and (2) that his goal was not to argue that hegemony was sufficient to bring about such a liberal economic order but rather to show that it was

necessary. He emphasizes as well that he believes that additional necessary conditions for an economic order would include the widespread expansion of liberal ideology and common interests among the major trading partners that they would gain from more closely integrated markets. See Gilpin, *Political Economy of International Relations*, pp. 72–73, 88, 91.

56. See Timothy J. McKeown, "Hegemonic Stability Theory and Nineteenth-Century Tariff Levels in Europe," *International Organization* 37 (Winter 1983):73–91; John A.C. Conybeare, "Public Goods, Prisoners' Dilemmas, and the International Political Economy," *International Studies Quarterly* 28 (March 1984):5–22; Arthur A. Stein, "The Hegemon's Dilemma: Great Britain, the United States, and the International Economic Order," *International Organization* 38 (Spring 1984):355–386; and Duncan Snidal, "The Limits of Hegemonic Stability Theory," *International Organization* 39 (Autumn 1985):579–614.

57. Robert O. Keohane, "The Theory of Hegemonic Stability and Changes in International Economic Regimes, 1967–1977," in *Change in the International System*, edited by Ole Holsti, Randolph Siverson, and Alexander George (Boulder: Westview Press, 1980), pp. 131–162.

58. Robert O. Keohane, *After Hegemony: Cooperation and Discord in the World Political Economy* (Princeton: Princeton University Press, 1984).

59. Bruce Russett, "The Mysterious Case of Vanishing Hegemony, or, Is Mark Twain Really Dead?" *International Organization* 39 (Spring 1985):207–231; and Susan Strange, "The Persistent Myth of Lost Hegemony," *International Organization* 41 (Autumn 1987):551–574.

60. See Joanne Gowa, "Rational Hegemons, Excludable Goods, and Small Groups: An Epitaph for Hegemonic Stability Theory?" *World Politics* 41 (April 1989):307–324; Gowa, "Bipolarity, Multipolarity, and Free Trade," *American Political Science Review* 83 (December 1989):1245–1256; and Gowa, *Allies, Adversaries, and International Trade*.

61. G. John Ikenberry and Charles A. Kupchan, "Socialization and Hegemonic Power," *International Organization* 44 (Summer 1990):283–315.

62. See Lake, *Power, Protection, and Free Trade*, especially pp. 91–118 and 184–215.

63. See Friedrich V. Kratochwil, "The Embarrassment of Changes: Neo-realism as the Science of Realpolitik Without Politics," *Review of International Studies* 19 (1993):63–80.

64. See John Lewis Gaddis, "International Relations Theory and the End of the Cold War," *International Security* 17 (Winter 1992/1993):5–58.

65. Robert O. Keohane, "Theory of World Politics: Structural Realism and Beyond," in *Neorealism and Its Critics*, ed. Keohane, p. 159.

66. Ibid., p. 179, emphasis in original.

67. John Gerard Ruggie, "Continuity and Transformation of the World Polity: Toward a Neorealist Synthesis," in *Neorealism and Its Critics*, ed. Keohane, p. 150.

68. Ibid., p. 151.

69. Ibid., p. 152.

70. See Alexander Wendt, "Anarchy Is What States Make of It: The Social Construction of Power Politics," *International Organization* 46 (Spring 1992):391–425; and Wendt, "The Agent-Structure Problem in International

Relations Theory," *International Organization* 41 (Summer 1987):335–370. The prospects for such identity transformation may be limited. John Mercer, writing not from a realist viewpoint but basing his ideas on social identity theory, suggests that the simple division of people into separate groups that we call nation-states, and not anarchy in the sense of the absence of effective centralized authority, may yield self-regarding and thereby self-help-oriented states in the international system. Such a condition may not yield interminable conflict and does not preclude some forms of international cooperation, Mercer suggests, but at the least it produces competition, and the cooperation it yields is frequently (if not usually) directed against a third party. Jonathan Mercer, "Anarchy and Identity," *International Organization* 49 (Spring 1995):229–252.

71. Gilpin, *War and Change*, p. 7; he uses the same words on p. 211.

72. Waltz, *Theory of International Politics*, pp. 65–66. For additional statements by Waltz emphasizing continuity over change in world politics, see, for example pp. 72 and 118–119.

73. Ibid., p. 69.

74. Kenneth N. Waltz, "The Emerging Structure of International Politics," *International Security* 18 (Fall 1993):45.

75. See Keohane, *After Hegemony*.

76. Barry R. Posen, *The Sources of Military Doctrine: France, Britain, and Germany Between the Two Wars* (Ithaca: Cornell University Press, 1984).

77. In addition to the works cited in footnote 23, the recent development of the democratic-peace literature—which emphasizes and explores the apparent empirical regularity that democracies do not fight one another—is a clear challenge to the realist argument that domestic institutional forces are secondary in importance in driving world politics in comparison with the impact of international-systemic constraints. Key contributions to the democratic-peace thesis include Michael Doyle, "Kant, Liberal Legacies, and Foreign Affairs," *Philosophy and Public Affairs* 12, part I (Summer 1983):205–235, and part II (Fall 1983):323–353; Doyle, "Liberalism and World Politics," *American Political Science Review* 80 (December 1986):1151–1169; and Bruce Russett, *Grasping the Democratic Peace* (Princeton: Princeton University Press, 1993). A new study by Edward Mansfield and Jack Snyder suggests that *democratizing* states might be especially war-prone. Although this argument might weaken the democratic-peace thesis somewhat, it also challenges realist theory, for it still suggests that variance in a domestic institutional variable may induce significant variance in the behavior of states irrespective of their international situation. See Mansfield and Snyder, "Democratization and the Danger of War," *International Security* 20 (Summer 1995):5–38.

78. Waltz, "Emerging Structure of International Politics," passim.

79. See Walt, *Origins of Alliances*, pp. 25–26, 32–33, 167–171.

80. Christensen and Snyder, "Chain Gangs and Passed Bucks," especially 138–139, 146, 167.

81. Posen, *The Sources of Military Doctrine*, pp. 173–175, 208–213.

82. Grieco, *Cooperation Among Nations*, pp. 24–25, 188–193, 198–209.

83. Stephen M. Walt, *Revolution and War* (Ithaca: Cornell University Press, 1996).

84. Barry R. Posen, "Nationalism, the Mass Army, and Military Power," *International Security* 18 (Fall 1993):80–124.

85. See Otto Hintze, "The Formation of States" and "Military Organization," in *The Historical Essays of Otto Hintze,* edited by Felix Gilbert (New York: Oxford University Press, 1975), pp. 157–215.

86. Aristide R. Zolberg, "Strategic Interactions and the Formation of Modern States: France and England," *International Social Science Journal* 22 (1980):713. I offer some additional thoughts on the subject of the internal implications of external interactions of states and bring together a number of essays on the subject, including Zolberg's, in Joseph M. Grieco, ed., *The International System and the International Political Economy*, vol. 2, *State Structures and Strategies* (Aldershot, UK: Edward Elgar Publishing, 1993).

87. Charles Tilly, "Reflections on the History of European State-Making," in *The Formation of National States in Western Europe*, edited by Charles Tilly (Princeton: Princeton University Press, 1975), p. 55. Gabriel Ardant notes that during the nineteenth century "accelerating economic change and increased state power went hand in hand"; though compulsory service meant that governments did not have to pay for mercenaries, "it was still necessary, however, to feed, lodge, and equip armies which were larger than ever. It was also necessary to buy more technically perfect arms at more and more burdensome costs." The result was that "governments built the large, stratified administrations which their predecessors had dreamed of." Gabriel Ardant, "Financial Policy and Economic Infrastructure of Modern States and Nations," in *Formation of National States*, ed. Tilly, p. 219. For a detailed discussion of the relationship between international military competition and the formation of the British, French, and Prussian/German states, see Samuel E. Finer, "State- and Nation-Building in Europe: The Role of the Military," in *Formation of National States*, ed. Tilly, pp. 84–163.

88. Theda Skocpol, *States and Social Revolutions: A Comparative Analysis of France, Russia, and China* (Cambridge: Cambridge University Press, 1979). Skocpol also puts forward her arguments about the importance of interstate political-military competition in accounting for the trajectories of development of even large countries in "A Critical Review of Barrington Moore's *Social Origins of Dictatorship and Democracy*," *Politics and Society* 4 (Fall 1973):1–34; "France, Russia, China: A Structural Analysis of Social Revolutions," *Comparative Studies in Society and History* 18 (1976):175–210; and "Wallerstein's World Capitalist System: A Theoretical and Historical Critique," *American Journal of Sociology* 82 (March 1977):1075–1090. These essays are reprinted in Grieco, ed., *State Structures and Strategies*.

89. Brian M. Downing, *The Military Revolution and Political Change: Origins of Democracy and Autocracy in Early Modern Europe* (Princeton: Princeton University Press, 1992).

90. However, for an extremely interesting study of the development of the French nation-state and the decline of city-states in Italy and the Hanseatic League that persuasively calls for qualification of the argument that the formation of nation-states can be attributed wholly to international political-military competition, see Hendrik Spruyt, *The Sovereign State and Its Competitors: An Analysis of Systems Change* (Princeton: Princeton University Press, 1994).

91. On Waltz's thinking about state socialization in the international system, see *Theory of International Politics*, pp. 74–77, 92–93, 127–128.

92. Markus Fischer, "Feudal Europe, 800–1300: Communal Discourse and Conflictual Practices," *International Organization* 46 (Spring 1992):427–466. Also see the excellent resulting scholarly exchange: Rodney Bruce Hall and Friedrich V. Kratochwil, "Medieval Tales: Neorealist 'Science' and the Abuse of History," and Markus Fischer, "On Context, Facts, and Norms: Reply to Hall and Kratochwil," *International Organization* 47 (Summer 1993):479–500.

93. See John J. Mearsheimer, "The False Promise of International Institutions," *International Security* 19 (Winter 1994/1995):5–49; in addition, see Waltz, *Theory of International Politics*, pp. 88, 115–116. For responses to Mearsheimer's essay by Robert O. Keohane and Lisa Martin, Charles A. Kupchan and Clifford A. Kupchan, John Gerard Ruggie, and Alexander Wendt, and Mearsheimer's rejoinder to them, see the exchange in *International Security* 20 (Summer 1995):39–93. Mearsheimer's understanding of the realist perspective on international institutions is challenged by Randall L. Schweller and David Priess, "A Tale of Two Realisms: Expanding the Institutions Debate," *Mershon International Studies Review*, forthcoming.

94. For a realist critique of the view that the European Community is an important supranational authority, see, for example, Aron, *Peace and War*, pp. 411–415. For Waltz the cooperation among the Western European countries through the EC in the post–World War II era can be explained largely by bipolarity and the solving of the Europeans' defense problems by the United States. Waltz, *Theory of International Politics*, pp. 70–71.

95. I explore the issues discussed in the next two paragraphs in "The Maastricht Treaty, Economic and Monetary Union, and the Neorealist Research Programme," *Review of International Studies* 21 (January 1995):21–40.

96. This line of discussion follows the suggestions offered by Morgenthau regarding the European Coal and Steel Community in the second edition of *Politics Among Nations* in 1958, and, beginning with the third edition in 1966, the European Community; see, for example, Morgenthau, *Politics Among Nations*, 3d ed., pp. 531–534. In a similar vein, Paul Schroeder argues that the constraining of choice of one's partners is a motivation for states in establishing military alliances; they want to balance against an adversary and constrain and modulate the behavior of their partners. Schroeder, "Alliances, 1915–1914: Weapons of Power and Tools of Management," in *Historical Dimensions of National Security Problems*, edited by Klaus Knorr (Lawrence: University Press of Kansas, 1976), pp. 227–262.

97. I develop this argument in "State Interests and International Rule Trajectories: A Neorealist Interpretation of the Maastricht Treaty and European Economic and Monetary Union," *Security Studies* 5 (Spring 1996):176–222.

98. On Germany's near-total domination of recent EU diplomacy regarding Europe's path to EMU, see, for example, Lionel Barber, "Bonn Sets Agenda for Monetary Union," *Financial Times*, October 2, 1995, p. 2. Also see the recent essay by the former governor of the Bank of Denmark, Erik Hoffmeyer, "Bystanders at the Infighting: The Real Debate on Monetary Union Is About the Relative Power of France and Germany," *Financial Times*, February 9, 1996, p. 22.

99. A superior discussion of this problem is presented in Arnold Wolfers, "The Pole of Power and the Pole of Indifference," in Wolfers, *Discord and Collaboration: Essays on International Politics* (Baltimore: Johns Hopkins Press, 1962), pp. 81–102. Wolfers frames the analytical problem of power versus security in terms of

the debate between realists and idealists; today the problem is likely to be grounds for debate among realists.

100. Randall L. Schweller, "Bandwagoning for Profit: Bringing the Revisionist State Back In," *International Security* 19 (Summer 1994):85.

101. Ibid., especially pp. 85–88.

102. Mearsheimer, "The False Promise of International Institutions," p. 11; also see Fareed Zakaria, "Realism and Domestic Politics: A Review Essay," *International Security* 17 (Summer 1992):190–196.

103. Mearsheimer, "The False Promise of International Institutions," p. 10.

104. Ibid., pp. 11–12.

105. Schweller, "Bandwagoning for Profit."

106. Arthur A. Stein, "Coordination and Collaboration: Regimes in an Anarchic World," in *International Regimes*, ed. Krasner, p. 134.

107. For examples of efforts by critics of realism to pursue this line of analysis—that is, to attribute to realism the view that states seek to maximize gains *and* gaps in power to their advantage, and then to argue that such a view is untenable—see Snidal, "Relative Gains," pp. 172–173.

108. Morgenthau, *Politics Among Nations*, 1st ed., pp. 13, 15.

109. Ibid., pp. 155.

110. This is the view of Morgenthau's theory of world politics that is expressed by Waltz in *Man, the State, and War*, pp. 16–41. For an example of how Morgenthau ultimately explains international politics in terms of the desire of men to dominate others, see his *Scientific Man vs. Power Politics* (Chicago: University of Chicago Press, 1946; Midway Reprint, 1974), pp. 191–203.

111. See Nicholas J. Spykman, *America's Strategy in World Politics: The United States and the Balance of Power* (New York: Harcourt, Brace, and Company, 1942), p. 7, emphasis added; also see p. 41.

112. John H. Herz, "Idealist Internationalism and the Security Dilemma," *World Politics* 2 (January 1950):157. Also see Morgenthau, *Politics Among Nations*, 1st ed., p. 45.

113. Waltz, *Theory of International Politics*, p. 117, emphasis added.

114. Ibid., pp. 118–119, emphasis added.

115. Gilpin, *War and Change*, p. 51.

116. Ibid., pp. 67–68, emphasis added.

117. Ibid., p. 74.

118. Ibid., p. 95.

119. This is the path taken by Christensen and Snyder in "Chain Gangs," and Snyder in *Myths of Empire: Domestic Politics and International Ambition* (Ithaca: Cornell University Press, 1991).

8

Domestic Structure and International Change

MATTHEW EVANGELISTA

Linking domestic politics to international relations constitutes one of the most traditional approaches to the study of international change. Indeed, the use of domestic explanations for international developments predates the creation of the discipline of political science. The central questions in the study of international relations have long focused on change—especially change from a state of peace to a state of war—and philosophers and historians have sought explanations at the level of domestic politics (Waltz 1959). Explanations linking representative forms of government to pacific foreign policies, for example, date back to Rousseau and earlier (Doyle 1986). Even Thucydides—best known among political scientists for the affinity of his explanations to realist, balance-of-power theories of war—highlighted the impact of the different domestic polities of Athens and Sparta.

What, if anything, then, do domestic explanations for international change have to offer that is new? Ironically, perhaps the most promising development in the field is the recognition among scholars inclined toward domestic explanations for foreign policy that these explanations are inadequate. Many scholars understand that they must incorporate factors at the level of the international system into their explanations and, moreover, that they must do so in ways that are more systematic than the mere assertion that "everything matters." In some respects, we might speak of a convergence of traditions, where scholars favorable to realist approaches and inclined to treat the state as a unitary actor have also sought to integrate other levels of analysis into their explanations and to collaborate with those who were already doing so (e.g., Mastanduno, Lake, and Ikenberry 1989). Even the unalloyed neorealist accounts of international stability and change recognize that the impetus for international systemic transformations—for example, uneven economic growth that leads to shifts in the international distribution of power—resides in many instances in domestic causes: demographic changes, development of new technologies, and so on (Waltz 1979; Gilpin 1981).

The approach generally identified under the rubric "domestic structure" seeks to link the domestic and international levels of analysis by focusing on the state as the nexus of the two. The early work on domestic structure focused on the relative strengths of state and society—with the state defined most simply as the central government decisionmakers and bureaucratic apparatus (Krasner 1978)—the nature of their relationship, and especially the "policy networks" that linked them (Katzenstein 1978).[1] Purveyors of domestic structural analysis of international relations sought, among other things, to use their approach to bridge the gap between internal and external explanations for foreign policy and state development.[2] Both in the field of international political economy and in security studies, proponents argued that domestic structure provided a means of specifying the conditions under which external (realist) or internal (liberal or bureaucratic-politics) explanations would be more or less applicable. In the first part of this chapter I discuss some research that proposes domestic structure as a bridge between these competing theoretical approaches.

The state, as J. P. Nettl (1968) pointed out in an influential essay, is by its nature Janus-faced—it looks both to the domestic polity and to the external environment. Thus it lends itself particularly well to the role of analytic link between domestic and international levels, especially when understood as a component of the domestic structure. Domestic structure represents the relationship between state and society. In addition to helping to identify the most salient level of analysis for a given type of country or issue-area, it is often conceived as an intervening variable between domestic and international politics. Domestic structure works in both directions, providing domestic political forces access to foreign policymaking (what Kenneth Waltz [1959] called the "second image") and filtering the impact of the international environment into domestic politics (what Peter Gourevitch [1978] dubbed the "second image reversed"). In the second part of this chapter I summarize examples of analyses that employ domestic structure as an intervening variable in this fashion.

The domestic structural approach seems especially appropriate to the study of comparative foreign policy, to answering the question of why states that face similar international pressures and constraints—including major changes in the external environment—often respond very differently. Its relevance to explaining major global change is more uncertain. If it has any role to play, it is in linking the forces of the external environment to domestic political change and showing how the foreign policies that result from such linkages contribute to the transformation of the international system. It is a tall order, and one that the present theoretical development of the domestic structural approach suggests will not soon be filled. In the third section of this chapter I make a tentative effort to sketch out a role for domestic structural analysis in accounting for global change, using the case of the end of the Cold War as an example.

Domestic Structure as a Theoretical Bridge

The literature on domestic structures has served as a way of bridging the debate between internal and external explanations for foreign policy in issue-areas ranging from international political economy to international security policy. In political economy the external-internal divide is often characterized as a debate between realism and liberalism. In the security field the realist approach is contrasted to the bureaucratic-politics approach, which, as Theda Skocpol (1985, 4) put it, treats government agencies as "pure analogues of the competing societal interest groups of classical pluralism." Thus it makes claims for security policy similar to what the liberal approach makes for political economy. In both fields scholars have identified cases in which countries with divergent domestic structures faced common international pressures. They tested propositions derived from the competing internal and external theories and found that the relative power of each theory's predictions depended on the domestic structure.

The pioneering effort in this vein was Peter Katzenstein's (1976) comparison of U.S. and French energy policy—the first study summarized here. The second comparison presented here is a summary of my own work on U.S. and Soviet security policy.

Domestic Structure and International Economic Change

Katzenstein sought to illustrate the role that domestic structure plays in mediating states' responses to international economic changes. He developed simple propositions from realist and liberal theories and tested them against cases of the United States and France. Both faced the same external shock—the energy crisis of the 1970s, triggered by the Arab oil embargo imposed in the wake of U.S. support for Israel in the 1973 war. Katzenstein argued that in the wake of the oil embargo and the dramatic increase in oil prices, realist, external explanations would predict that each state would act as a unitary actor to seek to secure a supply of oil at the lowest possible prices for the overall national interest. Liberal, internal explanations would predict that government policy in each state would vary depending on the strength of the relevant interest groups, including the oil companies; the policy would be a result of competition between groups. Drawing on the traditional distinction in the study of international relations, Katzenstein suggested that given the same external impetus or constraints, realist theories would predict the pursuit of power by state actors, whereas liberal theories would predict the pursuit of wealth by societal actors.

France Versus the United States

To these approaches Katzenstein contrasted one based on analysis of domestic structures. This approach held that the response of each state to the oil crisis would depend on its domestic structure, in particular on the relationship between state and society. Katzenstein characterized France as having a strong state and a weak society, where political power was highly concentrated. He considered the United States, in contrast, to have a weak state and a strong society, where politics was characterized by social pluralism.[3]

Katzenstein argued that the domestic structure of each country was mainly a product of its history. In France rationalization of authority structures preceded the development of participatory institutions—state power came first, then democracy. In the United States, the pattern was reversed. After the French Revolution, the centralized political institutions in Paris came over time to be seen as representing the broad public interest against the power of local elites. In the United States, in contrast, the notion of the public interest was seen as being best served by weak state institutions; decentralization and dispersion of government power were seen as the best way to protect individual rights.

For Katzenstein, the historical evolution of state-society relations in the two countries shaped their contemporary structures. Hence French governmental institutions are highly centralized and their functions are differentiated—each ministry knows for which policies it is responsible.[4] In the United States the structure is decentralized and functions are fused. Departments, congressional committees, and the White House have overlapping jurisdictions—each organization feels entitled to promote its own policies, leading to national policy that is often stalemated or inconsistent. Concentration of power in the French state enhances its authority, whereas U.S. state power is circumscribed by a system of checks and balances.

In contrasting U.S. and French societies, Katzenstein argued that the impact of society on bureaucracy is the key to influence on government policy. In France the public bureaucracy traditionally has appeared to be above partisan politics, whereas in the United States bureaucracy is part of the political struggle (thus the mass exodus from government to think tank whenever the presidency switches from one party to another).

Comparing Energy Policies

Katzenstein's domestic structural approach predicted that French policy would approximate the realist, state-dominated pursuit of power, whereas U.S. policy would resemble the liberal, society-driven pursuit of wealth. In France's energy policy the main goal seems to have been to increase the country's autonomy and its access to a secure supply of oil. This policy was not simply a reaction to the oil crisis of the 1970s but a long-range strategy, going back several decades, comprising several components. First, the government has played an active role in the oil market. It has directly owned 35 percent of the stock of the Compagnie Française de Pétroles (CFP) since 1924. In 1965 the government formed its own company, Entreprise de Recherches et d'Activité Pétrolières (ERAP), to exploit oil from Algeria.

The second component of its strategy was the government's support of French oil companies against foreign competition. Beginning in the 1920s, it maintained a system of quotas that limited the role of foreign companies in importing, refining, and exporting oil in the French market. Ninety percent of all finished oil products had to come from domestic refineries. As of 1964 no new retail gasoline outlets were allowed to be constructed without government approval—another means of limiting foreign access to the domestic market. As a consequence, by the mid-1970s the French government controlled 80 percent of the refining and 35 percent of the distribution of oil. U.S. and other foreign companies saw a steady decline in their share of investment in the French petroleum industry.

The third component of the strategy was the development of special relationships with former French colonies in order to make France less subject to supply fluctuations on the international market. This policy, too, predated the oil crisis. The French government supported the operations of its companies in French colonial areas, for example. It spent the equivalent of over a billion dollars to underwrite the cost of drilling for oil in the Sahara during the first fifteen years after World War II. In Katzenstein's estimation, this long-term strategy implemented by a strong state apparatus ensured that the realist goals of autonomy and security of supply were consistently and successfully pursued.

In the U.S. case, in contrast, a domestic structural analysis would predict that strong societal forces, especially corporations, would be interested more in economic wealth and profits than in enhancing state power and autonomy. Although U.S. dependence on foreign oil has increased since the end of World War II, the vast majority of it has been imported by U.S. companies. How have the companies achieved their goals of expanded profits? In Katzenstein's view, they took advantage of the government, especially during times of crisis, when a secure supply of oil was essential. During World War II and the Korean War, for example, the weak U.S. state had no way to secure the flow of oil without relying on the big oil companies; they, in turn, demanded concessions. The oil companies cooperated with the U.S. war effort in the 1940s only in return for a government commitment to drop all pending antitrust legislation.

Even during normal times the oil industry has been able to exert its influence to extract concessions from the government, for example, in tax policy, overseas investment insurance, tanker subsidies, dry-hole drilling allowances, and the like. These policies are also used by the French government, but selectively and mainly to support particular goals, such as promoting French firms and decreasing the market share of U.S. firms. In the U.S. case the policies are straight subsidies with no strings attached.

In the early postwar period the oil companies used the U.S. government to help them dominate Middle Eastern oil. Between 1947 and 1950, as part of the Marshall Plan, the United States gave Western Europe US$384 million of oil produced by U.S. companies in the Middle East. As a result, the relative share of U.S.-produced oil in the Middle East rose from 38 percent in 1947 to 45 percent in 1950. More significantly, the dependence of Europe on U.S.-produced oil increased from 43 percent in 1947 to 85 percent in 1950. The U.S. companies during this period began to replace British companies as the main exporters of Middle Eastern oil. The French government was also involved in its companies' business in the Third World, especially the former French colonies. An important difference, though, is that the French state stayed involved in order to increase security of supply and autonomy. The U.S. state, in contrast, once it had been used by the oil companies to obtain a dominant position in the Middle East, could no longer influence the companies, except indirectly through fiscal policy (Ikenberry 1986). In the aftermath of the first oil crisis in October 1973, it became obvious that U.S. oil companies supported the price increase imposed by the Organization of Petroleum Exporting Countries (OPEC) because it increased their profits. Oil interests and state policy coincided as the U.S. government came to favor decontrol of the industry so that market mechanisms would raise prices and provide incentives for domestic production and conservation (Ikenberry 1986).

To summarize: A realist, state-as-rational-actor approach would have predicted similar responses in France and the United States to the same external events. The state would seek to secure an oil supply and enhance the autonomy of the country's oil production. A liberal, domestic-interest-group approach would view the state's policies as the product of internal politics and pressure from corporations. External factors would only come into play as windows of opportunity, which the corporations would use to their advantage. The domestic structural approach seeks to reconcile these two competing perspectives. It holds that countries with strong states and weak societies would lean toward realist responses, whereas countries with weak states and strong societies would lean toward liberal responses. Katzenstein's presentation of the French and U.S. cases seemed to bear out these predictions.

Domestic Structure and the Security Environment

The literature on security policy, both within political science and in the broader policy discourse, has long been characterized by a debate between internal and external schools. It parallels the debate in international political economy, with realists favoring assumptions of the state-as-unitary-actor and proponents of domestic-level explanations focusing on the role of bureaucracies and interest groups. Both approaches are amply represented in the literature on security policy and, in particular, arms races (Gleditsch and Njolstad 1990). I have compared the arms policies of the United States and the Soviet Union—specifically the processes by which they developed major new weapons—drawing simple propositions from realist and bureaucratic-politics approaches (Evangelista 1988). I argued that realist theory would expect each country to develop weapons in response to those of the other side in an "action-reaction dynamic" (Rathjens 1969), directed from the top of the political-military system and resembling the behavior of a unitary actor. A bureaucratic-politics approach, in contrast, would expect the initiative for major weapons development to come unsolicited from weapons laboratories, military contractors, and military services (Allison and Morris 1975).

The United States Versus the Soviet Union

There is a long tradition of comparative historical analysis of Russia and the West—most notably the works of Alexander Gerschenkron (1962) and Barrington Moore Jr. (1966)—that identifies the importance of differences in domestic structures for both economic and security policy.[5] The Russian pattern was very different from that of the United States and Britain. Those "early industrializing" countries took advantage of favorable geographic circumstances and a relative absence of international pressures to industrialize at a gradual pace. Industrialization was carried out by private manufacturers and financed by private capital; the limited role played by a weak state allowed for the development of democratic institutions.

Russia differed as well from the second pattern, the "late industrializers." In Germany and Japan the pressure of the international system and competition from more advanced countries required the state to take a leading role, for example, in mobilizing capital for industrial investment. This pattern resulted in strong authoritarian states with weak societal forces and a consequent absence of democracy. The third pattern, "late,

late industrialization," is typified by Russia and China. Under extreme international pressure, communist elites in these countries undertook costly campaigns of forced-draft industrialization to catch up with their more advanced competitors. The political outcome of such "revolutions from above" included highly centralized, strong states with weak, even atomized societies.

The pattern of sensitivity to foreign pressure leading to strong centralization and state intervention finds antecedents far back in Russian history,[6] but for our purposes the early Soviet period is of most relevance. Here one finds a strong relationship between military requirements and centralized, forced-draft industrialization. Stalin's ruthless policies of collectivization of agriculture and rapid industrialization were plainly intended to contribute to the buildup of Soviet military power, albeit at terrible cost to the populace. It seems apparent, then, that the international pressures faced by a late, late industrializer such as the USSR affect the development of both military and economic policy by fostering the growth of a highly centralized, strong, hierarchically organized state at the expense of civil society.

Although in the realm of security policy—especially in the USSR—it is sometimes difficult to distinguish between state and societal actors, one can nevertheless make sharp comparisons between the United States and the USSR on the basis of historically conditioned domestic structures. In this respect, one could characterize the United States as a weak state whose fragmentation and decentralization of authority permit multiple inputs into the policy process from the "bottom up." Policy initiatives in the strong, centralized, hierarchical Soviet state, in contrast, came from the "top down."[7] Thus one would anticipate U.S. policy to come closer to the bureaucratic-politics model, whereas Soviet behavior would conform more closely to realist expectations.

Weapons Innovation

My examination elsewhere (Evangelista 1988) of eighteen cases of U.S. and Soviet weapons innovation confirmed the expectations derived from comparing the two countries' domestic structures. Neither side's policies corresponded exactly to ideal-type realism or bureaucratic politics. Yet in the U.S. case the degree of independent initiative exerted from below, the efforts of political and technological entrepreneurs, and the frequent irrelevance of actual Soviet behavior to the success of new U.S. weapons programs bring the U.S. pattern much closer to an internal, bureaucratic-politics model than to a realist, unitary-actor model. The "bottom-up" approach was especially striking in the case of the development of the nuclear-powered submarine, the multiple nuclear warhead, and tactical nuclear weapons.

Major Soviet arms innovations were most typically reactions to Western initiatives (including, for the early Cold War period, weapons developed by Nazi Germany during World War II). Though the structure of domestic Soviet institutions of military research, production, and deployment gave peculiar features to Soviet responses, the Soviet case comes close in many respects to what a unitary-actor assumption would predict. Initiative came from the top of the political system to mobilize resources to meet the external challenge. The development of jet interceptor aircraft and ballistic missiles in response to the German wartime initiatives and development of the Soviet atomic bomb and tactical nuclear weapons during the postwar period are among the clearest examples of this phenomenon. Even in the late Brezhnev era, when Soviet military-industrial production seemed to be propelled largely by inertia, with greater scope for institutional and group interests, many weapons innovations, especially in aircraft, were direct responses to U.S. initiatives (Chaiko 1985; Lambeth 1991; Twigg 1994).

Thus, in both the economic and security-policy issue-areas, proponents of domestic structural approaches attempted to integrate competing theoretical perspectives and specify the conditions under which one or the other would apply.

Domestic Structure as Intervening Variable

Students of international relations and comparative foreign policy have increasingly drawn insights from the literature on domestic structures to apply to issues and countries that had fallen outside the scope of the original work. The trend has been toward broadening the domain of relevance of the approach. One area neglected by domestic structural analysis was the comparative study of the foreign policies of the Soviet-type countries. Simply describing them in that fashion—as "Soviet-type"—tells much of the story. Traditionally the East European states of the Soviet bloc were considered sufficiently similar to one another and different from other states to merit a category all their own. One study of the foreign economic strategies of these states explicitly argued that Katzenstein's type of domestic structural analysis was not particularly useful for understanding political-economic systems modeled on the Soviet system (Comisso and Tyson 1986). It emphasized instead "the unique political and economic structure of members of the socialist bloc" (Comisso 1986, 195) and employed concepts that treated the Soviet-type system as sui generis.

In the first part of this section, I question such a rejection of the domestic structural approach to the East European states of the former Soviet bloc. I employ domestic structure as an intervening variable to compare how Poland and Romania responded to the oil crises of the 1970s and the problem of foreign debt in the early 1980s. I find the approach useful both for understanding the differences between the two countries and for understanding their similarities to non-Soviet-type states. Both aspects appear more relevant now that the adjective "Soviet-type" has lost its contemporary significance for the states of Eastern Europe, and the benefits of placing those states in a broader, comparative framework is widely recognized.

By the late 1980s several scholars had used domestic structural analysis to explore aspects of security policy, including alliance strategy, force posture, and weapons deployment (e.g., Platias 1986; Evangelista 1988; Barnett 1990), that were originally deemed irrelevant to the debates over the relative autonomy of the state (Krasner 1978). Thomas Risse-Kappen's discussion (1991) of the relationship between public opinion and security policy represents a further advance both in the scope of the inquiry (the focus on mass publics) and in the sophistication of the notion of domestic structure. Risse-Kappen's linking of the structure of domestic institutions with coalition-building processes benefited from previous critiques of the simple strong state–weak state dichotomy (e.g., Ikenberry 1986) as well as developments in the thinking of the original advocates of domestic structural approaches (e.g., Katzenstein 1978, 1985; Gourevitch 1986). The second part of this section summarizes his use of domestic structure as an intervening variable between public opinion and security policy.

Economic Crisis, Domestic Structure, and Adjustment

Using domestic structures to compare how particular East European states reacted to common external economic events represents an endeavor similar to Katzenstein's comparison (1976) of France and the United States and his later edited volume (1978) comparing several advanced industrial states. Indeed, the initial external events are the same in each comparison—the oil price shock of 1973—but the consequences for relatively poor states of the "Second World" could be expected to diverge considerably from those of the "First World."

At first glance it seems that until recently the states of the former Soviet bloc all had such similar domestic structures that we should expect them to have responded in similar ways to the constraints and pressures of the international economy. They were all, for example, highly centralized, single-party states, with state-owned industry and weak, dependent labor unions. Here, however, I argue that despite these similar characteristics, we can identify differences in responses that are linked with different domestic conditions, or, in essence, different domestic structures. Later, I draw such a comparison between Poland and Romania (before the events of 1989), but first I describe in more detail what external events triggered the states' responses.

International Economic Conditions

The same economic events that evoked divergent responses in the advanced industrial states had a substantial impact on economies of the Soviet bloc as well. First were the major increases in oil prices in 1973 and 1974 and then again in 1979 and 1980. These helped to trigger a recession in the industrialized countries and led to a slowdown in world trade. For the countries of Eastern Europe—as for many developing countries—the recession threatened to derail their strategies for outward-oriented growth, which were dependent on exporting products to the industrialized world (Tyson 1986).

In the wake of the oil price hikes, the abundance of "petrodollars" deposited in Western banks posed a temptation to East European regimes, as the banks offered loans on generous terms. Before the loans could be used to foster productive investment, however, the second oil-induced recession hit. The recession was the longest in postwar history, lasting from 1979 to 1983—and even longer in the Second and Third Worlds. The recession prevented the countries that had borrowed heavily from being able to pay back their loans: They were unable to sell their exports in order to earn dollars to make the repayments.

The possible policy responses to such a predicament were generally twofold. The state could find new markets for exports—the solution adopted by the newly industrializing countries of East Asia. Or it could implement austerity programs, as, for example, the government of Mexico did when it pushed real wages down by 24.3 percent in 1983 and another 7.5 percent in 1984. Poland and Romania were insufficiently flexible to shift their exports to new markets. Their governments chose austerity, and the comparative analysis of their domestic structures explains their relative degrees of success.

Domestic structure in Soviet-type systems includes not only state-society interactions but also the relationship of state and society to the Communist Party (or its equivalent). For purposes of this illustrative comparison domestic structure will not be defined as precisely as, for example, in Risse-Kappen's study. The contrast between Poland and Romania will be fairly striking, much as the differences between U.S. and Soviet domestic structures were in our consideration of arms policies.

Poland: The Party's Demise, Civil Society's Rise

Poland had a long history of economic crises preceding the oil shock of 1973.[8] In 1970 workers protesting price increases were put down so harshly that a public outcry forced the removal of Wladyslaw Gomulka, the party first secretary. His successor, Edward Gierek, immediately set out to transform the party. By the end of 1971 he had removed not only most of Gomulka's supporters but also many of the people who had helped him to get into office. He replaced these people with the youngest, best educated, party officials in Eastern Europe, people who saw the party as a career rather than as a mission. The careerist orientation of the young bureaucrats had two consequences. In their lack of interest in ideological purity, party members began to resemble society as a whole. At the same time, however, the party lost whatever coherence it had because it was no longer unified by a common mission.

As a by-product of an effort to streamline and reduce bureaucracy, the party transferred several of its functions in local regions to state institutions. The party lost some of its control over enterprises and ministries, especially on questions of investment. In dealing with society, the regime tried to improve relations with both the workers and the Catholic Church. Strikes were not legalized, but they were generally met with wage increases rather than repression.

Gierek's economic policy entailed an expansion of involvement in the international market. He was personally interested in improving relations with the West, was on good terms with French president Valéry Giscard d'Estaing, spoke French, and spent a lot of time in Paris. The initial result of the international focus and the looser domestic atmosphere was positive, as reflected in a growth rate of 9.4 percent for the period 1971–1975.

When the economic situation began to deteriorate, with high oil prices and an inability to sell Polish goods abroad for hard currency, Gierek had to look for new policies. As Laura Tyson (1986) has noted, one of the first things most of the East European regimes did was to cut back on capital investment (new firms, new machinery, etc.) because these required imported inputs of equipment and raw materials. Gierek had some trouble controlling the level of investment because of his earlier reforms, which had given enterprises and ministries some autonomy from the party.

Another common area on which to focus, in order to implement an austerity program, is wages and price policy. Here there were three options: raise prices, decrease wages, or slow employment growth and even institute unemployment. The third option was basically ruled out for ideological reasons—a socialist country is supposed to provide secure employment. At first Gierek tried to hold down wages. Yet one consequence of the decentralization of the party and division within the top political leadership was that workers felt better able to assert their rights. They responded to pressure on their wages by launching a wave of several hundred strikes in the late 1970s. The strikes were generally followed by concessions in the form of wage increases, thereby defeating the purpose of the austerity program. With the failure of wage restraint, Gierek tried price increases. These too were met with protests and were reversed. The workers interpreted Gierek's actions as a sign of weakness and pressed for more concessions. The failure of his last attempt at an austerity program in the summer of 1980 led to the rise of the Solidarity trade union movement.

In December 1980 Gierek was removed from office (later, in the new capitalist Poland, he made a small fortune selling his memoirs). Stanislaw Kania, his replacement, had no better success. Why not? Because the main tool that a centralized one-party state needs—the party—was disintegrating. From September to December 1980, 50,000 members resigned. By December 1981 a half million members, or 17 percent of the membership, had left (reducing the party from 3.2 to 2.7 million members). Solidarity—already recognized by the government as an independent trade union in September 1980—was becoming increasingly popular.

Central control of the kind necessary to impose an austerity program and dominate strong social forces like Solidarity was not reestablished until the military took over in December 1981. The initial objective of General Wojciech Jaruzelski's coup was to crush Solidarity, but once that was done he put through an austerity program in February 1982. Prices of all consumer goods increased by 300 to 400 percent, increasing the cost-of-living index by 100 percent in the course of a year. Some compensation in wages followed, but real wages still fell by 25 percent as a result of the price reform. These measures succeeded in reversing the trade imbalance. With domestic consumption down, Poland began exporting more than it imported. But it still owed some US$25 billion to Western banks and was spending a large proportion of its export earnings simply to service the debt rather than to reinvest in the economy, renovate the technological infrastructure, and improve people's standard of living.

To summarize the case of Poland: In a centralized, communist-party state, one would expect to see quick responses to international economic disturbances and a great deal of flexibility. Society is considered weak relative to the state, and the state would be expected to implement an austerity program without much protest. In fact, in Poland, weakness and divisions within the party gave societal groups, especially workers, an opening to exert more influence and prevent the government from making adjustments to the international economy at their expense. Only when the army came in was it possible to enforce centralized control of the economy again—yet even this "success" was short-lived, owing to the tumultuous events of 1989.

Romania: Stalinism Confronts Economic Interdependence

In Romania there was never an erosion of centralized control and there was no assertion of independent power by social groups—until the violent upheaval of 1989–1990.[9] Nicolae Ceauçescu, the last Romanian communist leader before the 1989 revolution, came into power in 1965. His first task was to increase the power of the already highly centralized party apparatus and, in particular, his own personal power. The role of the parliament, the

Grand National Assembly, was limited to a largely symbolic function, and the same was true for the local people's councils. Party secretaries became more responsible for the economy, and a number of party and economic positions were fused.

Ceauçescu also established a system of personal rule that bypassed the traditional party organizations. The year he came into office, he established a political executive committee in order to circumvent the Central Committee and its presidium (the politburo). In 1974 he established a Permanent Bureau limited to five close associates, later expanded to fifteen. He instituted a system of rotation to keep lower party officials from establishing themselves in Bucharest; he would send them out to the provinces for extended periods. The personal character of his rule can perhaps best be described by listing some of the offices he personally held: general secretary of the party; chairman of the council of state; president of the republic (a job created expressly for him); chairman of the national defense council; commander in chief of the armed forces. In comparison to this strong centralized authority, societal groups were relatively powerless: Trade unions and workers' councils, originally intended to convey people's concerns to the top leadership, were instead used, in the standard phrase, as "transmission belts" to implement government policy.

Romania was the least industrialized of the East European countries when communist regimes were imposed in the region after World War II. The highly centralized state and party apparatus was used to promote rapid industrialization on the Russian model. Romania was fortunate in having its own energy supply: oil and natural gas. For investment capital, it relied on restricting consumption, squeezing the population in the traditional Soviet fashion. Hence its early economic development was essentially self-sufficient.

When Ceauçescu entered the scene in 1965 he continued the industrialization drive, promoting what he called "multilateral development." In Ceauçescu's vision, Romania, which had traditionally been considered a producer of primary raw materials—it was known as the gas station and breadbasket of Europe—would now become a modern, balanced, industrial economy. This goal brought Ceauçescu into conflict with the Soviet Union, which had different plans for its regional economic organization—the Council for Mutual Economic Assistance (CMEA). The Soviets were arguing for specialization of the economies into areas in which each had a comparative advantage. They were happy to have Romania remain the gas station and breadbasket.

Economic performance was reasonably good in Romania during Ceauçescu's first decade in power, with a growth rate of about 6 percent per year. By the second half of the 1970s, things had taken a turn for the worse. The Romanians had been pretty much protected from the first oil-price shock, since they were self-sufficient in oil. In fact, they had invested heavily in oil refineries and so imported crude oil and reexported refined oil, thus benefiting somewhat from the price increases. By the late 1970s, though, domestic production had dropped off, and they began importing from the Soviet Union and the Middle East. They began to run up a trade deficit and borrowed money from the World Bank and the International Monetary Fund. Romania had been the first Soviet-bloc country to join the two institutions. It was also the first to recognize West Germany in 1967 and to develop economic relations with it. It maintained extensive contacts with China, despite Soviet criticism. This independence in foreign policy was also the product of Ceauçescu's role and was at the same time an instrument for supporting that role. He used independence from the Soviet Union to summon feelings of nationalism and thereby enhance his stature. Independence also gave him more options in the economic sphere than the other East European countries had.

By 1974 Romania was trading more with the Western countries of the Organization for Economic Cooperation and Development (OECD) than with those of the Soviet-sponsored CMEA. With the last of its oil reserves depleted, Romania also became the leading importer among the CMEA countries of OPEC oil.

Another innovation that Ceauçescu introduced was to recharacterize Romania, changing it from a "socialist country" to a "socialist developing country." This was part of his plan to improve relations with the Third World, which paid off later. While the other East European countries' trade balances were hurt by the recessions in the West and the consequent lack of demand for their products, Romania was able to reorient much of its exports to the Third World, and so its trade balance did not suffer as much.

By the second oil shock of the late 1970s and the recession of the early 1980s, however, Romania was forced to rely on the traditional solution of depressing domestic demand through an austerity program. Unlike Poland, Romania was able to carry out a suppression of domestic consumption without triggering mass unrest (at least not for a decade). Starting in 1979, personal consumption was severely limited, prices were increased for almost everything, electric power was reduced and restricted, and by 1981 even food was rationed. In the early 1980s Romania shifted its trade back toward the Soviet bloc and refused to take any further Western loans. As a result of these measures, the balance of trade improved and some of the debt was paid off. But Ceauçescu was not satisfied. In an effort to make Romania more economically independent, he continued to squeeze the population. This situation was in marked contrast to that in Poland, where in the late 1980s the communist government felt it had to submit a referendum to the voters to see if they were willing to make some sacrifices in the interest of reform and future economic benefits (they were not).

We can summarize the differences between Romania and Poland in their response to the debt and energy crises by focusing on their domestic structures. Romania had what Ellen Comisso (1986) called a socialist patrimonial system—power is concentrated in one person who could implement flexible adjustment policies at the expense of the population (with the help of a powerful security apparatus). Poland had, in Comisso's terms, a collegial system, where no single leader had the authority to enforce radical policies to make the country adjust to international economic disturbances. More important than the differences encapsulated in this taxonomy,[10] though, were the conditions of the main components of the domestic structure in each country: party, state, and society. In the 1970s Poland's state and party apparatus was crumbling while societal forces, particularly workers, were growing in strength. The result was an inability to respond to economic shocks with the type of austerity measures adopted by Romania. In contrast, Romania, like some authoritarian regimes in the Third World, was able to squeeze a weak society because Ceauçescu controlled the instruments of a still strong, centralized state.

Public Opinion, Domestic Structure, and Security Policy

In his pioneering study of the links between public opinion, domestic structure, and security policy, Thomas Risse-Kappen (1991) sought to solve a puzzle: Why, given similar trends in public opinion toward military spending and relations with the Soviet Union during the 1980s, did the governments of four liberal democracies behave so differently in their policies toward security and the USSR? His basic answer is that domestic structure mediated public opinion and that his four democracies—the United States, France, Japan, and Germany—vary in their domestic structures and, consequently, in their governments' responsiveness to public opinion on foreign policy.

Domestic Structure: The State of the Art

Risse-Kappen's description of what constitutes domestic structure represented the accumulated wisdom of fifteen years (following Katzenstein's 1976 article) of developing the concept for use in the comparative study of foreign policy. He refers to his approach as a mixed one, incorporating insights from the original state-society literature and the work on policy networks and coalition-building. Since his elaboration of domestic structure guides the coding of his four cases and has already proved to be valuable for subsequent comparative research (e.g., Evangelista 1995; Risse-Kappen 1994, 1995a), it is worth quoting in full:

I.   The nature of the *political institutions* and the degree of their centralization: Is executive power concentrated in the hands of one decision maker (president, prime minister, chancellor) who controls the bureaucratic infighting among governmental agencies? To what extent can the government control the legislative process?

II. The *structure of society* regarding its polarization, the strength of social organization, and the degree to which societal pressure can be mobilized: How heterogeneous is the society in terms of ideological and/or class cleavages? How well developed are social coalitions and organizations in their ability to express grievances and raise demands?

III. Finally, the nature of the coalition-building processes in the *policy networks* linking state and society:
   A. In countries with centralized political institutions but polarized societies and rather weak social organizations, the policy network is likely to be *state-dominated*. The policy-relevant coalition building would then be restricted to the political élites and would more or less exclude societal actors and/or public opinion.
   B. By contrast, *societal control* of the policy network is to be expected in countries with comparatively homogeneous societies and a high degree of societal mobilization but weak state structures. The policy-relevant coalition building would take place among societal actors; accordingly, public opinion would play a major role.
   C. Countries with political institutions and social organizations of comparable strength are likely to have a policy network characterized by *democratic corporatism*. Political and societal actors would be engaged in continuous bargaining processes in search of policy compromises in an environment of give-and-take. As a result, some sorts of middle-of-the-road policies are to be expected, reflecting the common denominator of public opinion. (Risse-Kappen 1991, 485–486.)

Risse-Kappen's coding does not produce a continuum but rather four distinct types of countries that share certain aspects of domestic structure (see Table 8.1). In this framework Germany and Japan are similar to each other, whereas France and the United States are virtual opposites. In this respect his categorization is largely consistent with what other comparative studies, drawing on notions of domestic structure, have found (e.g., Katzenstein 1976, 1978; Ikenberry 1986).

Responses to the Soviet Threat

Risse-Kappen is explicitly interested in testing the effect of domestic structures as an intervening variable. He identifies the prerequisites for conducting such a test as follows: "To isolate the role of domestic structures as the intervening variable between public opinion and policy decisions requires a case in which the influence of the international environment appears constant for the four countries and in which under ideal conditions public attitudes are also more or less similar" (Risse-Kappen 1991, 493). In Risse-Kappen's account, the dramatic change in Soviet behavior during the decade of the 1980s was reflected fairly uniformly in public perceptions of the Soviet threat and public attitudes toward military spending across his four cases. All four countries saw an increase in support for military spend-

TABLE 8.1   Risse-Kappen's Taxonomy of Domestic Structures of Liberal Democracies

	U.S.	*West Germany*	*Japan*	*France*
Political system	Decentralized	Intermediate level of centralization	Intermediate level of centralization	Centralized
Society	Heterogeneous weak organizations	Heterogeneous strong organizations	Homogeneous strong organizations	Heterogeneous weak organizations
Policy	Society-dominated	Democratic corporatist	Quasi-corporatist	State-dominated

Source: Thomas Risse-Kappen, "Public Opinion, Domestic Structure, and Foreign Policy in Liberal Democracies," *World Politics,* vol. 43, no. 4 (July 1991).

ing coinciding with the deterioration of East-West relations in the late 1970s and early 1980s, and most saw support for military spending decline as relations improved. Most countries showed a reduced perception of Soviet threat following the ascendancy of Mikhail Gorbachev and his conciliatory foreign policies (the anomalous case is Japan, which still perceived a Soviet threat in the late 1980s, probably owing to unresolved territorial disputes over the Kuril Islands and Sakhalin).

Yet the behaviors of the four governments diverged as a consequence, according to Risse-Kappen, of the way different domestic structures filtered societal influences, especially public opinion. U.S. policy was hostile toward the USSR from the late 1970s until just before the 1984 presidential election, when President Ronald Reagan softened his rhetoric. After Gorbachev came into office, the Reagan administration eventually began to respond favorably to his many conciliatory initiatives in security policy. Risse-Kappen argued that the initially hostile U.S. government policy of the late 1970s reflected elite and public disillusion with the arms-control process and Soviet activity in the Third World, as one would expect in a weak state easily influenced by societal forces. By the early 1980s public concern about the danger of nuclear war promoted a growing peace movement to which the administration felt obliged to respond by toning down its hostile rhetoric, maintaining existing arms treaties, and pursuing continued negotiations. The new administration policies were also the product of fluid internal competition in a weak, decentralized state apparatus, which eventually resulted in a new coalition in favor of at least the appearance of moderation in policy toward the USSR. The delayed but positive Reagan response to Gorbachev also tracked public attitudes toward the new Soviet leader, with some time lag, and reflected the consolidation of the moderates' position and the hard-liners' defection from the administration.

In France public opinion was far more conciliatory toward the USSR and more accepting of Gorbachev than was actual government policy. Public opinion had little impact on decisionmaking. Societal forces were weak and fragmented, as illustrated, for example, by the fractious and ineffectual French peace movement—a sharp contrast to its German, Dutch, British, and U.S. counterparts. These findings reconfirm the generalizations about the strong role of the French state in dominating public policy making.

German security policy mirrored the public's commitment to détente and arms control and the elite consensus that had emerged in the policy network during the 1970s. It maintained a fairly stable course despite the ups and downs of U.S.-Soviet relations. As the public became increasingly antinuclear and the peace movement flourished during the "new Cold War" of the early 1980s, however, government policy reflected the change. The main impact was felt in the coalition-building processes within the party system. The democratic corporatist state gradually forged a new consensus around changing societal and institutional values and was particularly well prepared to embrace the new Soviet policies pursued by Gorbachev.

At first glance Japanese policy seemed consistent with public opinion, as in the German case, and as one would expect from elements of domestic structure—intermediate degree of centralization and corporatist bargaining arrangements—that the two countries hold in common. Pacifist popular sentiments seemed to be embodied in the state's principle of spending no more on the military than 1 percent of the gross national product. And the public's concern about the northern islands would seem to bring it into accord with its government's skeptical and hard-line policy toward Gorbachev. Yet on closer inspection the views of state policymakers diverge considerably from popular opinion. The 1 percent ceiling on military spending, for example, gives prosperous Japan the second or third largest military budget in the world—and even this limit some Japanese leaders have found to be too constraining. As far as policy toward Gorbachev's USSR was concerned, despite the common popular and elite attention to the disputed territories, the public expressed considerable interest in engaging the Soviets in negotiations to seek their return, whereas the government refused to improve relations with the USSR until the Soviets conceded the Japanese position on the dispute. According to Risse-Kappen, this divergence of views has a muted impact on security policy because the quasi-corporatist policy network in Japan obliges its leaders to incorporate societal and opposition views on security that may be more moderate than their own.

Domestic Structure and Contemporary Global Change

Risse-Kappen's account suggests one way that major changes in the international environment—Gorbachev's successful efforts to end the Cold War as the case in point—are diffused throughout the system. The mechanism consists of public responses to international stimuli, which are filtered through domestic structures in particular countries and result in foreign policies that eventually produce new interactions among states, thereby reinforcing and "globalizing" the initial state-level transformation. This is my own tentative extrapolation of Risse-Kappen's findings, but it seems consistent with how a domestic structural approach would account for the momentous changes since the late 1980s.

The Gorbachev Phenomenon and the End of the Cold War

Clearly the end of the Cold War and the disintegration of one of its two main protagonists would be on anyone's list of major international changes in need of explanation. For our purposes the most important point to understand is that the initial impetus for the international transformation came from within the Soviet Union. Mikhail Gorbachev deliberately sought to end the Cold War as a prerequisite for carrying out fundamental internal reforms (Garthoff 1994; Gorbachev 1995). Soviet withdrawal from the political-military competition with the United States signaled the demise of the bipolar international system—long before most analysts would have predicted it on the basis of "objective," material factors (e.g., U.S.-Soviet military balance). Thus an explanation for this particular international systemic transformation must begin by explaining why Soviet foreign and domestic policy changed.

How should we account for the specific changes Gorbachev wrought? The candidate explanations are myriad (Deudney and Ikenberry 1991/ 1992; Evangelista 1991). A domestic structural approach would not at first glance seem to be a strong contender. A central tenet of the approach is that domestic structures are historically conditioned, especially by the interaction of the state with the external environment (Gerschenkron 1962; Moore 1966; Katzenstein 1984, 1985). The Gorbachev phenomenon, which entailed both domestic structural transformation (shifting the heavily skewed balance from the party-state to society) and international structural transformation (the move away from bipolarity), should not logically be explicable by an approach that takes structure as given.

Yet there are aspects of the domestic structural approach that seem applicable to the Gorbachev case. The simple fact that we associate the Soviet changes with his name is only possible because the Soviet-type political system gives its leaders scope to initiate major transformations as well as more modest policy innovations (Bunce 1981). Although the prerequisites for broad societal transformation—education, urbanization, professional diversification (Lewin 1988)—were decades in the making, they were not deterministic. They were satisfied long before Gorbachev came to power and would not have produced dramatic political change without someone like him as state leader. Domestic structural approaches to Soviet-type systems sensitize us to the likelihood of top-down policy initiatives (Brzezinski and

Huntington 1963; Evangelista 1988; Halpern 1989). The approach was far less successful, however, in anticipating the groundswell of popular response that overwhelmed an already ambitious liberalization initiated at the top.

Gorbachev's internal initiatives were directed primarily at reviving the economy. The Soviet economic crisis had many causes and it would be claiming too much to argue that the domestic structural approach holds any particular advantage in accounting for it. In that aspect of the crisis that concerned the lack of technological dynamism, however, analyses that stressed the domestic structure definitely got the trend right, and for the right reasons. These included studies of the overall level of Soviet technological development (Amann, Cooper, and Davies 1977), the potential for technological innovation (Amann and Cooper 1982), and comparative analyses of the civilian and military sectors and Soviet versus Western cases using domestic structure as a key variable (Evangelista 1988; Holloway 1977, 1982; Kaldor 1981, 1986).

Not only the consequences but also the origins of the Soviet transformation had an international dimension—or several (Deudney and Ikenberry 1991/1992). Even the economic crisis cannot be understood solely as a domestic issue. As several observers have pointed out, it is the comparative international aspect of the economic crisis, the relative rather than absolute failure of the Soviet economic order, that helped to stimulate reform—"the perceived inability of the Soviet system to catch up [with], let alone overtake, the West" (Halliday 1992, 133).[11] The "new thinking" in Soviet foreign policy, promoted by Gorbachev and his foreign minister, Eduard Shevardnadze, also derived in part from international—and transnational—sources. If domestic structure can serve, as the studies summarized in this chapter indicate, as an intervening variable between the international environment and domestic politics, then it should have something to say about these international influences on Gorbachev's policy. In turn domestic structure should be able to say something about the mechanisms by which internal societal and institutional forces were able to get their objectives pursued in the new foreign policy. Several studies do suggest an important role for domestic structure in understanding the international and transnational dimensions of Soviet change (Snyder 1987/1988, 1991; Risse-Kappen 1994; Evangelista 1995). Yet in this case, as in others, domestic structure must be supplemented by other approaches to provide a full account of major international change.

Conclusion: Future Directions for Domestic Structural Analysis

The application of domestic structure to understanding the international-domestic linkages in the transformation and disintegration of the Soviet Union is of more than historical interest. Many of the types of linkage are certain to recur with some frequency in the future course of international relations and they may bring further profound changes. These linkages include perceptions of relative economic (or social, or political) welfare and transnational relations of all sorts. Such external influences require points of access into domestic societies. Domestic structure might provide a way of indicating which countries are likely to be more or less receptive to such influences by calling attention to the links between domestic and international policy networks, coalition dynamics that might provide openings for transnational penetration, and so forth (Risse-Kappen 1995a, 1995b; Darst 1994). Domestic structure could also provide insights into how effectively a given country might take advantage of ideas and proposals of transnational coalitions or "epistemic communities" of specialists (Haas 1992; Darst 1994).

As the end of the Cold War shifts our attention away from superpower rivalry, it brings into focus the economic and security concerns of smaller states. Much of the most innovative work on post–Cold War foreign policies links politics, economics, and security through the medium of domestic structure. Domestic structural analysis has proved to be a powerful tool for understanding divergent state policies on such vital issues as nuclear proliferation, alliance policy, and regional security regimes (Barnett 1990, 1992; Gause 1990; Solingen 1994a, 1994b) as well as on issues of growing concern such as the environment (Darst 1994; Princen 1995). It continues to serve as a useful means of studying the differences between states' foreign economic policies—the original domain of domestic structural analysis (Hart 1992; Clark and Chan 1995).

Finally, much of the recent work in domestic structure has paid particular attention to the interaction between a country's domestic structure and the historically derived normative understandings embodied in its society. Much as the early work in domestic structure formed a theoretical bridge between realism and liberalism, this recent work offers the possibility of integrating the new "constructivist" challenge to international relations theory with more traditional approaches. Constructivism has so far lacked a model of domestic-international linkages to explain how international practices actually shape state interests and identities. In other words, what are the political mechanisms that facilitate or hinder the social construction of international reality? Recent work suggests that domestic structure might help to elucidate this question (Risse-Kappen 1995a, 1995b; Checkel 1995; Clark and Chan 1995; Katzenstein 1996).

As long as states play a role in initiating and responding to global change, they will do so through the vehicle of foreign policy, and they will do so in divergent fashions. As the international system changes in new and unexpected ways, scholars will debate in old and familiar ways the sources and consequences of those changes. In other words, international change will continue to be subject to rival theoretical interpretations. For those reasons, we can anticipate that the analysis of domestic structures will continue to provide a valuable means of comparing foreign policies and of reconciling competing theories, and that domestic structure itself will remain a crucial intervening variable linking domestic and international politics.

Notes

1. For further reflection on the definition of the state, see Rueschemeyer and Evans 1985, pp. 46–48.
2. For discussions of the internal-external debate, see Russett 1983 and Rogowski 1985.
3. Disagreements with or qualifications of Katzenstein's characterization of France have been expressed in Ikenberry 1986 and Milner 1987, and of the United States in Krasner 1978, Ikenberry 1986, and Ikenberry, Lake, and Mastanduno 1988.
4. Milner (1987) disagrees here as well.
5. This section draws on Evangelista 1989.
6. For discussion, see Pintner and Rowney 1980; Klyuchevsky 1958; Seton-Watson 1967; and Gerschenkron 1968.
7. The top-down versus bottom-up analysis draws on Brzezinski and Huntington 1963, pp. 202–230, and is developed in Evangelista 1984. Some of the generalizations concerning domestic structure are familiar to students of comparative politics, who more often write of "state structures." See, for example, Hall 1983 and Weir and Skocpol 1985.
8. This section draws almost entirely on Poznanski 1986, although he might not agree fully with my interpretation of his history.
9. My source for most of this discussion is Linden 1986.
10. These terms appear to be mainly a restatement of the standard distinction in Soviet politics between the totalitarian and oligarchic models. For a discussion, see Hough 1977, pp. 19–48.
11. The source of Gorbachev's policy innovation is familiar to students of U.S. public policy: "People define conditions as problems by comparing current conditions with their values concerning more ideal states of affairs, by comparing their own performance with that of other countries, or by putting the subject into one category rather than another" (Kingdon 1984, 20–21; see also Walker 1981, 88).

References

Allison, Graham, and Frederic A. Morris. 1975. "Exploring the Determinants of Military Weapons." *Daedalus,* vol. 104, no. 3 (Summer).
Amann, Ronald, and Julian Cooper, eds. 1982. *Industrial Innovation in the Soviet Union.* New Haven: Yale University Press.
Amann, Ronald, Julian Cooper, and R. W. Davies, eds. 1977. *The Technological Level of Soviet Industry.* New Haven: Yale University Press.
Barnett, Michael. 1990. "High Politics Is Low Politics: The Domestic and Systemic Sources of Israeli Security Policy, 1967–1977." *World Politics,* vol. 42, no. 4 (July).

_____. 1992. *Confronting the Costs of War: Military Power, State, and Society in Egypt and Israel*. Princeton: Princeton University Press.

Brzezinski, Zbigniew, and Samuel P. Huntington. 1963. *Political Power: USA/USSR*. New York: Viking Press.

Bunce, Valerie. 1981. *Do New Leaders Make a Difference? Executive Succession and Public Policy Under Capitalism and Socialism*. Princeton: Princeton University Press.

Chaiko, Lev. 1985. *Helicopter Construction in the USSR*. Falls Church, VA: Delphic Associates.

Checkel, Jeff. 1995. "Norms, Institutions, and National Identity in Contemporary Europe." Paper presented to the annual meeting of the American Political Science Association, Chicago, August.

Clark, Cal, and Steve Chan. 1995. "MNCs and Developmentalism: Domestic Structure as an Explanation for East Asian Dynamism." In *Bringing Transnational Relations Back In: Non-State Actors, Domestic Structures, and International Institutions,* ed. Thomas Risse-Kappen. Cambridge: Cambridge University Press.

Comisso, Ellen. 1986. "Introduction: State Structures, Political Processes, and Collective Choice in CMEA States." Special issue, *International Organization,* vol. 40, no. 2 (Spring).

Comisso, Ellen, and Laura D'Andrea Tyson. 1986. "Power, Purpose, and Collective Choice: Economic Strategy in Socialist States." Special issue, *International Organization,* vol. 40, no. 2 (Spring).

Darst, Robert G. 1994. "Leninism, Pluralism, and International Cooperation: The Internationalization of Environmental Protection in the USSR and Its Successor States, 1968–1993." Ph.D. diss., University of California, Berkeley.

Deudney, Daniel, and G. John Ikenberry. 1991/1992. "The International Sources of Soviet Change." *International Security,* vol. 16, no. 3 (Winter).

Doyle, Michael. 1986. "Liberalism and World Politics." *American Political Science Review,* vol. 80 (December).

Evangelista, Matthew. 1984. "Why the Soviets Buy the Weapons They Do." *World Politics,* vol. 36, no. 4 (July).

_____. 1988. *Innovation and the Arms Race: How the United States and the Soviet Union Develop New Military Technologies*. Ithaca: Cornell University Press.

_____. 1989. "Issue-Area and Foreign Policy Revisited." *International Organization,* vol. 43, no. 1 (Winter).

_____. 1991. "Sources of Moderation in Soviet Security Policy." In *Behavior, Society, and Nuclear War,* vol. 2, ed. Philip Tetlock, et al. New York: Oxford University Press.

_____. 1995. "The Paradox of State Strength: Transnational Relations, Domestic Structures, and Security Policy in Russia and the Soviet Union." *International Organization,* vol. 49, no. 1 (Winter).

Garthoff, Raymond L. 1994. *The Great Transition: American-Soviet Relations and the End of the Cold War*. Washington, DC: Brookings Institution.

Gause, F. Gregory III. 1990. *Saudi-Yemeni Relations: Domestic Structures and Foreign Influence*. New York: Columbia University Press.

Gerschenkron, Alexander. 1962. *Economic Backwardness in Historical Perspective.* Cambridge, MA: The Belknap Press of Harvard University Press.

_____. 1968. "Russia: Agrarian Policies and Industrialization, 1861–1917." In *Continuity in History and Other Essays.* Cambridge, MA: The Belknap Press of Harvard University Press.

_____. 1981. *War and Change in World Politics.* New York: Cambridge University Press.

Gleditsch, Nils Petter, and Olav Njolstad, eds. 1990. *Arms Races: Technological and Political Dynamics.* London: Sage.

Gorbachev, Mikhail. 1995. *Zhizn' i reformy* [Life and reforms]. 2 vols. Moscow: Novosti.

Gourevitch, Peter. 1978. "The Second Image Reversed: The International Sources of Domestic Politics." *International Organization*, vol. 32, no. 4 (Autumn).

_____. 1986. *Politics in Hard Times: Comparative Responses to International Economic Crises.* Ithaca: Cornell University Press.

Haas, Peter M., ed. 1992. "Knowledge, Power, and International Policy Coordination." Special issue, *International Organization*, vol. 46, no. 1 (Winter).

Hall, Peter A. 1983. "Policy Innovation and the Structure of the State: The Politics-Administration Nexus in France and Britain." *Annals of the American Academy of Political and Social Science,* vol. 466 (March).

Halliday, Fred. 1992. "A Singular Collapse: The Soviet Union, Market Pressure, and Inter-state Competition." *Contention*, vol. 1, no. 2 (Winter).

Halpern, Nina P. 1989. "Policy Communities in a Leninist State: The Case of the Chinese Economic Policy Community." *Governance*, vol. 2, no. 1 (January).

Hart, Jeffrey A. 1992. *Rival Capitalists: International Competitiveness in the United States, Japan, and Western Europe.* Ithaca: Cornell University Press.

Holloway, David. 1977. "Military Technology." In *The Technological Level of Soviet Industry,* ed. Ronald Amann, Julian Cooper, and R. W. Davies. New Haven: Yale University Press.

_____. 1982. "Innovation in the Defence Sector." In *Industrial Innovation in the Soviet Union,* ed. Ronald Amann and Julian Cooper. New Haven: Yale University Press.

Hough, Jerry. 1977. "The Soviet System: Petrification or Pluralism?" In *The Soviet Union and Social Science Theory.* Cambridge, MA: Harvard University Press.

Ikenberry, G. John. 1986. "The Irony of State Strength: Comparative Responses to the Oil Shock in the 1970s." *International Organization*, vol. 40, no. 1 (Winter).

Ikenberry, G. J., D. A. Lake, and M. Mastanduno, eds. 1988. "The State and American Foreign Economic Policy." Special issue, *International Organization*, vol. 42, no. 1 (Winter).

Kaldor, Mary. 1981. *The Baroque Arsenal.* New York: Hill & Wang.

_____. 1986. "The Weapons Succession Process." *World Politics*, vol. 38, no. 4 (July).

Katzenstein, Peter J. 1976. "International Relations and Domestic Structures: Foreign Economic Policies of Advanced Industrial States." *International Organization*, vol. 30, no. 1 (Winter).

_____, ed. 1978. *Between Power and Plenty: Foreign Economic Policies of Advanced Industrial States.* Madison: University of Wisconsin Press.

_____. 1984. *Corporatism and Change: Austria, Switzerland, and the Politics of Industry.* Ithaca: Cornell University Press.

_____. 1985. *Small States in World Markets*. Ithaca: Cornell University Press.

_____, ed. 1996. *The Culture of National Security: Identity and Norms in World Politics*. New York: Columbia University Press.

Kingdon, John W. 1984. *Agendas, Alternatives, and Public Policies*. Boston: Little, Brown and Company.

Klyuchevsky, Vasili. 1958. *Peter the Great*. Translated by Liliana Archibald. New York: Vintage.

Krasner, Stephen D. 1978. *Defending the National Interest: Raw Materials Investments and U.S. Foreign Policy*. Princeton: Princeton University Press.

Lambeth, Benjamin S. 1991. *From Farnborough to Kubinka: An American MiG-29 Experience*. Santa Monica, CA: Rand Corporation.

Lewin, Moshe. 1988. *The Gorbachev Phenomenon*. Berkeley: University of California Press.

Linden, Ronald H. 1986. "Socialist Patrimonialism and the Global Economy: The Case of Romania." *International Organization*, vol. 40, no. 2 (Spring).

Mastanduno, M., G. J. Ikenberry, and D. A. Lake. 1989. "Toward a Realist Theory of State Action." *International Studies Quarterly*, vol. 33, no. 4 (December).

Milner, Helen. 1987. "Resisting the Protectionist Temptation: Industry and the Making of Trade Policy in France and the United States During the 1970s." *International Organization*, vol. 41, no 4 (Autumn).

Moore, Barrington Jr. 1966. *Social Origins of Dictatorship and Democracy: Lord and Peasant in the Making of the Modern World*. Boston: Beacon Press.

Nettl, J. P. 1968. "The State as a Conceptual Variable." *World Politics*, vol. 20, no. 4 (July).

Pintner, Walter McKenzie, and Don Karl Rowney, eds. 1980. *Russian Officialdom: The Bureaucratization of Russian Society from the Seventeenth to the Twentieth Century*. Chapel Hill: University of North Carolina Press.

Platias, Athanassios. 1986. "High Politics in Small Countries." Ph.D. diss., Cornell University.

Poznanski, Kazimierz. 1986. "Economic Adjustment and Political Forces: Poland Since 1970." *International Organization*, vol. 40, no. 2 (Spring).

Princen, Thomas. 1995. "Ivory, Conservation, and Environmental Transnational Coalitions." In *Bringing Transnational Relations Back In: Non-state Actors, Domestic Structures, and International Institutions,* ed. Thomas Risse-Kappen. Cambridge, UK: Cambridge University Press.

Rathjens, George W. 1969. "The Dynamics of the Arms Race." *Scientific American* (April). (Reprinted in Bruce M. Russett and Bruce G. Blair, eds. *Progress in Arms Control?* San Francisco: W. H. Freeman, 1979.)

Risse-Kappen, Thomas. 1991. "Public Opinion, Domestic Structure, and Foreign Policy in Liberal Democracies." *World Politics*, vol. 43, no. 4 (July).

_____. 1994. "Ideas Do Not Float Freely: Transnational Coalitions, Domestic Structures, and the End of the Cold War." *International Organization*, vol. 48, no. 2 (Spring).

_____, ed. 1995a. *Bringing Transnational Relations Back In: Non-state Actors, Domestic Structures, and International Institutions*. Cambridge, UK: Cambridge University Press.

_____. 1995b. *Cooperation Among Democracies: The European Influence on U.S. Foreign Policy*. Princeton: Princeton University Press.

Rogowski, Ronald. 1985. "Internal vs. External Factors in Political Development: An Evaluation of Recent Historical Research." *PS: Political Science and Politics*, vol. 18, no. 4 (Fall).

Rueschemeyer, Dietrich, and Peter B. Evans. 1985. "The State and Economic Transformation: Toward an Analysis of the Conditions Underlying Effective Intervention." In *Bringing the State Back In,* ed. Peter B. Evans, Dietrich Rueschemeyer, and Theda Skocpol. Cambridge, UK: Cambridge University Press.

Russett, Bruce. 1983. "International Interactions and Processes: The Internal vs. External Debate Revisited." In *Political Science: The State of the Discipline,* ed. Ada Finifter. Washington, DC: American Political Science Association.

Seton-Watson, Hugh. 1967. *The Russian Empire, 1801–1917.* Oxford: Oxford University Press.

Snyder, Jack. 1987/1988. "The Gorbachev Revolution: A Waning of Soviet Expansionism?" *International Security*, vol. 12, no. 3 (Winter).

_____. 1991. *Myths of Empire: Domestic Politics and International Ambition.* Ithaca: Cornell University Press.

Solingen, Etel. 1994a. "The Domestic Sources of International Regimes: The Evolution of Nuclear Ambiguity in the Middle East." *International Studies Quarterly*, vol. 38, no. 4 (June).

_____. 1994b. "The Political Economy of Nuclear Restraint." *International Security*, vol. 19, no. 2 (Fall).

Twigg, Judyth L. 1994. "'To Fly and Fight': Norms, Institutions, and Fighter Aircraft Procurement in the United States, Russia, and Japan." Ph.D. diss., Massachusetts Institute of Technology.

Tyson, Laura D'Andrea. 1986. "The Debt Crisis and Adjustment Responses in Eastern Europe: A Comparative Perspective." *International Organization*, vol. 40, no. 2 (Spring).

Walker, Jack L. 1981. "The Diffusion of Knowledge, Policy Communities, and Agenda Setting: The Relationship of Knowledge and Power." In *New Strategic Perspectives on Social Policy,* ed. J. E. Tropman, M. J. Dluhy, and R. M. Lind. New York: Pergamon.

Waltz, Kenneth N. 1959. *Man, the State, and War: A Theoretical Analysis.* New York: Columbia University Press.

_____. 1979. *Theory of International Politics.* Reading, MA: Addison-Wesley.

Weir, Margaret, and Theda Skocpol. 1985. "State Structures and the Possibilities for 'Keynesian' Responses to the Great Depression in Sweden, Britain, and the United States." In *Bringing the State Back In,* ed. Peter B. Evans, Dietrich Rueschemeyer, and Theda Skocpol. Cambridge, UK: Cambridge University Press.

9

Institutions and Change

STEVEN WEBER

The 1990s have so far been a good decade for thinking about international institutions and the problem of change in world politics. Any casual observer living through the past several years would have noted at least the possibility of some connection between the two. The dissolution of the communist bloc and then of the Soviet Union itself was correlated roughly in time with the revival of serious activity in the United Nations (UN), the European Community (EC; now the European Union, EU), the Conference on Security and Cooperation in Europe (CSCE), and other institutions. The newly independent states of Eastern Europe made it an early priority to seek membership in as many of these existing institutions as possible as well as to form a variety of new ones of their own in almost every conceivable shape and size—the Visegrad Triangle, the Pentagonale, and so on. On first rendering, it did not seem to most observers that international institutions were an important *source* of the end of the Cold War or of the substantial changes in world politics that came with it—or at least not a critical source.[1] But for the moment, it seemed, international institutions were a substantial *beneficiary* of change.

As a natural consequence of having gone to graduate school in the middle 1980s I, along with others who shared the experience, was wary of these kinds of observations. The classical realist thinkers and their descendants still had convincing arguments about why change in the international system would remain a "political" rather than a "legislative" or "judicial" process and thus be subject more to the impact of power attached to states than to international institutions.[2] That was not to say that international institutions were irrelevant. Stephen Krasner's edited volume *International*

Regimes and Robert Keohane's *After Hegemony* contained equally convincing theoretical insights about why states might use international institutions to pursue their interests and why institutions might not be quite so
volatile with respect to changing power configurations among states.[3] But
what could not help but strike readers of both books—and of the large
number of empirical studies that followed them—was the concentration of
institutions in what seemed to be issue-areas of secondary significance for
states. Reducing transaction costs and the like was well and good for some
issues, such as the oceans and the regulation of radio frequencies, but when
it came to most of the "big" issues of "high" politics, states seemed to
choose stubbornly independence and autonomy of action, regardless of
how easy it was for political scientists to show that contracting outside of a
regime framework could be terribly inefficient.[4] On the central concerns of
international politics states seemed less attracted to efficiency and optimal
aggregate outcomes than they were to pursuing their own interests. As
Robert Jervis noted in the Krasner volume, security regimes were rare and
weak when they existed—and the reason was that powerful states wanted
it that way.[5]

The renewed assertion of U.S. power during the 1980s seemed to vindi-
cate Susan Strange, Bruce Russett, and others in their critiques of the
regime literature.[6] John Mearsheimer's provocative end-of-the-Cold War
article in *International Security* brought these critiques up to date in 1990
and asked the right questions about the robustness or volatility of the old
institutional arrangements as well as the new ones that were sprouting up:
Why should the United States in its supposed "unipolar moment" not make
use of a freedom to exercise power and try to shape in its own interests the
second fifty years of an American century? Why should a reunited
Germany no longer bound by the Cold War logic of *ostpolitik* and the need
for the U.S. nuclear umbrella not reclaim its full sovereign prerogatives
from the North Atlantic Treaty Organization (NATO) and then from the
EC? Why should Japan, released similarly from dependence on the United
States, continue to pay even lip service to the General Agreement on Tariffs
and Trade (GATT) (now the World Trade Organization, WTO) in a mer-
cantile pursuit of trading relationships around the world?[7]

Austere and compelling as the logic of the neorealist argument was, it did
seem to many who read Mearsheimer and took it seriously that too many
of his dogs were not barking. European states were not, for example, rush-
ing to form bilateral alliances with each other, with the United States, or for
that matter with the Soviet Union, to guard themselves against a reunited
Germany. The barking was coming instead from institutions with all sorts
of acronymic labels: WEU (Western European Union), CSCE, EBRD
(European Bank for Reconstruction and Development), and so on. No
doubt these conversations and debates were focused on day-to-day events

and the particularly high profile of institutions in 1990, but they did have within them the seeds of two potentially interesting observations, which John Ruggie set out in a simple way:[8]

1. In the short term at least, leaders of European states were *not* acting on the presumption that the end of the Cold War implied an inevitable or even likely return to the politics of multipolarity that their states had experienced in the 1920s and 1930s. Equally important, no one seemed to be acting on the assumption that others might think that way.

2. Again in the short term, there seemed to be concerted moves in Europe not to *exit* institutions but to reinforce those already in place. This seemed to be true even of institutions such as NATO whose major purposes were tightly linked to the Cold War and which were thus arguably redundant. At the same time, states were creating and binding themselves to new institutions. For the moment, politics in Europe seemed taken up with debates over the appropriate division of labor *between* institutions.

I label these observations only "potentially interesting" because the challenge of a strong theoretical argument cannot be met simply by short-term and probably "noisy" data points whose significance is hard to define. Yet there was indubitably also a secular trend during the twentieth century toward greater reliance by states on institutions to manage their relationships. In 1909 there were thirty-seven conventional intergovernmental organizations in the world, by 1951 there were 123, and in 1986, 337.[9] The life cycle of institutions during the immediate post–Cold War world had to be seen in that context, and the picture was at least mildly provocative. Indeed, trends in power that might have worked to the detriment of institutions were not new, and the repercussions might have been felt more keenly in Europe and elsewhere over the postwar period had the impact of the declining overall power position of the United States not been allayed by the Soviet threat and continuing U.S. predominance in military capability. But with that threat dissipating, military power could no longer be expected to substitute for the broader resources that are needed to keep stable an international system and sustain cooperation within institutions. The stark realist view was simply that underlying trends should now come to the fore, driving states' interests in different directions and undermining institutions.

In any case, there were soon to be additional data points subject precisely to this interpretation. The uncomfortable tension between specifically German preferences and European Community aspirations to develop a common foreign policy toward what was Yugoslavia set off the first alarm bells. The September 1992 crisis of the European Exchange Rate Mechanism, which also set into sharp relief the EC's difficulties with organizing trade concessions for the struggling economies to the East, made the alarm bells substantially louder. Apart from its unsettling effect on statesmen, periods of rapid change where data points proliferate at such a furious pace tend to reignite standing debates among social scientists. That should be seen as an opportunity, and in the mid-1990s international institutions were right at the center of the maelstrom. What does it mean to ask about institutions and change in world politics?

The academic literature has long debated and will continue to debate that very broad question. My aim in this chapter is to bring the debate into clearer focus by setting out three general schools of argument about international institutions, emphasizing for each their analytic slant on the problem of change.[10] I piggyback on Robert Keohane's very important 1988 article, "International Institutions: Two Approaches," but I argue that there is a third approach that should be considered distinct.[11] I look at what each of these approaches can do, from a problem-solving perspective, with two critical questions: Where do institutions come from, and What do they do? Finally, I discuss the possibilities of a research program in the context of the third approach, which I believe can do something particularly interesting with the problem of change.

My special interest in change is driven not only by the theme of this volume but also by a theoretical disposition for which I must, before proceeding, add a disclaimer. One of the sustaining features of the realist perspective on international institutions (as on other things) is that it is parsimonious. I eschew for the purposes of this chapter competing for parsimony with a theory that has just one crucial variable, because in international relations it is hard for me to imagine any single variable that could replace the distribution of capabilities as *the* variable with the single most explanatory power. Instead, I will try to compete on more forgiving grounds by looking for arguments that solve problems in a logically compelling way. Such arguments would have three characteristic elements: a clear statement of what is being explained; a similarly clear statement of what is being used to explain; and a picture of the lines of causality that go between those two things.

The last element is particularly important, I believe, when we are trying to talk creatively and systematically at once about change. To define change in a generic fashion would be difficult, but one point that would be a part of any definition is that the concept "change" incorporates some notion of process. Put differently, change implies a story that plays itself out as the system under study transits from state 1 to state 2.[12] Theoretical arguments that lead us to expect certain things and not others about that story ought to be open to evaluation. For this reason I start with a bias in favor of process-oriented arguments, or at least those that have clear implications for the process of change, over arguments that put most of their weight on the measurement of independent and dependent variables. Comparing static states one to another may be sufficient for many purposes, but it is a poor way of getting at the problem of change.

There is also a more practical reason for my predisposition. The 1990s having brought the Cold War to a close and ushered in a period of rapid large-scale transition in world politics, international relations theory should respond by putting into its central realm of puzzles and problems those phenomena in the world that are newly interesting, those we wish and need to understand in more detail. Change, even if it remains as a generic concept somewhat murky, will be at the heart of that interest in the coming years.

Three Approaches to Institutions

Having sneaked by the challenge of defining change, I will now sneak by the challenge of defining an institution. The reason for doing this is that the three approaches that I outline are sufficiently different that to develop one definition of institution that will travel across them would be difficult. As a starting point only, I will rely on the standard definition of an institution as "a persistent and connected set of rules that prescribe behavior, constrain activity, shape expectations," ignoring only for now the issue of the mysterious unnamed actor (who is behaving and acting? who has expectations?).[13]

Keohane labels his first category the *rationalist* approach. Rationalists are quite close to realists in their conception of the state as the principal actor in the story. "Rationality" as an adjective that describes state behavior need not be caricatured; the state is simply seen as a goal-seeking actor with central interests that derive principally from its position in the international system. As independent rational actors, states make individual utility calculations about how to pursue interests. But because states cannot get everything they want by themselves and because they live with other states in a world in which information is costly and imperfect, the problem becomes one of maximizing what comes out of an expected utility function with many uncertain terms. In other words, states respond strategically to cues in their external environment. Yet, as the Prisoner's Dilemma and other games remind us, it can become quite difficult for strategic actors to get what they want (and could, in principle, attain) when transaction costs are high or insuperable and when it is difficult or impossible to write contracts. Strategic actors constrained by these problems can take an additional step. They will sometimes recognize that the outcomes of their actions are individually and collectively suboptimal, and they may find it in their instrumental interest to provide themselves with means to get around the constraints. Hence the value of institutions.[14] States create and join institutions that function in various ways to reduce transaction costs and make it easier instrumentally for states to cooperate when it is already in their interest to do so.

The focus of the rationalist approach is:

Actors/Interests/Individual Utility Calculations/Exchange and
Contracting

Keohane's second category is the *reflectivist* approach. Reflectivists begin
with a different conception of the state that rejects the linked notions of autonomy, interests that are defined independently, and the exogenous nature
of environmental constraints. The state is still in some sense the principal
actor in the story, but it makes no sense to talk about states separately from
one another or from their environment. States "exist" only in conjunction
with other states and with their environment. The two are mutually constitutive, which means that a state is defined not so much by what it "is" as by
what it "does"—how it interacts with its environment—and part of what
states do in defining themselves is to enter into lasting relationships with
other states and to form institutions. Rather than seeking goals per se,
states are "identity-seeking" actors: they act so as to reinforce the special
characteristics of identity that set them off from the environment.[15]
Certainly the information, contracting, and market-failure problems that
rationalists identify are going on in the reflectivists' world, but to concentrate on those things misses the central point. States, in this model, are social entities constituted in their ongoing relationships with other states, and
thus in institutions.

The focus of the reflectivist approach is:

Values/Structures/Social Utility Calculations and Norms/Identity-
Seeking Behavior

I now introduce a third category, for which I borrow from James
Caporaso's recent work the label "institutionalist."[16] This, of course, is not
a "new" category. In practice, much of the empirical research work that international relations scholars actually do fits more comfortably here than in
either the reflectivist or the rationalist category. This, I think, reflects more
than just the inevitability of real-world examples struggling against ideal-
types and ending up resting in a netherworld somewhere in the middle. In
terms of theory, institutionalism is also hardly new. The new economics of
organization competes with historical institutionalism, the new sociological
institutionalism, and many other kinds of institutionalism for the label—
and not just (not even principally) in international relations.[17] I do not intend in this article to review the many and interesting differences in these
approaches, at least not directly. Instead I try to develop some core insights
that institutionalist arguments can bring to the problem of change. I shall
try to argue that the institutionalist approach has its own motivations for
and methods of inquiry that set it apart from the other schools, but that
these motivations and methods—particularly the latter—are frequently un-
derspecified. What has been missing from this line of research, in other

words, is two things: first, a partly philosophical, partly epistemological characterization of the institutionalist approach that could give it a firmer shape and set it apart more clearly from the rationalist and reflectivist schools; and second, a well-defined set of methods.

To a certain extent institutionalism is, in fact, a compilation of concepts from both rationalist and reflectivist arguments. Institutionalism borrows from the rationalist view its baseline questions: Who are the principal actors? What are their interests? What are the constraints under which they pursue those interests? It also shares with rationalists a view of the state as an independent and autonomous actor that exists, at least as a meaningful unit of analysis, prior to entering into relationships with others. Beyond that point the two approaches part company.

In the institutionalist view the state in the international system is not so much goal seeking as it is *purposeful*.[18] The difference is subtle but important, and it lies in the set of responses that is assumed to be within the repertoire of the actor and can be independently invoked. The simplest kind of goal-seeking behavior is that of a thermostat, which responds in a single and predetermined manner to changes in the temperature of a room. A more sophisticated goal seeker, such as a primitive neural network, can learn from its mistakes in pursuing a goal and can respond over time to the same repeated problem in different ways. The goals, in either case, are unchanged. Purposeful actors are capable of changing goals as well, and they may do this in the absence of or even in seeming opposition to exogenous signals from the environment. Purposes, then, go beyond interests as rationalists conceive of them. Purposes are infused by ideas, values, and norms and by the social-aggregate manifestations of cognitive structures, such as scripts, schemata, and habits, that are not reducible in any plausible way to exogenous environmental cues.

Where do these ideas, values, norms, and cognitive structures come from in the first instance? In principle, they are rooted in all sorts of murky places like national tradition, religion, language, culture, and the like; but the aim of the institutionalist approach is not so much to explain the primitive *sources* of these purposes as to understand their *consequences* for international relations. International institutions are critical here, because it is institutions that are the major vehicles through which those consequences are propagated. The notion is that states still make utility calculations and act strategically, but the purposes that generate preference schedules that, together with beliefs and expectations about other states' purposes and the nature of the international environment, generate strategic behavior are affected and changed by international institutions. Put simply, relationships are built not only on the distribution of capabilities but also on ideas, norms, and habits. Institutions are meaningful because they carry each of these things beyond the point at which they can reasonably be said to be supported by power, at least by power attached to states. For that reason institutions deserve a separate ontological standing and should not simply be folded into the so-called environment.[19]

There is a crucial difference here from the rationalist school that bears repeating for its myriad consequences. Purposes (as opposed to interests) stand outside the realm of methodological individualism: Purposeful actors' preferences cannot be defined exogenously, and their social relationships cannot be reduced to the aggregate products of self-interested calculations. For institutionalists states do more with what they take from international institutions than simply update their expectations about others' preferences and the nature of the environment in which they function. That is the essence of the rationalist school: that institutions alter the range of strategies that state actors can play, with *predetermined preferences*. In the institutionalist approach institutions do that—but they also *change the preferences* themselves.

There is also a crucial difference here from reflectivist views. Institutions may be more than functional by-products of individual utility calculations, but they are less than socially reified structures that are guaranteed "reproduction" through their hegemonic (in the Gramscian sense) hold on individual agents' sense of the possible. The institutionalist view bears more of the characteristics of cognitive than motivational or affective microfoundations, which lie behind much of the reflectivist view. The "emotional" bonds of congruence that Talcott Parsons saw between values and morals expressed in self, culture, and society—reproduced (with modifications) in reflectivist arguments—are less important than the "cold" cognitive elements of scripts and schemata that do things such as reducing uncertainty, organizing attention, and setting into motion "garbage cans" in which problems and solutions travel in decoupled antiparallel streams seeking each other out.[20] As I will discuss later, the microfoundations of institutionalism are not yet well worked out—but the cognitive flavor does leave greater room for contingency and debate. States question the institutions of which they are a part—maybe not continuously, but over time very little about the terms of a state's international relationships will in fact be taken for granted. Institutions are contested, their shape and the distribution of power therein always subject to dispute and renegotiation. There is constant pressure from individual interests, which in principle can undermine just as easily as reinforce the patterns of behavior and interaction that are institutions.

In abstract, general terms the distinction between these schools of thought sounds sufficiently clear that it is natural to wonder why the institutionalist approach seems to have lived in relative theoretical obscurity. I think the first-cut answer to this question is that when it comes to moving outside semitheological debate and actually doing empirical research and reporting results, the institutionalist approach is not easy to handle. It is simply easier to argue and defend explanations from the rationalist and reflectivist schools (although not always against critics from opposing camps) than to demonstrate empirically that what the institutionalist approach suggests should happen between states and institutions is actually happening in the real world. That stands as an important challenge, prior even to the challenge of constructing methodological tools for an institutionalist approach. To take a small step toward meeting these challenges, I next examine what the rationalist and reflectivist approaches each say about two central questions: Where do institutions come from? What do institutions do? This should identify some important gaps into which an institutionalist research program can grow.

Where Do Institutions Come From?

From a methodological individualist perspective the question "where do institutions come from" is really a compilation of two questions: Why are there institutions at all, and why one institution but not another when an excess of alternatives exists? Ernst Haas has pointed out that both questions are pivotal in international relations.[21] After all, states may define in incompatible ways issues that need to be dealt with on the international agenda, and they may propose cooperative solutions that make no sense from other states' perspectives. To reduce what participants see as debates over first principles to quarrels by euphemism over the distribution of simple quantifiable costs and benefits does not always make sense.[22] The European Union's Maastricht Treaty is perceived (whether rightly or wrongly) by most of those who will decide whether it takes effect as a step in an exercise in constructing a polity, not just developing mechanisms for coordinating policies between autonomous actors.[23] The basic definition of the issue, in this case what the emerging polity will be and what values it will represent internally and externally, is up for grabs, and more is on the line than just who will pay and who will benefit.

Even when that is not the case, as when states agree on the general definition of a problem, there typically exists more than one option for doing something about it. Sometimes there are many options (one of which could be no cooperation), and each entails different kinds of institutional arrangements. I take an example from my current research: By the end of 1989 the United States and its major West European allies agreed, broadly, about the nature of the challenge they were faced with in the attempted political and economic transitions of the Central and Eastern European (CEE) states. They also agreed in broad terms about the risks should reform fail. But the "problem" even in that broadly shared definition did not point to a single solution—or more realistically, to a single institutional form through which an appropriate set of policies could be pursued. The Western states did not quarrel much over the definition of the challenge, but they did offer different plans of action, each of which was matched logically with a particular arrangement of institutions. Each arrangement of institutions in turn promised to distribute differently the costs and benefits to the cooperating states. An explanation of the outcome, so far as it is known, should aspire to do more than just explain the existence of institutionalized cooperation in a case like this; it should differentiate between the particular institutional arrangements that might have been and favor one over the others. Even *within* this "case" there is interesting variance.[24] The European Bank for Reconstruction and Development, for example, represents a large-scale cooperative endeavor aimed in part at promoting the flow of private external capital toward bankable private sector projects in CEE, but there has been no substantial institutionalized cooperation on the issue of aid for safeguarding substandard and dangerous nuclear reactors in Eastern Europe.[25] How do the rationalist and reflective approaches stand up to this kind of challenge?

The rationalist story has states entering into long-term contractual relationships on the basis of self-interested cost-benefit calculations.[26] The purest version of this approach turns the arrows of explanation in the other direction to focus on the origins of the institutions and reduces to functional or efficiency arguments. Studies in this mold make scintillating reading but seem awkward at best when applied to cases that we know in the real world of politics. The seminal (and fascinating) "Law Merchant" paper of Paul Milgrom, Douglass North, and Barry Weingast on the revival of trade in early medieval Europe illustrates nicely this conundrum. This paper lists the minimal requirements for sustained trading relationships among autonomous actors (merchants) who cannot easily collect information about one another's reliability, as measured by their record of compliance with contracts. Market failure is guaranteed—until suddenly appears the Law Merchant, an institutional innovation that fulfills those minimal requirements, and the saga of market failure is no more.[27]

The problem with calling this an explanation is that it does not say why the Law Merchant appeared, and not something else. There are usually many functional solutions to a given problem, and there certainly were many in medieval Europe. Why the Law Merchant and not Leviathan, which would have also provided the necessary reputation information (perhaps by beheading merchants who cheated on contracts) and thus sustained a revival of trade? Can it be simply that the Law Merchant was the socially optimal solution, in the sense that it met at the lowest cost the precise institutional requirements for trade? (Leviathan, after all, has massive organizational costs, and maybe something less imposing would have been better.)

Even that is not obvious in an abstract sense. In any case, the notion that social institutions are driven by optimality criteria is discredited by theory and data as well as by common sense. If the Law Merchant happened to have been the optimal institution in this case, that observation is something to be explained not assumed; and the process by which it and not something else emerged should be of interest.[28]

Mainstream international relations theory fills this hole in the rationalist approach with hegemonic stability theory and its much-improved variants. The explanation of why one institution is selected over others rests somewhere within the hegemon's conception of how to advance most effectively its interests, and then in the story of how it coerces or pays others to join in.[29] When alternative institutions are clearly in sight, the selection of one over another reflects the powerful state's perceived valuation of the distributional consequences of that choice.[30] The argument is easier to make when power is in fact concentrated thoroughly in one state than when it is distributed more widely. When states have more nearly equal capabilities it is possible, at least in principle, for a small group to cooperate in what collective action theorists called a "k" or "privileged" group—but it is difficult and we do not know much about the conditions under which this "hegemonic committee" will form. The challenge ought to be particularly severe when the problem requires the creation de novo of new institutions rather than the perpetuation of what is already in existence. Given the clear list of impediments and the vaguely defined conditions for transcending them, it is not surprising that the rationalist school remains formally agnostic and informally pessimistic about the prospects for institutions arising in this way.[31]

The reflectivist approach rejects most of the basic elements of this story as well as its explanatory engine. For reflectivists institutions arise not in a stark world in which atomized states struggle to write enforceable contracts but instead within a social world in which communication and discourse play a central role in relationships. Problems, challenges, and opportunities for cooperation do not simply emerge from the environment to confront states but are instead constructed by those social processes. Multiple actors—which could include transnational epistemic communities, private nongovernmental organizations, existing international institutions, and others as well as states—offer their own sets of ideas that contest the definition of a problem or an issue. Power attached to states is less important, at least at the point at which institutions are being formed, because states generally are not equipped in the first instance to judge effectively the distributional consequences of the choices that they make.[32] Masking the payoffs to power is a veil of ignorance that arises from the complexity and uncertainty of the state of the world. This opens the door for knowledge claims (on which states have no monopoly) to define and package issues and problems in many different, and by no means static, ways. Institutions rest on a convergence among states on knowledge claims that "create" a package of issues and delineate things to do cooperatively in that area. Distributional questions may arise later but are in fact by that time only marginally important, since most of the real work of distribution has already been done by the process of defining the issue.

An important element of the reflectivist approach is the way in which it turns the process of building institutions back on the "definition" of what it means to be a state. In coming together to craft institutions, states define the extent, the terms, and thus the meaning of what they do. This is the central step in constructing identity as a social unit. In an imaginary world without institutions the concept of a state per se would have no meaning. In the language preferred by the reflectivist approach, states are "constituted" by their interaction in institutions just as institutions are constituted by the states that make them up. Neither states nor institutions are prior ontologically one to the other.

The problem with this perspective, as I understand it, is that although it can accommodate comfortably the existence of institutions in the international system, it is really no more precise (and possibly less so) than the rationalist view in explaining the selection of one among many possible institutions. When knowledge claims compete, as they almost always do, the core of the reflectivist approach offers no clear reason to expect any particular institution to emerge. That would require a supplemental argument about why one set of knowledge claims "wins" and why others are left behind. If it is a matter primarily of a powerful state picking a set of ideas that maximize (subject to constraints of uncertainty) its expected payoffs, then we are back at something that, stripped of fancy language, is very close to a rationalist argument. There are other possibilities that would distinguish more clearly the reflectivist approach. If there is something in the *ideas themselves*—a purely logical coherence, or a link to shared moral values, or a reinforcement of prevailing patterns of language and thought—then that would comprise a candidate argument for selection distinctive to the reflectivist approach. Or if states come to value *certain kinds* of institutions for their own sake and not for the sake of the outcomes they are expected to make possible—for example, multilateral institutions that have broad membership and norms of nondiscrimination, for the sake of multilateralism—then that would be another candidate argument for selection.[33]

It is possible to construct abstractly many such candidate arguments, but it is difficult to make any single one stand up to empirical evidence across a reasonably broad range of cases. It may very well be that in some situations the veil of ignorance is quite thick—more frequently perhaps for small and weak states than for large and powerful states but for the latter as well in situations of marginal importance where attention is low, and probably in some other special situations as well. I have myself adopted this type of approach in explaining peculiarly institutionalized forms of cooperation in cases related to strategic arms control during the Cold War in which there was little or no data that could test or otherwise differentiate among contending sets of ideas.[34] But this seems to be an exception and not the rule. In most real-world cases of interest to international relations scholars, states do seem to articulate independent interests that pierce the veil of ignorance at least part of the way. And they seem to be rather inventive in coming up with new ideas and new institutional structures when either or both are seen as necessary to promote those interests.

This point stands out from any review of the international institutions that exist today or have existed over the past several centuries. What is impressive is the *heterogeneity* of forms—a variety of voting rules, a variety of definitions of property rights, even a variety of conceptions of sovereignty, by which I mean here simply an answer to the question, What constitutes a state such that it is eligible in principle to be a member of an international institution? How can states be "constituted" by their interaction in institutions if these take so many and sometimes contradictory forms? A generative grammar, like any system of grammar, must have rules—but these are not evident in the network of institutions that dot the international system even at any one moment in history.

Stephen Krasner has suggested that what is evident over time in the state-institution nexus is a variant of the "garbage can" scheme, in which states that are faced with streams of problems and streams of solutions find matches between the two in ways that are weakly if at all constrained by language, prior practice, or more expansive definitions of sovereignty than the one I used earlier.[35] In a time of rapid change what seemed yesterday to be inviolable rules of international institutions can become today's anachronisms. The United Nations has put its imprimatur on territorial enclaves or "safe havens" for the Kurdish population within the sovereign territorial boundaries of Iraq. Members of NATO and the former Warsaw Pact have agreed essentially on a free-skies proposal for the monitoring of arms accords. What several years ago was considered to be purely domestic issues relating to human rights, citizenship, voting, and so on is rapidly becoming a legitimate realm for surveillance *and* action by international institutions. Parallel developments took place earlier in trade negotiations in which domestic industrial organization, business practices, and even what some people would call "culture" are now standard subjects of bargaining about trade, at least between the United States and Japan.[36] Some but not all of these new practices are likely to be institutionalized broadly and formally over the coming years.

It is important to recognize that this type of change is not by itself a challenge to the reflectivist approach; the central question is, What is driving the change? Here the reflectivist approach may be vulnerable. If it is states that are the primary innovators, if it is states that later agree to create or join institutions that simply coordinate or regulate their evolving practices, then we are not really in a world in which states and institutions are mutually constitutive in the reflectivist sense. Powerful states may agree to redefine part of what it is that they (and their weaker brethren) are, and then confirm that agreement within institutions, but the engine of change would remain in the state. If the two steps—innovation and confirmation—are logically separable and separate in time and history as well, then it makes sense from the researcher's point of view to analyze them separately. The story that reflectivists tell about the origins of institutions does not predispose research in that direction.

What Do Institutions Do?

Given its roots in functional and utilitarian reasoning the rationalist approach should make its strongest claims on answering this question.[37] Rationalists see institutions as having mostly distributive functions, allocating costs and benefits among members according to a scheme that must be removed to some degree from the distribution of power (otherwise, why say that institutions do anything?). An important part of the allocation scheme is to alter transaction costs so that deals considered legitimate within the institution are facilitated and, by implication or directly, illegitimate deals are made more difficult. Robert Keohane's various demonstrations that institutions "bridge" market-failure problems that would otherwise impede bargains of mutual interest between states stand as the exemplar of this kind of approach.[38]

The market-failure analogy is by no means as limiting as it might appear at first glance. By drawing imaginatively on theories of incomplete contracting, Keohane and others in this tradition have shown how more elaborate institutions can provide states with means to alter substantially the expected future costs of certain kinds of behavior, which in turn makes possible relatively credible promises to do or not to do certain things that would otherwise be difficult to promise. Consider how NATO's institutional structure affected the credibility of the promise that West Germany in the 1950s wanted to make to France and Britain not to use again reconstituted military force against its presumptive allies. NATO (after 1950) had a unified command structure centered in Brussels. The command functions of the German *Bundeswehr* were transferred from a German general staff to the NATO command. This raised substantially the expected future costs to Germany of taking independent military action—as did other institutional features of NATO. The subsequent evolution of something approximating a "security community" in Western Europe rested on the promise of states not to use force within the community to settle disputes, a promise that states (and particularly West Germany) would have found hard to make and even harder to make credible without the institutions of NATO.[39]

Viewing international institutions through the theoretical lens of incomplete contracting problems, as persuasive as it is, still leaves aside or takes as given the preferences that underlie states' demands for contracts at all. That is probably acceptable in certain cases, for example, in NATO during its early years where the collective good that the institution is going to provide is relatively clear to all involved, as is the nature of the promise that states want to make to each other. It may not be acceptable in other cases, when issues are not so readily defined or shared in conception. When the challenge is less well understood than the Soviet military threat was during the Cold War, it may not be sufficiently clear what kinds of promises states actually want to make to each other or what is the collective good an institution may be able to offer. Asking similar questions about NATO in the mid-1990s leads to a more confusing picture because the reform and reconfiguration schemes being worked out in Brussels are not simply the product of strategic games played out between actors with exogenous preferences. States are arguing instead about what the game is; most of the so-called assumptions that need to be in place before a rationalist analysis of institutions can proceed are up for grabs. This kind of debate is not uncommon in international politics, and we should expect to see it more frequently during periods of rapid change when the environment in which states act is unsettled and uncertain; but it is *not* something that the rationalist research program is well suited to interpret.

This is where the reflectivist approach makes its own very strong claims. The distributive functions of institutions are relegated to second place in this approach because the interesting action takes place earlier, in defining precisely what it is that is going to be distributed and to whom. Institutions are not only distributive but *creative*, in two senses. First, it is institutions that empower actors to make claims. That the range of actors so empowered remains confined generally to states per se does not negate the reflectivist argument, since what is a "state" may depend more on institutional recognition than on competencies. In the early 1990s, Bosnia-Hercegovina could press its claims at the United Nations and at the CSCE but Serbia-Montenegro could not, despite the fact that the former entity (government? state?) controlled almost no territory whereas the latter was clearly a functioning social entity with the ability to implement policies over a discrete piece of territory.[40] Again, I sound a note of caution: Bosnia-Hercegovina may not survive as an independent political unit. If other small self-declared states of the post–Cold War breakdown do, it will be an important opportunity for the reflectivists to show that the institutions of which they have become a part were an important cause of that outcome.

The second element of creativity lies in the process of generating preferences. The reflectivist approach presumes that state actors do not really have preferences over many issues prior to the process of interaction that takes place in institutions. Social units in (imaginary) isolation from one another may have an inherent desire to survive and to preserve their autonomy; but even if that assumption is granted, reflectivists doubt that preferences over most other issues in international relations can follow in a similarly independent way.[41] If issues themselves are defined intersubjectively, then preferences over those issues cannot reasonably be said to exist prior to interaction. Preferences arise, then, where there were none before. If identity is defined as a bundle of preferences, then this is necessarily a second part of what it means to say that states create and are constituted by institutions as identity-seeking actors.

If I have portrayed here the reflectivist logic as a closed circle of reasoning that is seemingly self-referential and nonfalsifiable, that is because I think it probably is. That does not mean that it fails or is not intriguing as description. But I think the reflectivist approach has not done well in reaching outside of closed circles to provide a consistent analytic lever, a means of understanding institutions that will travel *across* stories. Though I have great respect for Alexander Wendt's efforts to introduce from sociology structuration theory into this area,[42] I fear in the end that too much concentration on the so-called agent-structure debate clouds the real explanatory challenge. I have yet to find among international relations scholarship a serious claim that Wendt is wrong in an ontological sense or that "problematizing the state" would not help us to describe the world as it really is, which suggests that there may be less at stake in the agent-structure debate than some claim.[43] The principal gripe with a structuration approach is methodological, and I find it a legitimate complaint. My particular gripe is that there remain too many potential closer circles, too many possible self-fulfilling stories among which the approach cannot clearly distinguish. States and anarchy work well together, but global Leviathan and a hierarchically organized international system would have worked just as well for structuration theory, as would a large and possibly infinite number of other outcomes. This points back to the first weakness of the reflectivist approach, which is in some ways more fundamental: Why one of these agent-structure "solutions" and not another? There remains no clear answer.

Institutions and Change: Using History

It is awkward, at least on the surface, to juxtapose the two concepts, institutions and change, in international politics (as it would be in any complex environment). The concept "institution" implies by itself stasis and not change; institutions are at a minimum patterns of behavior and of interaction that are *resistant* to change. Economists know this kind of ambivalence well. The most pure microeconomic models rely on the persistent logic of an institution called "the market" or "the money economy" to generate internally valid statements about rational individuals or mass behavior.[44] When economists try to give an account of how people actually behave, however, they are drawn inexorably to the problem of institutions and change. Even the money economy developed gradually and unevenly over time; as Simon Kuznets reminded us, "the excogitation of its complicated logic as a highly developed and consistent type, while useful, necessarily reflects the concentration on a case at one point in a vast range."[45] Institutions evolve (not necessarily in Darwinian fashion, however), they mature, they decay—in short, institutions undergo change. To complicate matters further, they are likely to do so at different rates; and because a conglomeration of institutions is certain to be in operation at any given moment, some on the upswing while others decline, some dominant while others are weak, it is not a simple challenge to give even a good descriptive account of the institutional environment within which any single behavior sits. Having set out this warning flag, we still need a starting point to say something useful about how international relations theorists have tried to deal in practical terms with this problem and how it has affected our research.

A central issue that differentiates rationalist and reflectivist views on this score is, in my view, whether institutions can themselves be a *cause* of change, a locus of innovation; or is that possibility confined to states and power that attaches to states? This is really a subset of the question of what do institutions do, but it is a subset that makes particular demands on attention to process and to history. It may be possible to show in a perpendicular slice of history at time = t how institutions reduce transaction costs for certain kinds of deals or even how institutions define the contours of an issue for states. It is not easy, however, to talk about change without at least *two* perpendicular slices of history, taken at point 1 and point 2, between which change has intervened. (Each additional slice of history adds, in principle, another data point—which is why I started this chapter with a preference for arguments that incorporate some notion of process.) If institutions generate change, or if they simply reflect or legitimate change that has taken place for other reasons, it would not be possible to know that without examining history. Taken on their own terms, what use of history do these two approaches make in their attempt to comprehend change?

The rationalist school is generally intolerant of history simply because history is not necessary to the argument. The driving force here is a change in the environment, which is treated as an exogenous shift in an independent variable and is usually not itself a target of explanation. The dependent variable is modified behavior on the part of states. What "intervenes" is simply the change in incentives and/or capabilities of those states that follows directly from the change in the environment. It is possible that different incentives could drive states to change the forms of the institutions within which they interact, or even the boundaries of what is a state and what is an institution.[46] But the outcome of change is still explained primarily through comparative statics, based on efficiency criteria. This is what makes it possible to slice into a system at time = t and satisfy the missing terms in the argument by looking only at the relative positions of the actors within that discrete slice.

In its use (or really non-use) of history, the rationalist approach imitates what economic studies of industrial clustering have called "pure-necessity" models of location under independent preferences.[47] The notion common to both kinds of stories is that unit actors make decisions on the basis of separate preferences that are essentially unaffected by what other units do. Locational clustering of industry is preordained by factor endowments that are geographically based. It is these factor endowments that are the "external environment"; the presence or absence of other firms does not affect what the next firm about to decide where to locate can earn in each region. It is easy to show that under these assumptions neither chance events nor the sequence in which firms make their decisions about where to locate affects the outcome. History does not matter. If one could, as Stephen Jay Gould has put it, "play the tape of history over again" but with a different sequence of firm decisions and even the addition a few random shocks, Silicon Valley would still be the heart of the U.S. computer industry. At equilibrium, the observed spatial pattern of industry is a unique and efficient outcome. The same would apply to the nexus of states and institutions that make up the international system. Change is ergodic and equifinal; chance events and the sequencing of history do not matter to the "final" outcome of the rationalist story.

The reflectivist approach is also relatively intolerant of history, although in a peculiar and different way from the rationalist approach. The driving force in the argument here can also be an exogenous change in the environment; for reflectivists, however, that change does not alter incentives directly but instead is filtered heavily through a social system in which individual actors are deeply embedded. Change in any individual actor's behavior is less interesting than a change in the behavior of the system as a whole. In principle a driving force for change could arise endogenously as well, from processes ongoing within the social system itself, although it is not so clear where such forces would come from if the system were not challenged by external events. If structures and agents are mutually constitutive, if the nexus of states and institutions is strongly self-reinforcing, why (and how) would innovations arise from within in the absence of external challenge?

The point is that change in the reflectivist story is also difficult to grasp, because the approach is not really sensitive in a manageable way to the contingency and variability of structures over time. Reflectivists stress that what happens in the future is constrained by what has happened in the past, but the general nature of the logic behind this argument makes it almost too robust. The concept of change must have a broad sweep because it must confront deeply embedded structures that are powerfully reinforced. Change must move mountains and, as in geology, timing, duration, and the weight of forces driving change could all be essential. Small forces can make a big difference if they persist for long enough. Conversely, discrete chance events at critical moments in the process of forming the sturdy state-institution nexus can determine which of the many (perhaps infinite) "solutions" to the problem is chosen. The story comes close to a different model of industrial clustering called the "pure chance" model. In this kind of story new firms are born in a particular region by spinning off from existing firms in that region. If each new firm stays where it is founded and any existing firm is equally likely to give birth to a new firm, then the equilibrium pattern of location is utterly dependent on the sequence in which firms actually generate offspring.[48] Since that "cause" is random, the outcome is completely dependent on chance. Rerun the tape of history and other outcomes (possibly an infinite number) are equally likely to that which did emerge. This kind of radical indeterminism is, in my view, also ahistorical (albeit in an opposite manner from rationalist determinism). If history is made up of singular stories of pure chance it can be interesting as description, but not really as part of generalizable explanations.

This discussion is my way of pointing out how history, at least in the way I am using the term here, has been marginalized in both rationalist and reflectivist studies of international institutions. Why was history left behind? The "decision," I think, was largely a concession to methodology, a concession that was in turn made possible by faith in the appropriateness for international relations research of models tied to particularly static notions about equilibrium. Both the rationalist and the reflectivist approaches are so tied (albeit in different ways) by two central assumptions.

The first assumption lies on the "demand" side of international institutions: It is that the demand for organization in a social system increases directly with the degree of complexity in the environment. In other words, as the world becomes more complex social actors demand higher levels of formal organization just to stay even in terms of world order. The second assumption lies on the "supply" side: It is that there are increasing costs to social organization. Pure anarchy, as Kenneth Waltz pointed out, is a very *inexpensive* way of organizing politics; to set up, maintain, and enforce hierarchical government is very expensive.[49] Combine these two assumptions, and you have a function that describes diminishing returns past a certain point for institutional organization in the international system. Rationalists and reflectivists may differ on the precise shape of the curve and (sometimes more for normative than for analytic reasons) about how soon the point of diminishing returns is reached, but they share in the logic of equilibrium generated by the assumptions. The quantity of international organization tends toward an optimal level at which supply and demand meet; on either side of that point strong forces push back toward the center. That is the essence of equilibrium: Shocks, accidents, mistakes, and other exogenous forces may upset the balance in the short term but will not have longer-term consequences, as the system tends inexorably to rebalance itself at its central point.

It is difficult with equilibrium-based models of this kind to conceptualize processes of change that are more than marginal adjustment within a prevailing system, in this case an international system.[50] The *possible* weaknesses for understanding macrolevel change in international politics were recognized early on, but these were seen mainly as a dilemma for political philosophers and pure theoreticians. Everyone doing empirical research in international relations understood that equilibrium models were oversimplified abstractions, but the assumptions seemed to be plausible representations of reality. Equally important, the models did seem to generate decent approximations of the way the system actually behaved. We went about our research, then, with the faith that the knowledge we were gaining would cumulate in a continuing fashion. That faith might well have been justified had the system we were studying continued to conform to the assumptions and expectations of equilibrium models.

The events of the 1980s and 1990s to which I alluded in the introductory part of this chapter reveal new questions about that faith.[51] Taken together, these events suggest that we are in the midst of a change of international system, at least in Europe.[52] This process of change has thrown the system into turmoil, undermining some old institutions and generating new ones. It has also induced a series of small if sometimes intensely violent conflicts, which cause most people to raise their eyebrows when political scientists refer to what is happening as a kind of "peaceful change." But the point remains: There has been no large conflict involving the major state actors who had or have the largest stakes in the system and its transformation.

The new "post–Cold War era" has not been set off as sharply from its past as were previous new international systems that developed in the wake of systemic wars.[53] One important consequence is that "old" international institutions and patterns of interaction—although they have come under pressure—have not been discredited and wiped away. "Old" ideas have not been delegitimized; in some instances at least they have been reinforced. And power relationships have not been fully clarified; status and power remain intermingled in a network of established institutions.[54] If the political map of Europe is being transformed in the context of extant institutions and ideas that retain both power and legitimacy, then the evolution of the international system past 1990 will reflect, perhaps deeply, the legacy of how it arrived at its moment of change. Will the processes and outcomes conform then to the assumptions and expectations of an equilibrium model, in which the effects of a history that includes chance events and critically timed exogenous shocks are damped out? Perhaps not. Consider, for example, how different the political and economic environment would be in Europe today if there had been no NATO, no European Community, no generally accepted ideas about democracy, economic liberalism, human rights (and the relationship among those things—as well as between them and the possibility of security cooperation), and so on.[55] Chance events at particular moments may have had a major causal role in bringing about this change and may have important sequelae that will not dissipate over time. Consider how different the international system might look as an environment if the Soviet "withdrawal" from Eastern Europe had come ten years later than it did.[56] Neither the rationalist nor the reflectivist view of international institutions is inclined to ask such questions—although the answers to them may be central to understanding what happens in the state-institution nexus over the next decade.

An Institutionalist Research Agenda

It is this gap between the rationalist and reflectivist approaches—the questions they do not ask—into which in my own work I am struggling to introduce an institutionalist research agenda. Two researchable propositions underpin the argument. The first is that structures of power constrain but do not powerfully determine political systems; that even under relatively tight constraints there are substantial and significant alternatives for states organizing themselves into institutions. If, for example, the system of relationships that developed between the United States and its major European allies and in Europe in the 1940s after the last systemic war was substantially underdetermined by the exigencies of a bipolar world, then the system of relationships developing in the 1990s is likely to be even more so.

The second proposition is that the institutions now coming into being in Europe (some de novo, some adapted from extant ones) will affect conceptions of self-interest both in the established states of the West and the newly emerging states of the East. The institutionalist hypothesis I propose is that these particular changes in states' conceptions of self-interest and of institutions could be mutually reinforcing—that this historically contingent state-institution nexus could sustain and propagate itself as a stable system. The theoretical analogy is to a third model of industrial location known as "agglomeration economies," in which fixed geographical benefits of locating in a particular region are enhanced by agglomeration benefits from the number of firms that have already located in the region.[57]

In this model, more than one outcome is possible, but not all of the possible outcomes are equally likely. Regions that are well endowed with factors have a higher probability of selection, but chance events could early on drive the system to a lower probability location that is not "optimal." Once a certain number of firms have co-located in that place, agglomeration effects overwhelm the benefits for the next firm of choosing to locate in the "better-endowed" place. The outcome is due both to chance and necessity. Not everything is possible, but more than one thing is. The same could be true of the state-institution nexus if, for example, institutions were by one or another mechanism to create increasing returns to the adoption of a particular set of ideas about how to organize domestic political systems within states and international relations between them. If that is happening in Europe after the end of the Cold War, then it would be impossible to understand either the process or the outcome without attention to both structural/power factors and history. Of course, it is not enough to say only that. The main challenge to institutionalists is to explicate and demonstrate the causal pathways that are operating, the mechanisms by which history in the sense I use the term here exerts its effect.[58]

I have made the argument elsewhere that even in the late 1940s under maximum bipolar constraints of providing security, there existed a range of possibilities for institutions, of which NATO was only one. The United States could have offered security promises to allies on a discriminatory bilateral basis, as the Soviet Union did in Eastern Europe and as the British and French governments would almost certainly have accepted.[59] Instead, the United States sponsored the creation of NATO, a multilateral alliance in which an attack on one was to be considered an attack on all; all allies were to be treated equally; and diffuse reciprocity was to be the norm.[60] If security in NATO took on many of the characteristics of a public good, it was because the United States chose to make it that way. Put differently, this was an institutional choice and it must be explained, not assumed—as anyone living today in Poland, Hungary, and the Czech Republic (at least) understands perfectly well.[61]

Once the question of institutional structure is opened up in this way, the consequences of what were products of choice and not necessity become themselves contingent. That is important if NATO has had a lasting effect on the possibilities perceived by and the preferences of states that were included in the institution. I think it is possible to demonstrate such effects. Consider the consequences for intra-European relationships: The institutional structure of NATO forced France and Germany to come to terms and solve their century-old security problem in a way that had seemed impossible until then. Useful counterfactuals for this point are not just imaginary: Contrast the current Franco-German relationship with that between Poland, Hungary, and what was the Czech and Slovak Federal Republic (CSFR) to see at least in part the consequences of the U.S. institutional choice as against the Soviet one.[62] The argument can extend to the many other institutional relationships that were facilitated by or linked to NATO—the European Community being the most obvious example.

The EU is an institution that probably would have been impossible in the East and may still be impossible or unlikely there. Again, counterfactuals are not entirely imaginary. The Visegrad process—which includes Poland, Hungary, and the CSFR and then its successor states—began in 1990 as an effort to create a kind of miniature EC with extensive economic integration featuring free trade, and intergovernmental cooperation on foreign policies, including, most important, joint negotiation with Brussels over accession to the Community. In late 1992 this effort at extensive cooperation began to falter, due largely to the noncomplementarity of the economies of these states, different foreign-policy orientations, in particular with regard to the Yugoslav conflict and the looming presence of Ukraine in the East, as well as (natural) competition to join the European Community as quickly as possible. Meanwhile, the EU moves in fits and starts, despite severe challenges. The doubtful status of Maastricht and particularly its provisions for moving toward a single currency notwithstanding, certain things that have happened before—such as Paris's search for allies in Eastern Europe or Moscow (or even Washington) to oppose or balance German power—are certainly not happening today; and many things *are* happening within the European Union that signal a continued commitment on the part of states to further economic and (more haltingly) political integration.

A second important consequence of NATO and its associated institutions was the linkage established within the institution between security cooperation per se and the domestic characteristics of the cooperating states. Churchill's realpolitik view of a potential alliance with the devil was not a founding principle for NATO; and although NATO was never an ideal-type security community, it did establish political standards for its member states in the areas of democracy, human rights, and economic freedom.[63] This was done according to propositions that went far beyond what the exigencies of providing security against the Soviet threat demanded.

Power did not create these consequences; they were forged in the realm of ideas and purposes and manifested subsequently in international institutions that were in turn made possible by U.S. power. But neither appears to be particularly volatile in Europe today. Neither I nor anyone else should confidently predict the form or shape of security institutions that will evolve in Eastern Europe over the next decade, but the current expectations of states that I mentioned in the introductory section of this chapter do reveal something that is arguably at variance with the rationalist approach. Developments here should provide interesting data for partial tests that can differentiate among at least two of the three schools of thought on international institutions.

It is less clear to me how to set up an experiment that would evaluate the reflectivist approach in this kind of empirical context. I think it is safe to say now, contra the reflectivist argument, that very little in the ongoing discussion about security structures in Europe after the Cold War is being taken for granted and that there is nothing approaching a generative grammar for institutions. No one just assumes that the Franco-German security problem is consigned to history; and no one just asserts that security guarantees are linked existentially to democratic domestic governments. Both propositions are the stuff of political debates in Europe and in Washington; they are contested both in the realm of power and in the realm of ideas. Options are floated, considered, and rejected in conscious processes of choice that will likely become more transparent to research as real challenges (such as the many-faceted conflict in the former Yugoslavia) mount. The data will be there; it is up to the reflectivists to produce an experimental design that can advance their argument in a case that ought to be a strong one for them.

My own institutionalist research plan is not limited to security issues.[64] At the same time that old institutions are evolving, new institutions are being created in Europe and by new actors who are not predominant in the traditional resources of power. One institution that has attracted my attention is the European Bank for Reconstruction and Development, which was inaugurated in April 1991 with the primary purpose of facilitating and supporting the transition to market economies and pluralist democracies in the emerging states of the former communist bloc. The bank has several unique features.[65] First, it is self-consciously a "European" institution—the impetus behind the bank came from the European Commission and the French Government; EU member states along with EU institutions hold a majority of the voting shares; and (in an unprecedented step) the EU itself and the European Investment Bank (EIB) each hold shares in the bank and have a seat on the board of directors.[66] The EBRD is also an institution with explicit political purposes that go beyond the boundaries of previous development banks: Article 1 of the Charter states that the Bank's "purpose shall be to foster the transition toward free-market oriented economies and promote private and entrepreneurial initiative in Central and East European Countries *committed to and applying the principles of multiparty democracy, pluralism, and market economics.*"[67] Also in contrast to other development banks, the EBRD is committed by its charter to focus its efforts on the growth of the private sector in its countries of operations, a focus that reflects not only economic considerations but also political notions about the relationship between private enterprise (particularly small and medium-sized businesses) and the social evolution of modern democratic societies.

How did this new institution, which goes beyond the boundary of previous cooperative endeavors and extant institutions, emerge during a period of rapid international change?[68] The EBRD was not a product of concentrated power, and it was not an "efficient" functional or utilitarian solution to a clearly defined problem. Quite the contrary: In late 1989 when the "problem" of whether and how to assist postcommunist transitions first appeared on the agenda for Western states, the several major players (in particular France, Germany, the United States, and Japan) offered very different arguments about what if anything needed to be done by governments, and who should do it. Each of those arguments was matched with different putative institutional arrangements that would have not only distributed differently the costs and benefits of cooperation among the Western states but also would have meant very different terms of engagement for the East. For a time, each of the Western states pursued independently its own course according to its unilateral definition of interest vis-à-vis the East. Each acknowledged in principle that it would be desirable to develop a cooperative approach, but there was no agreement on what cooperation was going to be about and, by implication, on the institutional structure through which a mutually acceptable form of cooperation could be organized.

The rationalist argument about institutions should generate fairly clear expectations about the next chapter of this story. The baseline is a set of states, not one of which is predominant in power, positioning themselves along the vectors of their autonomous interests. Since the stakes are significant, the interests are diverse and sometimes conflicting, and there is no clear sense that cooperation is necessary to avoid some kind of disaster (a shared aversion), the expected outcome tends toward no agreement or a least common-denominator "agreement to disagree" that creates a bland institution as an overlay to states' pursuit of individual interests.

But neither the process nor the outcome of the story seems to match those expectations. Instead, the arguments over possibilities for cooperation are fought out over different issues.[69] One issue revolves around the question, What does "Europe" per se mean at the end of the Cold War? What does Europe do, who is to be included, and on what terms? As in 1949 at NATO's birthing, there were alternative conceptions floating around, but this time there was no United States or other hegemon imposing a particular outcome. An outcome did emerge, however, other than "no agreement." At EBRD, Europe is an intergovernmental affair of national states, cooperating for an outward-oriented, foreign-policy purpose, with a central role for the European Union as an independently represented actor, with the United States as primus inter pares associate, and with the Soviet Union (while it existed) included in an apprentice role.[70]

The central point, which I document elsewhere, is that neither this outcome nor the processes of bargaining that led to it reflect strongly the impact of power attached to individual states and serving autonomous interests. What both do reflect is a convergence on a broad set of ideas and purposes that came to be shared among an intermediate-sized group of powerful states about how "Europe" should be organized and what it should do as an aspiring foreign-policy actor at the end of the Cold War. These ideas and purposes are familiar: They represent updated versions of "Atlanticist" foreign-policy ideas associated with U.S. "hegemony" during the Cold War. The process of creating a new international institution to deal with a new problem in a rapidly transforming international environment spawned in this case a reexamination of interests among the major states that drove their conceptions of interest closer together, despite the different geopolitical positions of the major actors vis-à-vis the East and the lack of any hegemonic power, but in the context of extant institutions and ideas not delegitimated or wiped away by systemic war. A similar story can be told for the other central issue of debate, the political economy of development and democracy in Eastern Europe, with special attention to the role of the private sector in forging a link between economic progress and democratic governance.[71] The outcome on these two axes is more than just a charter for a bank in the City of London; it has been an important factor in setting basic terms for cooperation among the Western states in their approach to Eastern Europe, and in setting terms under which the East and the West move toward a new relationship.

Can the reflectivist approach deal more comfortably with what I see as having happened at EBRD? I think not. The emphasis that the reflectivist approach places on ideas may be reflected in the story that I tell, but the ideas that emerged eventually as a foundation for cooperation among states at EBRD were at no point in the process of bargaining taken for granted. They were contested and championed by states. Many of the more specific ideas that have come to underpin EBRD's operating doctrines did not even exist in practical form prior to autumn 1989 but were crystallized from diverse intellectual currents by bank personnel and negotiators of shareholder states in the process of creating and beginning to operate the bank. Intellectual entrepreneurship and chance events played a critical role in bringing those currents together and forging a practical foundation for cooperation. EBRD is not, then, a product of any kind of agent-structure circle. It is a cooperative endeavor that has partially supplanted an embryonic competition among autonomous actors in pursuit of self-interest narrowly defined. The ahistorical nature of the reflectivist approach conceals the fact that these two streams of behavior—competition and cooperation—were separated in time. A process intervened between them, a process that has left the two in a state of coexistence that is not going to be "finally resolved," at least not within the time span of a reasonable research project, to a degree that would satisfy the expectations of a reflectivist argument.

Conclusion: Institutions and Path Dependence

My effort to construct an institutionalist explanation for EBRD sees a story of states with autonomous and different interests coming together to discuss possible cooperative endeavors—in the context of preexisting institutions and ideas—and finding their interests modified by both. Europe, as it is defined at EBRD, bears the mark of U.S.-led postwar multilateralism and Atlanticism that were cemented together by NATO and other Cold War institutions, and the mark of a concept of Europe closely tied to that within the EU, which was also a part of the post–World War II institutional network. Political conditionality as defined at EBRD bears the mark of shared experiences of multilateral lending for development at the World Bank and other regional development banks, which were also part of that network. Both demonstrate quite explicitly a link between security commitments and the domestic characteristics of states, according to a particular set of historically contingent assumptions about what it takes for modern states to live together peacefully and prosperously on the small piece of land that is the European continent. The external environment does not answer the question, What do states have to look like, and how alike do they have to be in order to cooperate with each other? That critical question is being answered in Europe, at least at present, according to a set of ideas and associated institutions.

The central question for an institutionalist research program is, Can cooperation be sustained by this foundation? If ideas and institutions act as a source of convergent interests for the moment, this may be just a lag in history, anticipating the moment when institutions fail or are submerged in familiar patterns of multipolar politics. Or it may not be; but the evidence to distinguish between these outcomes may not become clear for some time to come. In the meantime, an approach to institutions that makes use of history can rephrase the question to ask, Will a convergence among conceptions of interests that occurs in the process of creating an institution be reinforced by what the institution does as it carries out its operations, or will it be undermined?

If a convergence of interests is reinforced over time, then presumably the institution and the interests it promotes within states could establish themselves along a sustainable trajectory different from the "efficient" outcome of the rationalist approach.[72] The institutionalist approach rests on the notion that the trajectories need not converge and that a "noneffecient" trajectory could have sufficient internal returns that states, which remain free to choose, would not see net gains in jumping off the path. Working out in more detail the mechanisms by which this could happen and specifying observable implications along the path are the crucial steps in developing a more serviceable elaboration of the institutionalist approach.

There are related theories on which institutionalists can draw for this purpose. Institutionalism is by nature a path-dependent approach to explanation in the same way as is the "agglomeration economies" model of industrial location. Both rest on possibilities for what economists call positive feedback—which means increasing rather than diminishing returns to adoption.[73] With diminishing returns—as in conventional economic theory—economic behavior engenders negative feedbacks that lead to a single predictable equilibrium for price and market share. In a world of increasing returns there are many possible equilibrium outcomes. Such a world has four important properties different from those of the more standard world of diminishing returns. It is nonpredictable, in the sense that an outside observer could not deduce from antecedent conditions at which of the potential equilibrium outcomes the system will stabilize. It is potentially inefficient: There may be other potential equilibrium outcomes more optimal on aggregate that the system cannot attain. It can be inflexible, with nonefficient outcomes locked in and impossible to exit from. Finally, it is non-ergodic, which means that small and/or chance events that influence the system's behavior early on in its development may not be damped out or averaged away over time. In agglomeration economies, a certain product or technology or behavior may not be the optimal or efficient solution to a problem, but it becomes increasingly beneficial in the eyes of the next actor choosing what to adopt, depending on how many other actors have already adopted it. In this world of positive returns not all things are possible, but more than one thing is. If a particular "solution" gains an edge over others and increasing returns to adoption are sufficiently large, that solution can be "locked in" and difficult to exit from.

Economic historians tell this kind of story about spatial industrial location, as I discussed earlier; about technology (the QWERTY typewriter keyboard is the most familiar example), and even about international trade.[74] Path dependence is central to each. The early history of choice and change—in part the consequence of chance events, preexisting institutions, and small unpredictable shocks—can determine powerfully which trajectory is established and eventually "prevails." The system as a whole is non-ergodic: It does not forget its history. My point is that nor can a research program that will try to understand a world in which a similar dynamic may be operating. I have suggested that the state-institution nexus that is evolving in Europe today may have such properties.

But how will an aspiring social science deal with the element of chance in these stories? At least in the case of EBRD, chance plays an important role in initiating a series of events that leads to the creation of a new institution.

Chance also is important in "selecting" this particular institution (in terms of both its structure and its purposes) from a menu of realistic alternatives. This illustrates an important limitation of the institutionalist approach, shared by the economic models I have employed as analogies: There is no logically based "theory" of selection. To the extent that chance is not just variation in variables below the resolution of our research tools, and small events are truly the products of chance, such a theory may be in principle, not just in practice, inconceivable.[75] The best we can hope for now is probably a series of narratives about selection that may, over time, suggest recurrent patterns. If a "theory" of selection emerges, it will likely be the product of inductive reasoning and made up of contingent generalizations rather than any elegant deductive statement.

This demonstrates the limits of an institutionalist approach, but it also says something positive about what kinds of explanations are possible for institutionalists. We can also construct narratives that focus on the mechanisms of reinforcement and try to differentiate sustainable paths from unsustainable ones given the constant pressure of states defining their own interests. Possible mechanisms by which path dependence can be established is something that we know about and can model in a more explicit way. Such mechanisms include increasing returns to adoption (a particular institution rides down a learning curve); network externalities (as more actors join a particular institution, the benefits of belonging increase); support network externalities (as more actors join a particular institution, other institutions with which the primary one interfaces become more attractive and the system as a whole shows increasing benefits); and institutional isomorphism.[76] Each mechanism in principle can be pushed to generate observable implications in specific empirical cases, to demonstrate the existence (or nonexistence) of positive feedbacks and path dependence, and perhaps to compare the strengths of these effects.

It is important to remember that the existence of multiple equilibria does not mean that anything is possible, and it does not mean that anything that gets started can sustain itself. The Concert of Europe was a wasting asset. Other forms of international organization have not been. Some are clearly "nonoptimal." This kind of problem should be a central focus of international relations research, particularly in trying to understand the broader problem of change. If we are living in an international political world that does not tend necessarily toward a negative-returns equilibrium, then understanding how states and international institutions fit together may mean understanding what is possible under specific circumstances, identifying critical junctures of change, delineating mechanisms under which a certain solution can be sustained as well as the forces that are pushing toward other paths. An institutionalist research program, in my view, has good potential to contribute to this kind of understanding.

Quite obviously, what I am proposing is different from the logical, deductive, deterministic, predictive orientation of the rationalist approach. But the attractions of that approach may diminish in a time of rapid, macrolevel change. International political theory can benefit more fully from the experiments that are taking place at a furious pace in the world today, if we are willing to revisit decisions about methodology that were made at a different time (and for different reasons). Above all, I think that the end of the Cold War presents fantastic opportunities to understand better the problem of innovation in world politics. Reuven Brenner has argued that when circumstances are expected to remain stable, people "memorize": They copy the institutions of their ancestors and at most tinker with them or maneuver within them. When circumstances are expected to change, people "think": They innovate, they take risks, they gamble.[77] International relations theory might well do the same.

Notes

I thought about and wrote this paper over a long period of time, during which I benefited from the writings of many people and discussions with so many others that I can not possibly recognize them all. Some are mentioned in footnotes; to the others I apologize and thank each one of you. I owe special thanks to the editors of the volume for inviting me to present my preliminary thoughts at a seminar at Princeton University in November 1991. The Council on Foreign Relations, the Institute on Global Conflict and Cooperation, and the Center for German and European Studies at the University of California at Berkeley provided needed research support.

1. This is not meant to denigrate the important contributions of the CSCE to legitimating and defending human rights groups in the Eastern bloc.

2. The classic argument is E. H. Carr, *The Twenty Years' Crisis, 1919–1939: An Introduction to the Study of International Relations* (London: St. Martin's Press, 1962).

3. Robert Keohane, *After Hegemony: Cooperation and Discord in the World Political Economy* (Princeton: Princeton University Press, 1984); Stephen Krasner, ed., *International Regimes* (Ithaca: Cornell University Press, 1983).

4. I adopt here, but only as a foil, the old distinction between high and low politics, which leaves trade in the latter category.

5. Robert Jervis, "Security Regimes," in *International Regimes,* ed. Krasner.

6. See, for example, Susan Strange, "Cave! Hic Dragones: A Critique of Regime Analysis," in *International Regimes,* ed. Krasner.

7. John J. Mearsheimer, "Back to the Future: Instability in Europe After the Cold War," *International Security* 15:1 (Summer 1990):5–57.

8. Ruggie elaborated these points in "Multilateralism: The Anatomy of an Institution," *International Organization* 46 (Summer 1992):561–598.

9. I thank Mark Zacher for sharing with me his research that produced these numbers. Zacher pointed out also that this secular trend cuts across multi-polarity/bipolarity, peace/war, and other such divides.

10. This involves the risk of simplifying and a bit of cartooning or at least a loss of some richness, but I will try to recapture some of that later.

11. Robert Keohane, "International Institutions: Two Approaches," *International Studies Quarterly* 32 (December 1988):379–396.

12. I am slipping in an assumption here, namely, that it is possible and useful to define such discrete "endpoints" as state 1 and state 2 as if they can be separated from the process of change, which may be ongoing. This may be to some a controversial move, but I will try to justify it later on.

13. I will also, for the sake of simplifying my analysis, pass over the considerable diversity among individual scholars and arguments within each category. All the usual "review article caveats" apply.

14. In an earlier work Keohane called this the "demand for institutions." See his "The Theory of Hegemonic Stability and Changes in International Economic Regimes, 1967–1977," in *Change In the International System*, ed. Ole R. Holsti, Randolph Siverson, and Alexander L. George (Boulder: Westview Press, 1980).

15. I borrow the term "identity seeking" from humanistic psychology. Identity seeking, apart from its particular philosophical orientation, has a number of implications that differentiate it from the concept of goal seeking. Two that stand out for international relations are: (1) that the preferences of an identity-seeking actor need not be transitive, nor are they sure to be consistent from one context to another; and (2) that survival may not take first priority. After all, human beings do commit suicide, which some psychologists interpret as an identity-seeking action, the sacrifice of life for the sake of a desired identity. For a related philosophical view, see Richard Rorty, "Inquiry as Recontextualization: An Anti-dualist Account of Interpretation," in *The Interpretive Turn*, ed. David R. Hiley, James F. Bohman, and Richard Shusterman (Ithaca: Cornell University Press, 1991).

16. James A. Caporaso, "International Relations Theory and Multilateralism: The Search for Foundations," *International Organization* 46 (Summer 1992): 633–680. Caporaso uses "institutionalist" in some different ways than I do here, but there are enough similarities (and I owe sufficient debt to his work) that I think using the term here is justifiable.

17. Others might want to collapse economic institutionalism into the rationalist school, and sociological institutionalism into the reflectivist. Arguably, different brands of historical institutionalism could be handled in different categories. Though there are some natural affinities here, I think this is a mistake—at least of overaggregation, and in many ways of plain mischaracterization, as I explain in the chapter.

18. See Russell Ackoff and Fred Emery, *On Purposeful Systems* (Chicago: Aldine-Atherton, 1972).

19. This deserves emphasis. "Rationalist" arguments that simply take all demonstrated influences on behavior into their independent variables and then claim to explain outcomes by saying that actors behave in accordance with these (expanded, ad infinitum) utility functions are no longer distinctively rationalist but have become something else—what I would call a descriptive compilation of what everyone else is saying about behavior.

20. For a sampling of the literature, see Talcott Parsons, *The Social System* (Glencoe, IL: Free Press, 1951); Parsons, "Prolegomena to a Theory of Social Institutions," *American Sociological Review* 55 (June 1990):319–333; Michael D. Cohen, James G. March, and Johan P. Olsen, "A Garbage Can Model of Organizational Choice," *Administrative Science Quarterly* 17 (1972):1–15; James G. March and Johan P. Olsen, *Ambiguity and Choice in Organizations* (Bergen: Universitetsforlaget, 1976).

21. Ernst B. Haas, *When Knowledge Is Power: Three Models of Change in International Organizations* (Berkeley: University of California Press, 1990).

22. I am not saying, of course, that it never makes sense. It is possible sometimes to reconstruct these debates in rationalist terms, but it is not always easy and the product is not always plausible. If it is done by manipulating ex post facto "assumptions" about states' short- or long-term utility calculations—which is simply a way of constructing utility functions to match observed outcomes—then it is illegitimate. Claiming that those functions explain in some sense what is happening is simply an exercise in nonfalsifiable "reasoning" and strips the rationalist approach of its greatest strengths.

23. Felicia Wong developed this point (in an unpublished paper, University of California, Berkeley, 1992) and passed it on to me. She noted that this kind of behavior sits at an interface between "cooperation," regional integration, and possibly "state building"—a more poorly specified concept which itself calls up a broad range of theories.

24. There are interesting issues here concerning how different perspectives on institutions would define a "case," but I will leave them aside for now.

25. In early 1993 the members of the Group of Seven agreed, after several years of difficult discussion, to create a small multilateral fund for nuclear safety in parallel with what remain primarily bilateral assistance efforts. (See Reuters, 5 February 1993.) Participants in the negotiations and the designated managers of the fund told me in several interviews that the multilateral fund would likely amount to less than US$700 million—whereas the problem is thought to be on the order of $50 billion. They agreed that the fund is a "supplementary mechanism" and more of a cosmetic overlay to principally bilateral organization than any substantive kind of multilateral cooperative endeavor.

26. And leaving the relationship when the marginal benefits that come with exit are equal to or greater than the marginal costs. See Robert Gilpin, *War and Change in World Politics* (Cambridge: Cambridge University Press, 1981). This "positive theory of institutions" is really only one step removed from the Coase theorem, in which (given the absence of transaction costs) the market achieves optimal allocation without any substantial need for institutions.

27. Paul R. Milgrom, Douglass C. North, and Barry R. Weingast, "The Role of Institutions in the Revival of Trade: The Law Merchant, Private Judges, and the Champagne Fairs," *Economics and Politics* 2 (1990):1–23. The Law Merchant refers to a set of legal codes governing commercial transactions, administered by private judges drawn from the commercial ranks, that arose between the tenth and thirteenth centuries and was largely in place over the commercially active regions of Europe by the end of the eleventh century.

28. Milgrom, North, and Weingast acknowledged that the Law Merchant evolved and changed over time; but they hardly discussed this evolution. What com-

manded their attention is the way in which the basic elements of the institution serve as a functional resolution to the problem of sustaining trade through contracts in the absence of a state and a complex legal infrastructure. The paper hints at a similarly functional explanation for the development of the more complex legal infrastructure later, when trading activity expanded still more quickly.

29. David Lake, among others, has done a lot of interesting work to uncover some of the different pathways this story can take. See, for example, Scott C. James and David A. Lake, "The Second Face of Hegemony: British Repeal of the Corn Law and the American Walker Tariff of 1846," *International Organization* 43 (Winter 1989):1–30.

30. See, for example, Stephen Krasner, "Global Communications and National Power: Life on the Pareto Frontier," *World Politics* 43 (April 1991).

31. Duncan Snidal has something to say about when a committee might coalesce to perpetuate extant institutions (those created by hegemonic power), but what he actually says points out just as clearly the general and diffuse nature of a "stretched-out" version of hegemonic stability theory. See Snidal, "The Limits of Hegemonic Stability Theory," *International Organization* 39 (Autumn 1985):599.

32. In Jon Elster's terms, ideas that define issues compete in something that is more like a forum than a market. See Elster, "The Market and the Forum: Three Varieties of Political Theory," in *Foundations of Social Choice Theory*, ed. Jon Elster and Aamund Hylland (Cambridge: Cambridge University Press, 1986), pp. 103–132.

33. Patrick Morgan and Anne Marie Burley have made arguments that verge on this kind of proposition. See Morgan, "Multilateralism and Security: Prospects in Europe," and Burley, "Regulating the World: Multilateralism, International Law, and the Projection of the New Deal Regulatory State," both in *Multilateralism Matters: The Theory and Praxis of an Institutional Form*, ed. John Ruggie (New York: Columbia University Press, 1993). I have seen some proponents of the rationalist approach try to recapture this argument by referring to the form of the institution as itself a "consumption good" for states; but this to me seems intellectual sleight of hand that covers up the trick of defining ex post facto utility functions. It seems clear to me that the logic of the rationalist approach demands that institutions be explained as instrumental.

34. Steven Weber, *Cooperation and Discord in U.S.-Soviet Arms Control* (Princeton: Princeton University Press, 1991), and "Cooperation and Interdependence," *Daedalus* 120 (Winter 1991).

35. Stephen Krasner made this point in "Westphalia and All That," in *Ideas and Foreign Policy: Beliefs, Institutions, and Political Change,* ed. Judith Goldstein and Robert O. Keohane (Ithaca: Cornell University Press, 1993), pp. 235–264. I owe thanks to Krasner also for some ideas that emerged from a discussion that he led about this paper in Berkeley in the autumn of 1991.

36. Of course elements of what some call "culture" others call "nontariff barriers," which is one way of smoothing the entrance of these issues onto the negotiating table.

37. It is also reasonable to expect the rationalist approach to be most well developed in this area, since it emerged principally in contrast to the stark realist argument that institutions do not do anything substantial in international politics except

as the agents of powerful states. The challenge of the first-generation literature on international regimes, as evidenced in the Krasner edited volume, was to show that institutions can act as independent or at least intervening variables and affect outcomes. Only once that role for institutions was firmly established did it make sense to start thinking seriously about the origins of institutions.

38. Keohane, *After Hegemony*.

39. I discuss these points in detail in Steven Weber, "Does NATO Have a Future?" in *The Future of European Security*, ed. Beverly Crawford (Berkeley: Institute of International Studies, 1992). I also turn the analysis around and ask, What kind of institutions would help states to make credible promises *to* use force, not within the community but against outsiders who attacked a member? This kind of argument helps to clarify the institutional structures of a "collective security system" and differentiate them from a security community—showing some of the strength of this kind of approach.

40. Obviously I intend no judgment on the justice of those policies.

41. Some would disagree that even this assumption is universally valid, but granting it does not really weaken the reflectivist position.

42. Alexander Wendt, *Social Theory of International Politics* (Cambridge: Cambridge University Press, forthcoming).

43. I borrow this phrase from David Dessler's article, "What's at Stake in the Agent-Structure Debate?" *International Organization* 43 (Summer 1989):441–473. My answer, after reading with particular care the conclusion to this article, is "not that much," since the kinds of research Dessler suggests we ought to do are almost indistinguishable from what many of us have been doing, albeit perhaps under slightly different labels.

44. For a particularly interesting statement of this position, see Wesley C. Mitchell, "The Prospects of Economics," in Mitchell, *The Backward Art of Spending Money and Other Essays* (New York: McGraw-Hill, 1937). This essay was written in 1924; in it Mitchell argued that "the money economy . . . is in fact one of the most potent institutions in our whole culture. In sober truth it stamps its pattern upon wayward human nature, makes us all react in standard ways to the standard stimuli it offers, and affects our very ideals of what is good, beautiful, and true. The strongest testimony to the power and pervasiveness of this institution in molding human behavior is that a type of economic theory that implicitly assumed men to be perfectly disciplined children of the money economy could pass for several generations as a social science." I've not seen a better statement of this position.

45. Simon Kuznets, "The Contribution of Wesley C. Mitchell," in Joseph Dorfman et al., *Institutional Economics: Veblen, Commons, and Mitchell Reconsidered* (Berkeley: University of California Press, 1964), p. 98. I thank David Spiro for pointing out to me the relevance of this literature.

46. There is a close analogy here to theories of industrial organization that rely heavily on transaction cost economics. In those stories, technological change alters the incentives to organize firms (particularly with regard to vertical integration), which changes in turn the "natural" boundaries of firms. Douglas North's *Structure and Change in Economic History* (New York: Norton, 1981) is a slightly different and intriguing attempt at a similar type of explanation in social organization beyond the scope of the firm. North relies heavily on changes in property-rights con-

cepts (an exemplar of an institution if there ever was one) to forge a more subtle link between technological change and social organization.

47. W. Brian Arthur wrote a helpful review of this literature in *Cities and Their Vital Systems*, ed. Jesse H. Ausubel and Robert Herman (Washington DC: National Academy Press, 1988).

48. Probability theorists call this a Polya process. Unit increments are added one at a time to one of N categories, with probabilities equal to current proportions in each category. It is easy to show that an equilibrium is reached with a constant proportion of industry in each category. But *which* equilibrium emerges is entirely dependent on the sequence in which firms spin off—and is thus a random outcome.

49. Presumably, there is a continuum of possibilities between these two extremes, with increasing costs as one moves along the continuum from anarchy to hierarchy. See Kenneth Waltz, *Theory of International Politics* (Reading, MA: Addison Wesley, 1979). For an interesting twist to the argument, see Giulio M. Gallarotti, "The Limits of International Organization: Systematic Failure in the Management of International Relations," *International Organization* 45 (Spring 1991):183–220.

50. Put differently, to explain movements along the curve presents less of a problem than trying to understand changes in its shape.

51. I present here some questions about whether the models are in fact generating decent approximations of how the system is behaving. Elsewhere I have begun to raise questions about the continuing validity of the assumptions, at least on the demand side (see "Cooperation and Interdependence"). Later in this chapter I will question as well the assumption about the supply side.

52. I rely here on Robert Gilpin's notion (in *War and Change in World Politics*, pp. 41–44) of a "systemic change" to refer to change in the governance of the system, which I think is clearly demonstrable as of 1992. Whether a more profound kind of change is occurring—what Gilpin calls "systems change," meaning a change in the nature of the actors—is more controversial, and I will not address the issue here.

53. Interesting debates are developing over the cause of this apparent difference, made particularly poignant because the system that is undergoing change was supposed (at least in the mainstream neorealist view) to have been extremely stable. I suggested rather quickly in the introductory section of this chapter that institutions were probably not a major cause, but that can be taken as a challenge to those who would argue differently.

54. Robert Gilpin contrasts "status" and "power" within international systems in *War and Change in World Politics*. See also Geoffrey Blainey, *Causes of War* (New York: Free Press, 1973), on the connection between legitimacy and "clarified" power relationships.

55. I explore the sources and consequences of this particular contingent linkage between security cooperation and broader concepts of what states that cooperate should—or must—be like in Steven Weber, "Shaping the Postwar Balance of Power: Multilateralism in NATO," *International Organization* 46 (Summer 1992): 633–680.

56. At which time the European Union might have been substantially closer to political union, and Japan might have had a much greater role in Europe and the United States a lesser one. I do not claim that these are anything more than plausi-

ble speculations, but I advance them to underscore the point that different timing and sequences of events could plausibly have led to very different outcomes. At the same time, it is important to recognize that counterfactuals like these are almost as easy to criticize as they are to write down.

57. Paul David explains that this effect would follow from economies of scale and network externalities in infrastructure, labor markets, legal and financial services, transportation, and so on. See David, "High Technology Centers and the Economics of Locational Tournaments," cited and discussed in Arthur, "Urban Systems and Historical Path Dependence."

58. I emphasize causal pathways and mechanisms because of the absence of agreed-upon knowledge about "outcomes"—a state we may be in for some (perhaps a very long) time.

59. See my "Shaping the Postwar Balance of Power." I document there how and why Britain and France expressed preferences for bilateral ties; and I argue that even if those preferences had been different, had the United States offered security on a bilateral basis, Britain and France would have had little choice but to accept the deal. See also Kenneth Oye's related argument about pressures on states to conclude bilateral deals once discriminatory bargaining begins, in *Economic Discrimination and Political Exchange* (Princeton: Princeton University Press, 1992).

60. The major principles here—nonexclusion, indivisibility, and diffuse reciprocity—are recognizable as part of what influenced the shape of U.S.-sponsored economic international institutions as well. John Ruggie opened this line of analysis to me by leading the collaborative project that led to the *Multilateralism Matters* volume.

61. To underscore the point that security in Europe is not objectively a nonexcludable good, I emphasize in "Shaping the Postwar Balance of Power" how certain states were excluded from NATO in the 1940s and 1950s and that many—including the three that I mentioned, each of which would very much like to be a member—are still excluded today.

62. I do not of course contend that this is the only source of difference in the context of security relationships between these states, but that it is an important one.

63. I discuss this point as well as the nature of exceptions to it in "Shaping the Postwar Balance of Power."

64. Many political scientists, though, will see security as a preferred ground for testing, since (in the traditional realist and neorealist view) security should be a strong case for explaining institutions on a rationalist basis with utilitarian or functional logic and without recourse to ideas.

65. I have written at length about the EBRD's founding and mission, in "Origins of the European Bank for Reconstruction and Development," Working Paper of the Center for European Studies, Harvard University. This section draws heavily on that paper.

66. To be precise, the twelve EU states plus the EU plus the EIB together make up a majority of the shares.

67. "Agreement Establishing the European Bank for Reconstruction and Development," May 1990 (my emphasis).

68. I answer this question with evidence in "Origins of the European Bank." What follows is the briefest summary of my argument there.

69. Anticipating the rationalist critique, I demonstrate in "Origins of the European Bank" that these issues and the positions of the major actors on them are not reducible in any reasonable way to power. Put differently, states were not simply bargaining over power and cost-benefit distribution under different labels.

70. For details and a discussion of what has happened to the Soviet issue, see "Origins of the European Bank."

71. Details in "Origins of the European Bank." I do not of course claim that these understandings were historically or even logically valid, only that as shared ideas they drove the process of cooperation.

72. It might bear resemblance to one of the many (infinite?) trajectories possible for reflectivists. What distinguishes the institutionalist approach is that it would concentrate specifically on two issues: selection—why one path rather than another was chosen—and reinforcement—the mechanisms by which the selected path sustains itself, given that other paths remain available.

73. A useful overview is W. Brian Arthur, "Competing Technologies, Increasing Returns, and Lock-In by Historical Events," *Economic Journal* 99 (March 1989):116–131.

74. The most frequently cited article is Paul David, "Clio and the Economics of Qwerty," *American Economic History* 75 (1985):332–337. The choice of AC over DC current or VHS over Beta format for VCRs are similar stories. On international trade, see E. Helpman and P. Krugman, *Market Structure and Foreign Trade* (Cambridge, MA: MIT Press, 1985).

75. Paul Humphreys offers an intriguing discussion of this issue in *The Chances of Explanation* (Princeton: Princeton University Press, 1989).

76. In a world in which competition is not intense and survival is not tenuous and the most important element of the environment is other institutions, institutions tend to look alike not because they are competing for limited resources and are driven to do the same tasks (the realist view of states competing for scarce security) but because they need to fit into the larger organizational environment in order to function. Organizational theorists posit three mechanisms for this type of isomorphism: coercion (pressure or expectations regarding what is legitimate); mimesis (copying, particularly when goals are unclear); and normative pressures in internal organization (converging recruitment standards). See Paul J. DiMaggio and Walter W. Powell, "The Iron Cage Revisited: Institutional Isomorphism and Collective Rationality in Organizational Fields," *American Sociological Review* 48 (1983):147–160.

77. Reuven Brenner, *Betting on Ideas* (Chicago: University of Chicago Press, 1985).

10

Conclusion: Continuity and Innovation in International Relations Theory

G. JOHN IKENBERRY
AND MICHAEL W. DOYLE

In an era of dramatic upheaval in world politics, it is not surprising that scholars of international relations tend to reflect on the adequacy of their ideas and theories. Moments of great historical change inspire some observers to advance grand assessments of the human condition and the pathways of world politics—but it humbles others. The collapse of the Soviet Union and the sudden end of the Cold War comprise one of those singular historical moments that inspire both theoretical ambition and humility. The Cold War's end is an event that reminds us that world politics is, in a profound sense, still very surprising. Our belief that deep forces of historical change are slowly but relentlessly at work is reconfirmed—but so too is our skepticism about the adequacy of our theoretical tools and knowledge. The world events of the 1990s have made professional students of international relations curious again—curious about change in world politics and curious about the status of our theories.

This volume is about "change" in two respects. In one sense, we asked scholars from a wide range of theoretical orientations to discuss their theories as guides to change in world politics. What are the commitments and hypotheses about international change that are lodged in their theories and ideas? In some chapters the authors have taken on this assignment directly, and in others the discussion of change is more implicit. What is clear is that the various theoretical traditions make very different claims about change. They find the sources of change in different places, and they differ on its importance as a basic problematic of international relations theory.

The chapters are also about change in another sense: They reflect the changing mix of theories and debates within the field of international relations. Fashions change and so do theoretical debates in international relations. This collection of essays is premised on the argument advanced by Miles Kahler—that the narrowing of theoretical debate in American international relations to a contest between various versions of neorealism and neoliberalism has been more a limiting than a progressive development. We argued in the introduction that there are strong epistemological and disciplinary reasons to encourage a "pluralism" of theory. In this spirit, the present volume seeks to showcase some of the important changes and innovations in the wider field of international relations.

Lurking in the shadows is neorealism. Stimulated by Kenneth Waltz's updated version of realist theory, neorealism has dominated American international relations theory since the early 1980s.[1] Its appeal has lain in its parsimony and its accommodation to scientific-styled research programs in both security studies and international political economy. Its theoretical premises are organized around basic and seemingly enduring features of world politics: anarchy, the distribution of power, and self-regarding states. Its pervasiveness is reflected in the fact that researchers in most other recent theoretical enterprises in the field have felt it necessary to engage neorealism. These critiques and debates have been waged on many fronts, but they all tend to share a basic view, namely, that neorealism cannot explain a great deal of what scholars find puzzling about world politics. Similarly, the essays gathered here share the view that basic theoretical questions are still in play—that there are intellectual virtues in expanding rather than narrowing the debate.

In this conclusion we discuss the essays in this volume along two lines: first, as they provide innovations or advancements to several basic areas of international theory; and second, as they grapple with problems of international change. These essays do not constitute a new "great debate" of the sort that seized the field in earlier decades. What we have is a scattered set of debates and research agendas that are pushing the boundaries of contemporary theory. If these essays at all reflect the wider theoretical discussions in international relations, what seems clear is that the intellectual contours of the field are slowly being rearranged.

Promising Lines of Inquiry

Although the essays come from very different parts of the field, they tend to focus on a few basic issues. Three issues are particularly noteworthy. One is the politics of "identity" formation in international relations. The issues in this area concern how the basic roles and identities of actors—individuals, groups, states—are constituted. A second agenda deals with issues of "structure" in international relations—both unpacking and going beyond the neorealist notion of anarchy. Finally, there is renewed attention to the character and consequences of international institutions. We can look at each of these clusters of "new thinking" in turn.

Identity Politics

One area of growing theoretical activity in international relations calls into question the basic roles and identities of actors—and it has been an inquiry tied primarily to poststructuralist analysis. In this sprawling intellectual area scholars have seen themselves engaged in a self-conscious and counter-hegemonic critique of the dominant concepts and categories of traditional international relations theory, particularly neorealism. The essays by James Der Derian and Jean Bethke Elshtain in this volume may be seen as part of this growing literature. There are many different clusters of work in this area—each with different assumptions and ambitions—but they are loosely united in their view that traditional, positivist international relations theory is itself a reflection of a socially constructed state-centered reality. Our empiricist tools and conventional theories are not neutral entities but rather mask and reinforce a particular configuration of dominance, inequality, and self-interest.

There are different strands in this enterprise. Elshtain's essay begins where many other feminist critiques of international relations end, namely, with the suggestion that gender roles and gender assumptions pervade the language of international theory. But she moves quickly to broaden her critique, arguing that the gender focus is itself part of a wider effort to challenge and reexamine our key concepts, such as identity, the state, and power. The argument is not that international theory is male-biased, as if the introduction of female constructions would remedy the situation. Rather, the tack is to use gender as a "prism" that can help to reveal the constructed character of our intellectual assumptions and frameworks. The purpose is to subvert or undermine our received images—to make them more contested and less secure.

Der Derian makes similar claims in elaborating a poststructural approach to international relations. He argues that a poststructuralist approach is essentially concerned with understanding "why one moral or political system attains a higher status and exercises more influence than another at a particular historical moment." Intellectual traditions and systems of thought are not as detached from politics and relations of power as Western rationalist and positivist social science would believe. The argument is not that there is "no truth" to be found in political inquiry but that there is no detachment from the objects of our scrutiny. What the analyst sees as the reality that must be explained is not an "object" or "other," it is a representation of reality that is at least partly constituted by the reigning intellectual frameworks of the moment. The investigator can never be fully outside his study. Moreover, Der Derian agrees with Elshtain that our intellectual constructions are not random; power lurks in the background. Indeed, as Der Derian makes clear, a central aspect of critical inquiry is to investigate the "interrelationship of power and representational practices" that privilege one "truth" or "identity" over another.

At a minimum, both these essays seek to disturb and upset. They want to bring into the realm of debate the intellectual frames that conventional theory in the field takes as given—to make our otherwise unexamined theoretical apparatus part of an expanding "contested terrain." Such efforts can be more or less compelling. But both authors want to do more. They also want to sketch the outlines of specific research programs that build on their own theoretical commitments. This is where the most promising innovations can be anticipated.

Elshtain proposes more explicit attention to the politics of identity formation—gender and otherwise. This would seem to be a very promising line of inquiry. Elshtain discusses her work on war and the construction of gender identities. War, she argues, has tended to call forth certain types of gender identities within society. These social images—such as the "just warrior" and the "heroine on the home front"—have in turn served to facilitate or reinforce certain collective views about the virtues of and justifications for war.

This type of inquiry is full of possibility. It suggests that we look comparatively across societies and history at the ways in which individuals, groups, and societies construe themselves as actors and endow their actions with meaning. As Elshtain argues, taking up identity politics "means that one cannot presume that all states work to maximize or secure their own power." It attempts to render problematic our basic concepts of state, sovereignty, and nationalism. The challenge is to unpack these notions and to provide an understanding of how these identities are collectively and historically constructed. At some point this "identity politics" agenda loses its unique association with feminism or poststructuralism. It takes us squarely into the traditional research domains of historical sociology and comparative politics—understanding variations in state ideologies and traditions, alternative forms of nationalism, different patterns of political and civic traditions, and so forth.[2]

Der Derian explores his notions of representation and constructed reality in terms of the U.S.-led war in the Persian Gulf. He argues that American images of conflict in the Gulf War were "constructed" in a representational reality that grew out of war simulations and media representations. War simulation imposed a reality on the events. Military leaders constructed images of what was at stake and how the war would unfold on the basis of technology that abstracted war out of its historical and human setting. Metaphors of gaming, video imaging, and simulated action all created perceptions within the military establishment that made the decision to launch the Gulf War seem feasible and desirable.

It is possible to be skeptical of the specific interpretation about the Gulf War yet also to be intrigued by the call to probe the language and images of foreign policy decisionmakers. Der Derian is careful to argue that there is a research agenda in poststructural international relations theory. It is not that "anything goes" in a poststructuralist account, it is that the analyst is implicated in the analysis. If there is a specific research agenda suggested by Der Derian's analysis, it may be one that combines the otherwise overlooked and diffusely connected role of technology, metaphor, and language with careful empirical research on foreign policy decisionmaking. The multiple layers of meaning and the social construction of roles and images that poststructuralists introduce into analysis, however, are so complicated and far-reaching that it is difficult to see how it can ever be pursued in traditional positivist terms.

The most intriguing questions raised by these essays deal with questions of identity formation—but good answers to these questions are not ones that poststructuralism is necessarily best equipped to provide. Some questions deal with the state as a rational and self-interested actor. The task would be to turn this "ideal" image of the neorealist state into a variable, exploring variations in the ways that states actually are constituted as such. Other questions deal with group identity. The task here is to explore variations in the congruence or fit between group loyalties and collective identities on the one hand, and territorial states and other political communities on the other.[3]

Scope and Structure

Innovation has also taken the shape of expanding the traditional parameters of theory and reclaiming lost traditions of scholarship. This is what Daniel Deudney does in bringing old and neglected theories of geopolitics back into the realist mainstream. Deudney surveys the various clusters of geopolitical writings—showing their underlying unity as materialist theories of politics. Although geopolitics and realism share common intellectual roots, geopolitical ideas were jettisoned in the evolution of postwar American realism.

Deudney's argument is important in reminding us—as Kahler does as well—how far contemporary American neorealism has evolved from its European intellectual origins. The realist ideas brought across the Atlantic by European scholars in the 1930s and 1940s were not readily embraced by the American academy. The "geopolitical" aspects of realism were too closely associated with Nazi Germany, and later during the Cold War the "materialist" aspects of realism were too closely associated with Marxism. Deudney argues that in adjusting to these new realities geopolitics was among the heavy baggage that had to be jettisoned during realism's emigration to the United States. As a result, a rich array of old and potentially powerful arguments about the importance of geography, technology, and the material conditions of politics were lost.

According to this view, the Americanization of realism has resulted in a severe narrowing of its explanatory parameters. In particular, postwar American realism has tended to focus more on explaining the interaction of the actors rather than on explaining their genesis. This was true of Morgenthau—who was concerned more with describing relationships than with analyzing the underlying conditions or forces that created those relationships. This narrow focus was reinforced by neorealism's preoccupation with the consequences rather than the causes of structure. Likewise, works produced in the revival of geopolitical thinking since the 1960s (by writers who are mostly outside the professional field of international relations) have made only superficial reference to geographic and materialist sources of world politics.

Deudney argues for a return to the old tradition that makes direct connections between nature (in the form of the physical characteristics of territorial space and the evolution of basic technology) and politics. In this reconstructed view, politics and political institutions are in some deep sense best seen as "adaptations" to the material realities of the age. Deudney is particularly interested in reclaiming a "security materialist" orientation. As suggested by the geopolitical writings of Mahan, Mackinder, Haushofer, and Spykman, it is the changing technological manifestations of the industrial revolution (such as railroads and the telegraph) that combine with the large-scale geographical features of the world to produce the structure of political units and security relations. Security materialism is ultimately a theory about the "deep structure" of international relations. It is not an alternative to neorealism; rather it ultimately seeks to put the realism of interstate relations in a wider historical and theoretical context.

International Institutions

Other essays in this volume attempt to advance or extend well-traveled traditions of theory, and many of these arguments converge on the question of how to think about international institutions. Steve Weber looks directly at theories of institutions, and Joseph Grieco's essay arrives at this point as it attempts to sort out limitations and promising leads in realist theory. Grieco's contribution involves both circumscribing what realism can explain and finding interesting ways to extend realism beyond its core hypotheses. In the process, the notion of collective binding is suggested as a way to extend realist theory in a way that might explain international institutions.

A central controversy in realist theory concerns the precise impact of anarchy on state goals. Realists agree that anarchy makes security an overriding imperative of states, but they disagree on what precisely this means for state goals. Does it mean, as Grieco asks, that anarchy leads "normal" states to maximize their power or to maximize their security? If realists want to argue, as many have, that states seek to increase their relative power position at every turn, the implications for international cooperation are far-reaching. In this formulation the problems of cheating and relative gains would loom very large, and international cooperation would be rare or impossible. Grieco advances the more modest claim that states seek to maximize their security. This means that states seek to "minimize gaps in power" that favor rivals; it is a more defensive notion of the state's preoccupation with relative power. States are more concerned with preventing disadvantages in their position than with extending any advantages that they may enjoy. States will still be led to balance and to avoid functional differentiation, but the impact of anarchy is less severe. More variation in the state's security goals is allowed, and specific expectations require the introduction of domestic and other nonsystemic variables.

The other line of inquiry concerns realism and international institutions. Grieco finds that the recent revitalization of the European Union poses difficult problems for realism. How can realist theory explain the decisions made by European states in recent years to shift policymaking authority away from national governments to the supranational level? These European developments would seem to fly in the face of realist claims that states will stubbornly protect their primacy and independence. Realism might argue that the Europeans are engaged in balancing, perhaps against Japan and the United States. Grieco suggests another alternative, arguing that European integration might best be seen as a form of collective binding, where states within the Europe community seek to tie down and render more predictable the strongest states within the group.

Steve Weber's arguments about international institutions attempt to delineate a "middle way" between so-called rationalist and reflectivist theories. Rationalist theories argue that institutions are essentially functional or utilitarian "solutions" to problems encountered by rational actors seeking to organize their environment in ways that advance their interests. Kenneth Shepsle describes institutions as "agreements about a structure of cooperation" that reduce transaction costs, opportunism, and other forms of "slip-page."[4] Reflectivist theories argue that institutions are actually crystalliza-tions of shared systems of identity and meaning problems. Institutions are overarching patterns of relations that define and reproduce the interests and actions of individuals and groups.

Weber challenges both of these views—or, more precisely, he articulates a position that draws on aspects of each. Rationalist theories are not equipped to appreciate the multiple and changing "purposes" of states, which are traced to ideas, norms, culture, and history. Reflective theories cannot appreciate the complex ways in which states can both create and ig-nore international institutions.[5] The key to a middle position, according to Weber, lies in relaxing the ontological primacy of either states (self-inter-ested states) or international institutions and in introducing interactive processes into the relation. States can be conceived as independent and prior to institutions, but institutions at a later stage may have a "creative" impact on states, either in empowering states to make claims or in the process of generating preferences.

Grieco's realism and Weber's institutionalism converge in the view that anarchy and the structures of power constrain but do not tightly determine state action. Grieco sees room for different strategies and techniques for the management of power distributions, including room for the "binding" arrangements of institutions. Weber would argue that part of what makes institutions binding is their capacity to shape (in ways not yet well ex-plored) the preferences of states. Likewise, to understand the specific char-acter of the institutions that emerge, it is necessary to trace the shared ideas and purposes of states and not just the configuration of power. Ideas and purposes matter, and this can only really be seen by careful attention to his-torical and political processes.

Approaches to International Change

The problem of explaining change in international relations has been of re-newed interest to scholars in recent years for two reasons. First, there is general agreement that neorealism does not have a good theory of change, particularly as it concerns the underlying generative structure of the system. Change occurs outside the parameters of the system—and states simply re-spond to it in the form of balancing actions that follow shifts in the distri-bution of power.[6] Neorealism is better prepared to explain "sameness" in international relations, that is, the continuity and repetition of world poli-tics over long stretches of history. Many theorists find this view too limit-ing, arguing that neorealist theory ignores basic processes of change and transformation that are occurring "offstage."

Second, the sudden end of the Cold War and the demise of Soviet communism has underscored the shortcomings of narrow and static international theory. In the wake of these recent events a vigorous debate is unfolding, advancing and evaluating different social and international theory as it relates to the end of the postwar era.[7] In the face of contemporary shifts in international relations, the silences of structural neorealist theory speak quite loudly.

The essays in this volume do not provide fully developed theories of change, but they do hint at the broad range of arguments and possibilities. Most of the contributions of the essays come in complicating basic theories of change. We can start by sketching some basic notions about change in international relations and place the essays in this context.

Varieties of Change

How do we think about the various dimensions of international change? Robert Gilpin provides a useful starting point. He distinguishes three levels or types of international change: systems change, systemic change, and interaction change.[8] "Systems" change involves change in the organizing structure of the international system itself, including the character of the actors themselves. A shift in a system of empire to nation-state would constitute systems change. "Systemic" change refers to "change in the governance of an international system"—which means "change in the international distribution of power, the hierarchy of prestige, and the rules and rights embodied in the system. ... "[9] This type of change involves basic shifts in power arrangements that facilitate or undermine the ability of hegemonic states to "govern" the world political order. Finally, Gilpin identifies "interaction change," which refers to more incremental change in the relations, processes, and specific agreements among states within the system. This is really a residual category, referring to the vast array of day-to-day events in world politics.

This categorization is not exhaustive and it can be expanded to distinguish additional types of change. A basic type of change not included in Gilpin's classification is the deep organizing principle of the international system. It is at this most basic level that Waltz distinguishes between anarchic and hierarchical systems, and it refers not to the character of the actors themselves but to the type of organizing principles that define their interrelationship.[10]

Another type of international change involves shifts in the character of states. Whereas Gilpin's "systems" change refers to transformations in the types of unit—such as change from empire to nation-state—the focus here is on long-term change in the nature of states themselves: absolutist states, constitutional monarchies, fascist states, liberal-democratic, late-industrial welfare states, and so on. Within and between particular historical eras, states as sovereign entities have ranged widely in their domestic political character. This level of change focuses on shifts in the basic character of states, particularly as groups of these states emerge and interact.

We can also identify shifts in collective meaning and normative order—that is, the shared sets of beliefs that individuals, groups, and polities embrace as they engage in international politics. This is simply to observe that material and structural characteristics of world politics may remain constant across time, whereas ideational shifts take place among those who comprise the international system. These shifts, however, presumably also are manifest in change within leading polities within the system.

Varieties of Theory

International theories also posit different basic understandings of change. The most fundamental distinction is between theories that see the world politics in terms of cycles and equilibria and those that see it as a process of unfolding and developmental change. This basic distinction between change as repetitive cycles and change as linear development is not unique to international relations theory; it is part of a more general division within the social sciences on how to think about historical change.[11] Likewise, it is here that neorealism and modern liberal theories of international relations part company.[12]

Neorealism tends to embrace either a cyclical or an equilibrium notion of change. Waltz's structural theory argues that the dominant reality of world politics is anarchy—the basic organizing principle of the system. Change in the system, which is manifest primarily as shifts in the distribution of power across units, come from within the units (or states) that comprise the system.[13] Shifts in the distribution of power are manifest as shifts in the material capabilities of states—which in turn trigger balancing adjustments by other states. As such, Waltzian neorealism has an equilibrium notion of change. Change occurs "offstage," which results in consistent and predictable state responses, bringing the system back to its "resting" position.

The cyclical notion of change is reflected in Gilpin's theory of hegemonic transition. According to Gilpin, international order is, at any particular moment in history, the reflection of the underlying distribution of material capabilities of states. Over time that distribution of power shifts, leading to conflicts and ruptures in the system, hegemonic war, and the eventual reorganization of order that reflects the new distribution of power capabilities. It is the rising hegemonic state, whose power position has been ratified by war, that defines the terms of the new world political order. According to Gilpin, history is a continual sequence of these hegemonic orderings and reorderings.[14]

Cyclical theories of hegemonic leadership vary widely. Adopting a long-cycle view of world politics, George Modelski advances a notion of "world leadership."[15] According to Modelski, a state comes to dominate an era by riding a wave of rising technological innovation, economic growth, and military power. This dominance takes the form of world leadership, as the powerful state diffuses political, economic, and technological innovations. World leadership has a positive impact on world order; coercion is low, stability is maintained, and follower states gain from exchange relations with the leader.[16]

In these equilibrium and cyclical notions of change world politics is ultimately seen as a repetitive process of adjustment. The character of the actors—their interests, goals, relationships—remain essentially the same, as does the underlying structure of the system. Moreover, for Gilpin and other realists, the principal mechanism for change is war. The disequilibrium in the system—that is, the disjuncture between the power capabilities and the "governance" arrangements—is brought back into adjustment through the coercive triumph of the new hegemonic power. The cycles of change create new leaders and new systems of governance, but the basic dynamics of the system remain the same. States adjust, they do not really "learn."[17]

An alternative view of change is advanced in various developmental and evolutionary theories. These theories see change—of states, societies, institutions, and so on—at the core of international relations. They differ on what the "engine" of international change is and on whether the nature of the change is "progressive" in any real sense.

The most straightforward notions of developmental change emerge from the liberal tradition, which contains notions about the evolutionary unfolding of society and economy. Change takes the shape of "development" or "modernization," that is, the maturation and extension of a logic that is contained in society and economy themselves. Specialization, exchange, technological progress—all these processes push political life and international relations along a developmental trajectory.[18] This liberal logic of change need not incorporate complex notions of learning or evolution in the perceptions or orientations of actors. It simply holds that the material conditions of industrial and political life are in a continuous process of evolutionary change—and international politics is transformed as a result. Politics and institutions adjust to the underlying change in the industrial and technological circumstances of society.

A very different notion of developmental change sees the basic engine of change as intellectual: It is ideational change that is ultimately the most profound and transformative process at work in international relations. It is not the evolution of the material capabilities of actors that alters world politics as much as basic shifts in the way individuals and groups think about their interests, goals, and relations. Individuals ultimately construct their political universe, and they do so with different intellectual and normative orientations. Innovations and change in the basic organization and relations of world politics stem from shifts in the social constructions of people as they inhabit states and societies.[19]

Most developmental theories of international change offer a mixture of these materialist and ideational views. Emanuel Adler proposes a "cognitive evolutionary" view of international change that tries to incorporate both institutional and cognitive aspects into a larger structural theory. The focus is on the complex evolutionary process whereby countries come to define national interests, expectations, and values and spread them to other states.[20] "Understanding how change in international relations occurs," Adler argues, "entails grasping how national interests are created and how their essence is transmitted to other nations."[21] The logic of change involves the interplay of intellectual and normative innovations and wide-ranging political processes. Crises and ruptures in domestic and international institutions provide openings for the redefinition of state interests and norms. Likewise, new values and expectations that are embraced by a leading state will be diffused to other states.

The essays in this volume also tend to advance arguments about change that combine institutional and ideational aspects. Deudney's geopolitical tradition is the most materialist in its view of change. It is "nature" as such—in the form of industrial society and technology—that is the master agent of change. Polities adapt to the changing material conditions, and the primacy of particular varieties of political organization—localities, states, and supranational organizations—rises or falls according to the logic of political association inherent in the changing material capabilities. But even Deudney argues that intellectual processes are at work. Material and technological change mix with ideas and values to alter the character of world politics. Industrialism and technology provide opportunities to specific political groupings, but the opportunities must be grasped and pursued—which is inherently a political process.

The essays by Elshtain and Der Derian approach change from the opposite direction. It is the social process in which particular identities, roles, and interests are crystallized that is at the heart of political change. But even these essays attempt to place this process in a complex historical and political process. In particular, Elshtain tries to place changes in identities in such a context. War, she argues, provides the impetus for the construction of certain collective understandings of gender roles and heroic wartime images of national identity. These roles and images in turn—in a process not fully spelled out—reinforce certain collective orientations and expectations about foreign policy and international conflict.

Weber's essay attempts to provide a more explicitly mixed and multi-causal theory of international change. It places at the center of analysis the "purposes" that states express in their policies and actions. In contrast to rationalist theories, here institutions are not simply expressions of functional or efficiency "needs" of states. The interests themselves are put on the table for discussion. At the same time, institutions are not simply "constructions" of collective yet disembodied intellectual processes. Weber suggests, as does Adler, that a profoundly political and contested process is involved in the creation and evolution of institutions.

It is a bit surprising that so many of the essays emphasize the importance of the formation of and change in state interests and identity. This view represents a disagreement with both neorealism and neoliberal institutionalism. The argument is that it is necessary to look more deeply into the character of societies and states to find out how they construct goals and expectations. In some respects this concern leads to the issue of "social purpose"—how the interests and goals of states are extensions or reflections of deeper social understandings of what politics is as a collective enterprise. Matthew Evangelista's discussion of domestic structures also raises this issue: Divergent institutional structures are at least partly a reflection of differences that persist across polities in the meanings and traditions of politics.

Likewise, to understand international change, it is necessary to understand how the social purposes of states change over long stretches of history. This is a proposition that is widely held across theoretical tradition. Gilpin, for example, argues that one of the major sources of international change is change in the character of the politics and social goals of the leading states. Weber's institutionalism and the poststructuralist agenda also make these claims. The agreement is simply that an adequate theory of change in international relations must "look behind" traditional frames of reference to the values and expectations of societies. This is not to say that international politics must collapse into comparative politics—Adler's cognitive evolutionary theory incorporates both domestic factors and processes of international selection and diffusion. In a very real sense international change is not intelligible without grasping the larger logic of change that infuses both internal societies and the larger global system.

Conclusion

World events act to stimulate theoretical debate, and these events, if they are sufficiently dramatic, can move the center of gravity of the field. In some respects the new multipolarity of the international system mirrors a similar multipolarity of theory. More than ever before, it seems that the theory in the field of international relations is scattered into a multitude of puzzles and debates. The methodological diversity of scholars in the field is certainly as wide-ranging as it has ever been. The substantive topics that interest scholars in the field have also widened; the Cold War and bipolar struggle no longer exist to focus and concentrate theory and debate. Likewise, the new interest in explaining international change has reinforced the diversity in theory and approaches. The sources and dynamics of change, many scholars argue, require a capacity to reach across domestic and international divides to fashion developmental and evolutionary concepts and to fit together material and ideational variables.

The composer Sergey Sergeyevich Prokofiev provided two endings for his Seventh Symphony, one optimistic, one pessimistic. The conclusion of this volume could also have two endings. One ending might announce the decline of grand theory and great debates in international relations. The diversity of theoretical views expressed in this volume suggests an absence of any great progress in the field. We are still struggling with fundamental issues—theoretical accumulation, validation, and normal science are still elusive. The other ending is more optimistic. The field of international relations has not perfected a single paradigm or research program—as achieved, for example, in mainstream economics—but the field has expanded and diversified its theoretical repertoire. As Miles Kahler argues, it is probably a virtue that the gene pool of theory is large and getting larger. The pluralism and diversity of views is a virtue. As Jean Bethke Elshtain reminds us, "no single standpoint or perspective . . . gives us transparent pictures of reality. Many perspectives and ways of seeing expand the horizons of international relations discourse and make more supple our thinking. . . . "

Notes

1. Kenneth Waltz, *Theory of International Politics* (Boston: Little, Brown and Company, 1979).

2. For a discussion of identity issues in the ongoing debate between neorealism and its critics, see Jonathan Mercer, "Anarchy and Identity," *International Organization* vol. 49, no. 2 (Spring 1995):229–252.

3. This is an agenda pioneered by Karl Deutsch. See his *Nationalism and Social Communication: An Inquiry into the Foundations of Nationality* (Cambridge, Mass.: MIT Press). For a discussion of the changing political identity of citizens in the Western industrial countries, see Daniel Deudney and G. John Ikenberry, "The Logic of the West," *World Policy Journal*, vol. 10, no. 4 (Winter 1993/1994):17–25.

4. Kenneth A. Shepsle, "Institutional Equilibrium and Equilibrium Institutions," in *Political Science: The Science of Politics*, ed. H. Weisberg (New York: Agathon, 1986), p. 74.

5. John Ikenberry has also tried to delineate a "middle position" between rational and reflectivist theories of institutions, in G. John Ikenberry, "History's Heavy Hand: Institutions and the Politics of the State," unpublished paper, 1994.

6. See the insightful comments by Robert O. Keohane on neorealism's problem with explaining change, "Theory of World Politics: Structural Realism and Beyond," in *Neorealism and Its Critics,* ed. Keohane (New York: Columbia University Press, l986).

7. For a survey of the range of theories relevant to explaining the end of the Cold War and the collapse of the Soviet order, see Daniel Deudney and G. John Ikenberry, "Soviet Reform and the End of the Cold War: Explaining Large-Scale Historical Change," *Review of International Studies,* vol. 17, no. 3 (July 1991): 225–250. For an evaluation of the impact of international forces on Soviet change, see Daniel Deudney and G. John Ikenberry, "The International Sources of Soviet Change," *International Security,* vol. 16, no. 3 (Winter 1991/1992):74–118.

8. Robert Gilpin, *War and Change in World Politics* (New York: Cambridge University Press), pp. 39–44.

9. Gilpin, *War and Change,* p. 42.

10. Waltz, *Theory of International Politics.*

11. For an evocative discussion of basic theoretical choices in thinking about change, see Stephen Jay Gould, *Time's Arrow, Time's Cycle* (Cambridge, Mass.: Harvard University Press, 1987).

12. See the discussion of cyclical and evolutionary theories in John Lewis Gaddis, "International Relations Theory and the End of the Cold War," *International Security,* vol. 17, no. 3 (Winter 1992/1993):5–58.

13. Waltz, *Theory of International Politics.*

14. Gilpin, *War and Change.*

15. George Modelski, *Long Cycles in World Politics* (Seattle: University of Washington Press, 1987).

16. For elaborations and extensions of this model, see William R. Thompson, *On Global War: Historical-Structural Approaches to World Politics* (Columbia: University of South Carolina Press, 1988).

17. For an attempt to incorporate learning notions into cyclical theory, see George Modelski, "Is World Politics a Learning Process?" *International Organization* vol. 44, no. 1 (Winter 1990):1–24.

18. See Edward Morse, *Modernization and Transformation of International Relations* (New York: Free Press, 1976).

19. See the various essays by Alexander Wendt: for example, "The Agent-Structure Problem in International Relations Theory," *International Organization,* vol. 41, no. 3 (Summer 1987):335–370; "Anarchy Is What States Make of It," *International Organization,* vol. 46, no. 2 (Spring 1992):391–425; "Constructing International Politics," *International Security,* vol. 20, no. 1 (Summer 1995):71–81.

20. Emanuel Adler, "Cognitive Evolution: A Dynamic Approach for the Study of International Relations and Their Processes," in *Progress in International Relations*, ed. Emanuel Adler and Beverly Crawford (New York: Columbia University Press, 1991), pp. 44–45.

21. Adler, "Cognitive Evolution," p. 51.

About the Book and Editors

This book of ten original essays provides a showcase of currently diverse theoretical agendas in the field of international relations. Contributors address the theoretical analysis that their perspective brings to the issue of change in global politics. Written for readers with a general interest in and knowledge of world affairs, *New Thinking in International Relations Theory* can also be assigned in international relations theory courses.

The volume begins with an essay on the classical tradition at the end of the Cold War. Essays explore work outside the mainstream, such as Jean Bethke Elshtain on feminist theory and James Der Derian on postmodern theory as well as those developing theoretical advances within traditional realms, from James DeNardo's formal modeling to the more discursive soliloquies of Miles Kahler and Steve Weber. Other essays include Matthew Evangelista on domestic structure, Daniel Duedney on naturalist and geopolitical theory, and Joseph Grieco on realist theory.

Michael W. Doyle is Director of the Center of International Studies and professor of politics and international affairs at Princeton University. He is author of *Empires* (1986), *UN Peacekeeping in Cambodia* (1995), and *Ways of War and Peace* (1997). G. John Ikenberry is professor of political science at the University of Pennsylvania. He is author of *Reasons of State: Oil Politics and the Capacities of American Government* (1988) and coauthor with John Hall of *The State* (1989).

About the Contributors

James DeNardo is professor of political science at the University of California at Los Angeles. He is author of *Power in Numbers: The Political Strategy of Protest and Rebellion* and *The Amateur Strategist: Intuitive Deterrence Theories and the Politics of the Nuclear Arms Race.*

James Der Derian is professor of political science at the University of Massachusetts at Amherst. He is author of *On Diplomacy: A Genealogy of Western Estrangement* (1987) and *Antidiplomacy: Spies, Terror, Speed, and War* (1992); editor of *International Theory: Critical Investigations* (1995); and coeditor with Michael Shapiro of *International/Intertextual Relations: Postmodern Readings of World Politics* (1989).

Daniel Deudney is assistant professor of political science at the University of Pennsylvania.

Jean Bethke Elshtain is the Laura Spelman Rockefeller Professor of Social and Political Ethics at the University of Chicago. Her books include: *Public Man, Private Woman: Women in Social and Political Thought,; Women and War; Democracy on Trial;* and *Augustine and the Limits of Politics.* She has written extensively on just war theory.

Matthew Evangelista is associate professor in the Department of Government and director of the International Relations Concentration at Cornell University. He is author of *Innovation and the Arms Race* (1988) and numerous articles in such publications as *The Nation, International Security, World Politics* and *International Organization.*

Joseph M. Grieco is professor of political science at Duke University. He is author of *Cooperation Among Nations: Europe, America, and Non-tariff Barriers to Trade* (1990) and *Between Dependency and Autonomy: India's Experience with the International Computer Industry* (1984).

Miles Kahler is Rohr Professor of Pacific International Relations and Director of Research at the Graduate School of International Relations and Pacific Studies at the University of California at San Diego. He is author of *Decolonization in Britain and France* (1984) and *International Institutions and the Political Economy of Integration* (1995) and coauthor of *Europe and America* (1996).

Steven Weber is associate professor in the Department of Political Science at the University of California at Berkeley. His current research includes a project examining changes in the business cycle and implications for firms and governments, and a project about globalization and the development of new stock markets aimed at raising equity finance for small and medium sized firms in Europe.

Index